50★STATES

5000

FACTS

50★STATES
5000
FACTS

EVERYTHING YOU EVER WANTED TO KNOW—AND MORE!

NATIONAL
GEOGRAPHIC

WASHINGTON, D.C.

CONTENTS

◀ **Acadia National Park, Maine**

ALABAMA

★ ★ ★

"We Dare Defend Our Rights"

★ ★ ★

CAPITAL: Montgomery **FLOWER:** Camellia **NICKNAME:** The Yellowhammer State **ENTRY:** 1819

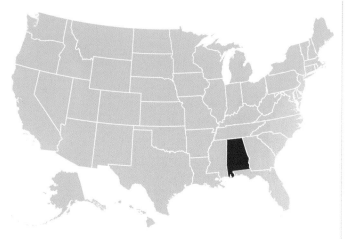

AL FACTS

- Alabama is located in the southeastern region of the United States.

- It was the 22nd state in the nation and is the 28th largest state by area.

- More than 10,000 years ago, people came to the area, some living near Russell Cave in what is now Bridgeport. Thousands of years later, Native American tribes such as the Cherokee, Chickasaw, Choctaw, and Creek settled throughout the territory.

- Beginning in the 1500s, control over the area changed hands from Spain to France to England. The British gained control of the area in 1763 by the Treaty of Paris, only to cede almost all the region after the American Revolution.

- The state's tallest point, Cheaha Mountain stands 2,407 feet (734 m) above sea level.

- The state has 50 miles (80.5 km) of beaches along the Gulf of Mexico and is home to popular Gulf Shores, which attracts nearly eight million visitors annually. ▼

▶ STATE BIRD
Northern Flicker
Colaptes auratus

Often referred to as a "yellowhammer" in Alabama, this woodpecker's persistent bursts of drumming are a familiar sound throughout the state during the spring. It gets its name from the bright yellow feathers under its tail and wings.

1886

The year Montgomery became the first U.S. city to initiate an electric streetcar system, known as the Capital City Street Railway Co.

AL

AK AS AZ AR CA CO CT DE FL GA GU HI ID IL IN IA KS KY LA ME MP MD MA MI MN MS MO MT NE NV NH NJ NM NY NC ND OH OK OR PA PR RI SC SD TN TX VI UT V

DAMN THE TORPEDOES, FULL SPEED AHEAD!

—Admiral David Farragut's famous command, issued at the Battle of Mobile Bay on August 5, 1864

▷ **THEIR LOSS …**
You can buy people's lost luggage at Scottsboro's Unclaimed Baggage Center.

- While the state is known for its natural resources and white barbecue sauce, it's football—especially the rivalry between the Auburn Tigers and the Alabama Crimson Tide—that reigns supreme. ▷

- The Confederacy was founded at Montgomery in 1861, and about 120,000 white Alabama men served in the Confederate forces during the Civil War.

- During a period in 1861, Montgomery served as the Confederate capital before it was moved to Richmond, Virginia.

- Alabama's state constitution has more than 300,000 words and more than 975 amendments. That makes it the longest state constitution and the most amended state constitution in the world.

- In the 1950s and 1960s, Alabama was at the center of the civil rights movement. In Montgomery, Rosa Parks refused to give up her seat on a bus in 1955, leading to the city's 381-day bus boycott.

- In 1965, Dr. Martin Luther King, Jr., led the Selma-to-Montgomery March. Later that year, Congress passed the Voting Rights Act.

- Condoleezza Rice, the first African American woman to serve as U.S. secretary of state, was born in Birmingham.

- Alabama has more than 132,000 miles (212,433 km) of streams and rivers.

- The Mobile-Tensaw Delta has more aquatic biodiversity than any other river system in the U.S.

- The state spirit is Conecuh Ridge Whiskey.

- The Perdido Key beach mouse and the Alabama beach mouse are two of North America's rarest species. ▷

STARS ★ OF ★ THE ★ STATE

HENRY LOUIS "HANK" AARON

(1934–2021) Born and raised in and around Mobile, "Hammerin' Hank" Aaron is considered one of the greatest baseball players of all time. A trailblazer who broke the sport's color line, he started off in the Negro Leagues before playing in Major League Baseball for the Atlanta Braves and the Milwaukee Brewers in a career that spanned 23 seasons. Aaron was the first player to have a combined 500 homers and 3,000 hits, and four years later broke Babe Ruth's record of 714 career home runs. Aaron retired from baseball in 1976 with 755 career home runs, a record that stood until 2007, when it was broken by Barry Bonds of the San Francisco Giants. Aaron's ties to Alabama remained tight, and there is now a baseball stadium named in his honor as well as a museum dedicated to his life and career in Mobile. ▷

▶ NO BEAR BRAWLIN'

It's illegal to wrestle a bear anywhere in the state.

WEIRD BUT TRUE

- There's a 12-lane bowling alley and a gym inside the Bridge Church in Birmingham.

- Mt. Nebo Baptist Church Cemetery, located in Clarke County, includes several tombstones featuring death masks that were cast from the people whose graves they mark.

- Anniston is home to the World's Largest Office Chair, which is made from 10 tons (9.1 t) of steel and weighs more than a car.

- In 1954, a woman from Sylacauga was badly bruised when a grapefruit-size meteorite crashed through the roof of her farmhouse and hit her as she napped on a couch. She was the first human known to have suffered an injury after being struck by a meteorite.

- Colbert County is home to Key Underwood Coon Dog Memorial Graveyard, the only one of its kind in the world.

- Scratch Ankle, Dogtown, and Bacon Level are all names of towns in Alabama.

- The town of Enterprise is home to the Boll Weevil Monument, acknowledging the role the pest played in encouraging farmers to grow crops other than cotton.

- Miss Baker, the first monkey to survive a space expedition in 1959, is buried in Huntsville. People sometimes leave bananas on top of her tombstone.

- Fire hydrants are made in a factory in Albertville, earning the town its reputation as the "fire hydrant capital of the world." ▪

▲ **STORY OF** THE SOUND Known as the "Hit Recording Capital of the World," Muscle Shoals Sound Studio is the birthplace of famous songs by Rod Stewart, Paul Simon, and many more. Formed in 1969 by four musicians in the working-class town of Sheffield, the studio eventually became one of the most sought-after locations in the country to record, and it created its own blend of southern music featuring country, rhythm and blues, and rock and roll. During times of racial unrest in the South, Muscle Shoals Sound Studio became a place that defied accepted societal standards on race relations, welcoming Black artists and producers. ▪

MISCELLANY

- **Hematite** is Alabama's official state mineral.

- The **star blue quartz** is the state's official gemstone.

- People from Alabama are called **Alabamians**.

- With 1,600-plus exhibits, the **Barber Vintage Motorsports Museum** is the world's biggest motorcycle museum.

- There's a hidden waterfall that drops 162 feet (49 m) into a limestone sinkhole at **Never Sink Preserve** near the town of Fackler.

- In **Mobile**, there's a popular cheese shop located inside an old gas station.

- Many artifacts and traces of prehistoric people have been found in **Russell Cave**, including human remains dating back more than 8,000 years.

- In 2015, **Civil War-era cannonballs** were discovered buried under sidewalks at the University of Alabama in Tuscaloosa.

- The Gulf Coast waterdog and the 20-inch (51 cm) eastern hellbender—**the biggest**

salamander species by weight** in North America—are both found in the state.

- **Birmingham** is the only known area on Earth with the raw materials needed to make iron: coal, iron ore, and limestone.

- About half of the peanuts grown in the United States are grown within a 100-mile (161 km) radius of Dothan, home of the **National Peanut Festival**.

- Alabama native **Mary Anderson is credited with inventing windshield wipers** in 1903. Nineteen years later, Cadillac adopted her "window cleaning device" as a piece of standard equipment on its cars.

RECORD ★ SETTERS

In 2002, Shelby County Habitat for Humanity set a record for the world's fastest home building. The Montevallo house took 3 hours, 26 minutes to complete.

BY THE NUMBERS

Natural Treasures

43% OF ALL SNAIL SPECIES IN NORTH AMERICA CAN BE FOUND IN ALABAMA.

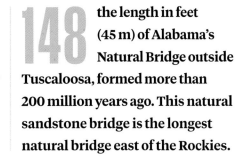

148 the length in feet (45 m) of Alabama's Natural Bridge outside Tuscaloosa, formed more than 200 million years ago. This natural sandstone bridge is the longest natural bridge east of the Rockies.

1982 the year that geology professor Dr. David T. King and his wife, Janet Abbott-King, discovered the most complete tyrannosaur ever found in eastern North America on a rural road in Montgomery County.

60,000 the age in years of an ancient underwater forest discovered by divers in 2012, off Alabama's Gulf Coast. Buried under a thick layer of sand and uncovered by giant waves during Hurricane Ivan, the trees are well preserved and rival the California redwoods in size.

1937 the year the Bangor Café Club opened inside Bangor Cave. It was billed as the first true underground nightclub in America.

11 the number of National Park Service properties in the state, including 2,040-acre (826 ha) Horseshoe Bend National Military Park in Daviston.

70% OF ALABAMA IS COVERED IN FOREST.

65 the length in miles (105 km) of the Little River, atop Lookout Mountain near Fort Payne, known as the longest mountaintop river in the U.S.

1972 the year Cathedral Caverns State Park was declared a national natural landmark. Located near the town of Grant, the cave was occupied by Native Americans as recently as 200 years ago.

133 the height in feet (41 m) of Graces High Falls, Alabama's tallest waterfall, found outside of Fort Payne

DESTINATION: ALABAMA

- The famed Tuskegee Airmen are honored at the national historic site in Tuskegee, where the first Black U.S. airmen once trained. Exhibits there showcase their contributions to World War II. ▷

- Step back to one of the most pivotal periods in U.S. history by following the U.S. Civil Rights Trail with several stops in Alabama, through cities like Birmingham, Selma, and Montgomery, that showcase historic landmarks that were part of the civil rights movement.

- The Monroeville courthouse where novelist—and future Pulitzer Prize winner—Harper Lee watched her father practice law (and was inspired to write her famous novel *To Kill a Mockingbird*) is now a museum devoted to the author. Visitors can often catch a dramatization of the book.

- Cullman is home to Ave Maria Grotto, a four-acre (1.6 ha) tribute to holy monuments created by Brother Joseph Zoettl, a monk who pursued monastic life at Alabama's only Benedictine Abbey.

- Visiting between January and March? Be sure to hit a Mardi Gras celebration in Mobile, which served as the French colonial capital and is the U.S. birthplace of the Carnival festival in 1703. The city's Carnival Museum keeps the party going all year long.

- The U.S.S. *Alabama* battleship earned nine Battle Stars for meritorious service during World War II. Now, the "Mighty A" is permanently docked in Mobile and is open for exploration, along with a spy plane and submarine.

- The Robert Trent Jones Golf Trail, made up of 26 public courses from Muscle Shoals to Mobile, is a bucket-list adventure for amateur and ace golfers alike. The trail includes more than 100 miles (161 km) of golf and 468 holes.

RECORD ★ SETTERS

The Vulcan statue, the city symbol of Birmingham, is the largest cast-iron statue in the world. Taller than a five-story building from toe to spear point, it depicts the Roman god Vulcan and was created in 1904 for an exhibit at the St. Louis World's Fair.

STARS ★ OF ★ THE ★ STATE

TALLULAH BANKHEAD
(1902–1968)
Known for her husky voice and exuberant—and sometimes scandalous—personality and behavior, Bankhead is considered one of the theatrical greats of her day. The granddaughter of a U.S. senator and the daughter of an 11-term member of Congress, Bankhead was born in Huntsville into tragedy: Her mother died soon after her birth. A natural performer, Bankhead's acting career took off on the stage in London, where she appeared in 16 plays before taking on the silver screen in Hollywood. Later in her career, Bankhead would return to the stage and also make appearances on TV and radio. Looks and acting chops aside, Bankhead stood out for her political involvement: A lifelong passionate Democrat, she prided herself in helping to elect both Harry S. Truman and John F. Kennedy to the presidency.

MADE IN AL

Alabama's agricultural outputs include:

- Poultry and eggs
- Cattle
- Fish
- Plant nursery items
- Peanuts
- Grains such as corn and sorghum
- Vegetables
- Milk and dairy
- Soybeans
- Peaches

Alabama's industrial outputs include:

- Iron and steel products
- Paper, lumber, and wood products
- Mining
- Plastic products
- Cars and trucks

SPORTING CHANCES

- Famous gold medal athletes from the state include Carl Lewis (track and field) and Mia Hamm (soccer).

- Alabama does not have any major sports teams, but college football is extremely popular. The University of Alabama has won 18 national championships.

- The Alabama and Auburn football teams go head-to-head in the game called the Iron Bowl. It gets its name from when it was played in Birmingham, which was known for its iron and steel production.

- Bryant-Denny Stadium in Tuscaloosa, is the seventh largest college stadium in the nation, with a seating capacity of 101,821.

- The Talladega Superspeedway motorsports complex has a seating capacity of 143,231 and is NASCAR's biggest track.

- From 1973 to 1980, Birmingham hosted the International Indoor Championships, a men's tennis tournament played on indoor carpet courts.

- Track star Jesse Owens, who won four gold medals in the 1936 Berlin Olympics, was born in the tiny town of Oakville.

- The state has hosted several professional golf tournaments, including the Mobile LPGA Tournament of Champions.

- Birmingham hosted the 2022 World Games, an international multisport event.

▶ **STORY OF** THE NAME Before European explorers staked claim in the territory in the 1500s, a number of Native American tribes called the area home, including a tribe known as the Alabamas, or Alibamons, whose territory was in what is now the central part of the state. One of the major waterways nearby was named for the tribe, and, eventually, the state took on the name, too. Although there were multiple variations of spelling—from Alebamon to Alibamon to Alabamu—documented over time, ultimately "Alabama" became the accepted version. And while no expert can quite agree on what Alabama actually means, it's widely believed to come from a mash-up of two Choctaw words: *Alba* and *Amo*, translating to "vegetation gathers."

MY FATHER JOINED OUR PARTY BECAUSE THE DEMOCRATS IN JIM CROW ALABAMA OF 1952 WOULD NOT REGISTER HIM TO VOTE. THE REPUBLICANS DID.

—American diplomat Condoleezza Rice

ALASKA

★ ★ ★

"North to the Future"

★ ★ ★

CAPITAL: Juneau **BIRD:** Willow Ptarmigan **NICKNAME:** The Last Frontier **ENTRY:** 1959

AK FACTS

- At 586,412 square miles (1,518,800 sq km), it's the largest state.

- The population is 733,583.

- The economy flourishes from oil, gas, and fishing, and the state is home to one of the world's largest fisheries. Other natural resources include gold, zinc, lumber, and jade.

- English and 20 Indigenous languages are the official languages.

- After gold was discovered near the Klondike River in 1896, thousands of treasure hunters braved freezing temperatures and harsh wilderness for the chance to make their fortunes in Canada's Yukon Territory. Soon, during what became known as the Klondike Gold Rush, prospectors were staking claims and building mining towns in Alaska as well.

- From black bears to reindeer to lynx, Alaska is known for its wildlife. Perhaps the most famous are the state's wolves, which are at the forefront of long-held debates over protection, sport hunting, and population control. ▼

▶ STATE FLOWER

Alpine Forget-Me-Not
Myosotis alpestris

Believed to represent perseverance, Alaska's state flower may be a tribute to the hardiness of the wild region's first settlers.

1867

When purchased in 1867, Alaska cost $7.2 million—approximately two cents per square acre (0.4 ha).

BLUE BABE

In 1979, gold miners discovered a 36,000-year-old mummified bison near Fairbanks. While buried underground, the skin reacted to silt and turned bluish, earning it the nickname Blue Babe.

> TO THE LOVER OF PURE WILDERNESS, ALASKA IS ONE OF THE MOST WONDERFUL COUNTRIES IN THE WORLD.
>
> —Conservationist John Muir, *Travels in Alaska*

- Home to many species of salmon, including Chinook, chum, coho, sockeye, and pink, the state is the world's top producer of wild salmon. Alaska prides itself on having a salmon industry that has been certified "sustainable" by the Marine Stewardship Council.

- The Athabascan people live in the interior and have the largest land base of any Alaska Native group. Although their society is traditionally matrilineal and has relied historically on nomadic subsistence hunting, it is made up of a widely diverse group of people whose practices and languages vary between clans.

- The area has been inhabited since at least 10,000 B.C., after nomadic peoples crossed the (now submerged) Bering Land Bridge between Siberia and North America. Today, their descendants make up 228 federally recognized Alaska tribes.

- Created by 13-year-old Benny Benson in 1927, the state flag showcases the North Star and the Big Dipper as symbols of Alaska's location and wilderness.

- In 1925, a devastating diphtheria outbreak hit Nome. When weather prevented planes from transporting lifesaving serum, the town was forced to rely on a group of dog-sledding teams to make the delivery. Twenty teams, including famous hero dogs Togo and Balto, raced against time in a relay lasting five days and covering 674 miles (1,085 km) to successfully save the town.

- During World War II, Japanese troops invaded Alaska's Aleutian Islands in an effort to control transportation routes in the Pacific. Although the islands were recaptured by the U.S. military in 1943, Native Unangax̂ people continued to suffer in prison camps for three more years, and they were never allowed to resettle in their homelands.

- In 1989, the Exxon Valdez oil tanker crashed into a reef in Prince William Sound, creating one of the worst oil spills in U.S. history. The impact was disastrous, resulting in hundreds of thousands of animal deaths as well as troubling the fishing industry. Thousands of people banded together in mass cleanup efforts, and the government passed stricter oil tanker regulations.

▶ **STORY OF** THE NAME The name "Alaska" was first used by Russian explorers who began to colonize the land around 1761, leading to conflict with the Unangax̂ people who inhabited the area. It is a derivation of the Unangax̂ word Aláxsxaq (or Alyeska), which translates approximately to "great land."

STARS ★ OF ★ THE ★ STATE

JEWEL
(b. 1974) is an esteemed author, actress, producer, and songwriter celebrated for her folk-inspired melodies and crooning vocals. Born Jewel Kilcher in Payson, Utah, she grew up in the small Alaska city of Homer, where she began singing at local venues. Jewel left home as a teenager, living in a van and singing in coffee shops throughout California. She was soon scouted by a label and released the 1995 album *Pieces of You*, which has sold 12 million copies to date. She went on to act in movies and television, publish a poetry collection and other books, and form a nonprofit organization dedicated to increasing access to clean drinking water around the world.

Many historians believe that more than 12,000 years ago, the region became the first place in the Americas settled by humans.

WEIRD BUT TRUE

- The city of Juneau can't be reached by road.
- Moose attacks are more common than bear attacks.
- The Reindeer Dog, a popular hot dog, is often topped with cola-marinated onions and cream cheese.
- Alaska is the only state whose name can be typed in one row on an English-language keyboard.
- Situated north of the Arctic Circle, Utqiagvik (Barrow) experiences 67 days of darkness each year.
- During the Midnight Sun Festival, Nome stages a mock bank robbery complete with costumes, bags of money, and an actor playing lawman and one-time resident Wyatt Earp.
- Alaska's glaciers are home to tiny worms called iceworms. One to three centimeters (0.39 to 1.18 inches) in length, these annelids thrive in cold temperatures and are believed to feed on snow algae.
- One man in Palmer set a record by growing a green cabbage that weighed 138.25 pounds (62.7 kg).
- At their closest point, which is between two small islands off their coasts, Alaska and Russia are only 2.5 miles (4 km) apart. That's about one-and-a-half times the length of the Golden Gate Bridge.
- Since 2006, Anchorage has hosted the Outhouse Races, an event where competitors must ride a homemade commode on skis to the finish line. ▷

▲ **STORY OF** THE ART Renowned for their beauty and as pieces of expert craftsmanship, totem poles have come to represent Alaska art. They have been made for centuries by peoples across the Pacific Northwest, including the Tsimshian, Haida, Eyak, and Tlingit cultures in Alaska. These poles are usually from 10 to 60 feet (3 to 18 m) tall—though some tower more than 100 feet (30.5 m) high—and depict carved animals, people, and mythological creatures meant to represent or commemorate events and ancestry. The art style varies by cultural group, though it is often highly structured and commonly makes use of symmetry, strong lines, and rich colors. ▪

MISCELLANY

- A traditional **Inuit dish** known as muktuk consists of whale blubber and skin, often eaten raw.
- The state marine mammal is the **bowhead whale**.

- The beginning of spring is known as **"breakup,"** as it marks the time when frozen rivers begin to break apart.
- **Jade** is the official state gem.
- **Fireweed jelly** is made from the juice of a seasonal flower known as fireweed.
- **Woolly mammoths** are the state fossil; research shows they existed in the area as recently as 5,600 years ago.
- Moose are the state land mammal. Moose is a popular regional meat, and **jellied moose nose** is considered a delicacy.

- **Alaskan malamutes**, the state dog, are believed to have existed in the area for more than 5,000 years. Their thick fur and powerful builds make them ideal for pulling heavy sleds.
- **King salmon** is the state fish.
- When Secretary of State William Seward negotiated the U.S. acquisition of Alaska as part of an 1867 territorial treaty with Russia, critics called the deal "Seward's Folly." To this day, **Seward's Day** is celebrated on the last Monday of March.

BY THE NUMBERS

20,310
feet (6,190 m): the elevation of Denali (formerly known as Mount McKinley), the tallest mountain in the United States

1,808
the highest recorded weight in pounds (820 kg) of an Alaska moose

50 ACTIVE VOLCANOES EXIST IN THE STATE.

24 the number of people who live in Alaska per every brown bear

1913 the year the Alaska territory granted the right to vote to women

1.3 the number of people per square mile (0.5 per sq km)

33,904 miles (54,563 km) of shoreline make up the coast.

483 THE NUMBER OF TIMES RHODE ISLAND COULD FIT INTO ALASKA

17 of the 20 highest U.S. peaks are in Alaska.

2 the number of times Alaska is larger than Texas

1,000 the estimated average number of earthquakes per month

3,000,000 THE APPROXIMATE NUMBER OF LAKES

−80°F (−62.22°C): the lowest recorded temperature

1741 the year the first European, a Danish explorer named Vitus Bering, reached the area

34,000 total area in sq mi (88,060 sq km) of Alaska's glaciers

- Home to 40 percent of the population, Anchorage is known for its arts, culture, and food. Among its many famous events is the Anchorage International Film Festival, which has been celebrating independent film since 2001.

- A popular cruise destination, the Inside Passage features fjords, glaciers, mountain views, and even temperate rainforests. Visitors have the chance to see wildlife such as bald eagles, whales, porpoises, and to visit Glacier Bay, a 24.3-million-acre (9,839,121 ha) World Heritage site.

- Fairbanks attracts visitors year-round for its summer festivals and its prime location for viewing the northern lights. Though it began as a mining city in 1901, Fairbanks also boasts a rich art culture, extensive Indigenous history, and a number of popular local breweries.

RECORD ★ SETTERS

Alaska was the first state to legalize on-site use of marijuana in dispensaries. Today, there are more than 150 across the state.

- Just 13 miles (21 km) from Juneau, Mendenhall Glacier is about 12 miles (19 km) long, half a mile (0.8 km) wide, and up to 1,800 feet (549 m) deep. Visitors can explore its luminous blue ice caves.

- Made up of 69 islands and numerous islets, the Aleutian Islands form an archipelago off the southwestern coast. They have been inhabited by Unangax̂ (Aleut) families for more than 8,000 years, who share their lands with seabirds, Steller sea lions, arctic foxes, and more.

- In 1917, 2,146,000 acres (868,455 ha) of wilderness were established as Mount McKinley National Park. Featuring abundant wildlife, open vistas, and the highest peak in North America, the park is now known as Denali National Park and is 4,740,091 acres (1,918,247 ha). It attracts up to 600,000 visitors annually.

AMERICA IS LOOKING FOR ANSWERS. SHE'S LOOKING FOR A NEW DIRECTION. THE WORLD IS LOOKING FOR A LIGHT. THAT LIGHT CAN COME FROM AMERICA'S GREAT NORTH STAR; IT CAN COME FROM ALASKA.

—Former Alaska governor Sarah Palin

- The aurora borealis, also called the northern lights, is a world-famous phenomenon caused by the collision of solar activity with Earth's magnetic field, resulting in multihued ribbons of light in the night sky. These lights are best viewed from mid-August to mid-April at northern latitudes.

- The Alaska Native Heritage Center (ANHC) in Anchorage offers educational and interactive exhibits on the 11 major Indigenous cultural groups to promote respect and value for the state's Native people.

- During the blueberry festival in Girdwood, visitors can partake in pie-eating and cooking competitions, take chairlift rides to forage for mountain blueberries, and more.

The rich coastal waters are inhabited by migrating whales, including orcas, humpbacks, gray whales, belugas, blue whales, and more, making Alaska a prime destination for whale-watchers.

◄ ROAD TRIP

Want to hit the road? A prime destination for those looking to get away from it all, the Alaska Highway winds through more than 1,350 miles (2,173 km) of remote wilderness.

MADE IN AK

Alaska's agricultural outputs include:

- Seafood (Pacific salmon, sockeye salmon, cod, pollack, crab, roe)
- Cattle
- Seafood-based flours
- Potatoes

Alaska's industrial outputs include:

- Ore (zinc, lead)
- Petroleum
- Coal
- Wood products
- Gold
- Civilian aircraft

SPORTING CHANCES

- Once the primary form of transportation, dog mushing was named the state sport in 1972.

- With mountains and snow aplenty, skiing is popular. At the Alyeska Slush Cup, competitors in costumes ski downhill toward a slushy pond with the goal of skimming across it.

- Since 1973, competing dog-mushing teams have retraced the famous 1925 Serum Run in the Iditarod Trail Sled Dog Race. In 1985, Libby Riddles became the first woman to win the Iditarod.

- Started in 1972, the NYO Games (previously known as Native Youth Olympics) pit young contestants against each other in events based on traditional games.

- In 1913, Walter Harper, an Alaskan of Athabascan and Irish descent, became the first person to reach the summit of Denali.

- Rage City Roller Derby, a women's derby league in Anchorage, has three times been voted the best Anchorage sports team.

- Other prestigious dog-mushing races include the Kuskokwim 300 and the Yukon Quest.

- Alaska Challenge is the longest hand-cycle race in the world. The race is held as part of the Challenge Alaska program, which aims to raise awareness and improve the quality of life for people with disabilities.

▶ **MUSH!**

A maximum of 14 dogs make up each dog sledding team in the Iditarod race.

STARS ★ OF ★ THE ★ STATE

IRENE BEDARD

(b. 1967) is an Indigenous American actress best known for her role as the voice of Pocahontas in the 1995 animated Disney film *Pocahontas*. Born in 1967 in Anchorage, Bedard is of Inupiat, Inuit, and Cree descent. At age 27, she was nominated for a Golden Globe and won a Western Heritage Award for her television debut in a production about the 1970s Lakota protest in Wounded Knee, South Dakota. In 2012, Bedard helped create two production companies devoted to telling inspirational Indigenous stories.

AMERICAN SAMOA

CAPITAL: Pago Pago **BIRD:** none **NICKNAME:** Motu o Fiafiaga **ENTRY:** 1900

★ ★ ★ *"Samoa—Muamua le Atua" (Let God Be First)* ★ ★ ★

AS FACTS

- The islands of American Samoa formed over millions of years, as the results of volcanic activity.

- It is believed that the first people to inhabit the Samoa Islands came by sea from Asia about 3,000 years ago.

- The entire territory of American Samoa consists of 117,500 square miles (304,300 sq km), about the size of Oregon.

- The territory is primarily made up of water, with only 76 square miles (197 sq km), or less than 0.1 percent of the territory, of dry land.

- American Samoa consists of five volcanic islands (Tutuila, Aunuʻu, and the Manuʻa islands of Ofu, Olosega, and Taʻū) and two coral atolls (Rose and Swains).

- Rose Atoll is the southernmost point in all of U.S. territory.

- The National Park of American Samoa is the only U.S. national park south of the equator. ▼

▼ OFFICIAL FLOWER
Paogo
Pandanus tectorius

The Samoan necklace, known as a *'ulafala*, is made from red beads from a pandanus fruit. It's traditionally worn by the village high chiefs or by Samoans in formal events.

1988
Congress established the National Park of American Samoa, created to protect tropical rainforests, coral reefs, fruit bats, and the Samoan culture.

THE ASTRONAUTS OF APOLLO 14 LANDED ON THE MOON, AND WHEN THEY RETURNED TO EARTH THE NEXT PLACE THEY STEPPED WAS AMERICAN SAMOA, AND THEY WERE WARMLY WELCOMED AND CHEERED AS HEROES HERE.

—Congresswoman Uifa'atali Aumua Amata Coleman Radewagen

- It is about halfway between Hawaii and New Zealand in the heart of Polynesia.
- American Samoa is neighbored by Samoa, an independent country that is not a U.S. territory.
- Roughly 90 percent of the population identifies as Pacific Islander.
- Around 95 percent of residents live on Tutuila, which is home to the capital city Pago Pago.
- English and Samoan are the official languages, and most residents are bilingual.
- American Samoa has a year-round tropical climate with two distinct seasons: the wet season, between October and May, and the dry season, from June to September.
- The territory has been called an "unsung South Pacific paradise" and "America's best kept secret" because of its tropical temps and stunning scenery.
- Rainforests are home to tropical birds, as well as indigenous species of fruit bats, including the Samoan flying fox.
- The super-rare spotless crake, a flightless bird native to the Pacific islands, has been spotted in the national park.

- Two species of sea turtles are commonly found in Samoan waters, the Hawksbill sea turtle (pictured) and the green sea turtle.
- Some 98 percent of the people follow Christianity, a religion first introduced to the area by British missionaries in the 1800s.

▶ **STORY OF** THE SONG American Samoa's official anthem is "The Star-Spangled Banner." (An official translation was made into Samoan in January 2006.) But perhaps the most traditional tune is a piece entitled "Amerika Samoa," written in the Native Samoan language by Mariota Tiumalu Tuiasosopo and adopted as the territory's own anthem in 1950. The anthem was composed by Napoleon A. Tuiteleleapaga, who wrote several popular songs and music for Hollywood feature films that were set in the Pacific islands.

STARS ★ OF ★ THE ★ TERRITORY

TULSI GABBARD

(b. 1981) Born on the main island of Tutuila, Gabbard was the first American Samoan to serve in the U.S. Congress. Her political career began at the age of 21 when she won election to the state House of Representatives for Hawaii, where she was raised after her family moved from American Samoa. Gabbard went on to serve two tours of duty in the Middle East as a major in the Hawaii Army National Guard before returning to politics, ultimately winning a seat in the House in 2012, becoming the first Hindu and one of the first two female combat veterans elected to Congress. In 2020, Gabbard threw her hat into the ring for the U.S. presidential election. She won two delegates in the primary contests, before ending her bid.

In 2021, Jacinta Migo became the Air Force's first American Samoan woman—and the first American Samoan Native—to be promoted to chief master sergeant, a distinction attained by just one percent of the enlisted force.

WEIRD BUT TRUE

- Large fruit bats native to American Samoa have up to three-foot (0.9 m) wingspans.

- Today in American Samoa is tomorrow in Samoa: Despite a distance of only 102 miles (164 km), the time difference between the two neighboring islands is 24 hours.

- On March 13, 2017, a Polish man became the first to travel through several time zones—from Samoa to Fiji to Australia to Hawaii to American Samoa—to complete the world's longest day of 49 hours.

- Researchers recently spotted what they called a "Cosmic Jellyfish" swimming in American Samoa's waters: Saucer-shaped, it sported two rows of tentacles and glowed bright red and yellow.

- Bright pink Venus flytrap anemones live in the territory's deep waters. They inject venom into their prey before swallowing it.

- U.S. astronauts splash-landed here after landing on the moon in the 1960s and '70s.

- In a traditional Samoan house, it is considered impolite to sit with your legs stretched out and uncovered.

- There are more American Samoans living in the mainland U.S. than there are on the island itself.

- The National Park of American Samoa is the only U.S. national park found in the Southern Hemisphere.

MISCELLANY

- **Pink coral** grows on Rose Atoll.

- American Samoa holds the **highest rate of military enlistment** of any U.S. state or territory.

- **Sea turtles are sacred**. According to local lore, they have the power to save fishermen lost at sea by bringing them safely to shore.

- In 2009, an earthquake struck near the islands, causing a tsunami with **waves more than two stories tall**.

- The **tsunami**, which resulted in about 200 deaths across the territory, devastated some areas and caused power and transportation disruptions.

- Approximately 90 percent of American Samoan land is **communally owned**.

- In order to establish American Samoa National Park, the U.S. federal government had to **lease the land** from local villages.

- It's Samoan tradition to cook in an *umu*, or earth oven made with hot volcanic stones.

- The movie *Moana* drew inspiration from the Samoan culture and language.

- Many Samoan men **sport tattoos** (also known as *pe'a*), which represent community, status, respect, and pride—a custom dating back thousands of years.

▼ FRESH INK

The ink or pigment used in the traditional tattoo rituals is made from the soot of burned candlenuts, mixed with sugar water.

▶ **STORY OF** THE NAME Home of one of the oldest Polynesian cultures in the world, with the first settlements thought to date back to 1000 B.C., the islands of American Samoa have been considered hallowed grounds for several centuries. (The name means "sacred earth" in Samoan.) But they've gone by other names, one of which is the "Navigator Islands," selected by French explorer Louis-Antoine de Bougainville in the late 1760s. He came up with the nickname after observing the impressive navigational skills of those sailing and trading among nearby islands.

BY THE NUMBERS

9 the record weight in pounds (4.1 kg) of the giant coconut crab, which climbs trees and skitters across sand throughout American Samoa

950 the number of species of fish found swimming in the territory's coral reef ecosystem

300 THE MAXIMUM NUMBER OF INCHES (762 CM) OF RAINFALL RECORDED IN A YEAR

3,000 the height in feet (914 m) of the cliffs on Taʻū Island. They are among the highest sea cliffs in the world.

3 the number of native mammal species, all of which are bats

184,440 the number of people with at least partial American Samoan ancestry living in the mainland United States

50 the length, in years, of the lease signed by village chiefs to enable the National Park Service to manage the rainforests, beaches, and coral reefs—and establish a national park

2,300 PEOPLE ARE EMPLOYED BY THE STARKIST TUNA CANNERY, THE LARGEST PRIVATE EMPLOYER ON AMERICAN SAMOA IN 2019.

19,200 the number of tourists received in 2019; in comparison, Hawaii had more than 10 million.

1722 THE YEAR DUTCH EXPLORER JACOB ROGGEVEEN BECAME THE FIRST EUROPEAN TO EXPLORE THE AREA

- Scale the top of Mount 'Alava for a panoramic view of the island of Tutuila. To get there, you must hike a 6.1-mile (9.8 km) loop through a tropical rainforest with stunning views.

- Tutuila Island's Two Dollar Beach picked up its moniker from the price of admission: At one time, two bucks would get you access to a pristine swath of white shoreline set against the gentle, shallow surf of the Pacific.

- The visitor center at the national marine sanctuary features family-friendly exhibits on all things found in the nearby ocean, particularly the coral reefs, plus ways to protect them.

- Follow the World War II Heritage Trail on Tutuila, and check out multiple installations that helped protect American Samoa from a Japanese invasion.

- Immerse yourself in all things Samoan at Fagatogo Square on Tutuila Island, featuring a bustling marketplace where visitors can sample local fare, such as fresh coconut milk and *poi fai* (banana pudding).

- Marvel (from afar) at the red quicksands at Pala Lake, close to top surfing spot Ma'ama'a Cove on Aunu'u Island.

- Ofu Lagoon is considered the top snorkeling spot on the island, thanks to crystal-clear water and a shallow protected reef. Keep your eyes peeled for octopus and sea turtles.

- A bloody battle between French sailors and Samoan villagers in 1787 is commemorated with a monument near the aptly named Massacre Bay. The monument was erected by the French government a century later.

- Take in a traditional *ava* ceremony and *fiafia* (traditional song and dance) in the village of Fagasa in the Eastern District of Tutuila Island.

TUNA
Over 90 percent of American Samoa's exports is canned tuna.

WHALE OF A TRIP
Depending on the season, visitors may spot eight species of whales in the surrounding waters, plus sea turtles and dolphins.

STORY OF THE CITIZENSHIP CHOICE American Samoa is the only U.S. territory that does not grant automatic citizenship at birth—a ruling that dates back to 1900, when the U.S. first took formal control over part of the territory. Unless Samoans have a parent who is a U.S. citizen, they are born noncitizen nationals, meaning they can travel freely and elect their own governor, but they cannot vote for the U.S. president, serve on a jury, or apply for certain federal jobs. American Samoans can apply for U.S. citizenship through an expedited naturalization process, but it requires extra steps to achieve that status. ∎

ANOTHER DAY IN PARADISE
Tutuila, with a shoreline that stretches 62.9 miles (101.2 km), is the largest island of American Samoa.

RECORD ★ SETTERS

"Big Momma," a 500-year-old, 20-foot-tall (6 m) coral head can be found off the coast. With a circumference of 135 feet (41 m), it is one of the largest Porites coral in the world.

SPORTING CHANCES

- American Samoa produces more American football players per capita than anywhere else in the world, earning it the nickname "Football Island."

- Over the past few seasons, some 50 NFL players were from American Samoa, and more than 200 played Division I collegiate football.

- It's estimated that a male born to Samoan parents is 55 times more likely to play in the NFL than the average American.

- American Samoa has competed in nine Summer Olympics, with its debut at the 1988 games in Seoul, Korea.

- The territory sent athletes to compete in the Winter Olympic Games for the first time at the 1994 games in Lillehammer, Norway, in the bobsleigh event.

- Two-sport Olympian Nathan Ikon Crumpton represented American Samoa in both the Tokyo Summer Olympics and the 2022 Winter Games.

- In 2022, Crumpton became the first athlete to represent the territory at the Winter Olympics since 1994, competing in the skeleton event.

- American Samoa has not won any Olympic medals. Its best performance to date is 15th place, by weightlifter Eleei Ilalio in 2004.

- A Philadelphia-born runner named Gary Fanelli represented American Samoa at the 1988 Olympics in the marathon. His time of 2:25:35 set an American Samoan record.

> **IT [IS] A COMMON THING WE SAY ON THE ISLAND. YOU KNOW THERE ARE ONLY TWO WAYS TO GET OFF THE ROCK: YOU ARE EITHER GOING TO BE IN THE NFL OR YOU ARE GOING TO JOIN THE MILITARY.**
>
> —Army Company Commander Captain Jordan Scanlan

- There is no Olympic-size training pool anywhere in the territory, but American Samoa has sent several swimmers to the Olympics.

- High-level swimmers opt to swim in the South Pacific Ocean for training.

- Talavalu, the rugby union team, is named after a traditional Samoan war weapon, originally carved out of hardwood.

- Kirikiti, a type of cricket, is played throughout American Samoa. Teams representing various villages once played festival-style matches that went on for days.

- In 1968, Tony Solaita became the first major league baseball player to come from American Samoa.

- American Samoa's World Cup soccer team was on the losing end of the highest ever score in an international match, which Australia won 31–0 in 2001.

MADE IN AS

American Samoa's agricultural outputs include:

- Bananas
- Coconuts
- Vegetables
- Taro
- Breadfruit
- Yams
- Copra
- Pineapples
- Papayas
- Livestock

American Samoa's industrial outputs include:

- Handicrafts
- Garments

STARS ★ OF ★ THE ★ TERRITORY

TROY POLAMALU

(b. 1981) "I am a first-generation American Samoan, and I'm proudly representing my family's lineage to America and to the NFL," Polamalu said at his 2021 induction into the NFL's Hall of Fame. After starring on the University of Southern California's team, Polamalu was drafted into the NFL in 2003. An illustrious career saw him play in three Super Bowls, winning two as a strong safety for the Pittsburgh Steelers. Off the field, Polamalu and his wife Theodora established an eponymous foundation aimed at giving back to communities in need.

ARIZONA

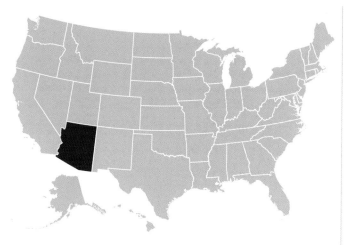

★ ★ ★

"God Enriches"

★ ★ ★

CAPITAL: Phoenix **BIRD:** Cactus Wren **NICKNAME:** Grand Canyon State **ENTRY:** 1912

AZ FACTS

- The population is 7,359,197.

- As the 48th state, Arizona was the last contiguous state to enter the U.S. It is the sixth largest in area.

- Top industries include aerospace, the manufacturing of electronics and semi-conductors, and a strong tourism industry for visitors seeking desert vistas and natural formations.

- Although famous for its deserts, the state contains a geographic variety of plateaus, mountainous regions, and forests, as well as a wide-ranging climate. While it is often arid, summers tend to bring heavy thunderstorms.

- The region has been inhabited since approximately 10,000 B.C., first by Paleolithic humans, and later by ancestral Puebloans. After the arrival of European explorers in the 1500s, the area became a Spanish settlement until Mexican independence in 1821. It was eventually ceded to the U.S. in 1848 after the Mexican-American War.

- In both population and reservation size, the Tohono O'odham Nation is the second largest in the state. The Nation is believed to be descended from Hohokam peoples of the Sonoran Desert, who created complex villages of irrigation canals and adobe structures.

- One of the largest Indigenous populations in the United States, the Navajo are one of 22 federally recognized native nations within the state, with a history that extends back thousands of years. A distinct Navajo culture developed around A.D. 1100, whose people traditionally lived in sacred homes known as hogans. Today, the Navajo Nation (Diné Bikéyah in the Navajo language) extends more than 27,000 square miles (69,930 sq km) through parts of Arizona, Utah, and New Mexico. ◄

▶ STATE FLOWER

Saguaro Cactus Flower

Carnegiea gigantea

These large flowers bloom on towering saguaros each spring thanks to pollination from local animals such as bats, birds, and insects.

1931

Begun in 1931 and completed in 1935, the Hoover Dam was built to control flooding along the Colorado River and has since become a national landmark. Sitting on the border of Arizona and Nevada, it is 726.4 feet (221.4 m) tall and weighs more than 6,600,000 tons (5,987,419 t).

LET THIS GREAT WONDER OF NATURE REMAIN AS IT NOW IS. YOU CANNOT IMPROVE ON IT.

—President Theodore Roosevelt about the Grand Canyon, 1908

▶ **LOOKING GOOD**
Official state neckwear: the bolo tie.

- Born in Phoenix in 1897, Frank Luke, Jr., went on to become a hero of World War I. Known for his flying prowess and bravery, Luke shot down 14 enemy observation balloons and four hostile airplanes during the war. His death remained a mystery for many years, until it was revealed that he was killed by enemy soldiers near Murvaux, France, after refusing to surrender.

- A native of Oklahoma, Lincoln Ragsdale became an instrumental leader of the civil rights movement in Arizona. After flying with the Black military pilots known as the Tuskegee Airmen in World War II, Ragsdale settled in Phoenix in 1946. There, he played a pivotal part in advocating for school desegregation and fighting housing discrimination.

- Tucson native Gabrielle Giffords is a politician known for her gun-safety advocacy. In 2011, Giffords survived a near-fatal injury during a shooting that killed six people. Since then, she has founded an organization devoted to promoting gun safety.

- The Hopi Tribe, a sovereign nation in northern Arizona, is known for pottery, basketry, textiles, and *katsinam* (kachina dolls). Katsinam, traditionally

carved from the roots of cottonwood trees, represent messengers from the spirit world. Although each piece varies with the artist, much of Hopi art features bold lines, vivid colors, and geometric shapes.

- Given its complex history, it is not surprising that Arizona is home to a diverse group of people. The state is 54.1 percent white (not Hispanic or Latinx), 31.7 percent Hispanic or Latinx, 5.3 percent American Indian, 5.2 percent Black or African American, 3.7 percent Asian, 2.9 percent two or more races, and 0.3 percent Native Hawaiian and other Pacific Islander.

▶ **STORY OF** THE PARK The Grand Canyon's history is a long one; the canyon itself is millions of years old and has been home to humans for up to 12,000 years. Ancestral Puebloans lived in and around the canyon and built large communities of diverse settlements. Today, 11 tribes have historic connections with the park lands. Spanish explorers began to arrive in the 16th century, and in the late 1800s American explorers, miners, and entrepreneurs flocked to the canyon to seek their fortunes. Initially designated a game preserve in 1903, the Grand Canyon was declared a national monument by President Theodore Roosevelt in 1908 and established as a national park in 1919.

STARS ★ OF ★ THE ★ STATE

SANDRA DAY O'CONNOR

(1930-2023) Sandra Day O'Connor was the first woman to serve on the United States Supreme Court. Though she was born in El Paso, Texas, O'Connor spent much of her childhood on her family's Arizona ranch. After completing her bachelor's degree and then law degree at Stanford University, she settled in Arizona in 1957 and was appointed to a seat in the Arizona State Senate in 1969. In 1981, President Ronald Reagan appointed O'Connor to the United States Supreme Court as the first female justice. O'Connor quickly became known for her work against gender discrimination, particularly in *Planned Parenthood v. Casey*, during which her swing vote reaffirmed abortion rights. After retiring, O'Connor advocated for the involvement of American youth in government.

- Arizona-born astronaut Timothy Creamer was the first person to live tweet from space.

- Local folklore features the Mogollon monster: a desert-dwelling version of Bigfoot who is said to lurk around the Mogollon Rim.

- On a March night in 1997, hundreds of Phoenix residents witnessed unidentified lights moving across the sky in a V formation. Though the military later claimed these were high-altitude flares, skeptics believe the mystery of the Phoenix Lights remains unsolved.

- When the London Bridge, originally erected in 1831, began sinking inch by inch, officials sold it to Lake Havasu City. The bridge in London was rebuilt, and the "real" London Bridge is now in Arizona.

- The movie *Oklahoma!* was filmed in Arizona.

- The horned lizard has an unusual defense: When threatened, it shoots blood from its eyes.

- Legend has it that when the city of Wickenburg lacked a prison in the 1800s, criminals were instead chained to a tree now known as the "jail tree."

- A Christmas-themed town called Santa Claus was established in 1937 and today is an abandoned ghost town.

- The state of Arizona does not observe daylight savings time, though the Navajo Nation does.

- Oatman is famous for its wild burros, which roam the streets and are protected by the U.S. Department of the Interior.

- At full height, a saguaro cactus can weigh more than a ton (0.9 t).

STORY OF THE NAME No one is positive where the name "Arizona" came from. Some believe it was given by a Spanish explorer, Juan Batista de Anza, who may have called the area the "place of oaks" in Basque. Others believe that it derived from a phrase used by the Indigenous Tohono O'odham people, meaning "place of the small spring."

RECORD ★ SETTERS

The state is home to the largest uninterrupted ponderosa pine forest, which stretches from Flagstaff all the way to the White Mountains.

MISCELLANY

- The state gem is **turquoise**.

- The **Gila monster** is the largest lizard native to the U.S., and one of the only venomous lizards in the world. It was named for its discovery along the Gila River Basin.

- Pluto was first discovered at the **Lowell Observatory** in Flagstaff.

- Arizona's small state mammal, related to raccoons and coati, is called the **ringtail**.

- **Ira Hayes**, of Pima descent, was one of the six soldiers famously photographed raising the American flag at Iwo Jima.

- Palo verde, meaning "green stick" in Spanish, is the state tree.

- The **Sonoran hot dog**, popular in Tucson, is wrapped in bacon and topped with a multitude of condiments including pinto beans, salsa, queso fresco, chilies, and more.

- The state amphibian, the **Arizona tree frog**, was chosen by the state's schoolchildren in 1985.

- The state colors are **blue and gold**.

- Arizona is the country's **top producer of copper**; its other natural resources include gold, silver, paper, lumber, and a variety of crops.

- Located outside of Wintersburg since 1988, the **Palo Verde Generating Station** is the largest nuclear power station in the country.

THERE'S SOMETHING WONDERFULLY HEALING IN ARIZONA AIR.

—Zane Grey, *The Call of the Canyon*

BY THE NUMBERS

20 the average length in inches (51 cm) of a Gila monster

18% OF THE POPULATION IS MADE UP OF PEOPLE AGED 65 AND ABOVE.

300+ the number of golf courses in Arizona

150 TO 175 years is the average life span of a saguaro cactus.

1912 the year women gained the right to vote in Arizona

1948 the year the state's Indigenous population finally gained the right to vote

5,970,000 THE NUMBER OF VISITORS TO THE GRAND CANYON IN 2019

277 miles (446 km) is the length of the Grand Canyon.

56,782 THE SEATING CAPACITY AT THE UNIVERSITY OF ARIZONA'S FOOTBALL STADIUM

Oraibi, a Hopi village established before A.D. 1100, is one of the longest continuously inhabited settlements in the U.S.

DESTINATION: ARIZONA

- The Grand Canyon, one of the Seven Natural Wonders of the World, was formed by six million years of erosion. The canyon is a mile (1.6 km) deep, and 18 miles (29 km) across at its widest point.

- Often called red rock country, Sedona boasts dazzling vistas of burnt sienna cliffs. The city is a favorite among those who love the outdoors, art galleries, or wellness resorts for massage, yoga, and more.

- Arizona is home to stunning natural formations such as Wave, an erosion-sculpted bluff of rippling color in the Coyote Buttes; Antelope Canyon, a winding, beautifully illuminated slot canyon near Page; and Horseshoe Bend, an oft-photographed site in Glen Canyon where the Colorado River bends suddenly against the desert backdrop.

- Arizona is perhaps most famous for its cliff dwellings. From around A.D. 1150, ancestral Puebloans built terraced homes of stone and adobe in cliff caves. Particularly impressive is Montezuma Castle, a 20-room dwelling that sits mid-cliff and was home to the Sinagua people more than 600 years ago.

- On October 26, 1881, in the town of Tombstone, lawman Wyatt Earp, gunfighter John Henry "Doc" Holliday, and Earp's two brothers faced down a group of outlaw cattle rustlers known as the "cowboys" in what came to be known as the Gunfight at the OK Corral. Today, visitors to Tombstone can see reenactments, historical exhibits, and the graves of famous Old West figures.

- More than 200 million years ago, a forest grew in what is now the Painted Desert. When nearby waterways flooded, these ancient trees fossilized into quartz, which visitors can still view at Petrified Forest National Park.

- Opened in 1876, the Yuma Territorial Prison of Old West fame housed inmates such as Pearl Hart, one of the only female stage-coach bandits. While the prison closed in 1909, the grounds and building remain as a state historic park.

- One of the nation's most quintessential desert sights is Monument Valley Navajo Tribal Park. Located in the Navajo Nation—and known in Navajo as Tse'Bii'Ndzisgaii—the park is made up of dusty plateaus and towering sandstone buttes.

- At three-quarters of a mile (1.2 km) across, 2.4 miles (3.9 km) around, and 550 feet (168 m) deep, Meteor Crater is Earth's best preserved meteorite impact site.

- Arizona is home to the world's most certified Dark Sky Places—areas best suited for stargazing. At Oracle State Park, the Grand Canyon, Tumacácori National Historical Park, Kartchner Caverns, Parashant National Monument, Petrified Forest National Monument, Sunset Crater Volcano National Monument, and Tonto National Monument, visitors can glimpse the Andromeda galaxy, Mars, and Jupiter.

I'M VERY OPTIMISTIC ABOUT MY HOME STATE OF ARIZONA.

—Senator John McCain

WILD WILD WEST

Following its acquisition as a U.S. territory, Arizona quickly became a land of ranching and cowboys. It also became a land of lawlessness—a hallmark of the Old West. In 1860, the Arizona Territorial Rangers formed to defend the region against outlaws and bandits.

MADE IN AZ

Arizona's agricultural outputs include:

- Beef
- Dairy
- Eggs
- Lettuce
- Spinach
- Wine
- Pecans
- Roses
- Cotton
- Grain

Arizona's industrial outputs include:

- Aircraft
- Transportation equipment
- Copper
- Appliances and components
- Electrical equipment
- Machinery
- Other metal products

SPORTING CHANCES

- Residents and visitors play more than 10 million total rounds of golf per year in Arizona.

- Arizonan wrestling superstar Billy Graham held the WWE Championship for nearly 10 months—longer than any other WWE "villain."

- Founded in 1884, the Payson Pro Rodeo is the world's oldest continuous rodeo.

- A member of the U.S. Women's Soccer team, Arizona native Julie Ertz was named Player of the Year in both 2017 and 2019.

- In 1949, Fred Batiste became the first Black athlete to play football for the University of Arizona.

- The Cardinals, founded in 1898, predated the NFL and are the oldest team in continuous operation in pro football history.

- At the U.S. Airways Center in Phoenix, Thunder Law of the Harlem Globetrotters made a basket shot from 82 feet, 2 inches (25 m) away—while facing backward!

- In 1996, Tucson-born gymnast Kerri Strug became famous for sticking her final vault landing—despite a painful ankle injury—to clinch the gold medal for her team.

- In 2022, Phoenix's NBA team, the Phoenix Suns, was purchased for a whopping $4 billion.

- The Phoenix Mercury hold the record for most WNBA wins in a season with 29 wins in 2014.

STARS ★ OF ★ THE ★ STATE

GERONIMO

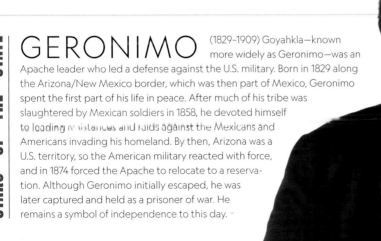

(1829–1909) Goyahkla—known more widely as Geronimo—was an Apache leader who led a defense against the U.S. military. Born in 1829 along the Arizona/New Mexico border, which was then part of Mexico, Geronimo spent the first part of his life in peace. After much of his tribe was slaughtered by Mexican soldiers in 1858, he devoted himself to loading in distances and raids against the Mexicans and Americans invading his homeland. By then, Arizona was a U.S. territory, so the American military reacted with force, and in 1874 forced the Apache to relocate to a reservation. Although Geronimo initially escaped, he was later captured and held as a prisoner of war. He remains a symbol of independence to this day.

ARKANSAS

★ ★ ★

"The People Rule"

★ ★ ★

CAPITAL: Little Rock **FLOWER:** Apple Blossom **NICKNAME:** Natural State **ENTRY:** 1836

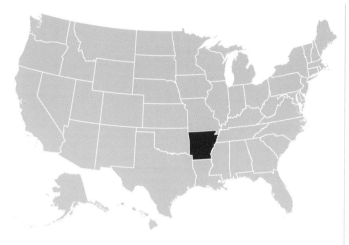

AR FACTS

- Arkansas is located in the southern United States bordering the Mississippi River.

- The state is known for its myriad natural resources, including bromine, natural gas, petroleum, and silica stone.

- The original inhabitants of the area include the Caddo, Chickasaw, Osage, Quapaw, Tunica, and Cherokee peoples.

- It was the 25th state in the nation and is the 27th largest state by area.

- The state's biggest city by population is Little Rock, with some 202,562 residents.

- Arkansas is the only state that produces diamonds, which were first discovered in 1906 on the surface of a field on a farm near Murfreesboro. The farmer, John Wesley Huddleston, known as Arkansas's "Diamond King," soon sold his land to a commercial mining company for $36,000.

- The state has six geographic regions, ranging from the mountainous Ozarks region in the north, to the swamps and bayous in the eastern delta region, to the forested Timberlands in the southwest.

▶ **STATE BIRD**
Northern Mockingbird
Mimus polyglottos

There are 428 species of birds calling Arkansas home, with 145 nesting within the state year-round. (The rest pass through seasonally.)

1972

In 1972, the state bought land that is now Crater of Diamonds State Park.

> ARKANSAS'S PEOPLE ARE SHAPED BY ARKANSAS IN RETURN: ITS TREES, ITS LAKES, ITS HILLS, ITS MOUNTAINS, AND A MYRIAD OF OTHER NATURAL WONDERS.

—Author Erin Dalton

▶ **POSSUM PIE**

A concoction of pecans, cream, chocolate custard, and cream cheese (but no parts of the animal!) is a signature dish in Arkansas.

- In 1957, Arkansas was the setting for one of the biggest milestones of the U.S. civil rights movement when nine African American students were escorted by Army troops into Little Rock Central High School, which previously had only allowed white students to attend. ▶

- Arkansas is one of the world's major producers of bromine, a highly corrosive, reddish brown element that's the basis for many widely used chemical compounds.

- The Louisiana Purchase of 1803 included the land that eventually became the state of Arkansas, which was the third state west of the Mississippi to be admitted to the Union, after Louisiana and Missouri.

- The change in landscape and altitude can cause major weather extremes throughout the four seasons. Arkansas experiences super cell thunderstorms, ice storms, and hot, humid summers.

- Tornadoes are also common, with some 37 twisters spawned in the state annually. On January 21, 1999, 56 tornadoes were recorded in Arkansas, the most on a single day in all the states. The year 1999 recorded a record-setting 107 twisters. ▪

▲ **STORY OF** THE NAME Decidedly rooted in the legacy of the American Indians who first lived on the land, and later interpreted by the French, the state's name took a circuitous route to its final destination. The name originated as *Acansa*, or *Akansea*, meaning "people who live downstream," a reference to the Quapaw tribe. The French later referred to it as both Arkansas and Arkansaw, leading to some confusion about its pronunciation in the early days of statehood. In 1881, the state's General Assembly passed a resolution deeming that the state's name should be spelled "Arkansas" but pronounced "Arkansaw," settling the matter once and for all. ▪

STARS ★ OF ★ THE ★ STATE

WILLIAM J. "BILL" CLINTON

(b. 1946) The only U.S. president who has hailed from Arkansas, Bill Clinton is a beloved son of the state. The first president to come from the baby boomer generation, Clinton was also the first Democratic president since Franklin D. Roosevelt to win a second term (and the second U.S. president to be impeached by the House). Today, a portion of State Highway 29 is known as Bill Clinton Drive, and the one-time Arkansas governor's first home in the tiny town of Hope—population 8,624—in now a museum, as is the one-bedroom brick Tudor where the Clintons made their first home in 1975. ▪

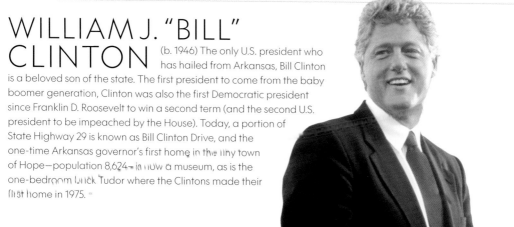

WEIRD BUT TRUE

- A Popeye statue welcomes visitors to the town of Alma, known as the "spinach capital of the world."

- One tiny shop in Mountain View has produced over 76,000 hand-crafted dulcimer instruments.

- For decades, witnesses have reported mysterious glowing orbs, known as the Dover Lights, on the hillside of an uninhabited valley of the Ozark Mountains.

- Since as early as 1834, Arkansans claim to have seen a creature that reaches well over seven feet (2.1 m) tall that's been called the beast of Boggy Creek or the Fouke monster.

- The World Cheese Dip Championship has drawn 10,000 visitors to this annual cheesy competition in Little Rock.

- Toad Suck, Flippin, Booger Hollow, Smackover, and Oil Trough are all names of towns in Arkansas.

- Dubbed Old Naked Joe, one Ozark mountain is said to be named after a man who lived at the top and preferred to roam around in his birthday suit.

- Visitors to Port of Pine Bluff are greeted by a full-size tugboat looming 30 feet (9 m) in the air atop two concrete pilings.

- Locals initially believed that Hell's Half Acre—a clearing of exposed rocks amidst an otherwise forested area—was an extinct volcano (and haunted).

- Beebe's Fallin' Blackbird Festival is named after two infamous days, in 2010 and 2011, in which thousands of blackbirds fell from the sky.

▶ STORY OF THE SOUND

What are you calling a violin? In Arkansas, the four-stringed instrument is lovingly known as a fiddle, and it has been making a prominent appearance in the fabric of the state's folklife since the 1800s. Today, fiddlers flock to Mountain View for the Arkansas State Fiddle Championship and Old-Time Fiddle Workshop, while a convention dedicated to the instrument is held each spring in Harrison. But it's not all about old-school music: In 2019, country star and Arkansas native Jenee Fleenor became the first fiddler to win the Country Music Association's Musician of the Year award in more than two decades.

▲ THIRSTY?

More than nine million gallons of water (34 million L) flow throughout Mammoth Spring State Park each hour.

MISCELLANY

- People from Arkansas are called **Arkansans or Arkansawyers**.

- Rogers is home to the **first Walmart store**, which opened in 1962.

- There are rock drawings created by Native Americans more than 500 years ago in a cave in **Morrilton's Petit Jean State Park**.

- In 1932, Jonesboro's **Hattie Caraway** became the first woman elected to the U.S. Senate. She served two terms for a total of 13 years.

- Ernest Hemingway wrote parts of *A Farewell to Arms* at his wife's family's home in Piggott, now a museum.

- The *Arkansaurus fridayi*, which lived some 113 million years ago, is the state's official dinosaur.

- Each year, Mount Ida hosts the **World Championship Quartz Crystal Dig**.

- Some 180 years old, Little Rock's redbrick **Old State House Museum** is the oldest standing state capitol building west of the Mississippi River.

- The **Magazine Mountain shagreen**, a species of snail, is only found in Arkansas.

- "Brown 'N Serve" rolls were first baked at Meyer's Bakery in Little Rock in the 1950s.

- **Square dance** is the official state folk dance of Arkansas.

- The **Chateau Aux Arc Winery** in Altus is the world's largest planter of Cynthiana grapes, and the largest Chardonnay vineyard in the country outside of California.

- Spanning 4,226 feet (1,288 m) over the Arkansas River, Little Rock's **Big Dam Bridge** is the longest enclosed suspension walker/biker bridge in North America.

- **Ouachita National Forest** (in Arkansas and Oklahoma), the biggest forest in the South, covers nearly 1.8 million acres (728,500 ha).

- In an effort to promote tourism, Arkansas changed its nickname from "Land of Opportunity" to **"The Natural State"** in 1995.

RECORD ★ SETTERS

An artist from Eureka Springs set a record for the world's largest set of wind chimes, measuring 35 feet 10 inches (10.9 m) tall.

BY THE NUMBERS

Natural Treasures

7 million acres (2.83 million ha) are harvested for crops, which is enough land to cover Puerto Rico and Rhode Island.

38 SPECIES OF ANIMALS AND PLANTS ARE THREATENED OR ENDANGERED, INCLUDING THE RED-COCKADED WOODPECKER, THE OZARK BIG-EARED BAT, AND THE SPECKLED POCKETBOOK MUSSEL.

143°F the average temperature (62°C) of the hot springs flowing from the southwestern slope of Hot Springs Mountain

10 the width in feet (3 m) of the top of the largest freestanding rock formation in Pivot Rock Park in Eureka Springs, home to several unusual geological features

2,753 the height in feet (839 m) of Mount Magazine, the highest point in the state

514,000+ the number of acres (208,000 ha) of lakes found throughout the state. At more than 40,000 acres (16,000 ha), Lake Ouachita is the largest lake in the state.

1,460 the length in miles (2,334 km) of the Arkansas River, the second longest stream to flow into the Mississippi-Missouri river system

55 THE LOWEST ELEVATION, IN FEET (16.8 M), IN ARKANSAS, FOUND IN THE OUACHITA RIVER

359 the length in miles (563 km) of Bayou Bartholomew, which stretches from Pine Bluff, Arkansas, to Sterlington, Louisiana, making it the longest bayou in the world

> ## AND SO I SAY TO ALL THOSE IN THIS CAMPAIGN SEASON WHO WOULD CRITICIZE ARKANSAS: COME ON DOWN ... SURE, YOU'LL SEE US STRUGGLING AGAINST SOME OF THE PROBLEMS WE HAVEN'T SOLVED YET. BUT YOU'LL ALSO SEE A LOT OF GREAT PEOPLE DOING AMAZING THINGS. AND YOU MIGHT EVEN LEARN A THING OR TWO.
>
> —President Bill Clinton

DESTINATION: ARKANSAS

- You can spend a day spelunking in Blanchard Springs Caverns, a system of limestone caves starting more than 200 feet (61 m) underground in the Ozarks. The caverns' features include an underground river, stalactites, stalagmites, and a "Cathedral Room" with a six-story stone column centerpiece.

- Visitors to Bentonville can pass a couple of hours perusing the Walmart Museum, outlining the history of the superstore as well as the story of its founder, Arkansas native Sam Walton.

- The state hosts a plethora of festivals dedicated to all things eating. From the Cave City Watermelon Festival to the World Championship Steak Cook-Off, there's something for every palate.

- Prospective prospectors are attracted to all that glitters in Crater of Diamonds State Park, where gemstones like diamonds, amethyst, garnet, jasper, agate, and quartz can be found.

- The gleaming Clinton Presidential Library in Little Rock is a treasure trove of memorabilia from the former commander in chief's time in the White House.

- Go way old-school in Little Rock's Quapaw Quarter, where most of the city's oldest buildings can be found. Dating back to the mid-19th century, some of the impressively restored homes and churches can be accessed through walking tours.

300 MILES (482 KM) OF HIKING TRAILS ARE ACCESSIBLE THROUGHOUT ALL 52 STATE PARKS.

- For decades, people have been visiting Hot Springs National Park. Nicknamed "The American Spa," famous (and infamous) soakers from Franklin D. Roosevelt to Al Capone have made trips here to dip into its reportedly restorative waters.

- Each year, movie buffs head to Hot Springs for the town's Documentary Film Festival. Launched in 1991, it's the oldest all-documentary film fest in North America.

- The Little Rock Zoo is home to some 500 animals, including six western lowland gorillas.

STARS ★ OF ★ THE ★ STATE

JOHNNY CASH

(1932–2003) Long before he sold 90 million records worldwide and won 20 Grammys, Johnny Cash was simply known as J.R., the fourth of seven children born to a Kingsland, Arkansas, cotton farmer. Cash joined the Air Force out of high school and eventually settled in Memphis, Tennessee, where his career took off. During his heyday, Cash played a raucous 1969 concert for inmates at the Cummins Prison in Gould, a move that brought attention to prison reform, a platform of importance for the musician. (He famously played shows at California's Folsom prison and San Quentin, among others.) Cash was inducted into the Rock & Roll Hall of Fame in 1992, and Arkansas still proudly claims him as its own. A museum operates out of his boyhood home.

SPORTING CHANCES

- During a spring training trip to Hot Springs in 1918, Babe Ruth stepped up to the plate and smacked a career-changing homer that launched him from simply a pitcher to one of the sport's greatest sluggers. ▶

- "Town ball" was the main spectator sport in the state until major league baseball games began broadcasting on the radio in the early 1900s.

- Baseball took off in the state in the 1860s, with games getting so heated that one umpire avoided disputes by wearing an unconcealed pistol.

- Born in Hamburg, Arkansas, Scottie Pippen went on to become a basketball legend, playing 17 NBA seasons and winning six championships with the Chicago Bulls in the 1990s.

- In the mid-1960s, Pine Bluff archery company Ben Pearson Inc. was manufacturing up to 5,000 arrows and 4,000 bows every day.

- Every Thanksgiving Week, Stuttgart hosts the World's Championship Duck Calling Contest, for a prize package worth more than $25,000.

- In 2021, some 144 of the best female golfers in the world competed in the Walmart NW Arkansas Championship.

- Tusk V, the University of Arkansas Razorbacks' live mascot, is a young male Russian boar.

- Wes McNulty, a Little League coach and a farmer of rice, soybeans, corn, and fish, is one of Arkansas's best golfers, with several amateur titles to his name.

- In 2005, 19-year-old Kerron Clement set a world record for the fastest indoor 400-meter run (44:57) on the track at the University of Arkansas in Fayetteville.

- The University of Arkansas is just one of two collegiate programs in history to win all six running championships: both men's and women's titles in cross country, indoor track, and outdoor track.

- Hailing from Ashdown, Hazel Walker was a pioneer in women's basketball. She founded the Arkansas Travelers pro team in 1949. ▪

MADE IN AR

Arkansas's agricultural outputs include:

- Cotton
- Catfish
- Beef cattle
- Dairy
- Poultry
- More than nine billion pounds (4.1 billion kg) of rice are grown annually, making the state the country's biggest producer of the grain.

Arkansas's industrial outputs include:

- Aerospace
- Defense
- Food and beverage
- Metals
- Technology
- The timber and paper products industry employs some 28,000 workers.

▶ HERE IT GROWS

Arkansas ranks fourth among all U.S. states in cotton production, with about 7 percent of the nation's crop.

▶ SOOIE!

The hog call "Woo pig sooie" is a popular chant at University of Arkansas sporting events.

▶ STORY BEHIND THE STATE FLAG'S STARS

When schoolteacher Willie Hocker first designed the Arkansas state flag in 1913, she included the 25 stars along the border as a nod to Arkansas being the 25th state to enter the union. The three stars at the center represent the governments that Arkansas has been ruled by in the past and present (Spanish, French, and the United States, respectively), while the star at the top—a symbol of the Confederacy—was added a decade later. Today, the fourth star is a hot-button topic in the state, with opponents lobbying to have it removed. ▪

RECORD ★ SETTERS

At a whopping 40.23 carats, the Uncle Sam diamond, discovered in 1924 at what is now Crater of Diamonds State Park is the largest diamond ever unearthed in the U.S.

CALIFORNIA

★ ★ ★

"Eureka!"

★ ★ ★

CAPITAL: Sacramento **BIRD:** California Quail **NICKNAME:** Golden State **ENTRY:** 1850

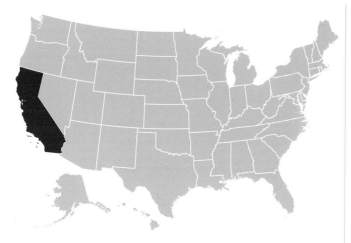

CA FACTS

- Population is 39,029,342, the largest in the country.

- The state is known for its technological, film, and agricultural industries, as well as its scenic beauty and beaches.

- The Indigenous people who first settled in the area that now makes up the state spoke as many as 135 different dialects. Today, the state is home to 109 federally recognized Indigenous tribes.

- California was the 31st state in the nation and, in terms of land area, is the third largest state.

- Agricultural crops include produce such as lemons, avocados, figs, grapes, dates, strawberries, nuts, and more. The state is also a source for gases, petroleum, and timber.

- In 1914, Cecil B. DeMille released the first feature-length film shot in Hollywood, encouraging others to open studios in the area. Today, "Tinseltown" remains the most influential of the world's movie industries. ▼

▶ STATE FLOWER

California Poppy
Eschscholzia californica

Unlike the more commonly known red poppy, the California poppy is a vibrant ocher shade. Native to the region, it is also known as *copa de oro* (cup of gold).

1821

In 1821, Mexico achieved its independence from Spain. As part of this new country, what is now California became home to the rancho system, a series of land grants for ranchers and cattle owners.

◀ GOLD! GOLD! GOLD!
When James Marshall discovered gold at John Sutter's sawmill in 1848, hundreds of thousands of fortune-seekers journeyed to California hoping to get rich quick.

CALIFORNIA IS A PLACE IN WHICH A BOOM MENTALITY AND A SENSE OF CHEKHOVIAN LOSS MEET IN UNEASY SUSPENSION.

—Author and journalist Joan Didion

- The San Diego Bay area was sighted in the mid-1500s by Spanish explorers searching for a fabled golden island. Spanish military officers later established a fort in the area in 1769, making San Diego the oldest California city.

- In 1846, a group of unlucky pioneers known as the Donner Party became stranded in the Sierra Nevada mountains after attempting to take a shortcut off the Oregon Trail. As food ran out, starving party members were forced to resort to cannibalism of the dead. The tragedy quickly became infamous.

- Today, the California population identifies as approximately 40.3 percent Hispanic or Latinx, 34.7 percent White, 16.3 percent Asian, 6.5 percent Black, 1.7 percent Indigenous American, and 0.5 percent as Native Hawaiian or Pacific Islander.

- Los Angeles was the birthplace of renowned rhythm-and-blues singer Etta James.

- In 1937, Ronald Wilson Reagan arrived in California to begin his career as an actor. He appeared in 53 films before pivoting to politics and becoming a proponent of conservatism. He served as governor from 1967 to 1975 and later as president.

- In the early 1940s, Mexican American children were forced to enroll in segregated schools. Sylvia Mendez and her family fought back against this and made history in the 1946 case *Mendez v. Westminster,* resulting in a bill that officially ended school segregation in the state.

- By the 1960s, San Francisco was dubbed the "Gay Capital of America." The city became famous for the country's first lesbian organization and first gay community center, and politician Harvey Milk made further history by becoming one of the first openly gay elected officials in America.

▲ STORY OF THE SOUND In 1961, three brothers from Hawthorne— Brian, Carl, and Dennis Wilson—joined with Mike Love and Al Jardine to form the Beach Boys. The band became famous for their feel-good vocal harmonies and relaxed sound. The Beach Boys pioneered "surf rock," creating albums that were distinctively West Coast with songs such as "Surfin' USA" and "California Girls." In 1988, they were inducted into the Rock & Roll Hall of Fame. To date, the Beach Boys have sold more than 70 million albums. ■

- In the late 20th century, the area to the south of San Francisco came to be known for a multitude of inventions that relied on a type of computer chip made of silicon—thus lending the region the moniker "Silicon Valley." Companies such as Google, Apple, and Facebook all originated here.

- In 1965, Filipino American farm workers appealed to Latino union leader Cesar Chavez to join them in a strike against working conditions and unfair pay. Chavez, who had previously founded the National Farm Workers Association in 1962, vowed both nonviolence and cooperation between Filipino and Latinx workers during what became known as the Delano Grape Strike. The strike achieved success in 1970, when farmers were finally awarded protection, benefits, and better pay. ■

On June 18, 1983, Encino native Sally Ride became the first American woman—and the third woman ever—to travel to space.

WEIRD BUT TRUE

- Founded in 1781 by settlers coming from Mexico, Los Angeles is older than Washington, D.C.

- As the result of a viral social media post, the thick San Francisco fog is nicknamed "Karl."

- At the Hollywood Forever Cemetery in Los Angeles, audiences can watch movies among tombstones.

- The state flag was designed by William Todd—a nephew of Mary Todd Lincoln.

- At a music festival in Lake Elsinore, attendees once skydived into the venue.

- At the Racetrack Playa in Death Valley, stones weighing hundreds of pounds seemingly move of their own accord. In 2014, researchers discovered that these "sailing stones" glide with the help of thawing sheet ice and wind.

- Located in Inyo National Forest and nearly 5,000 years old, Methuselah is one of the world's oldest living trees. "

▲ FOXY

The island fox is endemic to the Channel Islands off the southern coast.

MISCELLANY

- Historic **Route 66**, stretching from Chicago to Los Angeles, culminates at the Santa Monica Pier.

- The bear on the **state flag** was modeled after a real-life grizzly bear named Monarch.

- The state fossil is the **saber-toothed cat**.

- **Forest Lawn Memorial Park** in Glendale is the final resting place for celebrities such as Jimmy Stewart, Elizabeth Taylor, and Humphrey Bogart.

- **Winemaking** in the region dates back to the 1700s, when missionaries from Spain brought vines and cultivated the grape.

- The first Latina woman in space was L.A.-born **Ellen Ochoa**, who joined the crew of the space shuttle *Discovery*.

- California has **two state ghost towns**: Bodie, a gold rush town, and Calico, a silver rush town.

MARILYN MONROE

(1926–1962) Born Norma Jeane Mortenson in Los Angeles, Marilyn Monroe was an iconic actress. Raised in and out of an orphanage and foster care, Monroe catapulted to fame after she began modeling and caught the eyes of producers at Twentieth Century Fox. She appeared in multiple films, garnering a worldwide celebrity status despite personal and professional turmoil. Monroe was deeply interested in literature, humanitarian work, and philanthropy. Today she remains one of the preeminent symbols of Hollywood and continues to posthumously influence fashion, film, and music. "

BY THE NUMBERS

450 the length in feet (137 m) of the Hollywood sign

275 the height in feet (83 m) of the giant sequoia General Sherman, the largest tree in the world

14,494 feet (4,418 m) is the elevation of Mt. Whitney, the highest mountain in the continental U.S.

0 California grizzly bears are left after the species was hunted to extinction.

887,000 TONS (804,673 T) IS THE WEIGHT OF THE GOLDEN GATE BRIDGE.

1960 the year the Lakers moved from Minneapolis to Los Angeles

1906 the year of the Great San Francisco earthquake, whose 7.9 magnitude leveled buildings and unleashed a devastating fire

- Visitors to Hollywood can see the hand-prints and signatures of stars such as Clark Gable and Joan Crawford outside the famous Grauman's Chinese Theater.

- Upon its completion in 1937, the Golden Gate Bridge was the world's tallest and longest suspension bridge.

- Established as a national park in 1890, Yosemite is home to sweeping vistas and abundant wildlife.

- Disneyland, known as "The Happiest Place on Earth," opened in 1955 with just 18 attractions. Today, the park sees as many as 18 million visitors a year.

- Alcatraz Island, which first saw use as a prisoner outpost in 1861, was considered nearly impossible to escape due to its location in the San Francisco Bay. It is most famous for its term as a maximum-security prison.

- Napa Valley's more than 400 wineries produce world-class vintages. Although the first commercial vineyards were planted in 1861, the region did not get its reputation for fine wines until 1976.

- Visitors driving along the coastal cliffs of Big Sur's Highway 1 have the opportunity to glimpse California condors, stunning ocean views, and plentiful marine life such as sea otters, seals, and sea lions.

- As 18th-century Spain sought to expand its empire, Franciscan missionaries established religious outposts in the region. From 1769 to 1823, monks founded 21 of these missions, each still standing today.

- Located in Fresno, the Hmong Cultural New Year Celebration (HCNYC) is the largest Hmong American community event in the country.

CALIFORNIA IS ALWAYS IN MY MIND.

—Painter David Hockney

◢ COLOR FIELD

When spring arrives, Antelope Valley California Poppy Reserve bursts with more than 1,700 acres (688 ha) of wildflowers.

- Settled by Danish immigrants, Solvang resembles a sleepy hamlet in Denmark.

- Since 1978, Gilroy has held a festival devoted to garlic. Participants can braid the "stinking rose," enter cooking competitions, and sample delicacies such as garlic ice cream.

- Beginning in the 1880s, Sarah Winchester of the Winchester Repeating Arms fortune began renovating her home. Over the next 36 years, she molded the house into a labyrinthine structure of 160 rooms, today known as the Winchester Mystery House.

- Colonel Allensworth State Historic Park is the site of the first Californian town founded and governed by Black Americans.

- Wishtoyo's Chumash Village is an authentic re-creation of a Chumash village situated on a historic site in Malibu.

RECORD ★ SETTERS

In 2021, Kamala Harris, an Oakland native of Black and South Asian descent, became the first female vice president of the United States.

▶ **STORY OF** THE NAME Most scholars believe the origin of the state's name can be traced back to Spanish explorers in the 1500s, who named the region after a famous fictional island. The first reference appears in an early-16th-century romance novel by Garci Ordóñez de Montalvo, who tells the tale of California, a utopian island of Amazon-like women who use gold as their only metal and keep pet griffins. However, some scholars suggest that the legend is even older, reaching back to Spanish-Muslim relations and deriving from the Arabic word *khalif*, meaning spiritual and civil leader.

SPORTING CHANCES

- Born in Southern California, Tiger Woods is regarded as one of the greatest golfers of all time. His wins include more than 100 tournaments worldwide and 15 major championships.

- Valued at $7.56 billion, the Golden State Warriors are the most valuable NBA team and have six NBA championships to their name.

- Opened in 1922, the Rose Bowl football stadium in Pasadena is home to the annual Rose Bowl Game.

- Named after immigrants who flocked to California in search of gold in 1849, the San Francisco 49ers have won five Super Bowl Championships.

- Born in Hayward, California, figure skater Kristi Yamaguchi became the first Asian American woman to win an Olympic gold medal in 1992. Yamaguchi was the first Asian American inducted into the World Figure Skating Hall of Fame.

- Both celebrity icon and athlete, San Franciscan Joe DiMaggio achieved a 56-game hitting streak and was immortalized in the Baseball Hall of Fame.

- The third oldest continually used major league baseball park, L.A.'s Dodger Stadium is home to the Dodgers. Founded in 1883, the team has won seven World Series titles.

THE ATTRACTION AND SUPERIORITY OF CALIFORNIA ARE IN ITS DAYS. IT HAS BETTER DAYS, AND MORE OF THEM, THAN ANY OTHER COUNTRY.

—Essayist Ralph Waldo Emerson

- Beginning in the 1930s and '40s, San Francisco's Chinatown saw the creation of many Chinese American basketball leagues and sports groups for both men and women.

- Half a mile (0.8 km) off Pillar Point in Half Moon Bay is Mavericks, where waves commonly reach 30 feet (9 m) but can be 60 feet (18 m). Despite the dangers, people have been surfing this spot since the 1970s.

- The United States of America Snowboard and Freeski Association (USASA) based in South Lake Tahoe hosts more than 500 freeski and snowboard events annually.

- In 2016, California-raised NFL player Colin Kaepernick made history and raised widespread awareness by taking a knee during the U.S. national anthem to protest racial police brutality.

MADE IN CA

California's agricultural outputs include:

- Nuts, including almonds, pistachios, and walnuts
- Fruits, including grapes, strawberries, and oranges
- Dairy
- Wine
- Beef

California's industrial outputs include:

- Computers
- Other electronic products
- Aircrafts
- Electric motor vehicles
- Transportation equipment
- Machinery
- Chemicals
- Petroleum
- Diamonds
- Medical instruments

STARS ★ OF ★ THE ★ STATE

BRUCE LEE

(1940–1973) Bruce Lee, born Lee Jun Fan, was a celebrated actor and one of the world's greatest martial artists. Born to Chinese parents in San Francisco, Lee grew up learning boxing, dancing, and kung fu. After opening a school in Oakland, he developed his own martial arts technique known as Jeet Kune Do ("Way of the Intercepting Fist"). This method combined aspects of boxing, fencing, and kung fu to create a fluid and adaptable style, and it quickly caught the attention of a television producer. Lee soon rose to worldwide fame, popularizing martial arts movies and gaining innumerable fans.

COLORADO

★ ★ ★

"Nothing Without Providence or Deity"

★ ★ ★

CAPITAL: Denver **BIRD:** Lark Bunting **NICKNAME:** Centennial State **ENTRY:** 1876

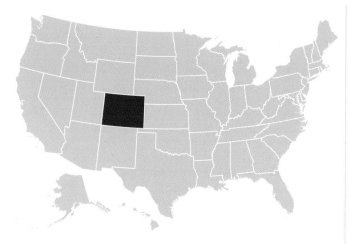

CO FACTS

- Hunters tracked bison and now extinct mammoths and mastodons through the land about 15,000 years ago.

- The first long-term settlements appeared in the southwest part of the state thousands of years ago in and around the area that is now Mesa Verde National Park.

- The Continental Divide—the natural boundary separating the watersheds that drain into the Pacific Ocean from the river systems that drain into the Atlantic Ocean—winds through Colorado.

- Over 80 percent of the population lives in the Front Range of the Rockies, which includes the 10 largest cities in the state.

- Native American tribes that settled in Colorado include the Ute, Cheyenne, and Arapaho tribes.

- The population was about 5.8 million in 2022, making it the 21st most populous state in the nation.

- Colorado's Rocky Mountains are home to bighorn sheep, mountain goats, black bears, mountain lions, beavers, golden eagles, and great horned owls. ▼

▶ **STATE FLOWER**
Columbine
Aquilegia coerulea

The lavender and white wildflowers bloom each spring and summer, and can be seen almost everywhere throughout Colorado, especially in the Rocky Mountain region.

1858

In 1858, the discovery of gold in Cherry Creek—which is now Denver—attracted the first U.S. settlers to the area.

COLORADO DOES NOT SHUT DOWN. COLORADO DOES NOT QUIT. COLORADO DOES NOT BREAK.

—Senator John Hickenlooper

▶ **FROZEN DEAD GUY**
The annual Frozen Dead Guy Days festival honors a resident whose remains were once cryogenically frozen inside a shed in Nederland.

- Animals like bison, prairie dogs, rattlesnakes, and burrowing owls can be spotted on Colorado's plains. ▶

- Covering 104,094 square miles (269,602 sq km), Colorado is the nation's eighth largest state by land area.

- The first European visitors were the Spanish conquistadors in the 1500s.

- There are more than 50 peaks above 14,000 feet (4,257 m) within the state.

- The U.S. government owns about a third of the state's 67 million acres (27 million ha), with most of that space open to the public for recreation.

- Colorado holds 75 percent of the land area in the continental U.S. above 10,000 feet (3,048 m).

- At an elevation of 6,800 feet (2,070 m) above sea level, Colorado has the highest mean altitude of the 50 states.

- Grand Mesa is one of the world's largest flattop mountains, spanning hundreds of square miles and standing more than 11,000 feet (3,353 m) above sea level.

- Denver is nicknamed the "Mile High City" because it sits at 5,280 feet (1,609 m) above sea level—exactly one mile. ▪

▶ **STORY OF** THE NAME When early Spanish explorers first locked eyes on a reddish, muddy river that ribboned through the land, they called it *Colorado*, meaning "colored red." Eventually, the name stuck, and it soon became the title of the territory as well as the river, which gets its rusty hue from the red sandstone soil of the region. ▪

STARS ★ OF ★ THE ★ STATE

WILLIAM "BUFFALO BILL" CODY

(1846–1917) Known for his cowboy-themed Wild West shows, Cody is considered one of the world's first global celebrities. His performances, which dramatized the culture of the American West with a cowboy's flair, made him a Western folk hero. Cody performed at Queen Victoria's 1887 Golden Jubilee and, in 1893, a run of shows in Chicago attracted a total of three million people. Cody is buried on Colorado's Lookout Mountain, and a nearby museum in Golden honors his life and work. ▪

▲ FOUR CORNERS MONUMENT

is the only place in the country where you can stand in four states—Utah, Arizona, New Mexico, and Colorado—at the same time.

- Each year, the town of Fruita celebrates "Mike the Headless Chicken Day," in honor of a bird who lived for 18 months without a head.

- Dove Creek is the self-proclaimed "pinto bean capital of the world."

- So many butterflies once migrated through a part of the state that they showed up on a weather radar map.

- On average, cats in Colorado live two years longer than cats in other states, one study found.

- A construction crew unearthed a 66-million-year-old *Torosaurus*, a relative of *Triceratops*.

- There is a UFO Watchtower in San Luis Valley.

- The state fair holds a Pet Rock competition, including a prize for the best-dressed rock.

- It was once illegal to have snowball fights in Severance.

- The world's first official "cheeseburger" is said to have been served in 1935 at the Humpty Dumpty Drive-In in Denver.

- Covering 53 square miles (137.8 sq km), Denver International Airport is twice the size of the island of Manhattan.

▲ BRIDAL VEIL FALLS

These waters in Telluride tumble down 365 feet (111 m) of craggy rock, making it the state's tallest free-falling waterfalls.

MISCELLANY

- At a depth of more than 1,000 feet (305 m), **Pagosa Springs** is the deepest measured geothermal hot spring in the world.

- The **Stanley Hotel** in Estes Park was the inspiration behind Stephen King's infamous horror novel *The Shining*.

- The **Kit Carson County Carousel** in Burlington dates back to 1905, making it one of the oldest surviving wooden merry-go-rounds in the U.S.

- Residents are called **Coloradans** or **Coloradoans**.

- The **United States Air Force Academy** is located near Colorado Springs.

- In 1996, miners in Larimer County unearthed the 28.3-carat **"Colorado Diamond."**

- Stretching over 53 miles (85 km), **Colfax Avenue** in Denver is the longest continuous street in America.

- "Spike," one of the most complete *Stegosaurus* skeletons ever found, was unearthed near Cañon City in 1992.

- **Rescue dogs and cats** are the official state pets.

- The state amphibian? The **Western Tiger Salamander**.

- The **Denver Mint** began producing silver and gold coins in 1906.

- With an elevation of 10,152 feet (3,094 m), **Leadville** is the highest incorporated city in the U.S.

- **No U.S. president or vice president** has been born in Colorado.

- Colorado is nicknamed the **Centennial State**, because it received its statehood 100 years after the Declaration of Independence was signed.

- Each year on August 1, residents celebrate **Colorado Day**, marking the anniversary of statehood.

- There are more than **100 fossilized dinosaur tracks** in Morrison.

- **President Theodore Roosevelt** visited Glenwood Springs so often, it was considered his home away from home.

- Colorado is home to **42 state parks**.

In 2015, 6,471 fans of the Denver Broncos wore faux bright orange mustaches to a football game, setting a world record for the largest gathering of people wearing false 'staches.

BY THE NUMBERS

1,900 THE NUMBER OF DINOSAUR TRACKS FOUND AT PICKET WIRE CANYONLANDS IN LA JUNTA, HOME TO ONE OF THE LARGEST PRESERVED SETS OF TRACKS IN THE WORLD

14,130 the elevation in feet (4,307 m) of the Mount Blue Sky Scenic Byway, the highest paved road in North America

1,440 THE LENGTH IN MILES (2,317 KM) OF THE COLORADO RIVER, ONE OF THE LONGEST IN THE COUNTRY. IT PASSES THROUGH SEVERAL STATES, INCLUDING COLORADO.

56 the height in stories of Republic Plaza in Denver, the tallest building in Colorado

158,000 the estimated number of dogs living in some 99,000 Denver households—more than the number of children

750 THE HEIGHT IN FEET (229 M) OF THE TALLEST SAND DUNE IN AMERICA, LOCATED IN GREAT SAND DUNES NATIONAL MONUMENT OUTSIDE OF ALAMOSA

250 the number of parks in Denver, which has the largest city park system in the nation

355 inches (9 m) of snow fall annually at Breckenridge Ski Resort.

DESTINATION: COLORADO

- Check out a city carved in the cliffs by ancestral Puebloans in Mesa Verde. Built somewhere between 550 and 1300, these ancient dwellings feature more than 4,000 identified sites.

- The largest self-built castle in the country, Bishop Castle near Pueblo is complete with a grand ballroom, soaring towers and bridges, and a fire-breathing dragon.

- There are hundreds of ghost towns, the last gasps of Colorado's mining boom in the late 1800s. Some, like Independence and St. Elmo, are well preserved and accessible to the public.

- A national historic landmark on wheels, the Cumbres & Toltec Scenic Railroad was featured in *Indiana Jones and the Last Crusade*. Visitors can chug back in time on this 1880 vintage train, which steams 64 miles (103 km) over the Rocky Mountains.

RECORD ★ SETTERS

Running two city blocks long, Glenwood Springs is the world's largest hot springs "pool." And at a temperature of 122°F (50°C), it's one of the hottest, too.

- Rifle Falls offers triple the view: A trio of waterfalls 60 feet (18 m) over a travertine dam on East Rifle Creek, this scenic state park also offers limestone caves for exploration.

- Towering monoliths, red rock canyons, giant boulders, and plenty of wildlife spotting: You'll experience it all with a visit to Colorado National Monument, a 31-square-mile (80 sq km) swath of protected landscape.

- The iconic ski town of Vail is a magnet for winter-activity enthusiasts around the world, but the area is just as energetic during the warmer months, with zip-lining, mountain coaster rides, and excellent entertainment options.

▽ RED ROCKS AMPHITHEATRE

Nature puts on a show, literally, at Red Rocks Amphitheatre, located outside of Denver. Surrounded by iconic ocher sandstone rock formations, it's the world's only naturally occurring acoustically perfect amphitheater.

A CRYSTAL CLEAR COLORADO SKY OPENS ABOVE US, A BLUE SO DEEP IT MAKES YOU DIZZY.

—Cyclist Neil Hanson, *Pilgrim Wheels*

SPORTING CHANCES

- Each year, the town of Leadville hosts a trail run and a mountain bike race, each 100 miles (161 km) long and considered to be among the toughest courses in the world.

- A golf ball flies here on average 10 percent farther than in other states because of the altitude.

- One of the world's first rodeos was held on July 4, 1869, in Deer Trail.

- In 1976, Colorado representatives made the decision to opt out of hosting the Winter Olympics in Denver, making it the only state to turn down that opportunity.

- The highest ski lift in North America can be found at Breckenridge Ski Resort, dropping skiers off around 13,000 feet (3,962 m) up.

- Future and current Olympians reside and train at the U.S. Olympic Training Center, a 35-acre (14 ha) campus in Colorado Springs.

- Runner Emma Coburn, the first U.S. woman to win a world medal in the steeplechase event, grew up in Crested Butte and graduated from the University of Colorado.

- Denver is the least populated city in the country with five major professional sports teams: Denver Broncos football, Denver Nuggets basketball, Colorado Rockies baseball, Colorado Avalanche hockey, and Colorado Rapids soccer.

- The Colorado National Speedway in Dacono features the state's only NASCAR track, a 3/8-mile (603.5 m) paved oval.

- Olympic swimmer Amy Van Dyken, who won six gold medals in her career, was born in Denver and attended Colorado State University.

- Although they have won three Super Bowl championships, the Denver Broncos also share the NFL record for the most losses at the Big Game, with five defeats.

▶ **STORY OF** THE SONG When poet Katharine Lee Bates set sight on the breathtaking vistas of Pikes Peak in 1893, she was moved to put pen to paper. The resulting verses would eventually become the lyrics to "America the Beautiful," one of the best-known songs in American history.

STARS ★ OF ★ THE ★ STATE

ELLISON ONIZUKA (1946–1986) The first Asian American to fly in space, Onizuka honed his aeronautical acumen at the University of Colorado, where he earned both a bachelor of science and a master of science degree. After joining the U.S. Air Force, Onizuka was ultimately selected as one of over 8,000 applicants for NASA's astronauts for the space shuttle program. In 1985, he earned a spot as a mission specialist on *Discovery* and later was selected for the space shuttle *Challenger* flight. While he lost his life on that mission when the *Challenger* exploded 73 seconds after liftoff, Onizuka's impressive legacy lives on.

CONNECTICUT

CAPITAL: Hartford **FLOWER:** Mountain Laurel **NICKNAME:** Constitution State **ENTRY:** 1788

★ ★ ★ *"He Who Transplanted Still Sustains"* ★ ★ ★

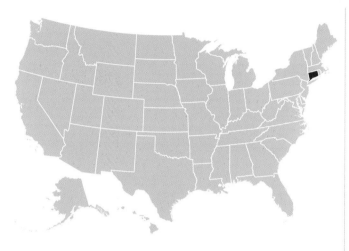

CT FACTS

- One of the 13 original colonies, Connecticut is the southernmost of the New England states.

- Connecticut's "Constitution State" nickname refers to the Fundamental Orders of Connecticut of 1638–39, considered history's first written constitution.

- With a population of about 3.6 million, Connecticut is one of the most densely populated states. The largest city is Bridgeport, home to 148,377 people.

- The Connecticut River, which flows for 410 miles (700 km), is one of the longest rivers in the nation without a major port at its mouth.

- Connecticut is known for being the home of several famous inventors including Charles Goodyear (vulcanized rubber), Elias Howe (sewing machine), Eli Whitney (cotton gin), and Eli Terry (clockmaker).

- Yale University, founded in 1701 in Saybrook, is one of the oldest colleges in the country. (The campus moved to New Haven in 1718.)

▶ STATE BIRD
American Robin
Turdus migratorius

The beloved red-breasted bird is a common sight in Connecticut, where it nests high in pine trees all year long.

1614

Dutch colonists, who arrived in 1614, were the first Europeans in the state. Dutch fur traders built a fort near present-day Hartford.

◀ NUTMEG STATE

Connecticut is sometimes called the "Nutmeg State," although no one is exactly sure why. One theory is that the nickname reflects the earlier inhabitants of the state, who were "so ingenious and shrewd that they were able to make and sell wooden nutmegs," but there is no proof that these early New Englanders actually sold wooden nutmegs.

- Connecticut contains three major regions: the Western Upland, the Central Lowland, and the Eastern Upland. Its unique landscape is marked with mountains, lakes, waterfalls, rivers, sandy shores, rocky coastlines, and forests.

- It was the fifth state to be added to the union, in 1788, and it is the third smallest state by area. (Only Delaware and Rhode Island are smaller.)

- Native American tribes including the Eastern Pequot, Golden Hill Paugussett, Schaghticoke, Mashantucket Pequot, and Mohegan lived on the land long before European colonization.

- Hartford is known as "Insurance City" because several insurance companies are headquartered there.

- Among U.S. states, Connecticut ranks highly in several economic factors, including annual individual salary, median household income, and teachers' salaries. It also ranks highly in access to primary health care.

- President George W. Bush was born in New Haven while his father, President George H.W. Bush, was a sophomore at Yale. He remains the only U.S. president born in the state.

- Connecticut is covered in woodland, and forests are one of the state's top natural resources.

- A 2,380-foot (725 m) spot on the south shoulder of Mount Frissell is the state's highest point. The mountain's peak, at 2,453 feet (748 m), actually lies in Massachusetts.

- Resident Samuel Colt, the inventor of the revolver, was influential in making the state a leading producer of guns and other arms during the Civil War.

- In 1902, Theodore Roosevelt became the first U.S. president to make a public appearance by automobile while in office when he took a car ride to Hartford's Pope Park.

- Connecticut is home to many mammals, including black bears, bobcats, muskrats, and white-tailed deer.

- On average, there are only 12 days a year when the temperature goes above 90 degrees, and about six days when it falls below zero.

▶ **STORY OF** THE SONG "Yankee Doodle" was adopted as Connecticut's state song in 1978, but the tune's roots reach much further back than that. The song was written by an Englishman in 1755, poking fun at the poorly dressed New England soldiers. Later, during the Revolutionary War, the song was picked up by American soldiers and eventually served as a morale booster between battles.

STARS ★ OF ★ THE ★ STATE

KATHARINE HEPBURN

(1907–2003) Born to a suffrage activist and a doctor in Hartford, Hepburn went on to become a cultural icon and one of the most recognizable actors of all time. A prolific performer, Hepburn won four Best Actress Oscars during her career, a feat that has yet to be matched by any other actress. Despite being one of Hollywood's brightest stars, she stayed true to her Connecticut roots and kept a home in Old Saybrook, which she called "paradise." A museum in her honor remains there today.

> OF ALL THE BEAUTIFUL TOWNS IT HAS BEEN MY FORTUNE TO SEE [HARTFORD] IS THE CHIEF. YOU DO NOT KNOW WHAT BEAUTY IS IF YOU HAVE NOT BEEN HERE.

—Author Mark Twain

WEIRD BUT TRUE

- In 1948, two men were arrested in Connecticut for selling rotten pickles.

- In 1901, Connecticut imposed the first law regulating the speed of a motor vehicle, restricting drivers' speeds to a maximum of 12 miles an hour (19.3 kph).

- The largest pair of googly eyes, measuring some 12 feet (3.7 m) tall, were made in Norwalk, Connecticut, in 2019.

- The first telephone book in the U.S. was issued in New Haven in 1878. It featured just 50 names.

- Some 3,000 puppets from all over the world are on display at the University of Connecticut in Storrs, which offers a degree in puppetry.

- It was believed that vampires lived in Jewett City during the 1800s.

- Westport's Staples High School class of 2014 had 16 pairs of twins enrolled in one academic year—a world record at the time.

- In 2014, a 15-year-old from East Hampton once solved a 250-piece puzzle in 13 minutes and seven seconds to set a world record at the time.

In 1809, Mary Kies of South Killingly became the first woman to apply for and receive a U.S. patent in her own name, for a method of weaving straw with silk.

> STORY OF THE NAME   Connecticut has a river to thank for its unique name. And, of course, the Mohegan who came up with it. They called the territory *Quinnehtukqut*, an Algonquian word meaning "beside the long tidal river." As European settlers came to the area in the 1630s and set up colonies along the river, the original spelling was anglicized.

▲ HUCK'S STORY

American writer Mark Twain wrote *Adventures of Huckleberry Finn* while living in Hartford.

MISCELLANY

- It is known as the **"Provision State"** since it sent many supplies and cannons to the Continental Army during the Revolutionary War.

- Watch manufacturer **Timex** is headquartered in Middlebury.

- First published in 1764, the **Hartford Courant** is the country's oldest continuously published newspaper.

- Until 1875, Connecticut had **two capitals**, with the state's General Assembly conducting business in both New Haven and Hartford on a rotating schedule.

- Transforming from a copper mine in 1773, the **Old New-Gate Prison & Copper Mine** in East Granby is the oldest surviving state prison in the nation.

- George Smith of New Haven invented the **lollipop** in 1908 after adopting the idea that putting candy on a stick would make it easier to eat.

- Residents are sometimes called **Nutmeggers** or **Connecticuters**. New Haven is known as **"The Elm City"** because of the many elm trees planted on the town's green since 1686.

- **Lyme disease**, which is spread by ticks in the Northern Hemisphere, was first identified in 1975 in Old Lyme, Connecticut.

- The **first American cookbook** was written by Amelia Simmons of Hartford in 1796.

- The **European praying mantis** is the state insect.

- Connecticut is said to be home to the **first hamburger**, which was served in a New Haven eatery in 1900.

▷ CATCH!

The world's first Frisbee—simply an empty pie tin—was thrown in 1871 in Bridgeport.

BY THE NUMBERS

500 THE NUMBER OF HISTORIC SHIPS IN THE COLLECTION OF THE MYSTIC SEAPORT MUSEUM, A RE-CREATION OF A 19TH-CENTURY COASTAL VILLAGE WITH A WORKING SHIPYARD

44 the number of singles tennis courts that would fit inside the largest single trading floor in the world, located in Stamford

33 HOURS 4 MINUTES the length of the longest ever bocce ball game, achieved by the Ridgefield 8 in Ridgefield, June 2019

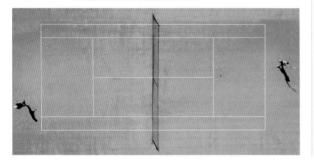

1965 the year the first Subway sandwich shop opened, in Bridgeport

14 the number of the nation's *Fortune* 500 companies headquartered in Connecticut

60% **of Connecticut is covered in woodland.**

5,828 THE LENGTH IN MILES (13,518 KM) OF RIVERS WITHIN THE STATE OF CONNECTICUT

15,032 the weight in pounds (6,818 kg) of the world's largest wedding cake, which was made by chefs at a hotel in Uncasville in 2004

A longtime staple at the Children's Museum in West Hartford, the "World's Biggest Sperm Whale" (also known as Conny) is so large that people can walk right into its belly. Made of concrete and steel, the structure measures 60 feet (18 m) long.

▲ SUBS!

The state is home to the world's first nuclear-powered submarine, U.S.S. *Nautilus*, commissioned in Groton in 1954.

DESTINATION: CONNECTICUT

- The Bush-Holley house in Greenwich, the home of the first Connecticut art colony, was once the center of American Impressionism. Today, the historic site offers tours and art exhibits.

- Search for Captain Kidd's buried treasure in Silver Sands State Park on Charles Island. Legend says the captain hid his treasure under the sand in 1699 and never reclaimed it.

- Located in downtown Mystic, the Mystic Aquarium offers a dive into ocean life, with exhibits featuring sharks, seals, stingrays, Steller sea lions, and the endangered African penguin.

- The Mark Twain House in Hartford showcases the work of this writer of classic American novels such as *Adventures of Huckleberry Finn* and *Tom Sawyer*.

- Stonington's Lighthouse Museum showcases exhibits about sealing, whaling, and farming. Check out the sprawling, 14-room Victorian mansion next door, once owned by captains Nathaniel Brown Palmer and Alexander Smith Palmer.

- Each fall, Bristol hosts a popular mum festival, a tradition stemming back 60 years, reflecting the town's heyday as a top producer of chrysanthemums.

- The seaside town of Old Saybrook offers colorful marinas, windswept beaches, and a quaint Main Street lined with shops and restaurants. ▼

> STAY IN CONNECTICUT OR MOVE TO CONNECTICUT! WE ARE THE MOST FAMILY-FRIENDLY STATE IN THE COUNTRY.
>
> —Governor Ned Lamont, 2022 State of the State Address

- The headquarters of World Wrestling Entertainment (WWE) is located in Stamford.

- ESPN, the world's first sports cable channel, launched in Bristol in 1979.

- In 2016, golfer Jim Furyk posted the lowest single round score (18 holes) in PGA Championship history, during the Travelers Championship, in Cromwell.

- In 1841, lawmakers banned nine-pin bowling because of excessive gambling. In response, players simply added another pin, which is how the game is still played today.

- Connecticut is home to the WNBA's Connecticut Sun, and several other minor league sports teams.

MADE IN CT

Connecticut's agricultural outputs include:

- Ornamental shrubs
- Flowers
- Clams
- Oysters
- Dairy
- Chicken eggs
- Sweet corn
- Maple syrup
- Tobacco
- Hay
- Fruit

Connecticut's industrial outputs include:

- Aerospace manufacturing
- Shipbuilding
- Machinery and machine tools
- Gravel, sand, and crushed stone
- Jet aircraft engines
- Metalworking
- Electronics

SPORTING CHANCES

- In 1995, Hartford-born Rebecca Lobo led the University of Connecticut women's basketball team to its first national championship, sparking a basketball dynasty.

- The University of Connecticut Huskies women's basketball team has won 11 NCAA Tournaments, including a record-setting four in a row.

- Geno Auriemma, the UConn Huskies women's basketball coach since 1985, has launched his own line of Italian wines, sauces, and restaurants.

STARS ★ OF ★ THE ★ STATE

JULIE CHU

(b. 1982) One of the most standout athletes to come out of Connecticut, Chu, born in Fairfield, is the first Asian American woman to play for the U.S. Olympic ice hockey team. Chu competed in four Olympic Games between 2002 and 2014, collecting as many medals—three silver, one bronze—in the process. In 2014, Chu was selected to be Team U.S.A.'s closing ceremony flag bearer at the winter games in Sochi, Russia, solidifying her status as one of the most decorated U.S. females in Olympic Winter Games history.

DELAWARE

★ ★ ★
"Liberty and Independence"
★ ★ ★

CAPITAL: Dover **BIRD:** Blue Hen Chicken **NICKNAME:** First State **ENTRY:** 1787

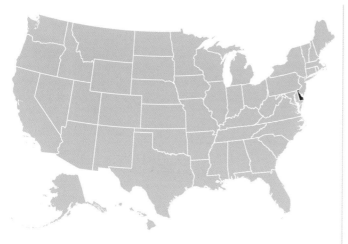

DE FACTS

- The population is 1,018,396.

- In a state known for its boardwalks, beaches, and fishing industry, Delaware's economy is also bolstered by pharmaceuticals, agriculture, manufacturing, and mining.

- For centuries, the Algonquian-language tribes of the Lenni Lenape, Nanticoke, Assateague, and Choptank peoples as well as the Iroquoian-language tribe of the Susquehannock lived in the region. Today, there are no federally recognized tribes in the state, although communities such as the Nanticoke Lenni-Lenape still live there.

- Following the arrival of Dutch explorers in the 17th century, Dutch and Swedish settlers established colonies. After the Dutch defeated the Swedes, Delaware became part of New Netherland, but the area was soon taken by the English and made into the Delaware colony.

- The 1776 Continental Congress was ready to put independence from Britain to a vote. But one of Delaware's delegates, Caesar Rodney, was absent. When Rodney heard the vote was tied, he rode through the night, covering 80 miles (129 km) and braving thunderstorms on horseback. He arrived just in time to cast the deciding vote: The colonies would declare independence.

- Following the assassination of Martin Luther King, Jr., in 1968, protesters took to the Wilmington streets. The National Guard soon moved to occupy the city. The occupation lasted nine months—the longest of any place in the nation during this period.

- Mabel Vernon, the prominent women's suffragist from Wilmington, served as secretary for the National Woman's Party (NWP). ◀

▶ STATE FLOWER
Peach Blossom
Prunus persica

At the time that this vibrant bloom was designated the state's official flower, Delaware was home to more than 800,000 peach trees.

1787

On December 7, 1787, Delaware was the first state to vote in favor of, or ratify, the new U.S. Constitution, making it the nation's first state.

OH, OUR DELAWARE, OUR BELOVED DELAWARE, FOR THE SUN IS SHINING OVER OUR BELOVED DELAWARE.

—from "Our Delaware," the state song

◄ WHEELY NICE Delaware is ranked as one of the most bicycle-friendly states.

- During the War of 1812, U.S. naval officer and Delawarean Thomas Macdonough led his fleet to successfully defend against a British attack off the coasts of New York and Vermont, thus saving the Northeast from invasion. ▲

- In 1738, the Quakers began meeting in Wilmington. Many Quakers would go on to play important roles campaigning to abolish slavery and aiding Delaware's Underground Railroad.

- Absalom Jones became America's first Black priest in 1802. Born enslaved, Jones was able to attend a Quaker-run night school for Black people until he became free in 1784.

- After discovering his love of skating at the age of 12, Johnny Weir (b. 1984) and his family moved to Newark to continue his training. Weir went on to become an Olympic figure skater and three-time U.S. National Figure Skating Champion. He has since expanded his work to include television commentary, fashion designing, and LGBTQ+ rights advocacy.

- In 1802, Éleuthère Irénée du Pont founded the DuPont company in Wilmington. The company, which at first produced explosives, became one of the country's largest chemical manufacturers.

▶ **STORY OF** THE NAME In 1610, British adventurer Samuel Argall accidentally happened upon a bay when his ship was blown off course during a storm. He named this bay and the connected river "Delaware" after the then governor of Virginia: Thomas West, Baron de la Warr.

STARS ★ OF ★ THE ★ STATE

JOSEPH "JOE" BIDEN

(b. 1942) Joseph Biden was elected the 46th president of the United States in 2020, along with the first female vice president, Kamala Harris. A politician and the former 47th vice president of the United States, Biden was born in Pennsylvania but raised from the age of 10 in Claymont. He began his career in politics after earning a law degree in 1968, and he was elected to the U.S. Senate in 1972. Winning reelection five times, he became Delaware's longest-serving senator. Biden became presidential nominee Barack Obama's running mate in 2008, and the pair were sworn into office in 2009. Biden is running for reelection as president in 2024.

IT'S GOOD BEING FIRST.

—Former state slogan

WEIRD BUT TRUE

- In 1905, Delaware became the last state to abolish the pillory, a punishment device similar to the stocks.

- The famous Dover International Speedway is guarded by a 46-foot-tall (14 m) statue of a monster known as Miles.

- For nearly 30 years, Sussex County held the "Punkin Chunkin" event, a world championship where competitors use a variety of mechanical trebuchets, slingshots, and air guns to hurl pumpkins as far as possible.

- Some eateries still serve muskrat, a large, water-dwelling rodent traditionally eaten by trappers. It is said to taste somewhat bitter and gamy.

- In Rehoboth Beach, it is illegal to pretend to sleep on a boardwalk bench.

- A house in the city of Lewes still bears a cannonball from a British attack.

- The Delaware gray fox is one of the only members of the canid family that can climb trees.

RECORD ★ SETTERS

In 1923 at the University of Delaware, language professor and WWI veteran Raymond W. Kirkbride launched the country's first study abroad program.

▶ There are more than 250 million chickens living in the state.

▲ LUCK BE A LADY
State bug: the ladybug

MISCELLANY

- People from Delaware are called **Delawareans**.

- The official state star is **Delaware Diamond** in Ursa Major.

- With a mean elevation of 60 feet (18 m), it is the **lowest state**.

- It does Delaware good: The state beverage is **milk**.

- Delaware is one of just five states **without a sales tax**.

- There are **only three counties** in Delaware.

- Wilmington is home to the exquisitely manicured **Nemours Estate**, whose 200 acres (81 ha) include the largest French-style gardens in North America.

- Due to its high number of visitors hailing from Washington, D.C., Rehoboth Beach is known as the **"Nation's Summer Capital."**

- During World War II, Delaware built **coastal watchtowers** that remain today.

- During the 1700s, pirates often visited—or raided—the coast, and they may have included the infamous **Blackbeard** and **William Kidd**.

- **Mary Ann Shadd Cary**, born in 1823, became the first Black female newspaper editor in North America.

- The **horseshoe crab**, the state marine animal, has existed on Earth for some 450 million years.

- **New Sweden**, the area's first Swedish settlement, was formed in 1638.

- Henry Heimlich, inventor of the **Heimlich maneuver**, was born in Wilmington.

- For one year, **the golden retriever** was the state dog. Today, rescue dogs hold the honor.

- The endangered **Bethany Beach firefly** can be found only within a 20-mile (32 km) range along the coast.

- **Scrapple**, a popular pan-fried loaf of pork scraps, has a festival devoted to it: the Bridgeville Apple-Scrapple Festival.

- At Rehoboth Beach's **Sea Witch Festival**, visitors dress in costumes and attempt to solve the clue-based Sea Witch Hunt.

- The state fossil is the **belemnite**, a squid-like animal that lived during the Jurassic and Cretaceous periods.

▶ **STORY OF** THE WORD Though since misappropriated into the English language to describe a gathering of any kind, the noun "powwow" comes from Algonquian-speaking peoples of the Northeast. The word originated as *pau wau*, meaning "medicine man" in the Algonquian languages. Today, it is used by many Indigenous nations—including the Nanticoke Indian Tribe of Delaware—in reference to "a cultural event that features group singing and dancing by men, women, and children."

BY THE NUMBERS

3 THE AVERAGE LENGTH IN FEET (0.9 M) OF THE GRAY FOX

447.9 feet (136.5 m): the highest point in the state

60% of all publicly traded and *Fortune* 500 companies have incorporated in Delaware. This is because of the state's many corporate friendly policies—such as no minimum requirement for a company bank account, no state income tax on out-of-state companies, and simple registering processes.

33,000 Delawareans served during WWII

8,000,000 the approximate number of people who visit Rehoboth Beach each year

381 miles (613 km) of shoreline in the state, thanks to bays and inlets

700 THE NUMBER OF FAMILY FARMS RAISING CHICKENS

1934 the year the U.S. Supreme Court confirmed Delaware's control of the Delaware River

- A top vacation spot for beachgoers across the country, Rehoboth Beach has been a tourist destination for around 150 years. The area first hosted guests as a camp in 1873, during which time the boardwalk was built. In 1925, a paved road between Rehoboth and the inland town of Georgetown was completed, making travel to mid-Atlantic cities easier and cementing the area as a seaside destination for families.

- When first built for the du Pont family in 1839, the Winterthur home contained 12 rooms. By the time Henry Francis du Pont opened his home to the public, it was a sprawling estate of 175 rooms and 1,000 acres (405 ha). Today, visitors can tour the home.

- At the Nanticoke Indian Museum in Millsboro, visitors learn about Nanticoke culture and history from artifacts dating back to 8,000 B.C. The only Indigenous museum in Delaware, the Nanticoke museum was designated a national historic landmark.

- Founded as a gunpowder works in 1802, the DuPont Company went on to become one of the engines driving the state's economy, and it remains a thriving corporation to date. Today, the site of the original works has been turned into the Hagley Museum and Library, which contains restored mills and workers' communities, the original du Pont home and gardens, and a library dedicated to American research and business.

At 1,982 square miles (5,133 sq km), Delaware is the second smallest state in the nation.

- In New Castle Court House, Quaker abolitionist Thomas Garrett was tried for his prominent role in Delaware's Underground Railroad. Having helped the previously enslaved Hawkins family achieve freedom, Garrett was sued by the Hawkinses' former owners for violating the Fugitive Slave Act of 1793. Convicted, fined, and left in financial ruin, Garrett was aided by friends and continued helping others live in freedom.

- In 1682, William Penn established Cape Henlopen as one of the nation's first public lands. Today's visitors can enjoy an abundance of water sports and hiking trails, horseshoe crabs and sea birds, as well as a nature center and the historic Henlopen Lighthouse.

- One of the state's longest-running events, Dover Days Festival, celebrates Delaware's heritage and culture. Events include traditional Maypole dancing, historical reenactments, hot-air balloon rides, and a parade.

- Legend holds that when it first opened in the 1730s, Dover's Golden Fleece Tavern became the de facto meeting place for revolutionaries. Supposedly, legislators voted to ratify the U.S. Constitution while drinking the locally brewed Fordham beer—still served today.

- Completed around 1859, Fort Delaware was built to guard the ports of Wilmington and Philadelphia. Today, costumed guides teach visitors about the fort's role in the Civil War, when it was a prison to as many as 12,595 Confederate soldiers.

▼ **BRIGHT IDEA**
The Lightship *Overfalls,* located in Lewes, is one of the last remaining U.S. lightships—lighthouses that float.

▲ BOUNTIFUL HARVEST
Natural resources include soybeans, field corn, sweet corn, watermelons, potatoes, peas, and more.

MADE IN DE

Delaware's agricultural outputs include:

- Chicken
- Soybeans
- Field corn
- Eggs
- Wheat
- Dairy
- Barley
- Other plant products
- Other grains
- Cattle

Delaware's industrial outputs include:

- Pharmaceuticals
- Motor vehicles and parts
- Plastics
- Industrial machinery
- Petroleum
- Coal products

SPORTING CHANCES

- Basketball player Elena Delle Donne, Wilmington native and University of Delaware alumna, was named WNBA MVP in 2015 and again in 2019.

- In 2003, former University of Delaware football coach Tubby Raymond was inducted into the College Football Hall of Fame.

- Bicycling is the state sport.

- Located in Delmar, the Delaware Motorsports Complex houses the Delaware International Speedway, the U.S. 13 Dragway, and the U.S. 13 Kart Track.

- Point-to-Point, located in Winterthur, is a National Steeplechase Association–sanctioned Steeplechase that was started in hopes of raising interest for the historical Winterthur museum.

- The Delaware Fightin' Blue Hens men's lacrosse team of the University of Delaware has produced several notable athletes, including John Grant, Jr., one of the world's best lacrosse players.

- In 2019, the Harrington-based Delaware Thunder professional hockey team officially became members of the Federal Prospects Hockey League (FPHL).

STARS ★ OF ★ THE ★ STATE

WILLIAM "JUDY" JOHNSON

William "Judy" Johnson (1899–1989) was a Hall of Fame baseball player known for playing with great finesse. Johnson grew up in Wilmington, playing baseball on the city's sandlots. Despite his skill, he was barred from professional baseball because of Jim Crow laws, until 1920 when Rube Foster founded a professional Black baseball league called the Negro National League. Johnson joined in 1921, quickly becoming a standout third baseman and playing in the first Negro World Series in 1924. After retiring as a player, Johnson went on to become a manager, and he was inducted into the Hall of Fame in 1975.

FLORIDA

★ ★ ★

"In God We Trust"

★ ★ ★

CAPITAL: Tallahassee **BIRD:** Mockingbird **NICKNAME:** Sunshine State **ENTRY:** 1845

FL FACTS

- In 1845, Florida officially became the 27th state.

- Native peoples inhabited the Florida peninsula around 12,000 years ago. They were nomadic, and first hunted prehistoric big game like camels, bison, and horses. Later, as those big-game animals became extinct, these tribes hunted small mammals and shellfish for survival.

- Over centuries, several Native American tribes settled throughout Florida, including the Timucua, Apalachee, Calusa, and Creek.

- Warm year-round, the average temperature ranges from 68.4°F to 73.1°F (20.2°C to 22.8°C) in the north and from 74.2°F to 78.1°F (23.4°C to 25.6°C) in the south.

- The Great Florida Reef is the only living coral barrier reef in the continental U.S., and the third largest in the world after the Great Barrier Reef and the Belize Barrier Reef. ▼

▶ STATE FLOWER

Orange Blossom
Citrus sinensis

One of Florida's most fragrant flowers, the blossom of the orange tree is said to bring good fortune and is popular in bridal bouquets.

1565

The year Spanish explorer Pedro Menéndez de Avilés established the first permanent European settlement in what would become the United States at St. Augustine.

FLORIDA IS A GOLDEN WORD ... THE VERY NAME FLORIDA CARRIED THE MESSAGE OF WARMTH AND EASE AND COMFORT. IT WAS IRRESISTIBLE.

—Author John Steinbeck

▶ SOMETHING WILD

Florida has not only alligators and crocodiles, but also panthers, sea turtles, manatees, and dolphins— and over 500 recorded species of birds.

- Residents are called Floridians.

- Florida was named on April 2, 1513, by Spanish explorer Ponce de León, who arrived after looking for gold and silver and found a lush land-scape of fertile farmland and sprawl-ing coastline instead. He called it "La Florida" possibly in honor of Pascua Florida—the Spanish Feast of the Flowers.

- For two centuries, Great Britain, France, and Spain all tried to establish settle-ments in Florida before the British took control in 1763. Two decades later, Spain took charge again, but only until 1821, when they traded the territory to the United States in exchange for Spanish rule over Texas.

- The Seminole people began with bands of Creek people from Georgia and Ala-bama who migrated to Florida in the 1700s, and they still live in Florida. They refer to themselves as the "Unconquered People" and have reservations through-out the state.

- The most southeastern state in the U.S., Florida is also the only state to border both the Atlantic Ocean and the Gulf of Mexico.

▲ LAKE DEFUNIAK in DeFuniak Springs is one of only two almost perfectly circular freshwater lakes in the world.

- Florida has the second longest coastline of any U.S. state. Only Alaska's coastline is longer.

- With over 20 million residents, it is the third most populated state in the country.

- Florida's highest point is only 345 feet (105 m) above sea level. It is also the flattest state in the country.

- You are never more than 60 miles (97 km) from the ocean no matter where you go in Florida.

- Covering more than 840 square miles (2,175 sq km), Jacksonville is the largest city in area in the contiguous United States. Roughly 970,000 people live there.

- Greater Miami is the only metropolitan area in America with two national parks: Everglades National Park and Biscayne National Park. ▪

STARS ★ OF ★ THE ★ STATE

ZORA NEALE HURSTON

(1891–1960) Hurston, an author and anthropologist, drew inspiration from her childhood in Florida's Eatonville, the nation's first incorporated Black town-ship. Her books, which included *Mules and Men* and *Their Eyes Were Watching God,* spoke to the African American experience and racial struggles in the South. While Hurston received some acclaim as an author during her lifetime, her works experienced a revival posthu-mously when the writer Alice Walker published a feature story about her in a 1975 edition of *Ms.* magazine. Today, visitors to the city of Fort Pierce near St. Lucie on the eastern coast of Florida can walk through Hurston's former home and follow the Dust Tracks Heritage Trail to learn more about her achievements. ▪

- The "Beethoven's Babies" bill requires state-funded childcare centers to play one hour of classical music a day.

- The Poozeum in Orlando boasts the world's largest collection of coprolites—aka prehistoric poop.

- In 1982, Key West seceded from the U.S. and declared itself the Conch Republic—for about one minute.

- Between 1957 and 1970, the University of Florida used a live alligator, named Albert, as its official mascot.

- There's an eight-hole putting green at the Palm Beach International Airport.

- Some alligators in Florida have been known to eat sharks.

- During a hurricane, 30 flamingos at a zoo in Miami were herded into a bathroom for their protection.

- Kissimmee, Florida is home to the American Nudist Research Library. Clothes are optional for visitors.

- Florida's own Bigfoot—a human-size, hairy primate called the Skunk Ape—is said to skulk around the swamps of the Everglades.

- Some people have been known to scatter their loved ones' ashes in Disney World's Haunted Mansion.

- Each year as part of the Mullet Toss, Floridians compete to see who can throw a dead fish farthest over the state line into Alabama.

- The town of Carrabelle boasts the world's smallest police station—housed inside a telephone booth.

- There are so many mediums living in the town of Cassadaga that it is known as the "psychic capital of the world."

RECORD ★ SETTERS

In 2019, 633 scuba divers gathered at Deerfield Beach International Fishing Pier to set the record for the largest underwater cleanup in 24 hours. All told, the group removed more than 1,200 pounds (544 kg) of trash and 60 pounds (27 kg) of fishing line from the water.

STORY OF THE FLAG Between 1868 and 1900, the flag that flew over Florida was a simple white design with the state seal at the center. But Francis Fleming, who served as Florida's governor from 1889 to 1893, thought it looked too much like a flag of surrender. So he led a push to redesign the flag with diagonal red bars—forming the Cross of Burgundy, a nod to the Spanish rule of the territory—plus a seal depicting a Seminole woman spreading flowers with a steamboat, the state tree (a Sabal palmetto palm), and the sun in the background. The seal was updated again in 1985.

MISCELLANY

- The **rare ghost orchid**, which draws its moisture from the air and has no leaves, grows only in Cuba and the flooded forests of South Florida.

- With its warm waters, **Blue Spring State Park** in Orange City is a popular hangout for manatees during the winter.

- The largest single-site collection of **Frank Lloyd Wright** architecture in the world is in Lakeland at Florida Southern College.

- **Orange juice** is the state drink.

- A scheduled **passenger airboat service** between St. Petersburg and Tampa launched in 1914—the world's first of its kind.

- Averaging 223 lightning events per square mile per year, Florida is the **lightning capital of the country** based on strikes per square mile.

- The St. Johns, **Florida's longest river**, is one of the few major rivers that flows from south to north.

- Venice is known as the **"shark tooth capital of the world."**

CAPE CANAVERAL is a launchpad for manned space flight including the Mercury, Gemini, Apollo, and space shuttle missions.

BY THE NUMBERS

375,302 — AMOUNT IN ACRES (151,879 HA) OF CITRUS ORCHARDS IN FLORIDA

137,600,000 — the number of visitors Florida receives per year, making it one of the top travel destinations in the world

54% of Miami residents were born outside of the United States, making it one of the most diverse cities in the world.

60 — the approximate number of six-toed cats currently living at the Ernest Hemingway Home and Museum in Key West—descendants of the famed writer's pet cat, Snow White

67 counties within the state, comprising over 400 cities, towns, and villages

75,000 — the number of employees of the Walt Disney World Resort, the largest number of people employed by one company in a single location anywhere in the U.S.

550,000+ the number of students enrolled in the state's colleges and universities

4,000 weight in pounds (1,814 kg) of the Christ the Abyss Statue, submerged in the ocean within John Pennekamp Coral Reef State Park in Key Largo

9,200 MILES (14,806 KM) OF HIKING, BICYCLING, EQUESTRIAN, AND SHARED-USE TRAILS IN THE STATE

$1,000,000,000,000 gross domestic product (GDP). If Florida were an independent nation, it would have the 15th largest GDP in the world, ranking above Turkey, the Netherlands, Saudi Arabia, Switzerland, and Argentina.

63

DESTINATION: FLORIDA

- Street artists show off their stuff in the Wynwood neighborhood of Miami, where building facades are covered with colorful murals, including the famed Wynwood Walls. ▲

- Each year, some 60 million people visit the four parks encompassing the Walt Disney World Resort in Orlando.

- Spanning 400 square miles (1,036 sq km), Tampa Bay is the state's largest open-water estuary. A paddling trip or boat tour on the bay may reveal glimpses of some of its wildlife, from birds to manatees, and more.

- The southernmost city in the continental U.S., Key West is steeped in an island vibe. With a lively nightlife, visitors can recharge after a day in the sun on Duval Street, the main drag that is lined with bars and restaurants.

- In 1976, singer Jimmy Buffett finished writing his hit song "Margaritaville" in Key West; today, Buffett has built an international empire of the same name including restaurants and resorts.

RECORD ★ SETTERS

Miami is the only major American city founded by a woman. In 1874, Julia Tuttle visited her father there, eventually inheriting his land, purchasing more, overseeing the construction of a railroad, and incorporating the city of Miami in 1896. Today, a 10-foot-tall (3 m) statue honoring Tuttle stands in the city's Bayfront Park.

THE STATE WITH THE PRETTIEST NAME, THE STATE THAT FLOATS IN BRACKISH WATER, HELD TOGETHER BY MANGROVE ROOTS.

—Poet Elizabeth Bishop

- Delray Beach's Morikami Museum and Japanese Gardens is the only museum in the United States dedicated purely to the living culture of Japan. There's a 16-acre (6.5 ha) park of renowned Japanese gardens, a world-class bonsai display, and galleries of historical and contemporary Asian art.

- Expect to see it all in Everglades National Park, the largest subtropical wilderness in the United States. Located on the southern tip of the state, it's the only place on Earth where both alligators and crocodiles coexist in the wild.

- In the early 20th century, both Thomas Edison and Henry Ford, two of America's most famous inventors and friends, wintered in side-by-side vacation homes in Fort Myers. Today, those estates—and their sprawling grounds—are available for tours.

768 the number of consecutive sunny days St. Petersburg received between February 1967 and March 1969, a standing world record

- The Gulf of Mexico barrier islands of Sanibel and Captiva boast 50 miles (80 km) of white, sandy shores. Sanibel is also home to the Bailey-Matthews National Shell Museum, which houses hundreds of shells from around the globe.

- Exhibits at the John and Mable Ringling Museum of Art in Sarasota feature old circus costumes, wagons, and the world's largest miniature circus.

- Watch a rocket blast off from the Kennedy Space Center on Merritt Island—home to two launchpads, the Astronaut Hall of Fame, and plenty of artifacts and exhibits telling the story of America's space program.

◀ **JUST KEEP SWIMMING**

In 2013, resident Diana Nyad became the first person to swim from Cuba to Florida without a shark cage or fins.

MADE IN FL

Florida's agricultural outputs include:

- Bell peppers
- Oranges
- Grapefruits
- Sugarcane
- Tomatoes
- Watermelons
- Sweet corn

Florida's industrial outputs include:

- Computer and electronic products
- Food, beverage, and tobacco products
- Aviation and aerospace
- Chemicals

SPORTING CHANCES

- Florida boasts at least 10 professional sports teams across football, basketball, hockey, soccer, and baseball.

- All told, Florida teams have won three Super Bowl titles, three NBA championships, two MLB championships, and three Stanley Cups.

- Florida has more than 1,000 golf courses, more than any other state.

- Baseball has been a Florida pastime for more than 100 years, with a number of major league teams getting in spring preseason training in the Sunshine State.

- Daytona Beach's City Island ballpark was the site of the first integrated professional baseball game. That stadium now is named after Jackie Robinson.

- Miami has hosted the NFL Super Bowl 11 times, the most played in one city.

- The Daytona International Speedway has been considered the "World Center of Racing" since opening its gates in 1959. It's also home to the Motorsports Hall of Fame of America.

- In 1972, the Miami Dolphins became the first team in the NFL to reach the Super Bowl with a perfect record, closing the season out with 17 straight wins.

- University of Florida's Ben Hill Griffin Stadium is known as "The Swamp."

- St. Petersburg's Shuffleboard Club had 5,000 members in 1944, making it the world's largest club of its kind. Today, membership stands at more than 2,600.

- Fort Lauderdale's International Swimming Hall of Fame features a museum packed with memorabilia, artifacts, and art representing different movements in the sport's history.

- In 2021, 59 synchronized dance waterskiers in Auburndale set a world record by being towed together by a single boat.

- Florida has produced more than 900 world fishing records, more than any other state, or even country.

GLORIA ESTEFAN

(b. 1957) The pop star, born in Cuba, came to early fame in the 1980s as the lead singer of the Miami Sound Machine. Several of the band's songs, including "Conga," "1-2-3," and "Rhythm Is Gonna Get You," were chart-toppers. All told, Estefan has won seven Grammy Awards, is in Billboard's Top 100 Best Selling Musical Artists, has received a star on the Hollywood Walk of Fame, and was honored in 2015 with a Presidential Medal of Freedom for her contributions to American music. She still resides in Miami, where she continues to perform and often gives back to the local community through her eponymous nonprofit foundation. ▪

GEORGIA

★ ★ ★

"Wisdom, Justice, and Moderation"

★ ★ ★

CAPITAL: Atlanta **FLOWER:** Cherokee Rose **NICKNAME:** Peach State **ENTRY:** 1788

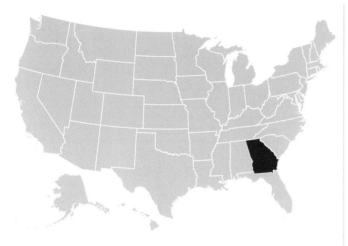

GA FACTS

- The population is 10,912,876.

- Georgia became the fourth state and is the 21st state in size.

- About three years into the Revolutionary War, the British captured Savannah, a key port city. The next year during the fall of 1779, Savannah became the site of the war's second deadliest battle when American forces attempted to liberate it in what is now known as the Siege of Savannah.

- The earliest known inhabitants were the Paleolithic peoples of the Clovis culture. As permanent settlements increased, the region became dominated by the Woodland peoples until the arrival of Spanish explorers in the 1500s.

- Coastal Georgia is home to the Gullah Geechee people. The Gullah Geechee are the descendants of enslaved peoples from numerous ethnic groups in Western and Central Africa who formed the unique traditions, art, music, and Gullah Geechee language that are still part of the culture today. ▼

▶ STATE BIRD

Brown Thrasher
Toxostoma rufum

The state bird is well known for its melodious song, which males use both in courtship and as a way to claim territory.

1732

Although British settlers had reached the area by the 1600s, Georgia did not become the 13th colony until 1732, when it was established by military leader James Oglethorpe.

> **I HAVE A DREAM THAT ONE DAY ON THE RED HILLS OF GEORGIA, THE SONS OF FORMER SLAVES AND THE SONS OF FORMER SLAVE OWNERS WILL BE ABLE TO SIT DOWN TOGETHER AT THE TABLE OF BROTHERHOOD.**
>
> —Civil rights leader Martin Luther King, Jr.

- The country's oldest historically Black college for women, Spelman College was founded in 1881. It began as a school in a church basement but is now one of the preeminent centers of education for Black women.

- In 1944, Lillian Smith published her novel *Strange Fruit*, a tale of interracial love. Smith, who grew up in Clayton, was an anti-segregation advocate often called a "traitor to the South" for her views on equality.

- On January 15, 1929, Martin Luther King, Jr. (born Michael Luther King, Jr.) was born in Atlanta. A Baptist minister and an activist, King became one of the most prominent leaders of the civil rights movement of the 1950s and '60s. Perhaps best known for his "I Have a Dream" address at the March on Washington, King received the Nobel Peace Prize in 1964. He was assassinated four years later.

- During the 18th century, Scots-Irish immigrants in the northern mountains of Georgia began distilling fruit or corn into alcohol—known as moonshine. Although moonshiners historically ran illicit operations to avoid federal taxes, their methodology has also come to be used by mainstream distillers.

- Ann Morgan "Nancy" Hart was a real-life Revolutionary War figure who became something of a folk hero. While her husband was away with the militia, Hart was known to dress herself as a man and wander through British camps to gain important information.

- From the late 1700s, Georgia's economy relied largely on cotton plantations and the perpetuation of enslaved labor, particularly after Eli Whitney's 1793 invention of the cotton gin, a production-increasing farming tool.

- Although peaches, the state fruit, had been grown in the region since they were brought by Franciscan monks in the 1500s, it wasn't until the end of the Civil War—when plantation owners could no longer exploit enslaved labor to grow cotton—that they became a horticultural mainstay.

- In 1961, Hamilton Holmes and Charlayne Hunter-Gault became the first two Black students admitted to the University of Georgia after challenging the state's segregation practices.

STARS ★ OF ★ THE ★ STATE

RAY CHARLES

(1930–2004) Ray Charles was a legendary musician and pioneer of soul music. Born Ray Charles Robinson in Albany, Charles began playing piano at a very young age. At age six, he developed glaucoma, which left him blind by age seven. Charles learned to read and write music in Braille, and he went on to also learn the clarinet, alto saxophone, and organ. As his career progressed, Charles emerged as a leading creator of soul music, combining jazz with gospel and R&B. In addition to winning 17 Grammys, the Grammy Lifetime Achievement Award, the President's Merit Award, and more, Charles also excelled at humanitarianism, founding the Robinson Foundation for Hearing Disorders (now the Ray Charles Foundation).

NUTS!

Famous for its peaches, but reliant on the peanut! The largest peanut-producing state, Georgia grows more than half of the peanuts produced in the U.S. each year.

WEIRD BUT TRUE

- Among its more than 30,000 Elvis-themed items, the Loudermilk Boarding House is home to a wart supposedly removed from Elvis's wrist.

- Georgia has two official state BBQ cook-offs: one for pork and one for beef.

- There is a three-quarters-scale replica of the White House in a neighborhood within the city of Atlanta.

- The secret formula for Coca-Cola, which was first invented in Atlanta in 1886, is kept locked away in a giant vault in the city.

- The winning pig at the state fair pig races gets an Oreo cookie.

- Possibly the world's largest tick collection is located at Georgia Southern University.

- Pear salad, a southern classic, contains pears, cheese, and mayonnaise.

- Known as "Georgia's Little Grand Canyon," Providence Canyon is a 150-foot-deep (46 m) canyon caused by human-made erosion.

- Peanuts, the state crop, are not actually nuts; they are legumes.

- In 1970, daredevil Karl Wallenda crossed Tallulah Gorge on a 750-foot-high (229 m) tightrope.

- The Georgia Capitol Museum in Atlanta contains a taxidermic two-headed calf.

- Although the official grave of Old West gunfighter John Henry "Doc" Holliday is in Colorado, some believe his true resting place is in Griffin. ▪

▶ **STORY OF** THE NAME Georgia was named for King George II of England, who approved the colony's charter in 1732. ▪

RECORD ★ SETTERS

James Oglethorpe laid Savannah out into 24 designated squares (22 of which still exist), making it America's first planned city.

MISCELLANY

- The **"adoptable dog"** is the state dog.

- Born enslaved in Clarke County in 1837, **Harriet Powers** is remembered as a pre-eminent American folk artist for her textile needlework.

- **Delta Air Lines**, one of the largest airline companies in the world, was founded in 1925 in Macon. Today, the company is headquartered in Atlanta.

- **Grits** are the official state prepared food.

- Known as the **Battle of Bloody Marsh**, a 1742 skirmish on St. Simons Island was Spain's only attempt to claim Georgia.

- The **shark tooth** is the state fossil.

- The state mammal is the **white-tailed deer**.

- **Quartz** is the state gem.

- **Joel Chandler Harris**, a folklorist best known for his tales of Uncle Remus and Br'er Rabbit, was from Eatonton.

- Organized in 1773, the **First African Baptist Church of Savannah** is one of the oldest continually operating Black churches in the U.S.

- In 1932, Franklin Delano Roosevelt had the **Little White House** built at Warm Springs as a base for his polio treatments.

- The **one-toed amphiuma**, a protected animal in Georgia, is a rare, eel-like amphibian with tiny legs.

DO-SI-DO

The square dance, a partnered dance involving four or eight couples who perform a series of steps announced by a caller, is the state folk dance.

BY THE NUMBERS

729

THE HEIGHT IN FEET (222 M) OF AMICALOLA FALLS, THE STATE'S TALLEST WATERFALL

586 the depth in feet (179 m) of Walker County's Fantastic Pit, the deepest unobstructed underground cave in the country

18 girls became the first members of the Girl Scouts when Georgian Juliette Gordon Low founded the organization in 1912.

1915 The boll weevil arrives in Georgia and devastates the cotton crop.

75 million+ people passed through ATL in 2021, making it one of the busiest airports in the world.

60 years: the life span of a gopher tortoise, the state reptile

700 square miles (1,813 sq km): the area of the Okefenokee Swamp, the largest swamp in North America

45,000 THE NUMBER OF UNION SOLDIERS IMPRISONED AT CAMP SUMTER/ANDERSONVILLE, THE LARGEST CIVIL WAR PRISON CAMP

38 inches (91 cm): how long copperhead snakes can grow

1 POUND 12 OUNCES (816.5 g): the weight of the world's heaviest peach, grown in Georgia

- Georgia's capital is also its largest city. The center of much history, it features Civil War ruins dating back to Sherman's march, the site of Booker T. Washington's Atlanta Compromise speech, the Jimmy Carter Library and Museum, Martin Luther King, Jr.'s childhood home, and more.

- Famed for its picturesque Spanish moss, Savannah is home to historic sites, unique architecture, and a vibrant cultural scene. It is also considered by many to be one of the country's most haunted cities.

- Stone Mountain Park includes a lake, golf courses, nature trails, rides, and more. Begun as a simple tower attraction on top of Stone Mountain in 1838, the park now draws around four million visitors a year and is the state's number one attraction. It also houses the world's largest Confederate monument, an ongoing source of controversy and debate.

- Situated in Georgia and Florida, the Okefenokee Swamp was largely designated a national wildlife refuge in 1937. The area is home to many animals, including black bears, river otters, cottonmouth snakes, alligators, and ospreys.

- Georgia is home to some of the largest archaeological mound sites in North America. The Kolomoki people, who may have lived in one of the most populous settlements north of Mexico from 350 to 600, constructed burial mounds up to 56 feet (17 m) tall—seven of which remain outside of the city of Blakely. The largest mounds lie outside of Cartersville and were constructed by the Etowah people of the Mississippian culture from around 1000 to 1500.

- Visitors to the Vidalia Onion Festival celebrate the festival's namesake, one of the state's top crops. These locally cultivated onions are said to be sweeter than any other kind. *

222 points earned by Georgia Tech during a 1916 football game, earning the college a record for the highest non-NFL team score

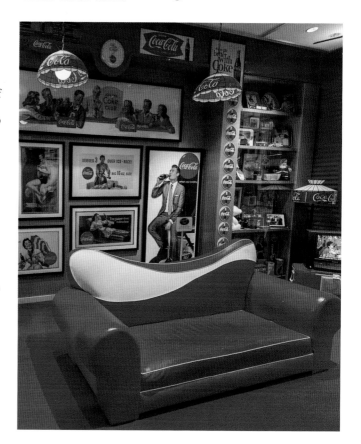

▲ VISIT THE REAL THING
Since it opened in 1990, the World of Coca-Cola has welcomed more than 18 million guests. The attraction celebrates the history of the local drink and features a theater, memorabilia, an open-to-the-public bottling line, and the famed Vault of the Secret Formula.

▶ **STORY OF** THE SOUND Georgia—and Atlanta in particular—has long been a center of musical innovation by Black artists. Folk music styles, such as the "ring shout," developed through the 19th century. Jazz artists Fletcher Henderson, Horace Henderson, and Mary Lou Williams stormed the music scene in the 1920s, and Ma Rainey ushered in the sounds of the blues. In 1949, WERD in Atlanta became the country's first Black-owned radio station; several years later, Ray Charles became internationally famous for pioneering soul music. Around 1995, when hip-hop duo OutKast won Best New Rap Group at the Source Awards, Atlanta gained further recognition on the world stage. Since then, Atlanta has become venerated for its sonic innovation, such as the development of trap music, and for being the home of a multitude of award-winning artists. Today, the city is hailed as one of the world's preeminent centers of music. *

RECORD ★ SETTERS

Chartered in 1836 and opened in 1839 in Macon, Wesleyan College was the world's first women's college to grant degrees.

SPORTING CHANCES

- Nicknamed "The Georgia Peach," Hall of Famer Ty Cobb from Narrows is known as one of the best all-around baseball players of all time.

- In 1933, the Augusta National golf club was opened by banker Clifford Roberts and Georgia-born golf champion Bobby Jones. A year later they began the Masters Tournament, which remains the country's preeminent golf tournament.

- Savannah-born golfer Hollis Stacy is the winner of three U.S. Women's Open tournaments as well as a Peter Jackson Classic. She was inducted into the World Golf Hall of Fame in 2012.

- In 1996, Atlanta hosted the city's largest event to date: the Centennial Summer Olympics.

▶ DOG DAYS

From Uga I through Uga X, a line of pure white English bulldogs has been the beloved University of Georgia mascot since 1956.

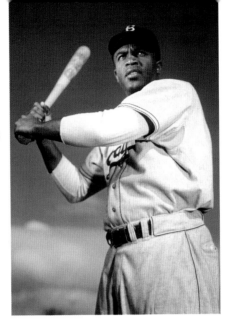

MADE IN GA

Georgia's agricultural outputs include:

- Poultry
- Pecans
- Peanuts
- Cotton
- Timber
- Eggs
- Dairy
- Corn
- Cattle

Georgia's industrial outputs include:

- Aircraft
- Machinery
- Motor vehicles
- Gas turbine parts
- Medical equipment
- Insecticides
- Paper

- Born in Cairo, Georgia, legendary baseball player Jackie Robinson was the first Black athlete to join Major League Baseball. Robinson was instrumental in desegregating the sport and was inducted into the Hall of Fame in 1962.

- Originally known as the Boston Red Stockings, the Atlanta Braves became a Georgia team in 1965, going on to win the 1995 and 2021 baseball World Series.

- Born in Vidalia, football player Mel Blount went on play in five Pro Bowls and start in four Super Bowl victories.

- A mere quarter-mile (400 m) drag strip can draw crowds of more than a half million people as cars speed by at Georgia Motorsports Park outside of Valdosta.

STARS ★ OF ★ THE ★ STATE

GERTRUDE "MA RAINEY" PRIDGETT

(1886–1939) Born Gertrude Pridgett in Columbus, Ma Rainey was a bisexual advocate and vocalist known as the "mother of blues." Rainey began her singing career in vaudeville performer with her husband, known as Pa Rainey. After hearing blues singers while traveling in Missouri, Rainey began to infuse her vaudeville performances with Black folk music. She also penned lyrics that focused on her bisexuality. In addition to directly influencing other renowned blues singers such as Bessie Smith, Rainey's work brought Black female experiences to mainstream audiences. She recorded some 92 songs and was inducted into the Blues Hall of Fame in 1983.

GUAM

★ ★ ★

"Where America's Day Begins"

★ ★ ★

CAPITAL: Hagåtña **BIRD:** Ko'ko' or Guam Rail **NICKNAME:** Land of the Chamorro **ENTRY:** 1950

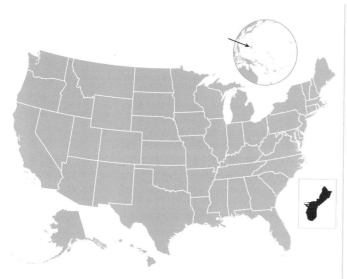

GU FACTS

- A U.S. territory, it is the largest and southernmost island in the West Pacific Ocean's Mariana Islands chain.

- 5,000 miles (8,047 km) west of San Francisco and 1,500 miles (2,414 km) east of Manila, Guam is closer to North Korea than it is to the continental United States.

- Guam covers an area of about 217 square miles (562 sq km), which is approximately the size of Chicago.

- In the last four centuries, it has been ruled by Spain, Japan, and the U.S.

- It was the site of the first Roman Catholic mission and formal European colony in the Pacific islands.

- There are two official languages: English and Chamorro, the Indigenous people's language.

- People from islands off Southeast Asia settled Guam and the Marianas more than 4,000 years ago.

- Most of the island is surrounded by a coral reef, which acts as a natural break-water protecting the shoreline. ▼

▶ OFFICIAL FLOWER

Bougainvillea
Bougainvillea spectabilis

Known as the paper flower by locals, this year-round plant produces brilliant blooms of red, pink, purple, orange, and white.

1898

The U.S. acquired Guam as a territory in 1898, as part of the Spanish-American War, with the signing of the Treaty of Paris between Spain and the U.S. formalizing the handover.

HÅFA ÅDAI!

—A widely used Chamorro greeting that means "Hello!"

AL AK AS AZ AR CA CO CT DE FL GA GU HI ID IL IN IA KS KY LA ME MP MD MA MI MN MS MO MT NE NV NH NJ NM NY NC ND OH OK OR PA PR RI SC

◀ SPAM FEVER

Each year Guamanians eat more than 16 cans of Spam per person—more than any other country or territory.

- With a strategic position between North America and Asia, Guam is a huge hub for the U.S. military: Around 30 percent of the island's total land area is occupied by U.S. Air Force and Navy bases.

- During World War II, Guam was bombed by the Japanese soon after they hit Pearl Harbor. Japanese troops then seized control and stayed for three years. After allied forces reclaimed the territory, Guam officially became a part of the U.S. With the signing of the 1950 Organic Act of Guam, the island was put under the administration of the Department of the Navy.

- The Organic Act of Guam, signed by President Harry Truman, also established the branches of Guam's government and Hagåtña as the island's capital, and it granted all residents American citizenship.

- In 1970, Guam elected its first governor, Carlos Camacho. He served one term.

- Guam does not carry any Electoral College votes, so residents can only vote in U.S. congressional elections and presidential primaries—and not in the presidential general election.

- A limited self-government is made up of a popularly elected governor, a small legislature, and a limited-voting delegate in the U.S. House of Representatives.

- Each of the 19 villages are represented by their own mayor.

- Guam's mean high temperature is 81°F (27°C), and its average low is 76°F (24°C). Dry months are December through June, while the rainy season is July through November.

- Typhoons, or tropical cyclones, can occur sporadically throughout the year, but they are more likely to occur during the rainy season. ▪

▶ STORY OF THE MOTTO Good morning, Guam—good night, New York. Guam's proximity to the International Date Line puts the island some 14 hours ahead of the East Coast of the U.S., and it gave the territory its motto of "Where America's Day Begins." But experts say that's actually a stretch of the truth: Wake Island, an atoll of three tiny islands in the Pacific Ocean, houses a U.S. military base. So, really, Wake Island is where America's day begins. ▪

STARS ★ OF ★ THE ★ TERRITORY

MADELEINE BORDALLO

(b. 1933) The first woman to represent Guam in Congress, Bordallo got her start in politics as Guam's Democratic National Committeewoman in 1964. By 1981, Bordallo, who moved with her family to Guam from Minnesota as a teenager, became the first woman from the Democratic Party to win a seat in the island's legislature. Her upward trajectory continued as she was elected Guam's first woman lieutenant governor, and, ultimately, a nonvoting member of the U.S. House of Representatives, serving from 2013 to 2019. Prior to leaving Congress, Bordallo lobbied for and passed a war claims measure, authorizing reparations to the survivors and descendants of the victims of the Japanese military occupation of Guam during World War II. ▪

CORAL LANE ▶

Many of Guam's paved roads are made of crushed coral mixed with cement.

WEIRD BUT TRUE

- On a map, Guam is shaped like a footprint.

- An Imperial Japanese Army sergeant hid out in the jungles of Guam for nearly 30 years after World War II ended.

- Umatac Village is home to one of the world's few "gravity hills," where cars and other items appear to roll uphill, but it's just an optical illusion.

- In the late 1800s, Asan Beach was the site of a leper colony, which was used for only a handful of years before it was destroyed by a typhoon.

- In Dededo, there's a cemetery for trained military dogs who participated in combat during World War II.

- Chamorro legends tell of a giant fish that ate the central part of the territory, creating the hourglass shape of Pago Bay.

- Spicy pickled mango is a popular treat.

- According to myth, a rock formation in the Fouha Bay is said to be the resting place of a goddess who created the world and its people.

- There are shipwrecks from both World War I and World War II below Apra Harbor—the only place in the world where wrecks from two different countries and two different wars are nearly touching.

▲ HÅFA ÅDAI

Chamorro culture has been shaped by former rulers, drawing from Spanish, Filipino, and Mexican food, clothing, and traditions.

MISCELLANY

- Up to two feet (60 cm) of rain fell on some parts of the island during Typhoon Mawar in 2023.

- Guam is a major hub for **subsea fiberoptic communications cables** between the western United States, Hawaii, Australia, and Asia.

- The **Austronesian people** settled Guam around 1500 B.C.

- **Kelaguen** is a traditional seafood or meat dish marinated in lemon juice and spices.

- **Two Lovers Point** gets its name from a local legend telling of a couple leaping to their death so they could be eternally linked.

- **Dededo's mall** is the largest shopping mall in Micronesia.

- During the **Vietnam War**, Guam served as a base for B-52 bombers headed for missions in Southeast Asia and was used as a transit point for evacuating Vietnamese refugees.

- Each December 8, residents celebrate **Santa Marian Kåmalen Day** in honor of the island's patron saint. Offices, schools and most

banks close as residents head to Hagåtña for a procession around the island's capital.

- The celebration centers around a 300-year-old statue of the **Virgin Mary** that survived the Japanese bombing on December 8, 1941.

- Another major celebration on the island is **Liberation Day** on July 21, which marks the anniversary of Guam's liberation from Japanese occupation during World War II.

- Festivities include a queen contest and a **mile-long parade** (1.6 km) in Hagåtña.

- Guam has **no sales tax**.

- At least 304 vehicles lined up in Guam to stage the world's longest **parade of Nissan cars**.

RECORD ★ SETTERS

On June 5, 2015, Guam became the first U.S. territory to legalize same-sex marriage after a pair of 28-year-old women filed a lawsuit upon being denied a marriage license.

BY THE NUMBERS

3.5 the duration in hours of a direct flight between Tokyo and Guam

85% of Guam residents are Roman Catholic

830 number of people who live within one square mile (320 per sq km), making Guam the 43rd densest place in the world

4 the width in miles (6 km) at the territory's narrowest point

5 THE NUMBER OF NUCLEAR-POWERED FAST-ATTACK SUBMARINES HOUSED AT NAVAL BASE GUAM

2,500 the number of tires dumped in the ocean by the Department of Agriculture to build an artificial reef to increase the fish population in Coco's Lagoon

$250,000 the estimated cost to dismantle the reef, once experts realized the tires were causing additional damage

7 the depth in miles (11 km) of the Mariana Trench, the deepest point in Earth's oceans, which is closer to Guam than to any other landmass

7 the number of publicly accessible golf courses

9,700 military members live on the island with their families—totaling about 16% of the population.

69°F THE COLDEST TEMPERATURE (21°C) EVER RECORDED ON GUAM, IN JANUARY 2021

DESTINATION: GUAM

- Photographs and memorabilia linked to Guam's role in World War II are housed at the Pacific War Museum, which features exhibits showcasing both American and Japanese items.

- At the cultural village at Gef Pa'go in Inarajan, visitors can experience what life was like in the early days of the island as Chamorro elders demonstrate traditional arts, crafts, and cooking.

> **BORN AND RAISED ON AN ISLAND, FAR FROM THE GOVERNING POWERS, MISUNDERSTOOD BY THE REST OF AMERICA, BUT INSTILLED WITH VALUES THAT EXEMPLIFY MY CULTURE.**
>
> —Guam native and artist Jerrold Castro on the plight of the Chamorro people

- Shark's Cove Beach is only reachable by a half-mile (800 m) hike, making it one of Guam's most exclusive beaches. The hidden cove is lined with palm trees while the water, ideal for snorkeling, is teeming with colorful tropical fish.

- The Dulce Nombre de Maria Cathedral-Basilica stands in the spot where the first Catholic church in Guam was built in 1669 and later demolished during World War II. The newer structure,

◀ WINDOWS TO THE SEA

The top deck of Fish Eye Marine Park in Piti offers sweeping views of the ocean and mountain ranges. Head below to the underwater area, which offers 24 windows to look into the ocean—and see some of the hundreds of species of fish that swim around the island.

built in 1958, serves as a memorial as well as a symbol of the island's devotion to the Catholic faith.

- Each weekend, bargain hunters browse and haggle at the Dededo Flea Market, where everything from home appliances to fresh, local produce is peddled.

- Tucked behind a nondescript parking lot in the village of Piti is a unique waterway in a turquoise hue so bold and clear that it almost looks fake. Known as Emerald Valley, this is a prime place to swim and spot soft corals, starfish, and sea urchins.

- Underwater World, Guam's premier aquarium, showcases life under the sea. Visitors can get up close and personal with sharks, rays, sea turtles, and more while learning about Guam's natural ecosystem.

- The aptly named Waterfall Valley features a quintet of flowing falls, somewhat hidden away in the depths of Inarajan on the south end of the island. A hike is required to get there, but a swim in the multiple natural pools near the falls can help to relieve weary legs.

RICARDO J. BLAS, JR.

(b. 1986) In 2012, Blas made Guam Olympic history when the super-heavyweight judoka won his match the first time a Guamanian advanced to the next round of competition by winning a preliminary round. The son of an Olympian and Guam's flag bearer at the opening ceremonies of the 2008 games, Blas also received worldwide attention when he weighed in to compete at 481 pounds (218 kg), making him the heaviest athlete in Olympics history. ⁕

In 2022, a pair of Guam residents built the world's tallest toy timber structure measuring nearly 26 feet (8 m) high.

MADE IN GU

Guam's agricultural outputs include:

- Papayas
- Bananas
- Breadfruit
- Mangoes
- Copra (sun-dried or smoked coconut meat)
- Bok choy
- Eggs
- Pork
- Poultry

Guam's industrial outputs include:

- Beauty products
- Scrap iron
- Electric batteries
- Food products
- Beverage products
- Scrap copper

SPORTING CHANCES

- Baseball, which arrived with the Americans at the turn of the 20th century, remains a popular pastime on the island.

- The Guam Major League was formed in 1974 and became the island's premier baseball league. In 1982, the league launched the Western Pacific Invitational Baseball Tournament, which brought in teams from Korea, Chinese Taipei, Japan, and the Micronesian region during its 13-year run.

- "Barefoot runner" and resident Eddie Vilbar Vega ran 101 marathons in one year without shoes on, a world record.

- In 2008, the national rugby team crushed the Brunei team with a 74–0 victory, its biggest-ever win.

- Guam has hosted the Pacific Games—an Olympic-like event with participation exclusively from archipelagic countries around the Pacific Ocean—twice: once in 1975 and then again in 1999.

- In 2019, the men's basketball team, the three-on-three men's basketball squad, and judo fighter Joshter Andrew all won gold medals at the Pacific Games.

- Guam made its Olympic debut in 1988, sending athletes to participate in track and field, swimming, and wrestling.

- Guam Olympians have competed in every Summer Games since 1988, participating in mountain biking, wrestling, athletics, swimming, and judo.

- The first—and so far only—winter Olympian representing Guam is Michigan-born Judd Bankert, who competed in the biathlon event at the 1988 games in Calgary.

- Bankert, a computer consultant, learned to cross-country ski for the occasion, and finished 71st in Calgary.

- The Fiestan Tasi (Festival of the Sea), held annually in Merizo, celebrates the importance of the ocean to the island's history and culture. It often includes boat races and water sports competitions and exhibitions.

▶ **WHEELS UP**
For 21 years, racing enthusiasts went to Guam International Raceway for events like motocross and drifting.

HAWAII

★ ★ ★

"Ua Mau ke Ea o ka ʻĀina i ka Pono"
("The life of the land is perpetuated in righteousness")

★ ★ ★

CAPITAL: Honolulu **BIRD:** Nene (Hawaiian Goose) **NICKNAME:** Aloha State **ENTRY:** August 21, 1959

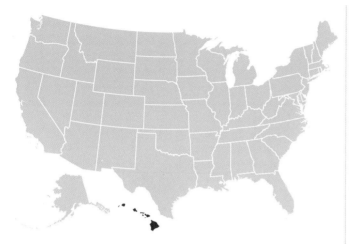

HI FACTS

- Hawaii encompasses a string of 137 islands stretching over a land area of 6,423 square miles (16,635 sq km) in the north central Pacific Ocean.

- Some 2,400 miles (3,862 km) from the West Coast of the continental U.S. and 3,850 miles (6,196 km) from Japan, Hawaii is the most isolated population center on Earth.

- There are eight major islands that make up the state of Hawaii: Niihau, Kauai, Oahu, Molokai, Lanai, Maui, Kahoolawe, and the Big Island of Hawaii.

- From east to west, Hawaii is the widest U.S. state, measuring 1,500 miles (2,414 km) from the island of Niihau to the island of Hawaii.

- Hawaii's population of some 1.4 million ranks 40th among all states. Honolulu, which is on Oahu and is Hawaii's capital and largest city, claims around 340,000 people.

- ▽ The Hawaiian Islands were formed by volcanic activity. Kauai is the oldest of the eight islands, formed about

▷ STATE FLOWER

Pua Aloalo
Hibiscus brackenridgei

Also known as the yellow hibiscus, the endemic (and endangered) plant is recognizable by its large, brightly hued flowers with a reddish center.

1778

In 1778, Britain's Captain James Cook named the group of islands the Sandwich Islands in honor of the Earl of Sandwich. A year later, Cook was killed in a battle with Hawaiians at Kealakekua Bay on the island of Hawaii.

THE LOVELIEST FLEET OF ISLANDS THAT LIES ANCHORED IN ANY OCEAN.

—Author Mark Twain

◀ HOT STUFF

There are six active volcanoes in Hawaii, including Kilauea, among the world's most active volcanoes, which has been erupting almost continuously since 1983.

5.1 million years ago. The Big Island is the youngest island, formed more than 500,000 years ago.

- More than 1,500 years ago, Polynesians first arrived in Hawaii from the Marquesas Islands, some 2,000 miles (3,219 km) away, traveling in canoes. Later, Tahitians settled there.

- In 1810, Hawaii's first king, Kamehameha the Great, conquered and united the eight major Hawaiian Islands, ruling until his death in 1819.

- The 1887 Constitution of the Hawaiian Kingdom (aka the "Bayonet Constitution"), empowered the legislature and foreign landowners and stripped the Hawaiian monarchy of much of its authority.

- The islands were annexed by the U.S. in 1898 and made a territory, which remained the case until Hawaii was granted statehood as the 50th state in 1959.

- On December 7, 1941, "A Date Which Will Live in Infamy," the Japanese launched a surprise attack on Pearl Harbor during World War II. Killing more than 2,300 Americans, the act forced U.S. involvement in the war.

- A heavy U.S. military presence remains, with a total of 12 bases in the state.

- Prior to 1820, Hawaii lacked a written language. Records were passed through storytelling, songs, and chants.

- Christian missionaries who arrived in the early 19th century developed the written Hawaiian language, which has just 12 letters: five vowels and seven consonants.

- Today, Hawaii is the only state with two official languages, English and Hawaiian.

- The 'okina mark (similar to an apostrophe) and kahakō mark (line above a vowel) are used to clarify pronunciation.

▶ **STORY OF** THE SONG The Hawaiian state song, "Hawai'i Pono'ī" has a royally interesting history. In fact, the lyrics were written by King David Kalākaua, the last king of Hawaii, who ruled from 1874 to 1891. In 1874, King David wrote the lyrics for a new state song, which includes lyrics about "Hawaii's own true sons" and pays homage to King Kamehameha, who unified the Hawaiian Islands into one kingdom. Music for it was later composed by Henry Berger of the Royal Hawaiian Band. It served as the national anthem of Hawaii starting in 1876 and was later made into the state song after Hawaii joined the union.

STARS ★ OF ★ THE ★ STATE

BARACK OBAMA

(b. 1961) The only president from outside the continental U.S., Barack Hussein Obama II was born on August 4, 1961, in Hawaii. After a brief stint living in Indonesia as a child, Obama returned to Hawaii as a fifth grader, attending (and playing varsity basketball at) the Punahou School, a private prep school. He then left Hawaii for college, ultimately graduating from Columbia University and later Harvard Law School before starting his career in politics. Even during his time in the White House from 2009 to 2017, the Obama family made frequent trips to Hawaii, often visiting over the Christmas holiday. Now, the president and former first lady Michelle have a home in Waimanalo on the island of Oahu.

WEIRD BUT TRUE

- There's a small patch of land at Kealakekua Bay on the Big Island that's owned by Britain.

- Astronauts training for missions to the moon and Mars have trained on the barren surface around Mauna Loa volcano.

- There's a golf course on the rim of the active Kilauea volcanic crater.

- Free coconuts are on offer at the Hoolehua Post Office on Molokai, and customers can decorate them and ship them anywhere in the world.

- Wayward skunks—one of the several species prohibited in Hawaii—have been captured on multiple islands.

- Hawaii's black coral, which is the skeletal remains of coral polyps, is the only state gem that's not a mineral.

- The humuhumunukunukuāpua'a (also known as the triggerfish) is the state fish.

- Volcanic smog that's released into the air from the active Kilauea volcano is known as "Vog."

- Snow drifts of three to five feet (0.9 m to 1.5 m) were reported at Mauna Kea after a blizzard struck in 2021.

Keck Observatory telescopes at the summit of Mauna Kea are the world's largest optical and infrared telescopes, measuring 32.8 feet (10 m) across and housed in domes spanning 700,000 cubic feet (19,822 m³).

RUFF SEAS

The Hawaiian name for the monk seal, *ilio-holo-i-ka-uaua*, translates to "dog running in the rough seas."

MISCELLANY

- Hawaii celebrates **King Kamehameha Day** every June 11, feting its first king with floral parades and parties.

- **Ka Lae** on the Big Island—also known as South Point—is the southernmost point in the U.S.

- The **highest (100°F/38°C)** and **lowest (12°F/-11.11°C)** temperatures in Hawaii's history were both recorded on the Big Island.

- **Sixty-three percent** of Hawaiians are Christian; of those, 25 percent identify as Evangelical Protestant and 20 percent report as Catholic.

- From 1866 to 1969, Hawaiians afflicted with leprosy—some 8,000 people—were sent to live at Kalaupapa on Molokai, which was one of a handful of **leper colonies** in the U.S.

- According to legend, Molokai is the **birthplace of the hula**, and a festival honoring the Native dance occurs on the island every May.

- The **Cathedral Basilica of Our Lady of Peace**, founded in downtown Honolulu in 1843, is among the oldest Catholic cathedrals in continuous use in the country.

- Many of the 10,000-strong herd of mother cows at **Parker Ranch** on the Big Island are descendants of the first ones brought to Hawaii in the late 18th century by the British.

- Hawaii is one of **only two U.S. states to grow coffee**. Porous volcanic soil and amenable weather contribute to coffee production totaling close to $60 million annually.

- In 1889, a Portuguese immigrant introduced the first **ukulele** to Hawaiians. And in 1885, a Hawaiian teenager invented the **steel guitar**; both instruments later became widely used around the world.

- The custom of offering a **lei**—a gift made with flowers, leaves, seeds, or nuts that's a symbol of love, friendship, gratitude, appreciation, and honor—was first introduced to Hawaiians by early Polynesian voyagers.

- Of the 50 states, Hawaii accounts for **99 percent of pineapple acreage**, as well as 96 percent of taro acreage, and more than 50 percent of the country's banana acreage.

- Hawaii's **Kalawao County** is the country's smallest county, occupying just 12 square miles (34 sq km) with a population of 82.

BY THE NUMBERS Natural Wonders

60 the height in feet (18 m) of the banyan tree in the center of Lahaina on Maui. Spanning 1.9 acres (0.8 ha), the tree is the largest of its kind in the U.S.

582,578

THE AREA IN SQUARE MILES (1,508,870 SQ KM) THAT PAPAHĀNAUMOKUĀKEA MARINE NATIONAL MONUMENT COVERS IN THE PACIFIC OCEAN. HOME TO SEABIRDS AND MARINE LIFE, IT'S BIGGER THAN ALL THE COUNTRY'S NATIONAL PARKS COMBINED.

3,000 the height in feet (914 m) of the cliffs on East Molokai's northern coast, the highest sea cliffs on Earth

730 the approximate depth in feet (223 m) of the Halemaʻumaʻu lava lake at Kilauea volcano's summit, the legendary home of Pele, the Hawaiian volcano goddess

840 THE SIZE IN ACRES (340 HA) OF HALALIʻI LAKE ON NIIHAU, THE LARGEST NATURAL LAKE ON THE HAWAIIAN ISLANDS

450 the amount of rain, in inches (1,143 cm), that falls on Mount Waialeale on Kauai, one of the world's wettest places

$10,000 the price for which Elizabeth Sinclair purchased the island of Niihau from the Kingdom of Hawaii in 1864 (she paid in gold). Known as the "Forbidden Island," it remains privately owned.

1,450 the height in feet (442 m) of Hiilawe Falls on the Big Island. The tallest waterfall on Hawaii, it's the same height as the Empire State Building.

33,500 the height in feet (10,211 m) of Mauna Kea from its submarine base, making it the tallest mountain in the world. The massive mountain reaches 13,796 feet (4,205 m) and can be seen above water.

3 THE NUMBER OF SQUARE MILES (7.8 SQ KM) COVERED BY A REEF FOUND IN THE ʻAUʻAU CHANNEL IN MAUI, THE LARGEST UNINTERRUPTED MESOPHOTIC CORAL ECOSYSTEM EVER RECORDED

- The country's only royal palace, the 'Iolani Palace in Honolulu was built by King Kalākaua in 1882. A modern marvel at the time, the palace was wired for electricity in 1887, four years before the White House. After the monarchy was overthrown in 1893, the palace became a government building and was eventually converted to a museum in 1978.

- One of the most popular tourist destinations in Hawaii, the U.S.S. *Arizona* at Pearl Harbor takes visitors back in time to the events of December 7, 1941. A museum features exhibits showcasing major moments in the history of Hawaii and a boat ride takes you out to the U.S.S. *Arizona* memorial, built over the remains of the sunken battleship.

- Hawaii's most recognized landmark, Diamond Head on the eastern edge of Waikiki's coastline, is a saucer-shaped crater that formed about 300,000 years ago. Today, the spot offers a top-notch hike with sweeping coastal views and a dose of military history, too.

- Located on the southeastern Kau coast on the Big Island, Punalu'u Black Sand Beach is a top spot to view large honu (Hawaiian green sea turtles) and hawksbill turtles sunbathing on the shore. Just be sure to watch from a distance and never touch wildlife.

- A boat ride, paddle, or helicopter ride along the 17-mile (27 m) Nāpali Coast on Kauai's North Shore reveals breathtaking beauty including soaring cliffs, plummeting waterfalls, and turquoise-hued water. And if it looks like it's straight out of *Jurassic Park*, that's because it is: Parts of the movie were filmed there.

- Hawai'i Volcanoes National Park on the Big Island is home to two of the world's most active volcanoes: Kilauea and Mauna Loa. While hiking is an option, those who prefer to drive can take either the Chain of Craters Road (where you can spot trails of recent lava flows) or the Crater Rim Drive (which skirts the edge of the Kilauea Caldera).

- Officially known as the Hana Highway, the Road to Hana is a 64-mile (104 km) stretch following the northeast coastline of Maui. With hairpin turns, tight one-lane bridges, and blind corners, the drive is not for the faint of heart, but the pit stops (think: towering waterfalls and roadside stands) and sweeping views along the way make it all worth it.

▲ SEEING GREEN
Papakōlea Beach, on the Big Island, has a green sand beach.

A descendant of Chinese immigrants to Hawaii, Hiram Fong became the first person of Chinese descent elected to Congress, and in 1959, the first Asian Pacific American elected to the Senate. Also a multimillionaire who was president for nine different companies, Fong served as a Hawaiian senator for nearly two decades.

SPORTING CHANCES

- Outrigger canoe racing, a sport with roots stemming to the days of Polynesian ocean voyagers in 300 A.D., is popular throughout Hawaii. Today, the 38-mile-plus (61 km) Moloka'i Hoe event from Molokai to Waikiki welcomes hundreds of paddlers each year. ▲

- Considered one of the greatest Hawaiian athletes of all time, Duke Kahanamoku of Honolulu earned three golds and two silvers in swimming at the 1912, 1920, and 1924 Olympic Games, and is also known as the father of modern surfing after popularizing the sport around the world.

- The NFL held its annual Pro Bowl at Aloha Stadium in Honolulu from 1980 to 2009, from 2011 to 2014, and in 2016. The stadium also served as the site of the Hula Bowl for top college football teams.

- At the 2020 Tokyo Olympics (held in 2021), native Hawaiian Carissa Moore won the first gold medal in the history of Olympic surfing.

- There are no major professional sports teams in Hawaii, and the only NCAA Division I athletics program in the state is at the University of Hawaii at Manoa.

- Each year, the University of Hawaii at Manoa hosts the Diamond Head Classic, a three-day invitational college basketball tournament featuring some of the top programs in the country.

- In 1993, Waimanalo-born Chad Rowan became the first non-Japanese grand champion in the 1,500-year history of sumo wrestling.

- Hawaii has served as the site of the Ironman Triathlon World Championships since 1978, except for 2020 and 2021. The event, which features a grueling 2.4-mile (3.8 km) swim, 112-mile (180 km) bike ride, and a 26.2-mile (42.2 km) run, was first held in Oahu before moving to Kona, on the Big Island, in 1981.

- Native Hawaiians may have started surfing as early as 1,000 years ago, calling the sport *he'e nalu* (wave sliding) and using wooden boards weighing up to 175 pounds (79 kg) and measuring up to 16 feet (5 m) long.

- Since 1965, top professional golfers have played at the Sony Open in Hawaii—formerly known as the Hawaiian Open. A stop on the PGA Tour, it's held at Waialae Country Club in Honolulu. ▪

MADE IN HI

Hawaii's agricultural outputs include:

- Sugarcane
- Pineapple
- Cattle and calves
- Coffee
- Macadamia nuts
- Floriculture
- Chicken eggs
- Bananas
- Papayas

Hawaii's industrial outputs include:

- Petroleum and coal products
- Transportation equipment
- Food products
- Computer and electronic products
- Beverages and tobacco products

▶ HAWAII TIME

Hawaii has its own time zone, Hawaii Standard Time, and does not observe daylight saving time.

STARS ★ OF ★ THE ★ STATE

MICHELLE WIE WEST

(b. 1989) A native of Honolulu, this star golfer started playing when she was four and was rewriting record books by the time she was a tween. At age 10, Wie became the youngest golfer to qualify for a United States Golf Association (USGA) amateur championship, and she qualified for an event on the Ladies Professional Golf Association (LPGA) tour at 13. She continued to rack up accolades, including becoming the youngest player to win any adult USGA event, and ultimately turned pro a week before her 16th birthday. Wie's success continued on the pro scene, including five titles at the HSBC Women's World Championship, all solidifying her status as one of golf's greats. ▪

IDAHO

★ ★ ★

"Let It Be Perpetual"

★ ★ ★

CAPITAL: Boise **FLOWER:** Syringa **NICKNAME:** Gem State **ENTRY:** July 3, 1890

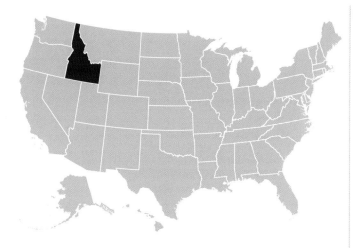

ID FACTS

- At a total surface area of 83,557 square miles (216,412 sq km), it is the 11th biggest state in the country.

- Idaho is twice as large as all six New England states combined.

- There are an estimated 1.9 million people living in the state. And with just 23 people for every square mile of land (8.8 per sq km), it is the seventh least densely populated state in the U.S.

- With more than 230,000 people, Boise, the state's capital, is the largest and most populated city.

- Forests cover approximately 21,500,000 acres (8,700,000 ha) and make up 40 percent of land cover. Nearly 90 percent of the forestland that existed in 1630 is still present today.

- The United States government owns 76 percent of all Idaho land and manages more than three-quarters of the forest. The rest is divided between public and private ownership.

- Idaho is home to more than 2,000 lakes.

- The state sits in the rain shadow of mountains in Washington and Oregon, meaning that it receives much less rain than those states do.

- Prior to the arrival of European and Mexican explorers, some 8,000 American Indians inhabited the state, including the Shoshone, Nez Perce, and Kootenai peoples.

- Native animal species include the grizzly bear, the woodland caribou, the fisher, the North American lynx, the pygmy rabbit, and the gray wolf.

- Explorer William Clark attempted to find a passage across the Salmon River—also known as "The River of No Return"—but was stalled by churning rapids and steep rock walls.

▶ **STATE BIRD**

Mountain Bluebird
Sialia currucoides

For most of the year, this easy-to-spot bird will remain in Idaho, living throughout the state in mountainous areas, valleys, meadows, and forests.

1896

In 1896, Idaho gave women the right to vote, making it the fourth state in the nation to do so.

ALL MY FATHER'S STORIES WERE ABOUT OUR MOUNTAIN, OUR VALLEY, OUR JAGGED LITTLE PATCH OF IDAHO.

—Tara Westover, Idaho native and author of best-selling memoir *Educated*

◄ CHEERS!
Idahoans are first in the nation for the most wine consumption per capita, according to a recent study.

- Because of its remote location, Idaho was one of the last states to be explored by European Americans. It wasn't until 1805 when Meriwether Lewis and his fellow members of the Corps of Discovery entered the area.

- Following Lewis and Clark's expedition, French-Canadian fur trappers arrived. Their influence is seen today in places like Coeur d'Alene (French for "heart of the awl") and Boise ("les bois" is French for "the trees").

- Despite signing the act creating the Idaho Territory, passing bills funding public colleges, protecting Native tribes, and encouraging people to migrate west and settle there, President Abraham Lincoln never visited Idaho.

- The "Gem State" nickname reflects the abundance of gold, silver, lead, zinc, cobalt, copper, and many other rare minerals that have been found in the state.

- Idaho is the only place in the world other than India where you can find star garnets, the state gem. The 12-sided crystals can be mined in Idaho Panhandle National Forests. ▪

▼ SERIOUS SPUDS
Nearly one-third of all U.S. potatoes are produced in Idaho, weighing in around 13 billion pounds (5.9 billion kg) of spuds each year.

▶ STORY OF THE NAME What does Idaho mean? Well, perhaps nothing at all. Researchers believe that in 1860 a Philadelphia-born doctor named George Willing presented the name to the U.S. Congress, insisting that it meant "Gem of the Mountains" in the Shoshone language. Willing actually wanted to give the name to the Colorado Territory, but that idea was nixed when lawmakers discovered it was not, in fact, a Shoshone word. (Some speculate Willing was inspired by a girl named Ida, or simply made it up.) But the name Idaho persisted and, by 1868 when the state gained its present borders, it became official. ▪

STARS ★ OF ★ THE ★ STATE

ELVINA MOULTON (1837–1917)

The first Black person to reside in the city of Boise, Moulton was a pioneer for both women and African Americans. Born enslaved in Kentucky, Moulton fled via the Oregon Trail, walking from Missouri to arrive in Boise before 1867. In Boise, she found work as a seamstress and a housekeeper, making enough money to buy her own home. Affectionately known as Aunt Viney, she never married but was known in the community for her kindness, including for the cookies she often baked for local children. She is also credited for helping to launch the First Presbyterian Church in Boise in 1878, of which she was the only African American member. ▪

- Idaho spans two time zones: The panhandle observes Pacific Standard Time, while the southern part of the state follows Mountain Standard Time.

- Almost the same number of men and women reside in the state.

- The Museum of Clean in Pocatello details the history of cleaning and features a collection of vacuums, including the world's first, which dates back to 1860.

- In 2004, the mayor of Wallace proclaimed the town to be the Center of the Universe—a statement that has never been proved (or disproved).

- The geyser in Soda Springs is set on a timer to go off every hour on the hour, making it the world's only "captive" geyser.

- Measuring 25 inches (63.5 cm) long and 14.5 inches (36.9 cm) wide, the world's largest potato chip is on display at the Idaho Potato Museum in Blackfoot.

- The Bear Lake monster, a massive marine creature with rows of razor-sharp teeth, is said to stalk a lake at the Idaho-Utah border.

- Boise, Idaho, is the state-plus-capital combination with the fewest letters.

- Cottonwood's Dog Bark Park Inn features a guesthouse built in the shape of a beagle. ▼

Among all states, Idaho ranks third in milk production and third in production of cheese.

MISCELLANY

- There are three lava fields in **Craters of the Moon National Monument and Preserve**, formed around 2,000 years ago.

- 67 percent of Idahoans are **Christian**, and approximately 21 percent of those residents identify as Evangelical Protestant.

- Built between 1850 and 1853, the **Cataldo Mission in Coeur d'Alene's Old Mission State Park** is the oldest surviving mission church, and the oldest standing structure in the state.

- Dipping down more than 7,900 feet (2,408 m), **Hells Canyon** is the deepest river gorge in North America.

- **Silver Mountain Resort** is home to North America's longest gondola, a 3.1-mile (5 km) journey from Kellogg's downtown to high up on Silver Mountain.

- Idaho has **80 recognized mountain ranges**, with nine peaks topping out at more than 12,000 feet (3,658 m), and hundreds reaching between 9,000 and 11,000 feet (2,743 and 3,353 m).

- At 12,662 feet (3,859 m) above sea level, the highest point, **Borah Peak**, is one of just a few in the lower 48 states that climbs more than 5,000 feet (1,524 m) from trailhead to summit.

- In 1955, **Arco** became the first town in the world to use electricity generated from nuclear power.

- Boise's **capitol building** was the first in the U.S. to be heated with geothermal water.

- Idaho attracts **37 million tourists** annually.

- **The Appaloosa**, a breed of horse favored by the Nez Perce, is Idaho's state horse.

- Flowing from an elevation of nearly 7,000 feet (2,134 m), Idaho's **St. Joe River** is the highest navigable river in the world.

RECORD ★ SETTERS

In 1914, Idaho became the first state in the nation to elect a Jewish governor. Moses Alexander, who was re-elected in 1916, is credited with starting the state highway system.

BY THE NUMBERS

25¢ the cost per ride on the first alpine chairlift when it was first used at the Sun Valley ski resort in 1936

6,500 weight in pounds (2,948 kg) of Boise's 11-foot-tall (3.4 m) statue of Abraham Lincoln, the world's third largest seated statue of the 16th president

72 different types of gemstones are found in Idaho, including rare star garnets, amethysts, rubies, and diamonds.

107,651 LENGTH IN MILES (173,248 KM) OF RIVERS THAT RIBBON THROUGHOUT IDAHO, 891 OF WHICH ARE FORMALLY PROTECTED

-60°F the coldest temperature (-51.11°C) ever recorded in the state, on January 18, 1943, in Island Park Dam

409 species of birds that fly around Idaho, including yellow-billed cuckoos, great horned owls, downy woodpeckers, Lincoln's sparrows, and bobolinks

$233 the cost of a weekday adult daily lift ticket at the Sun Valley resort during peak ski season

219 HEIGHT IN FEET (67 M) OF ONE OF THE WORLD'S LARGEST WESTERN WHITE PINE TREES, NEAR ELK RIVER

DESTINATION: IDAHO

- Home to Idaho State University, Pocatello oozes with old-school charm. Several of its turn-of-the-century buildings are on the National Register of Historic Places.

- Explore 111 miles (179 m) of shoreline in Sandpoint, which sits on the sizable Lake Pend Oreille. Surrounded by soaring peaks, Sandpoint is home to the popular Schweitzer Mountain Ski Resort.

- Known as the "Niagara of the West," Shoshone Falls in Twin Falls descends 212 feet (65 m) and spans 900 feet (274 m).

- Soak up info on all things spuds at the Idaho Potato Museum in Blackfoot, which offers "free taters for out of staters."

- Take a dip in one of Idaho's geothermal swim spots, such as Lava Hot Springs, which offers five pools, ranging in temperature from 102°F to 112°F (39°C to 44°C).

- There are 19 ski resorts scattered throughout the state, combining to offer a total of 28,000 vertical feet (8,534 m) of terrain on more than 18,000 acres (7,284 ha). Sun Valley attracts some 3,500 skiers per day on average.

- A vast swath of lava flows, Craters of the Moon National Monument and Preserve formed between 15,000 and 2,000 years ago, and is ripe for exploring. Stick around past sunset for spectacular stargazing.

- Pocatello's Fort Hall replica, a carbon copy of a trading post from 1834, features artifacts that retell the stories of those who passed through during the 19th century.

- Arguably the shining star of the state, Coeur d'Alene is known for its breathtaking beauty and has a bevy of activities to offer, from golf (where you'll find the world's only floating green) to zip-lining to skiing to shopping.

SPORTING CHANCES

- The University of Idaho's mascot is the Vandal, named after the school's 1917 basketball team that was said to be so good, it "vandalized" their opponents.

- Each fall, top college football teams battle it out in the Famous Idaho Potato Bowl at Boise's Albertsons Stadium.

- Some of the fastest boats from around the country go stern-to-stern at the annual Idaho Regatta on the Snake River.

- Billed as "the toughest half marathon in the Northwest," the Race to Robie Creek features around 2,200 feet (671 m) of climbing over the first 8.5 miles (15 km).

- Idaho is home to two of the top professional rodeo events in the country: the Snake River Stampede in Nampa and the Caldwell Night Rodeo.

- In 2019, an eight-year-old girl broke Idaho's catch-and-release record by snagging a 36.5-inch (92.7 cm) rainbow trout.

- Coeur d'Alene hosted an Ironman triathlon for nearly 15 years; the town still offers a half-Ironman each June.

- Boise is home to the Idaho Horsemen professional indoor football team, plus pro-affiliate squads including hockey's Steelheads and baseball's Boise Hawks and Idaho Chukars.

- The Idaho Stampede, an NBA Development League team, played in both Boise and nearby Nampa between 1997 and 2016.

- The Boise State Broncos football team was the first school to play on a blue field, known as the Smurf Turf.

◀ LAND (UN)LOCKED

It's possible to sail from the Pacific Ocean to Idaho.

- One of the greatest home run hitters in baseball's history, Harmon "Killer" Killebrew of Payette, racked up 573 home runs during his pro career, which spanned 22 years from 1954 to 1975.

- Considered one of his generation's best jockeys, Boise's Gary Stevens is a three-time winner of the Kentucky Derby.

- A standout basketball player at Moscow High School, Andrea Lloyd went on to win an NCAA title with the University of Texas in 1986 and followed that up with an Olympic gold in 1988.

MADE IN ID

Idaho's agricultural outputs include:

- Potatoes
- Trout
- Barley
- Plums
- Onions
- Sugar beets
- Mint
- Hay

Idaho's industrial outputs include:

- Computer electrical components
- Food, beverage, and tobacco products
- Wood
- Fabricated metal
- Machinery

> I THINK PROBABLY ONE OF THE IMPORTANT THINGS THAT HAPPENED TO ME WAS GROWING UP IN IDAHO IN THE MOUNTAINS, IN THE WOODS, AND HAVING A VERY STRONG PRESENCE OF THE WILDERNESS AROUND ME. THAT NEVER FELT LIKE EMPTINESS. IT ALWAYS FELT LIKE PRESENCE.

—Novelist Marilynne Robinson

STARS ★ OF ★ THE ★ STATE

PICABO STREET

(b. 1971) Born in Triumph, Idaho, as the only girl among eight children, Street strapped on her first pair of skis at the age of five and began racing soon after. She went on to become one of the world's best downhill skiers, first capturing attention at the 1994 Winter Olympics in Lillehammer, Norway, with her silver-medal finish, exuberant attitude, and uncommon name (a Native American word meaning "shining waters"). Four years later, Street captured a gold medal in Nagano, Japan, in the slalom, only to have a devastating crash weeks later, suffering severe injuries to her leg. Despite that, Street qualified for the 2002 Olympic Games, where she finished 16th before retiring from competitive skiing.

ILLINOIS

★ ★ ★

"State Sovereignty, National Union"

★ ★ ★

CAPITAL: Springfield **BIRD:** Northern Cardinal **NICKNAME:** Prairie State **ENTRY:** 1818

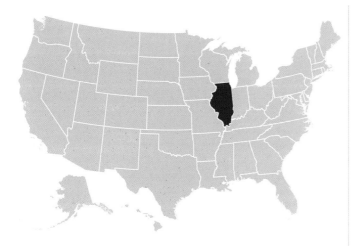

IL FACTS

- The population is 12,582,032.

- Illinois is the country's 21st state and the 24th largest state.

- Known for its bone-chilling winters, enthusiastic sports fans, and Chicago-based tourism, the state also boasts robust health care, manufacturing, and education industries. It relies on its fertile soil as well, farming corn, soybeans, apples, and more.

- The area has been inhabited for around 12,000 years, from Paleolithic peoples to the Mississippian cultures of around 900 to 1500 that included the Illinois, Miami, Ho-Chunk (Winnebago), Sac and Fox, Kickapoo, and Pottawatomie tribes. There are no federally recognized tribes in the state today, though many Illinois peoples now live in Oklahoma due to forced relocation.

- From 1754 to 1763, Illinois was a central location in the American phase of the Seven Years' War, known in North America as the French and Indian War, largely fought over imperial control of the so-called New World. After nearly a decade of battles, during which many Indigenous peoples sided and fought with either the French or British, Britain and the colonies defeated France, and Illinois was ceded to the British.

- After being forced out of Missouri, many members of the Church of Jesus Christ of Latter-day Saints sought refuge in Illinois. In 1839, founder Joseph Smith purchased a tract of land and named it Nauvoo. However, as the population of Nauvoo grew, so did tensions between Mormons and outside parties. This culminated in Joseph Smith's murder and the 1846 expulsion of the Mormons from Nauvoo (which was officially reversed in 2004). Annually, about a million Mormon pilgrims still visit Nauvoo.

▶ **STATE FLOWER**

Violet

Viola

In 1907, schoolchildren across the state voted to select this strikingly hued flower as the state's official bloom. It became law in 1908.

1893

In 1893, Chicago hosted the World's Columbian Exposition to showcase international culture and innovation. The fair was held in the neoclassical "White City," constructed entirely for the purpose by some of America's leading architects, and featured inventions such as the electric light bulb, Ferris wheel, zipper, and more. ▼

> ## BEING FROM ILLINOIS AND FROM THE MIDWEST, WE BELIEVE IN PRETTY BASIC FAIRNESS.
>
> —Senator Dick Durbin

► **AMERICA'S SNACK**

Twinkies, invented in Chicago, were originally filled with banana creme. During a WWII shortage, the switch was made to vanilla.

- In 1832, Sauk leader Ma-ka-tai-me-she-kia-kiak (also known as Black Hawk) led a confederacy of Sauk, Fox, and Kickapoo with the intention of peacefully reclaiming Native lands then occupied by the U.S. The American government responded with military force, resulting in the slaughter of most of the group in what is now known as the Black Hawk War. Though Ma-ka-tai-me-she-kia-kiak escaped, he was eventually forced to surrender.

- In 1858, Illinois senatorial candidates Abraham Lincoln and Stephen A. Douglas engaged in a series of debates concerning slavery and popular sovereignty. Although Douglas narrowly retained his seat as Senator during the election, the debates brought prominence to rising political star Lincoln.

- Following the arrival of New Orleans–style jazz in the 1920s, Chicago artists began developing their own sounds. This Chicago-style jazz, which featured solo work and rhythm, was pioneered by artists such as the legendary Nathanial Adams "Nat" King Cole. ◄

- By October 10, 1871, a raging fire had burned one-third of the city of Chicago in an event that came to be known as the Great Chicago Fire. Although legend held that the fire was started by a cow kicking over a lantern, the actual cause remains unknown.

- Though many lay claim to its invention, most historians trace the origin of deep-dish pizza (also called Chicago-style pizza) to Ike Sewell in 1943. Both Sewell's restaurant chain, Pizzeria Uno (now called Uno Pizzeria and Grill), and deep-dish pizza remain Chicago icons.

- Born in Peoria, Betty Friedan was a pioneering American feminist. In 1963, she wrote *The Feminine Mystique*, an analysis of social expectations for women.

- For more than 100 years, Illinois, and Chicago in particular, has been a hub of immigration.

- In 2008, Barack Obama was elected the first Black president of the United States. President Obama, who had lived and worked in Chicago's South Side and previously served in the Illinois Senate, made a victory speech in the city's Grant Park. ▪

ABRAHAM LINCOLN (1809–1865)

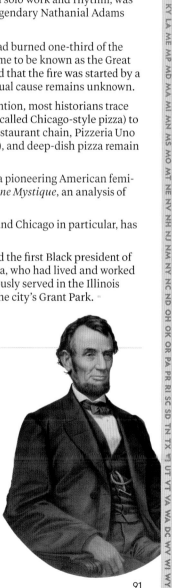

The 16th president of the United States, Abraham Lincoln is remembered for issuing the Emancipation Proclamation and leading the nation through the Civil War. Born in Kentucky and raised in Indiana, Lincoln settled in Illinois at the age of 21. He entered politics in the 1830s and was elected president in 1860. Following his election, seven states seceded from the Union in protest over Lincoln's antislavery views, with four more to follow as war began. In 1863, with the Civil War underway, President Lincoln issued the Emancipation Proclamation, declaring all enslaved people within the Confederacy free. After leading the Union to victory in 1865, Lincoln was assassinated by Confederate sympathizer John Wilkes Booth. Though the Emancipation Proclamation was only the nation's first step toward freedom and equality, Lincoln endures as an American hero whose legacy lives on. ▪

STARS ★ OF ★ THE ★ STATE

WEIRD BUT TRUE

- During St. Patrick's Day, the Chicago River is dyed bright green.

- In Niles, a half-size Leaning Tower of Pisa stores water.

- The nose of a large bronze bust of President Lincoln's head, situated before his tomb, has been rubbed for good luck so many times it has become shiny.

- Thanks to engineering and the construction of canals, the Chicago River flows backward.

- Berwyn is home to the (self-proclaimed) World's Largest Laundromat.

- In 1778, Virginia claimed Illinois as part of its territory (but later ceded it to the U.S.). ▪

> **IN ILLINOIS, WE HONOR THE LEADERS WHO HAVE MADE HISTORY SO THEIR LEGACY MAY GUIDE US TO THE FUTURE.**
>
> —Lieutenant Governor Juliana Stratton

▶ **STORY OF** THE NAME Historians believe that the state's name comes from the Illiniwek, or Illini, people who lived in the area. "Illinois" was likely a French pronunciation of the word, which means "best people." ▪

RECORD ★ SETTERS

In 1993, Chicago-born Carol Moseley Braun was sworn in as a senator from Illinois, making her the country's first Black female senator.

MISCELLANY

- No one knows exactly where Chicago's moniker, the **"windy city,"** comes from. While it may refer to the weather, common lore claims that the nickname refers to the local "windbag" politicians of the 19th century.

- The state insect: the **Monarch butterfly**.

- The world's first nuclear reactor, **Chicago Pile 1**, was built in 1942 below the campus of the University of Chicago.

- The icy winter wind that whips off Lake Michigan has its own nickname: **The Hawk**.

- **The Tribune Building** in Chicago contains pieces of the Great Pyramid of Khufu, the moon, Abraham Lincoln's tomb, the Roman Colosseum, and the Alamo.

- **Popcorn** is the state snack.

- **Route 66** begins in Chicago.

- The state exercise is **cycling**.

- A **Chicago-style hot dog** is a frankfurter served in a long roll and topped with yellow mustard, relish, onions, tomato wedges, pickles, sport peppers, and celery salt.

- **St. Frances Xavier Cabrini**, a Catholic missionary from Italy who became naturalized, was the first U.S. citizen to be canonized. One of her arm bones is enshrined at the National Shrine in Chicago.

- In 1972, engineer **Martin Cooper** led the Illinois-based team that invented the world's first cell phone.

- Chicago-born actress **Nichelle Nichols** shared one of the first on-screen interracial kisses with William Shatner as Star Trek's Lieutenant Uhura and Captain Kirk.

- Opened in 1933, the **Museum of Science and Industry** is housed in one of the only remaining buildings from the 1893 Chicago World's Fair.

- The state pie is **pumpkin**.

- The **eastern tiger salamander** is the official amphibian of Illinois.

- **Fluorite** is the state mineral.

- **The Italian beef**, supposedly created in Chicago's Little Italy in 1938, is a messy sandwich made with thinly sliced roast beef, spicy giardiniera, and sweet peppers piled onto a French roll and served dry or au jus (with beef drippings).

- The state fossil is a prehistoric marine animal called the **Tully Monster**.

◀ **HOW DO YOU DO?**
The largest and most complete T. Rex—on display in Chicago—is nicknamed SUE.

BY THE NUMBERS

-38°F (–38.9°C): THE LOWEST RECORDED TEMP IN ILLINOIS—LOWER THAN THE AVERAGE TEMPERATURE AT THE NORTH POLE

2,160 people could fit into the world's first Ferris wheel, which debuted at the 1893 World's Fair.

2 to 3 the average depth in inches (5.1 to 7.6 cm) of deep-dish pizza

925 THE DEEPEST POINT IN FEET (282 M) OF LAKE MICHIGAN

1,450 THE HEIGHT IN FEET (442 M) OF THE WILLIS TOWER

30,000 pieces of glass make up the Chicago Cultural Center's Tiffany Dome.

6 the number of nuclear power plants in Illinois

97 Nobel laureates have been alumni, faculty members, or researchers at the University of Chicago.

◀ METROPOLIS

Outside of Collinsville lies the Cahokia Mounds, the archaeological remains of what may once have been the greatest American civilization north of Mexico. Covering up to 4,000 acres (1,600 ha), the settlement was built by the Mississippian peoples from around 700 to 1400, making it a larger city than London was at the time. Today, it is a UNESCO World Heritage site.

DESTINATION: ILLINOIS

- Willis Tower (formerly Sears Tower) was the world's tallest building until 1998. Though its height was eventually surpassed, it remains a top tourist destination for its sweeping views. The building features 110 stories and a glass-bottomed Skydeck.

- The world-famous Art Institute of Chicago holds one of the country's largest permanent collections. Its architecture and exhibits include art and artifacts from around the globe and from all periods of history. It is especially known for its Impressionist and Post-Impressionist collections.

- Architect Frank Lloyd Wright based his home—and many of his buildings—in Illinois. His unique Prairie style relied on simplicity, organic design, and leaded glass windows. Visitors can follow the Frank Lloyd Wright Trail in Illinois to discover 13 of his architectural marvels.

- After settling in Galena, Ulysses S. Grant went on to become the Union's general-in-chief during the Civil War, and president of the United States in 1869. Grant's Galena home remains open to the public and is listed on the National Register of Historic Places.

- Chicago's Second City Comedy Club first opened its doors in 1959 as a small improvisational comedy theater. Since then, the theater has become famous for producing top-talent performers, and boasts alumni such as Tina Fey and Stephen Colbert.

- Known for its natural beauty, Starved Rock State Park offers 18 glacially formed canyons and opportunities for ice climbing during the winter.

- Casey is famous for its large statues: It claims the world's largest replicas of a birdcage, a golf tee, a mailbox, knitting needles, a pitchfork, a rocking chair, wind chimes, and wooden shoes.

- After comic book superhero Superman "adopted" Metropolis as his hometown in 1972, the Illinois city's name took on new meaning. Today, Metropolis is known as the "home of Superman," and features a 15-foot-tall (4.5 m) statue of the hero, a Superman museum, and a Superman festival.

▼ WHERE HAVE YOU BEAN?

Situated along Chicago's lakefront, Millennium Park features 24.5 acres (9.9 ha) of public space. In addition to the curated grounds, visitors can see Cloud Gate (also known as The Bean), a stainless-steel sculpture that reflects Chicago's skyline.

▶ STORY OF THE MOB Evoking images of Thompson submachine guns, fedoras, and suits, 1920s Chicago has become almost synonymous with mobsters. Following Prohibition in 1920, the city saw a rise in bootleggers and gangsters who ran illegal alcohol rackets. It also saw the rise of Al "Scarface" Capone, who ruthlessly eliminated rival gangs after taking over as boss of the Chicago Mob (also known as the Chicago Outfit). Things came to a head in 1929, when members of a rival mob run by George "Bugs" Moran were slaughtered—most likely by Capone's men—in what is now known as the St. Valentine's Day Massacre. While the murders effectively confirmed Capone's hold on Chicago, they also drew federal attention, leading to Capone's eventual arrest and a gradual decline in the mob's power—although it still exists to this day.

AIR JORDAN

Established in 1966, the Chicago Bulls are perhaps best known for former player Michael Jordan, widely regarded as possibly the greatest basketball player of all time. With Jordan as shooting guard, the team won six NBA championships between 1991 and 1998. Other notable Bulls players include Scottie Pippen, Dennis Rodman, Charles Oakley, and Horace Grant.

RECORD ★ SETTERS

In 1900, Margaret Ives Abbott, who grew up in Chicago, became the first American woman to win an Olympic event.

MADE IN IL

Illinois's agricultural outputs include:

- Soybeans
- Corn
- Animal feed
- Processed grain products
- Pork
- Wheat
- Cattle
- Dairy
- Hay
- Oats
- Sheep

Illinois's industrial outputs include:

- Machinery
- Chemicals
- Computer and electronic parts
- Transportation equipment
- Light oils
- Dump trucks
- Cell phones
- Immunological products

SPORTING CHANCES

- In 1945, a local tavern owner attempted to bring his billy goat to the World Series at Wrigley Field. After being denied admission, he proclaimed that as long as he couldn't bring a goat onto the field, the Cubs would never win a championship again. The "Curse of the Billy Goat" was born. The team could not seem to shake the goat's revenge ... until 2016, when they won their first World Series since 1908. The "curse" was finally lifted.

- Born in Chicago in 1956, Chicago native Dorothy Hamill is a former figure skater known for her inventive new moves and for winning the gold medal at the 1976 Olympic Games.

- Formed in 1920 as the Decatur Staleys, the now Chicago Bears are one of the two NFL charter members still in existence and have the most NFL Hall of Famers to date.

- Raised in Roscoe, racer Danica Patrick became the first woman to win a NASCAR Cup Series pole. She also holds the highest finishing position for woman in the Great American Race and was the first woman to host ESPN's sports award show, the ESPYs.

- Often called the South Siders, the Chicago White Sox became a major league team in 1901. They have won three World Series titles, and in 1984, former shortstop Luis Aparicio became the first Venezuela native to be inducted into the Hall of Fame.

GWENDOLYN BROOKS

(1917–2000) Gwendolyn Brooks was a poet and author who became the first Black poet to win the Pulitzer Prize. Born in Kansas, Brooks was raised in Chicago. She began writing at a young age and had her first poem published at 13, going on to publish her first collection in 1945. Brooks quickly became known for her varying style, vivid depictions of Black city life, and ability to merge expertly executed art with social commentary. In 1949, she published *Annie Allen*, a series of poems about a Black girl growing up in Chicago, which won the 1950 Pulitzer Prize. Brooks was also named Poet Laureate of Illinois and was the first Black woman to become poetry consultant to the Library of Congress. She remains one of the most esteemed authors and poets of the 20th century.

INDIANA

★ ★ ★

"Crossroads of America"

★ ★ ★

CAPITAL: Indianapolis **FLOWER:** Peony **NICKNAME:** Hoosier State **ENTRY:** 1816

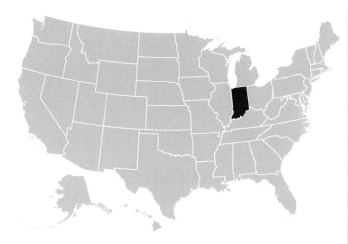

IN FACTS

- The population is 6,833,037.

- Indiana was admitted as the 19th state and is the 38th state by size.

- Known for aerospace and aviation, agriculture, and manufacturing, the state also relies on its defense and national security industry and is a contributor to technology and energy development.

- From around 1000 to 200 B.C., a group of interconnected communities known by historians as the Adena-Hopewell culture lived in what is now Indiana. The area was later home to Mississippian tribes, and eventually became dominated by the Illini, Miami, and Shawnee. There are no federally recognized tribes there today.

- Due to the lack of a decent road system, travelers moved primarily via the Ohio River. In the 1840s, the railroad dominated transportation, passing frequently through Indianapolis, eventually turning it into the state's largest city.

- In 1947, famed sexologist Alfred Kinsey established the Institute for Sex Research in Bloomington.

▶ STATE BIRD

Northern Cardinal
Cardinalis cardinalis

One of the most popular birds, the northern cardinal is famed for its vivid coloring, jaunty crest, and cheerful whistle.

1842

Founded in 1842 by French priest Rev. Edward Sorin, the University of Notre Dame was chartered by the Indiana Legislature in 1844. The Catholic university's notable alumni include U.S. Secretary of State Condoleezza Rice, talk-show host Regis Philbin, NFL star Joe Montana, and others. ▼

> I LIVE IN INDIANA AND TEACH AT PURDUE UNIVERSITY ... MY COLLEAGUES ARE POWERFUL AND INTELLIGENT AND KIND. THE COST OF LIVING IS LOW, THE PRAIRIE IS WIDE, AND ON CLEAR NIGHTS, I CAN SEE ALL THE STARS IN THE SKY ABOVE.
>
> —Author Roxane Gay

- The Ku Klux Klan (KKK), an American hate group that champions white supremacy, arrived in Indiana in the 1920s. *The Indianapolis Times* launched a series of investigations that exposed politicians as Klan members and revealed political corruption, ultimately leading to a decline in KKK membership. The newspaper won a Pulitzer Prize for its work in 1928.

- From the 1500s, French and British settlers moved into the Ohio Valley area. Tensions between the two colonizing groups, each allied with different Indigenous communities, erupted in the 1750s, leading to the American phase of the global Seven Years' War, known as the French and Indian War (1754–1763).

- After the Revolutionary War, Americans began to flood into the region. To stave off encroachment in their lands, Shawnee brothers Tecumseh and Tenskwatawa formed a pan-tribal confederacy, and in 1808 founded a village known as Prophetstown. In 1811, U.S. forces defeated Tenskwatawa and burned Prophetstown in what is now known as the Battle of Tippecanoe.

- "Hoosier," the demonym for inhabitants of Indiana, seems to have come into popular use in the 1830s, thanks to the poem "The Hoosier's Nest" by John Finley. However, no one is certain of the word's origin—one theory ventures that it comes from the greeting commonly shouted from indoor Indiana pioneer cabins when visitors arrived: "Who's yere?"

- Manufacturing took off at the turn of the 20th century. Perhaps the most notable was automobile manufacturing, pioneered by Elwood Haynes in Kokomo. By 1916, Haynes had sold more than 7,000 vehicles, and automobile companies were producing in more than 40 Indiana cities.

- In the 1930s, John Dillinger began his notorious criminal career by robbing five banks within four months. He became famous for his prison escapes, including one during which he used a fake pistol carved from wood and covered in shoe polish. Dillinger's spree came to an end when he crossed state lines into Illinois and became an FBI target.

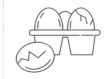

▲ CRACK!

A Hoosier holds the record for "most eggs broken with a whip in 30 seconds."

▶ ORIGINS

Indiana means "Land of the Indians," referring to the many varied Indigenous tribes who originally lived in the area.

STARS ★ OF ★ THE ★ STATE

JAMES DEAN

(1931–1955) Born in Marion, James Dean was an American actor and Hollywood icon. After moving with his family to California at the age of six, Dean studied violin, dancing, and art. He later moved to New York to pursue acting, where he worked as a busboy before appearing on Broadway. Dean then broke out into the acting scene in 1955 in the film adaptation of John Steinbeck's *East of Eden*. The same year he starred in *Rebel Without a Cause*, which solidified him as the embodiment of the restless youth of the 1950s, and also filmed *Giant* (released 1956). Sadly, on September 30, 1955, Dean was killed in a highway accident. Despite having appeared in just three movies, he remains an enduring influence in film and culture.

▶ WANDERLUST

The Mount Baldy sand dune "wanders" at a rate of 5 to 10 feet (1.5 to 3 m) each year.

WEIRD BUT TRUE

- At France Park, visiting divers can explore abandoned—and now under-water—mining equipment.

- Southern Indiana's cave system is home to the rare, blind northern cavefish.

- Indiana's quarries provided the limestone for the Empire State Building in New York, the Pentagon in Virginia, and multiple federal buildings around the country.

- Indiana is home to the first rotary jail, a now defunct form of prison built on rotating platforms meant to limit access to cells.

- A tree in Indianapolis was grown from a seed that had been transported to the moon and back.

- One Hoosier built a working roller coaster in his backyard.

- To combat sand dune Mount Baldy's erosion, officials have "fed" the dune four "meals" of sand over the past 50 years.

- In Mitchell, there is an annual festival dedicated to persimmons.

- Freshwater jellyfish can be found in Indiana.

- Indiana's RV/MH Hall of Fame commemorates those who have made "significant contributions" to recreational vehicles.

MISCELLANY

- Indiana has a state aircraft: the **P-47 Thunderbolt**.

- Hoosiers celebrate **Indiana Day** on December 11, the day the state was admitted to the Union.

- A traditional dessert, **persimmon pudding** is a dense, moist cake made with persimmon pulp.

- The state rifle is the **Grouseland Rifle**.

- Indiana was the site of the country's **first train robbery**.

- **"On the Banks of the Wabash, Far Away"** is the official state song.

- **Lake Michigan** is the only Great Lake entirely within the U.S.

- **Salem limestone** is the state stone.

- The state tree is the **tulip poplar**.

- In the 1820 case *State v. Lasselle*, an enslaved Indiana woman named **Polly Strong** sued for—and won—her freedom.

- **Wilbur Wright**, one of the two Wright brothers who achieved the first powered airplane flight, was born near Millville.

RECORD ★ SETTERS

In 1885, Sylvanus Freelove Bowser created the world's first gasoline pump and sold it to a grocery store in Fort Wayne.

STARS ★ OF ★ THE ★ STATE

COLE PORTER

(1891–1964) Cole Porter was a celebrated composer and lyricist known for his wit and sophistication. Born in Peru, Indiana, to a wealthy family, Porter began playing violin at age six and piano at eight. When he was 10, he composed his first operetta, and published his first waltz the following year. After attending Yale, Porter made his Broadway debut at age 16. Although openly gay, Porter married Linda Lee Thomas, who continually supported his career. From the 1930s to 1950s, Porter dominated Broadway with his comedic musicals, and he also worked on films. His many songs, such as "Night and Day," "I Get a Kick Out of You," and "I've Got You Under My Skin," received both critical and popular acclaim. Porter was inducted into the Songwriters Hall of Fame in 1970.

BY THE NUMBERS

3 the length in inches (7.6 cm) of the endangered Indiana bat

150 the number of rescued and rehabilitated felines at the Exotic Feline Rescue Center in Center Point

570 to **240** million years ago, Indiana's limestone bedrock formed.

174,000 THE NUMBER OF DAIRY COWS IN INDIANA

15% of the state's population fought for the Union during the Civil War.

190.7 miles an hour (306.9 kph) is the fastest average winning speed at the Indy 500.

86 THE HEIGHT IN FEET (26 M) OF CATARACT FALLS, THE HIGHEST WATERFALL IN INDIANA

1,180 cubic miles (4,919 km³) of water are in Lake Michigan.

2,500 the number of caves in the state

- Before it was founded as the capital of Indiana in 1821, Indianapolis had been the home of various Lenape peoples. Over time it became known for its meatpacking and metalworking industries, automobile manufacturing, education, and culture. Visitors flock to the Indiana Soldiers and Sailors Monument, museums and theaters, picturesque canals, and more.

- Indianapolis's White River State Park houses some of the state's top attractions, such as the Eiteljorg Museum of American Indians and Western Art, the Indianapolis Zoo, the National Collegiate Athletic Association (NCAA) Hall of Champions, and more.

- The Basilica of the Sacred Heart, consecrated in 1888, is the mother church of the U.S. Congregation of Holy Cross. Part of the University of Notre Dame campus, the Gothic Revival church started as a small log cabin at the time of the school's founding. Today, the building is famous for its detailed frescoes by Vatican artist Luigi Gregori, 100 stained-glass windows, and towering organ.

▼ SWEEPING SANDS

Located on the southern shore of Lake Michigan, Indiana Dunes National Park covers 15,000 acres (6,070 ha) and draws campers, birders, hikers, and beachgoers. The park's tallest dune, reaching 192 feet (59 m) and known as Mt. Tom, is the site of numerous events such as the athletic Three Dune Challenge and year-round dune sledding.

Indiana native Don Larsen remains the only baseball pitcher to throw a perfect game during a World Series, which he did in 1956.

- Fort Wayne, the second largest city, is home to the Fort Wayne Museum of Art and the Foellinger-Freimann Botanical Conservatory. The city is known for its art and culture, as well as its dining and nightlife options.

- Perfect North Slopes and Paoli Peaks offer skiing, snowboarding, and snow tubing.

- Abraham Lincoln spent his childhood living the frontier lifestyle in Little Pigeon Creek. Today, the Lincoln Boyhood Memorial stands on the site, featuring a living historical farm, memorial building, and cabin site memorial.

- Now a national natural landmark, Marengo Cave was originally discovered in 1883 by two children. Created by the underground erosion of limestone, the cave contains many geological formations, as well as bats, salamanders, and blind crayfish. It is Indiana's most visited natural formation. ▪

STARS ★ OF ★ THE ★ STATE

MADAM C.J. WALKER

(1867–1919) Madam C.J. Walker, founder of the Walker Method, was a businesswoman, philanthropist, and one of the first Black female millionaires in the U.S. Born Sarah Breedlove in Louisiana, Walker grew up under Reconstruction. After an experience with hair loss, she turned her attention to inventing and selling her own haircare regimen. In 1910, Walker relocated to Indianapolis and founded the Walker Manufacturing Company, where she provided job opportunities for more than 40,000 African American women and men in the U.S., Central America, and the Caribbean. She created a line of care products for Black women and started multiple beauty colleges. Today, she is remembered for her philanthropy, activism, and entrepreneurship. ▪

MADE IN IN

Indiana's agricultural outputs include:

- Corn
- Soybeans
- Animal feed and other grains
- Pork
- Dairy
- Chickens
- Eggs
- Popcorn

Indiana's industrial outputs include:

- Vehicles
- Machinery
- Pharmaceuticals
- Electric machinery
- Chemicals
- Medical instruments and parts
- Mining and metals, such as iron and steel
- Plastics
- Wood office furniture
- Hardwood veneer

SPORTING CHANCES

- At five foot six (1.7 m), Daniel Eugene "Rudy" Ruettiger was initially told he would never be able to play football due to his smaller stature. Despite his height, Ruettiger not only joined Notre Dame, but secured a now famous victory over rivals Georgia Tech in 1975.

- Larry Bird, born in West Baden in 1956, went on to become a basketball legend known for his shooting skills. Winning three MVP awards and three NBA Championships, Bird was inducted into the Basketball Hall of Fame in 1998.

- In 1987, Indianapolis hosted the Pan American Games, an intercontinental summer sports competition held since 1937.

> **BASKETBALL MAY HAVE BEEN INVENTED IN MASSACHUSETTS, BUT IT WAS MADE FOR INDIANA.**
>
> —Former Indiana Hoosiers coach Bob Knight

- Notre Dame's Fighting Irish likely originated as an insulting nickname given by opposing teams in the 1920s. However, as Notre Dame began to earn recognition in the sports world, the nickname instead came to represent their athletes' determination and fighting spirit.

- Football player Peyton Manning is considered one of the greatest quarterbacks ever. He played with the Indianapolis Colts for 14 seasons, winning the Super Bowl with them in 2007.

- When founded in 1903, Major League Baseball joined the minor leagues in excluding Black Americans from their ranks. In 1920, pitcher and team owner Andrew "Rube" Foster, fed up with unequal treatment and booking opportunities for independent Black teams, chartered the Negro National League. That year, the first game was held in Indianapolis, where the Indianapolis ABCs beat the Chicago American Giants.

- Founded in 1967, the Indiana Pacers' name honors the Indianapolis 500. The team has won three American Basketball Association (ABA) championships and six NBA division titles.

- The Indianapolis Colts moved to Indiana in 1984. The Colts have won two Super Bowls and three NFL championships.

- Seven winners of the Indianapolis 500 were born in Indiana: Joe Dawson, Howdy Wilcox, L. L. Corum, George Souders, Louis Schneider, Bill Cummings, and Wilbur Shaw.

- Born in Lafayette, Ray Ewry went on to win eight Olympic gold medals in individual track events despite having contracted polio as a child.

▶ **STORY OF** THE RACE On May 30, 1911, the first 500-mile (804.7 km) race took place in Indianapolis. The 2.5-mile (4 km) track, which is located at the Indianapolis Motor Speedway, was originally built as an automotive testing facility in 1909. Soon, the four Indiana owners turned their attention to racing, and decided upon the longer distance in order to lengthen the racing time and raise public appeal. The original race drew much attention—visitors were excited by the $10,000 prize, possibility of collisions, and state-of-the-art vehicles—and today the event is one of the highest-attended single-day sporting events in the world.

IOWA

★ ★ ★

"Our Liberties We Prize and Our Rights We Will Maintain"

★ ★ ★

CAPITAL: Des Moines **BIRD:** American Goldfinch **NICKNAME:** Hawkeye State **ENTRY:** 1846

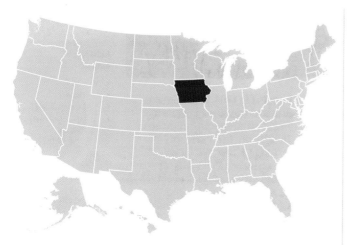

IA FACTS

- Iowa is bordered by Minnesota to the north, Wisconsin and Illinois to the east, Missouri to the south, and South Dakota and Nebraska to the west.

- It's the only state bordered by two navigable rivers: the Missouri River to the west and the Mississippi River to the east.

- The state flag reflects French influence; it has vertical blue, white, and red stripes similar to the French flag.

- The Dakota Sioux, Illini, Ioway, Missouria, and Otoe lived on the land that is now the state. The word "Iowa" comes from the American Indian tribe of the same name.

- With a land area of 55,875 square miles (144,716 sq km), Iowa is the 23rd largest state.

- The population is about 3.2 million, placing it 31st in the United States.

- Farms make up about 85 percent of Iowa's land, yet some 61 percent of Iowans live in urban areas, including around 211,034 who reside in Des Moines, the capital. ▼

▶ **STATE FLOWER**
Wild Prairie Rose
Rosa pratincola

This flower blooms throughout the summer across Iowa in varying shades of pink.

1972

Iowa began holding the presidential nominating contests known as caucuses in 1972.

I HAD TO GO TO FRANCE TO APPRECIATE IOWA.

—"American Gothic" artist Grant Wood

HIGH ON THE HOG
There are more hogs than humans in Iowa.

- Originally claimed by France, the land shifted between Spanish and French control for a century before the U.S. acquired the territory through the Louisiana Purchase in 1803.

- Elevation changes 1,190 feet (363 m), from the low point of 480 feet (146 m) above sea level to a high point of 1,670 feet (509 m) above sea level. To compare, Florida has an elevation change of 345 feet (105 m).

- Temperature averages 15°F (−9°C) in January and 75°F (24°C) in July. The annual average temperature is 49°F (9°C).

- In 1868, the Iowa Supreme Court deemed that segregated "separate but equal" schools were unlawful, 85 years before *Brown v. Board of Education* ruled the same thing on a federal level.

- The Red Delicious apple, also known as the "Hawkeye," was first grown in Iowa in 1856.

A MIGHTY WIND
Iowa produces more than 57 percent of its electricity with wind power, the highest percentage in the U.S.

STARS ★ OF ★ THE ★ STATE

HERBERT HOOVER

(1874–1964) The 31st president of the United States was born in West Branch, making him the first U.S. president born west of the Mississippi River. Orphaned as a child, Hoover went on to attend Stanford University and worked for mining companies before stepping into the political arena, becoming the Republican presidential nominee in 1928. Just months after he won the election, the stock market crashed, the nation spiraled into depression, and his presidency faltered as a result. Still, Hoover is fondly lauded as a son of the state. The Herbert Hoover Presidential Museum is located in West Branch, where his birthplace cottage still stands.

- A three-story brown and white bull beckons to visitors in Audubon.
- The town of Riverside is the fictional future birthplace of *Star Trek* character Captain James T. Kirk, who, according to the town plaque, is supposed to be born there in 2228.
- Burlington's Snake Alley, which has five half-curves, two quarter-curves and drops 58 feet (18 m) over a distance of 275 feet (84 m), is considered one of the crookedest streets in the world.
- A 15-foot (4.5 m) fiberglass sculpture of a strawberry welcomes visitors to the city of Strawberry Point.
- Iowa is the only state name that starts with two vowels.
- Otto Frederick Rohwedder, of Davenport, invented the machine to slice bread.
- Woolly mammoth bones have been found in southern Iowa.
- It's home to one of the world's largest frying pans—and largest popcorn balls.
- Le Mars is known as the ice cream capital of the world.
- Correctionville, Defiance, and Gravity are all towns in Iowa.
- There's a 2,200-pound (998 kg) stalagmite from New Mexico at West Bend's Grotto of the Redemption, a Catholic shrine made up of rocks and minerals from all over the world.
- The world's largest clog dance was achieved by 2,605 people during the Tulip Time festival in Pella on May 8, 2010.

THAT'S WHERE THE TALL CORN GROWS.

—from "Iowa Corn Song," the unofficial state song of Iowa

▲ LITTLE ENGINE THAT COULD
The Fenelon Place Elevator in Dubuque has been called the world's steepest and shortest scenic railway.

- A **skate park** in downtown Des Moines is bigger than a city block.
- Based in Des Moines, the **World Food Prize Foundation** recognizes achievements in food improvement and sustainability.
- Western Iowa's **Loess Hills** features sand dunes created by windblown soil during the Ice Age.
- The **Haunted Bookshop** in Iowa City has more than 45,000 used, rare, out-of-print, and antiquarian books.
- Sioux City is home to one of the **largest popcorn processing plants** in the country.
- Des Moines is the center of the state's **insurance industry**, with nearly 80 of Iowa's insurance companies headquartered in the region.
- Each year, the town of Britt **hosts the National Hobo Convention**, which honors migratory workers who traveled on freight trains to find work throughout the country after the Civil War.
- Iowa City is designated a **UNESCO City of Literature**, thanks to the prestigious Iowa Writers' Workshop, a graduate-level creative writing program with a long list of published alumni, including Flannery O'Connor and Ann Patchett.
- **Winnebago motor homes** come from Winnebago, Iowa.

RECORD ★ SETTERS

In 1869, the Iowa Supreme Court ruled that women should be allowed to practice law, making Iowan Arabella Mansfield the first female lawyer in the U.S. Born in 1846, Mansfield did not attend law school, but she spent two years studying in her brother's Mount Pleasant law office to prepare for the bar exam, which she passed.

BY THE NUMBERS

795,000 pounds (360,606 kg) of wool is produced by Iowa's sheep every year

40,000,000 copies of the *Better Homes and Gardens Cookbook* have been sold, originally released by a publisher headquartered in Des Moines

6 the number of covered bridges featured in the hit movie *Bridges of Madison County* that still exist, out of 19

84,900 the number of farms in Iowa

1,100 the number of species of fish and wildlife that live in Iowa, including shorebirds, raptors, songbirds, many small mammals and bats, amphibians, reptiles, many small fish, butterflies, dragonflies, and more

1853 the year doors opened at Cornell College, the first college in the state to admit women

600 the amount of butter, in pounds (272 kg), used to make a cow sculpture at the Iowa State Fair—enough to cover more than 19,000 slices of toast

15 the height in feet (4.5 m) of the world's largest concrete gnome, located at Reiman Gardens in Ames, which weighs 3,500 pounds (1,588 kg)

$6,000,000 the estimated value of the Shrine of the Grotto of the Redemption in West Bend, aka the "Eighth Wonder of the World," considered to be the world's most complete human-made collection of minerals, fossils, and shells

$71,700,000 the total grants and scholarships provided to students at Grinnell College in 2023, whose $3 billion endowment is among the largest of undergraduate liberal arts colleges in the U.S.

- At Effigy Mounds National Monument, explore the four-square-mile (10 sq km) area of prehistoric American Indian burial and ceremonial mounds.

- Along the High Trestle Trail, a 25-mile (40 km) paved path from Woodward to Ankeny, is a soaring, 13-story-high footbridge across the Des Moines River Valley.

- As Iowa's only island city, tiny Sabula, is situated in the Mississippi River. Sabula is just a mile (1,600 m) long and a quarter mile (400 m) wide, and is home to two churches, a park, and a pizza shop.

- One of the oldest and largest agricultural and industrial expos in the country, the Iowa State Fair is also famous for its various snacks on a stick, from apple pie to pickles to peanut butter and jelly sandwiches.

- The largest rural Danish settlement in the United States, Elk Horn and Kimballton offer a European vibe in the heart of the Midwest. The stars of the villages are the working windmill (relocated from Denmark) and the Morning Star Chapel.

- The Ice House Museum in Cedar Falls, which celebrated its centennial in 2022, offers an in-depth look at the arduous task of collecting ice from lakes for cold storage.

- Dedicated in 1920, Backbone State Park—named for the "Devil's Backbone," the narrow and steep ridge of bedrock carved by the Maquoketa River—is a popular hiking destination, with 21 miles (34 km) of trails. There's also rock climbing, fishing, boating, and camping available.

- The eagle population rises to about 3,500 birds each winter. Catch a glimpse of the majestic fliers at #11 Lock Dam along the Mississippi River in Dubuque from mid-December to early March.

- Music Man Square in Mason City offers a streetscape modeled after the set of the 1962 motion picture of the musical.

- Saunter through the real-life setting for the novel and movie *The Bridges of Madison County*. Stroll across the surviving historic covered bridges, all constructed between 1870 and 1884 and most listed on the National Register of Historic Places.

- Visit the oversize art at the John and Mary Pappajohn Sculpture Park, a 4.4-acre (1.8 ha) green space in Des Moines.

The average size of a farm in Iowa is 359 acres (145 ha).

STORY OF THE ART Perhaps one of the most recognizable paintings in the world has a direct link to Iowa. "American Gothic" was inspired by artist Grant Wood's visit to Eldon, Iowa, where a particular white farmhouse with a large Gothic window caught his eye. Wood drew influence from that home, using it as the backdrop in the iconic painting, depicting a sullen-faced farmer and his equally dowdy daughter. Built in the 1880s, the "American Gothic" house still stands, now serving as a museum dedicated to Wood.

RECORD ★ SETTERS

One of the world's first electronic digital computers was built and operated by researchers at Iowa State College (now Iowa State University) from 1937 to 1942. The Atanasoff-Berry Computer, later named the ABC, was designed by a mathematician to solve systems of up to 29 linear equations simultaneously.

SPORTING CHANCES

- Although Iowa has no professional major league sports teams, the state has minor league sports teams in baseball, basketball, and hockey.

- The National Sprint Car Hall of Fame and Museum in Knoxville is the only museum in the country dedicated to preserving the history of sprint car racing.

- Baseball great Bob "the Heater from Van Meter" Feller hailed from Iowa. He played 18 seasons in the major leagues for the Cleveland Indians between 1936 and 1956.

- Jack Trice, an African American football player, helped break the color barrier in the early 1920s at Iowa State College (now University). The school's football stadium bears his name.

- Ventura's Lynne Lorenzen remains the nation's all-time leader in scoring for 6-on-6 high-school basketball with 6,736 points, set in 1987.

- The classic baseball film *Field of Dreams* was set in Dubuque; today the movie set, located in Dyersville, serves as a popular tourist destination.

- In 2021, Major League Baseball began staging a game at the Field of Dreams in Dyersville, with the players emerging from cornstalks, just like they did in the movie.

- Since 1920, at least one wrestler in Iowa has represented Team U.S.A. wrestling in the Olympics; 13 have won gold medals.

- Chow's Gymnastics and Dance Institute in West Des Moines has produced two Olympic gold medalists: Shawn Johnson and Gabby Douglas.

▲ GO HAWKS!
The University of Iowa mascot is named Herky the Hawk.

- Iowa's RAGBRAI, which stands for *Des Moines Register*'s Annual Great Bicycle Ride Across Iowa, attracts around 10,000 riders annually to cycle an average of 468 miles (753 km) from one side of the state to the other.

- David Armbruster, a longtime swim coach at the University of Iowa, is one swimmer credited for inventing and perfecting the butterfly stroke in the 1930s.

- Each year, more than 35,000 people head to LeClaire to take in Tugfest, a tug-of-war competition.

MADE IN IA

Iowa's agricultural outputs include:

- Iowa has led the nation in corn production since 1994.
- Hogs
- Soybeans
- Oats
- Cattle
- Eggs
- Dairy products

Iowa's industrial outputs include:

- Top U.S. producer of ethanol
- Food, beverage, and tobacco products
- Machinery
- Chemical products
- Computer and electronics
- Fabricated metal

STARS ★ OF ★ THE ★ STATE

JOHN WAYNE
(1907–1979)

Born Marion Robert Morrison in Winterset, Iowa, John Wayne is one of the most popular actors of the 20th century. Known for his roles in films like *Stagecoach* and *Red River*, Wayne won an Academy Award in 1969 for his portrayal of outlaw cowboy Rooster Cogburn in *True Grit*. Wayne's career was so impactful the U.S. Congress posthumously honored him with a Congressional Gold Medal, and California's Orange County airport was renamed after him. More than a million visitors have traveled to Madison County to check out his birthplace home, where there is a museum dedicated to the actor.

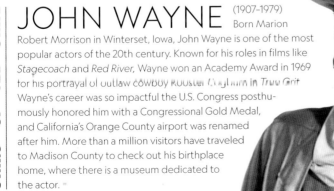

KANSAS

★ ★ ★

"To the Stars Through Difficulties"

★ ★ ★

CAPITAL: Topeka **FLOWER:** Wild Native Sunflower **NICKNAME:** Sunflower State **ENTRY:** 1861

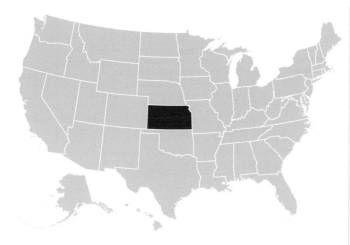

KS FACTS

- The population is 2,937,150.

- Kansas is the 34th state in the nation in population and the 13th state in size.

- In addition to its wide plains, the state is known for its wheat farming, aerospace industries, advanced manufacturing, oil, and natural gas.

- In 1806, shortly after Lewis and Clark began their famous expedition to the West, American officer and explorer Zebulon Montgomery Pike led the lesser known "Southwestern Expedition" into what is now Kansas.

- In 1830, President Andrew Jackson enacted the first of many major policies denying the legal and political rights of Indigenous Americans. Under the Indian Removal Act, tribes within state borders were forcibly removed to lands west of the Mississippi, including Kansas. Today, there are four federally recognized tribes in the state: the Iowa, Kickapoo, Prairie Band Potawatomi, and Sac and Fox.

- In 1854, Congress passed the Kansas-Nebraska Act. It created two new

▶ **STATE BIRD**

Western Meadowlark
Sturnella neglecta

Featuring arresting yellow chests and spotted wings and backs, these birds create their nests on the ground out of local grasses.

1872

In 1872, the iconic "Cowboy Capital of the World" was established at Dodge City. ▼

> ## WHEN I WRITE, I AIM IN MY MIND NOT TOWARD NEW YORK BUT TOWARD A VAGUE SPOT A LITTLE TO THE EAST OF KANSAS.
>
> —Author John Updike

◀ BUZZ BUZZ

After a petition was signed by more than 2,000 schoolchildren in 1976, the honeybee became the state insect.

territories and repealed the Missouri Compromise, which outlawed slavery anywhere above 36° 30' N. Instead, the act called for popular sovereignty, which allowed the people of the territories to decide whether or not to consider slavery legal. This measure caused a rush of proslavery and antislavery proponents to the state. The conflict turned bloody, triggering four years of guerrilla warfare known as Bleeding Kansas.

- Kansas's population did not see significant growth until the end of the Civil War, when freed Black Americans began to seek new opportunities away from the South. The Homestead Act of 1862 also drew settlers, including German, Swedish, and Mexican immigrants.

- In the 1920s, Buster Keaton took the world of silent film by storm. Born in Piqua, as Joseph Frank Keaton IV, Keaton became famous for his visual comedy in films such as *Sherlock, Jr.* and *The General*.

- Born in Kansas City in 1920, Charlie Parker was a musician who is considered one of the greatest jazz saxophonists and is known as one of the pioneers of bebop.

- Raised in Abilene, Dwight D. Eisenhower would go on to become the 34th president of the United States.

- The Topeka chapter of the National Association for the Advancement of Colored People (NAACP) worked with local attorneys and families to challenge the Supreme Court on the legitimacy of segregation. *Brown v. Board of Education of Topeka* succeeded in 1954, and segregation was ruled unconstitutional.

- Two years before the famous 1960 Greensboro sit-ins in North Carolina, Black students in Wichita staged a sit-in at a local drugstore. After a month of protest, they were victorious, and their actions inspired the further desegregation of other establishments.

- Early agricultural settlements thrived in Kansas until around 1500, when tribes instead became migratory. The area was home to many nations, including the Arapaho, Pawnee, Kaw (Kansa), Kiowa, Osage, Otoe, Missouri, and Comanche.

- In 1866, Congress established six new peacetime army regiments consisting only of Black men. These men, who were stationed along the frontier in order to remove Plains Indians, were soon nicknamed buffalo soldiers by local tribes. Many of these buffalo soldiers were stationed in Kansas, either at Fort Leavenworth or Fort Hays. The regiments served until 1951. ▪

▶ STORY OF THE NAME

Kansas takes its name from the Siouan-speaking Kaw people, often referred to by Europeans as "Kansa" or "Kanza." ▪

STARS ★ OF ★ THE ★ STATE

HATTIE McDANIEL (1895–1952)

Hattie McDaniel was the first Black actor to win an Academy Award. Born in Wichita to previously enslaved parents, McDaniel showed a gift for singing and acting from a young age. She left high school to perform with various minstrel and vaudeville troupes, and by the 1920s had become one of the first Black women to sing on radio. McDaniel also appeared in small parts on screen, though roles for Black actors were extremely limited and stereotypical. In 1934, she landed a breakout role in *Judge Priest*, which led to more opportunities and recognition. Her most widely known role is that of Mammy in 1939's *Gone with the Wind*, for which she won an Oscar. McDaniel continued acting throughout her life but passed away from breast cancer in 1952. She continues to be remembered both for her talent and for shattering barriers. ▪

In 1918, Kansas City native Nora Douglas Holt became the first Black woman to earn a master's degree, which she achieved in music.

▲ I'M KING OF THE WORLD

Wichita native and National Geographic Explorer-at-Large Bob Ballard discovered the remains of the shipwreck *Titanic*.

WEIRD BUT TRUE

- One Kansas food chain once served a burger with peanut butter, jelly, jalapenos, and bacon.

- A gallery in Norton features only the losing candidates of U.S. presidential races.

- A water tower in Wilson once doubled as the city's jail.

- The geographic center of the U.S. is located in Kansas—at the site of a former pig farm.

- Kansas has its own cryptid known as Sinkhole Sam.

- A group of scientists used mapping techniques to prove that Kansas is actually flatter than a real pancake.

- *The Wonderful Wizard of Oz* was originally titled *From Kansas to Fairyland*. ▽

MISCELLANY

- People from Kansas are called **Kansans**.

- The state amphibian is the **barred tiger salamander**, which can grow to be 14 inches (35.5 cm) long.

- The state soil is **Harney silt loam**.

- The state animal is the **American buffalo**.

- Although the exact origin is unknown, the term **Jayhawker**, which rose to prominence during the Civil War and eventually came to stand in for native Kansans, may have originally referred to antislavery Union soldiers.

- **Tylosaurus**, once a carnivorous reptile, is now the state marine fossil.

- The state flying fossil is the **Pteranodon**.

- Kansas native **Nina Allender** became famous for her political cartoons.

- **Cottonwood** is the state tree.

- **Barbed wire** played a unique role in Kansas history, as it became one of the only ways to separate livestock and crops and establish property.

- The state reptile: **the ornate box turtle**.

- **Bierocks** are popular pastries often stuffed with cabbage, meat, and onions.

- **"Home on the Range"** is the state song.

- American settlers on the prairie often **made their homes from sod**.

- In 1958, two brothers in Wichita borrowed $600 from their mother and opened the **first ever Pizza Hut** restaurant.

- At 109 feet (33.2 m) deep and 32 feet (9.8 m) in diameter, the **Big Well** in Greensburg is the world's largest hand-dug well.

TOTO, I HAVE A FEELING WE'RE NOT IN KANSAS ANYMORE.

—Dorothy Gale, *The Wizard of Oz*

BY THE NUMBERS

112 THE NUMBER OF TORNADOES OCCURRING ON AVERAGE EACH YEAR FROM 2003 TO 2012

11,000,000 the weight in pounds (5 million kg) of Big Brutus, the world's largest electric shovel

80,000,000 years: the estimated age of Monument Rocks

8,617 acres (3,487 ha) is the size of the tallgrass Konza Prairie Biological Station.

4,000+ species of plants thrive at the Botanica gardens in Wichita.

4,039 height in feet (1,231 m) of the highest point in Kansas

5 feet (1.5 m): the height that the flowering stems of the state grass, little bluestem, can grow

41,000 THE SIZE IN ACRES (16,590 HA) OF CHEYENNE BOTTOMS, THE LARGEST MARSH IN THE INTERIOR U.S.

DESTINATION: KANSAS

- Most of North America's tallgrass prairie, which once covered 170 million acres (68,796,560 ha), remains only in the Kansas Flint Hills. Covering 11,000 acres (4,452 ha), Tallgrass Prairie National Preserve offers visitors the chance to observe a unique ecosystem. ▲

- Filled with historical sites, family-friendly activities, and a vibrant musical scene, Topeka is a popular stop. Top destinations include the Evel Knievel Museum, the Kansas Children's Discovery Center, and Brown v. Board of Education National Historical Park.

- Home to the Kansas Speedway, Kansas City is a destination for race car enthusiasts. The city also offers plenty of history and culture, such as at the Amelia Earhart Birthplace Museum and many galleries, theaters, and museums.

- Known as the "Air Capital of the World," Wichita has long been a pioneer in aviation. Visitors can learn more at the Kansas Aviation Museum, or explore the city's rich Old West history, outdoor attractions such as hot-air ballooning, and a dinosaur theme park.

- Standing 44 feet (13 m) tall, the Keeper of the Plains sits where the Big and Little Arkansas Rivers join in Wichita. Made by Comanche-Kiowa sculptor Blackbear Bosin in 1974, the steel landmark weighs five tons (4.5 t) and is surrounded by a Ring of Fire.

- At the Wilson After Harvest Czech Festival, attendees celebrate the region's Czech heritage with polka, traditional dress and food, and a Princess Pageant.

- Monument Rocks, also known as the Chalk Pyramids, is a group of Niobrara chalk formations in western Kansas. The 70-foot-tall (21 m) structures were originally seabed and were formed by erosion during the Cretaceous period around 80 million years ago.

- Located in Hutchinson, the Strataca Underground Salt Museum offers visitors a peek at a historical salt mine 650 feet (198 m) below the surface—as well as the opportunity to ride an underground train or take a tour in the dark. ▪

RECORD ★ SETTERS

After being nominated in 1887 by several men as a "joke," Susanna Madora Salter surprised her detractors by winning two-thirds of the vote to become mayor of Argonia—and the first female mayor in the U.S.

STARS ★ OF ★ THE ★ STATE

AMELIA EARHART

(1897–1937) Amelia Earhart was a legendary aviator and the first woman to fly solo across the Atlantic. Born in Atchison, Earhart determined to become a pilot after her first airplane ride in 1920. Soon after, she set a record by becoming the first woman to fly at 14,000 feet (4,267 km). In 1928, Earhart became a sensation when she joined pilots Bill Stultz and Louis Gordon as a passenger in crossing the Atlantic, becoming the first woman to do so. In 1932, she completed the flight solo, making her the first woman and second person ever to make the trans-Atlantic flight alone. In 1937, when attempting to become the first woman to fly around the world, Earhart and her co-pilot disappeared. Both the mystery and Earhart's legacy live on, inspiring aviators across the globe. ▪

TRIPLE-DOUBLE

At the 2019 United States National Gymnastics Championships in Kansas City, Simone Biles became the first woman to land a triple-double, a triple-twisting double backflip.

MADE IN KS

Kansas's agricultural outputs include:

- Beef
- Wheat
- Soybeans
- Corn
- Dairy
- Hides
- Grain
- Oilseed
- Flour

Kansas's industrial outputs include:

- Transportation equipment
- Chemicals
- Machinery
- Processed food products
- Pharmaceuticals and medical products
- Dog and cat food
- Radio navigational equipment
- Pneumatic tires

- In 1912, the Jayhawk mascot of Kansas University was given its first iteration by cartoonist Henry Maloy. He drew from the term's origin (referring to the state's antislavery advocates of the 1850s), fashioning a bird that resembled both a jay and a hawk, and he added shoes—for "kicking opponents."

- Representing Kansas State University, the royal purple Wildcats began as a baseball team in 1863.

- Born in 1885, Forrest Allen, known as Phog Allen, played basketball at the University of Kansas. Allen went on to be basketball's first great coach, and he spearheaded the addition of basketball to the 1936 Olympic Games.

- Born in Wichita, Judy Bell became the Kansas state women's amateur golf champion at age 15. She set a record for the lowest score in the Women's Open in 1964 and won multiple titles, including the Broadmoor Invitational three times.

SPORTING CHANCES

- Hosting its inaugural race in 2001, the Kansas Speedway features a 2.37-mile (3.8 km) road course and hosts four NASCAR Cup Series races and the ARCA racing series championship race.

- Raised in Kansas, Billie Moore became the first women's basketball coach to lead two different schools to national championships. In 1976, she coached the first women's Olympic basketball team, earning a silver medal. She was inducted into the Basketball Hall of Fame in 1999.

- In 1936, John McLendon became the first Black student to earn a degree in physical education at the University of Kansas. In 1958, he also became the first head coach to win three straight national championships, and in 1966 the first Black head basketball coach at a predominantly white university.

- In 1925, Walter Beech founded the aviation company Travel Air Company. In 1932, he and his wife, Olive Ann Beech, opened Beech Aircraft Company.

- Over the course of his career as a running back, Seneca native John Riggins played in two NFC championship games and Super Bowls XVII and XVIII. In 1983, he was named MVP of Super Bowl XVII and All-Pro.

> **KANSAS IS INDISPENSABLE TO THE JOY, THE INSPIRATION, AND THE IMPROVEMENT OF THE WORLD.**
>
> —Senator John J. Ingalls

▶ **STORY OF** THE SOUND Originally a garage band from Topeka, Kansas has become one of the country's most iconic classic rock bands. They released their debut record in 1974 before rising to stardom in 1976 with the smash hit "Carry on Wayward Son." Since then, Kansas has sold more than 30 million albums worldwide and produced 15 studio albums, eight of which were gold.

KENTUCKY

★ ★ ★
"United We Stand, Divided We Fall"
★ ★ ★

CAPITAL: Frankfort **BIRD:** Northern Cardinal **NICKNAME:** Bluegrass State **ENTRY:** 1792

KY FACTS

- Located along the western side of the Appalachian Mountains, Kentucky ranks 36th in area, covering 39,732 square miles (102,907 sq km).

- With a population of about 4.5 million, Kentucky is the 26th most populous.

- The Ohio River flows 664 miles (1,068 km) along the northern and western borders of the state.

- During the 1600s and 1700s, the Ohio River was the border of the region later called the Northwest Territory. During the French and Indian War between 1754 and 1763, the river was an entryway to the area for European settlers. And it was a dividing mark between British settlements and American Indian communities until the end of the American Revolution.

- The land may have been named "Ken-tah-ten" (land of tomorrow) by the Wyandot, who lived in the area in the 1600s.

- Lexington, home to more than 450 equine farms, is known as the "Horse Capital of the World." ▼

▶ STATE FLOWER

Goldenrod
Solidago

The bold yellow blossoms of this leggy plant—which can grow up to eight feet (2.4 m)—can be spotted throughout the state all summer long.

1792

Kentucky was a part of Virginia until 1792, when it was admitted to the union as the 15th state and the first state on the western frontier.

◀ DOES A BODY GOOD
Kentucky's official state beverage is milk—a nod to the state's thriving agriculture industry. (Although many people argue it should be bourbon.)

KENTUCKY ... IS ALSO A PLACE FILLED WITH INTRIGUING MYSTERIES.

—Author Barton M. Nunnelly

- The term "Kentuck" is sometimes used to describe a native or resident.

- The Cumberland Gap, a natural pass through the Cumberland Mountains near the point where Kentucky, Virginia, and Tennessee meet is known as "the way west." It's where American frontiersman Daniel Boone helped build the first trail through the pass—called the Wilderness Road—which eventually became the main route used by as many as 300,000 settlers between 1775 and 1810.

- In 1818, the Jackson Purchase saw the U.S. buy the westernmost region of the state—5.7 percent of Kentucky's total area—from the Chickasaw people. The price: $300,000.

- Of the four states in the U.S. that call themselves commonwealths, Kentucky is the only one that wasn't one of the 13 original colonies.

- Remaining neutral during the Civil War, Kentucky supplied some 100,000 troops to the North and 40,000 troops to the South.

- Frankfort became the capital of Kentucky in 1792.

- Kentucky has over 1,000 miles (1,600 km) of commercially navigable waterways, more than any other state except Alaska.

- About 48 percent of Kentucky's land area is forested. These woodlands are mostly comprised of white oak, red oak, walnut, yellow poplar, beech, sugar maple, white ash, and hickory.

- Kentucky's highest point is Black Mountain in Harlan County, 4,145 feet (1,264 m) above sea level; its lowest point, the Mississippi River in Fulton County, sits 257 feet (78 m) above sea level.

▲ STORY OF THE SONG Named as an homage to Kentucky, the twangy strains of bluegrass music's roots are firmly planted in the state. Bill Monroe, known as the "Father of Bluegrass," was born and raised on a farm in rural Rosine—his boyhood home is now a landmark—and was instrumental in sparking the popularity of the genre across the South and into other parts of the United States. ▪

STARS ★ OF ★ THE ★ STATE

MUHAMMAD ALI

(1942–2016) He may be remembered as "The Greatest," but Ali started off simply as Cassius Marcellus Clay, Jr., of Louisville. After taking up boxing at the age of 12, Ali (he changed his name after joining the Nation of Islam in 1964) went on to become the first boxer to win three World Heavyweight titles (in 1964, 1974, and 1978). He also earned an Olympic gold medal in boxing in the 1960 games. Today, several spots in Kentucky honor Ali's legacy, including a boulevard named after him, as well as the Muhammad Ali Center, a museum that is dedicated to "respect, hope and understanding" and outlines his accomplishments and influence both in and out of the ring. ▪

> ## TO BE BORN IN KENTUCKY IS A HERITAGE; TO BRAG ABOUT IT IS A HABIT; TO APPRECIATE IT IS A VIRTUE.
>
> —Author Irvin S. Cobb

▲ DUMMY LUCK

Vent Haven, the world's only museum dedicated to ventriloquism, is home to around 1,000 dummies, with some dating as far back as the Civil War.

WEIRD BUT TRUE

- Muhammad Ali claimed he threw his Olympic gold medal from a Louisville bridge into the Ohio River, but no one has ever found it.

- What else may lie at the bottom of the Ohio River? A small airplane that crashed in the 1970s.

- Post-it Notes are produced at the 3M plant in Cynthiana, about 30 miles (48 km) northeast of Lexington.

- A "meat shower" once poured over Olympia Springs, likely the result of vulture vomit.

- At Chubby Ray's restaurant in Jeffersontown, Kentucky, customers were challenged to eat a five-pound (2.3 kg) hamburger in less than an hour.

- A dog beat a cat, a donkey, and a chicken to become mayor of Rabbit Hash, Kentucky.

- Before they take office, politicians in Kentucky must pledge that they have never fought in a duel.

- To get to Kentucky Bend, a peninsula surrounded by the Mississippi River on three sides, you must drive through Tennessee. The bend is not actually attached to Kentucky.

- Ancient mummies have been discovered within Kentucky's caves.

- A hotel in Lexington allows guests to check in with their houseplants—and offers a "tea" for the greenery, served in a pink mug.

- The town of Cynthiana inspired the zombie-themed TV show *The Walking Dead*. Today, the world's largest mural dedicated to the show can be found on Walnut Street.

MISCELLANY

- **Burgoo**, a traditional Kentucky stew, consists of chicken and beef with cabbage, potatoes, okra, and lima beans.

- **Cumberland Falls**, the second largest waterfall east of the Rocky Mountains, produces the Western Hemisphere's only regularly occurring moonbow: a rainbow produced at night by lunar light.

- **Historic Old Louisville**, the third largest historic district in the United States, has the country's highest concentration of residential homes with stained-glass windows.

- A bloody Civil War battle took place in **Perryville** on October 8, 1862, with 7,621 total casualties.

- **Washington, Kentucky**, was the first town in the U.S. to be named after George Washington, in 1786.

- President **Abraham Lincoln** was born in a log cabin in Hodgenville, Kentucky, on February 12, 1809.

- Some claim **Mother's Day** was first observed in Henderson by teacher Mary S. Wilson.

- The **"old-fashioned"** drink was created in Louisville at a gentleman's club in the 1880s and is considered the city's official cocktail.

- Bibb lettuce was first cultivated by **John M. Bibb** in Frankfort, Kentucky.

- Eastern Kentucky has been home to so many country music stars that a stretch of highway was renamed the **"Country Music Highway."**

- The **spotted bass** is Kentucky's state fish.

- At 240 feet (73 m) above the Kentucky River in Lawrenceburg, **Young's High Bridge**, a railroad crossing built over a century ago, is one of the tallest bungee-jumping platforms in North America.

RECORD ★ SETTERS

Cardiothoracic surgeons at the University of Louisville performed the world's first successful artificial heart implantation on a woman in 2021.

BY THE NUMBERS

20 the number of recipes included in a booklet of Col. Harland Sanders's favorite recipes, including spoon bread and "Kentucky" biscuits, the Kentucky Fried Chicken biscuit recipe written by the originator of the popular fast-food chain

95 THE PERCENTAGE OF THE WORLD'S BOURBON THAT'S PRODUCED IN KENTUCKY

100 the approximate number of acres (40.5 ha) covered by the Louisville Mega Cavern, a former mine turned underground adventure attraction—and the largest building in Kentucky

3 the number of lakes in Kentucky that are natural; the rest were human-made

15,876 the number of elk roaming the state, the highest population of elk in the eastern part of the United States

34 the weight in tons (30.1 t), of the giant baseball bat marking the entrance to the Louisville Slugger Museum. The bat stands 120 feet (36.6 m) tall.

379 the depth in feet (116 m) of Mammoth Cave near Brownsville. At more than 400 miles (644 km) long, it is the longest known cave system in the world.

12 the height and width in feet (3.7 m) of the World Peace Bell in Newport, which is one of the largest free-swinging bells in the world

82 THE NUMBER OF STAINED-GLASS WINDOWS FOUND IN COVINGTON'S ST. MARY'S CATHEDRAL BASILICA OF THE ASSUMPTION. THE DESIGN FOR THE CHURCH WAS INSPIRED BY THE NOTRE-DAME CATHEDRAL IN PARIS.

1,000,000 the number of Corvettes manufactured at the General Motors plant in Bowling Green, the only plant in the world to produce the sports car

- Churchill Downs is the site of the famous Kentucky Derby. Visitors can tour the grounds and check out the ins and outs of the historic racetrack. There are also two floors of interactive exhibits at the Kentucky Derby Museum.

- Marked by its bright red visitor center (a historic stable), the Kentucky Music Hall of Fame in Mount Vernon offers a vibrant look at musicians who hailed from the state, from bluegrass and country stars to crooners.

- Some 41 distilleries are found through the state, making up Kentucky's Bourbon Trail. The art of distilling in the state is a tradition stemming back 230 years.

Kentucky's bluegrass region is named for its abundance of meadow grass. The "blue" is a nod to the hue of flowers that bloom when the grass is two to three feet (0.6 to 0.9 m) tall.

- Foodies, whiskey afficionados, and history buffs revel in Lexington, where top-rated restaurants, bars, and museums abound. Order up a hot Brown—a baked open-face sandwich with turkey, tomato, bacon, and creamy cheese sauce invented by a Louisville chef in 1926—then saunter around downtown to check out historic sites like the Louisville Slugger Museum.

- With more than 400 miles (644 km) of explored caverns and passages, Kentucky's Mammoth Cave National Park is the world's longest known cave system. A spelunker's playground, tours of Mammoth Cave's limestone labyrinths are offered daily.

- The nation's 16th president is honored at Abraham Lincoln Birthplace National Historical Park in Hodgenville. Built in 1916, the park features a neoclassical memorial building dedicated to Lincoln in 1911, complete with 56 steps—representing Lincoln's age at his death. There's also a replica of the one-room cabin where he was born in 1809.

- Occupying a swath of land that cuts through 21 counties in eastern Kentucky, Daniel Boone National Forest is 708,000 acres (286,517 ha) of pristine wilderness. The forest's shining star is Natural Arch, a sandstone arch spanning nearly 100 feet (30.5 m) and rising nearly 50 feet (15 m) above the forest floor. Accessible by hiking trails, it is one of Kentucky's largest natural landmarks.

- Butcher Hollow in Eastern Kentucky is the hometown of Loretta Lynn. The country music star—whose song about her childhood in the coal mining community topped charts in 1970—is honored with a museum packed with memorabilia, housed in a four-room cabin.

GEORGE CLOONEY

(b. 1961) The prolific actor, screenwriter, and director grew up far from the spotlight of Hollywood in the sleepy town of Augusta (population: 1,238). Born in Lexington to a former beauty queen mom and a talk-show host dad, Clooney was more into sports than acting. As a teen, he even tried out (unsuccessfully) for the Cincinnati Reds baseball team. He went on to enroll in Northern Kentucky University before dropping out to pursue acting. Selling lemonade on the streets of Augusta helped him fund his trip to California. The move worked out: Clooney has won two Academy Awards and is one of the highest-grossing actors of all time.

I DON'T KNOW HOW AT THIS POINT ANYTHING COULD BE BIGGER THAN THE KENTUCKY DERBY.

—J. Paul Reddam, owner of 2012 Kentucky derby winner I'll Have Another

SPORTING CHANCES

- The Kentucky Derby, held in Louisville, is the oldest horse race held continuously in the U.S.

- Kentucky has one professional sports team: the women's soccer club Racing Louisville FC.

- Louisville hosted two NFL teams in the 1920s: the Brecks from 1921 to 1923 and the Colonels in 1926.

- The University of Kentucky Wildcats men's basketball squad is one of the winningest teams in NCAA history, with eight national championships, 17 Final Four appearances, and a winning percentage of about .765.

- Kentucky fans flocked to a 2003 game between the University of Kentucky and Michigan State University. An arena in Detroit welcomed a crowd from both schools totaling 78,129— a record attendance for a college basketball game.

- The University of Kentucky started a women's basketball team in 1902, one year before the men organized a team.

- An archery tournament at the Kentucky State Fair in 2013 included 9,426 players, breaking a world record for this type of sporting event.

- In 2012, the University of Louisville was the setting for the fastest ever underwater 50-meter swim in a 25-meter pool, by Jordan Proffitt in 27.86 seconds.

- Louisville-born swimmer Mary T. Meagher set world records in 100- and 200-meter butterfly and followed that up with three gold medals at the 1984 Olympics.

- Basketball star Dan Issel was the University of Kentucky's all-time leading scorer and one of the top scorers in professional basketball with 27,482 points during his 15-year career.

- In 2018, an angler reeled in a state-record-setting blue catfish weighing 106.9 pounds (48.5 kg) from the Ohio River.

- Born in Corydon in 1898, A.B. "Happy" Chandler served as governor of Kentucky and as a U.S. state senator. He was also the second commissioner of Major League Baseball and is in the Baseball Hall of Fame.

▲ RUN FOR THE ROSES

The Kentucky Derby is held on the first Saturday in May. It is known as "The Most Exciting Two Minutes in Sports."

RECORD ★ SETTERS

In 2018, attorney and community activist Nima Kulkarni became the first Indian American elected to the Kentucky Legislature. She represents District 40, which includes the University of Louisville, Churchill Downs, and portions of south Louisville.

LOUISIANA

★ ★ ★

"Union, Justice, Confidence"

★ ★ ★

CAPITAL: Baton Rouge **BIRD:** Eastern Brown Pelican **NICKNAME:** Pelican State **ENTRY:** April 30, 1812

LA FACTS

- Louisiana lies in the southeastern region of the United States and shares its border with Texas, Arkansas, and Mississippi.

- Today, Louisiana's 4.6 million residents include almost every nationality on Earth, contributing to its "cultural gumbo."

- A flag resembling the Stars and Stripes was adopted during the Civil War; in 1912, the current "Pelican State" flag became official.

- Thirteen states or parts of states were carved out of the Louisiana Purchase territory, including Louisiana, Missouri, Arkansas, Iowa, North Dakota, South Dakota, Nebraska, and Oklahoma.

- President Thomas Jefferson negotiated the Louisiana Purchase with Napoleon in 1803.

- The cultural mix in Louisiana's population reflects its earliest days when its original Native American inhabitants; enslaved and freed peoples from the Caribbean and Africa; plus settlers from Europe, the West Indies, and more all made their home in the area. ▼

▶ STATE FLOWER

Magnolia
Magnolia grandiflora

The evergreen Magnolia trees grow throughout the state and burst with fragrant, creamy-white blooms each March and April.

1682

The French gave the then territory its name in 1682. "La Louisiane" ("Land of Louis") was named for King Louis XIV.

▶ **GATOR COUNTRY** Along with Florida, Louisiana has the largest alligator population in the U.S. There are an estimated two-million-plus gators living in the state, most of which are concentrated in coastal marshes.

IT IS IMPOSSIBLE TO CAPTURE THE ESSENCE, TOLERANCE, AND SPIRIT OF SOUTH LOUISIANA IN WORDS.

—Author Chris Rose

- Louisiana has flown more flags than any other state: Spain, France, Great Britain, the Republic of West Florida, and the United States all controlled the territory before 1812.

- Spanning 24 miles (38 km), the Lake Pontchartrain Causeway outside New Orleans is the world's longest continuous bridge passing over water.

- Louisiana is the only state to have parishes, instead of counties. Why? Under both French and Spanish rule, Louisiana was officially Roman Catholic. Because the boundaries dividing the territories mostly coincided with church districts, the area's primary civil divisions became officially known as parishes.

- Louisiana is one of the flattest states: At 535 feet (163 m) above sea level, Driskill Mountain in Shreveport is its highest point. Its lowest point is the city of New Orleans, which sits eight feet (2.4 m) below sea level.

- Louisiana has an average annual rainfall of 56.9 inches (144.5 cm).

- Louisiana has no official language.

- Historically, Louisiana has been a hotbed for agriculture.

- Louisiana is known for its many bayous, including Bayou Bartholomew, the longest in the world, which stretches from Arkansas into Louisiana. ◭

- In 2020, three hurricanes and two tropical storms made landfall, breaking the state record for the most strikes in a single season.

- The discovery of sulfur (1867) and oil (1901) led Louisiana to become the country's top producer of oil and natural gas, and a center of petroleum refining. ◾

STARS ★ OF ★ THE ★ STATE

LOUIS ARMSTRONG

(1901–1971) "Satchmo" got his start in New Orleans, where he first picked up the bugle as a kid and played in various New Orleans watering holes until he caught his big break around 1922. Armstrong's music was so popular that his 1964 hit "Hello, Dolly!" knocked the Beatles off the top of the pop charts. In 1967, he released the single "What a Wonderful World" and later became the oldest male at the time to top the U.K. Singles Chart. While Armstrong's prolific career took him all over the world, New Orleans will always claim Armstrong as its own. Today, the city's airport as well as a 32-acre (13 ha) public park in the Tremé neighborhood are both named after the musician. ◾

- In the 1970s, a Cajun chef placed a deboned chicken inside a deboned duck and then stuffed both inside a deboned turkey—and popularized the Turducken.

- There have been sightings of a rare pink dolphin in the Calcasieu River.

- Some of Louisiana's swamps are said to be haunted by a voodoo priestess.

- The town of Jean Lafitte was once a hideaway for pirates.

- A woman in Houma was once struck by lightning while grocery shopping inside a store. (She survived.)

- Cajun lore tells of a toothy, bloodthirsty werewolf called a *rougarou* that stalks Louisiana swamps.

- Each year, the town of Abbeville turns out for the Giant Omelette Celebration, which honors the state's French heritage by cooking a 5,000-egg omelet in a 12-foot (3.7 m) skillet.

- The nutria, a semiaquatic rodent with webbed feet and bright orange buck teeth, is an invasive species in the Louisiana wetlands.

- The National Hansen's Disease Museum in Carville is the only national museum honoring leprosy patients, who once quarantined on-site there.

- The largest ever portion of gumbo, weighing 6,800 pounds (3,084 kg), was served in Shreveport in 2018.

- A coffin floated away from a cemetery during a flood in St. Francisville—it was later found in a pond and returned to its original resting spot.

- More than 35 concrete statues of frogs can be found in Rayne, which calls itself the "Frog Capital of the World." ■

▶ **STORY OF** THE SONG It's a beloved tune sung in nurseries and preschool classes across the country, but only Louisiana can claim it as its own. "You Are My Sunshine," first popularized by country crooner Jimmie Davis, is one of four state songs of Louisiana, but by far the most well known. (Davis served as Louisiana's governor from 1944 to 1948 and again from 1960 to 1964; he used the song for his campaigns.) In 1977, "You Are My Sunshine" was named as an official song of Louisiana to honor Davis's contributions to the state. ■

◀ **SLURP!**
At an eating contest in Metairie, a woman once set a world record by slurping down 420 oysters in eight minutes.

MISCELLANY

- **The Catahoula leopard dog** is Louisiana's state dog.

- **The Sazerac,** a concoction of whiskey with sugar and bitters is the official cocktail of New Orleans.

- Established in the 1800s, Albany is home to one of **the country's oldest settlements of Hungarians**.

- At about 20 miles (32 km) in width from east to west and 140 miles (225 km) in length, Atchafalaya Basin is **the largest swamp in the country**.

- After opera made its U.S. debut in New Orleans in 1796, the city soon became known as **"The Opera Capital of North America."**

- What's the difference between **Creole and Cajun food**? Though both are native to Louisiana, Creole food typically uses tomatoes and tomato-based sauces while traditional Cajun food does not.

- Connecting communities for 106 miles (171 km) between Donaldsonville and the Gulf of Mexico, Bayou Lafourche is considered one of **the longest "main streets" in the world**.

- Built in 1922, Baton Rouge's St. Ann Church—also known as **"The Church That Won't Die"**—has withstood several major hurricanes, including Katrina.

- Louisiana goes by **several nicknames**, including the Sugar State, the Bayou State, the Creole State, and the Pelican State.

- A great majority, 84 percent, of Louisiana residents practice **Christianity**, with evangelical Protestants being the most common group among them.

- 2005's **Hurricane Katrina**, which first hit Louisiana at Burrwood, then moved to New Orleans, is considered one of the worst natural disasters in the history of the United States.

- Louisiana boasts the **tallest state capitol** in the U.S. at 450 feet (137 m) high with 34 floors.

RECORD ★ SETTERS

In 2004, Louisiana elected its first female governor. Kathleen Blanco served in office until 2008; prior to that she was lieutenant governor of the state from 1996 until 2004, and was also the first woman in Louisiana elected to the Louisiana Public Service Commission.

BY THE NUMBERS
Mardi Gras

1837 the year the first Mardi Gras parade took place, on Shrove Tuesday in New Orleans

1,400,000 people visit New Orleans for Mardi Gras each year.

301 THE DISTANCE IN MILES (484 KM) OF THE COMBINED MARDI GRAS PARADE ROUTES, LASTING A TOTAL OF 204 HOURS

250 the number of people who can fit on the largest superfloat in the Mardi Gras parade, "The Pontchartrain Beach, Then and Now"

$3,000 THE AVERAGE PRICE TO RIDE AS A VIP ON A MARDI GRAS FLOAT

93,000 pounds (42,184 kg) of beads were found clogging New Orleans' storm drains after Mardi Gras in 2018.

3 the number of colors designated as the official Mardi Gras hues: purple, green, and gold

500,000 the number of king cakes sold in New Orleans each year around Mardi Gras, with another 50,000 shipped across the country

Jungle Gardens boasts one of the world's most complete collections of camellias. The public garden contains more than 900 varieties.

DESTINATION: LOUISIANA

- While in the French Quarter, check out one of New Orleans' most recognizable landmarks: the St. Louis Cathedral in Jackson Square. The oldest continuously active Roman Catholic cathedral in the United States, it was originally built in 1727. The first building burned down during the great fire of 1788; the present structure dates to 1794.

- Locally, it's called Vieux Carré ("Old Square"). Globally, this parcel of New Orleans is known as the French Quarter. Soak up old-world charm, satisfy your sweet tooth with a beignet—fried dough doused in powdered sugar—at Café Du Monde, and people-watch on Bourbon Street, which buzzes with energy all day—and night—long. ▷

- New Orleans' Garden District was created by Americans after the 1803 Louisiana Purchase. There, you can ogle grand historic homes that line the streets, from stately Victorians to colorful Creole cottages.

NEW ORLEANS HAS ITS OWN MIND, ITS OWN THING. IT HAS A REAL SPIRIT. IT'S THE MOST AUTHENTIC OF ALL AMERICAN CITIES.

—Actor Brad Pitt

2,482

There are 2,482 islands in the state, totaling 1.3 million acres (526,091 ha).

- Get to know more about Louisiana's Creole culture in Cajun Country; aka Lafayette. Perhaps best known for its eclectic fare, visitors can sample a variety of Cajun customary dishes, from gumbo to po'boys to jambalaya.

- Louisiana's Old State Capitol building in Baton Rouge is fondly referred to as the "castle-on-the-river" for its unique architecture and position high on a bluff looming over the Mississippi River.

- Avery Island is the home of Tabasco hot sauce, but it's also a popular habitat for thousands of egrets and other birds that come to nest each winter. Nicknamed "Bird City," this area in Louisiana's flat coastal marshes is a great place to spy various feathered friends during a tropical garden tour.

- The Creole Nature Trail All-American Road is a 180-mile (290 km) scenic byway through "Louisiana's Outback." Pass through national wildlife refuges (Sabine, Cameron Prairie, and Lacassine), where you can look for alligators, birds, and other animals in the untouched wilderness. Craving a beach day? The area features 26 miles (42 km) of pristine coastline along the Gulf of Mexico.

- The village of Abita Springs, in the North Shore area of Lake Pontchartrain, has two claims to fame. The Abita Brewery, where the award-winning beer is bottled—and the Abita Mystery House, featuring oddball artifacts (think art cars and UFO replicas) curated into a curious collection. ◾

SPORTING CHANCES

- Louisiana hosts two major pro athletic teams, both based in New Orleans: the Pelicans in the NBA and the Saints in the NFL.

- The state is also home to minor league baseball, rugby, soccer, and hockey teams, plus 12 universities and colleges that offer NCAA Division I athletic programs.

- The New Orleans Pelicans are named after the state bird of Louisiana, which was once considered endangered.

- In 2010, the New Orleans Saints won their first—and so far, only—Super Bowl, beating the Indianapolis Colts 31–17.

- Drew Brees, the star quarterback of the 2010 Super Bowl championship team, still resides in New Orleans with his family after retiring from the NFL in 2021.

- New Orleans will host the Super Bowl for the eleventh time in 2025, which will tie Miami for the record of the city to host the most Big Games.

- Louisiana State University's Tiger Stadium was nicknamed "Death Valley" by an opposing coach whose team never won there.

- With a crowd capacity of 102,321, Tiger Stadium is the sixth largest on-campus football stadium in the country.

- The country's oldest fishing tournament, the Grand Isle Tarpon Rodeo, has been attracting anglers to the barrier island in the Gulf of Mexico for nearly a century. The biggest tarpon ever caught in the competition? A 208-pounder (94 kg), hooked in 2018.

- Evelyn Ashford, the first woman in U.S. track and field history to win four Olympic gold medals, was born in Shreveport in 1957. She earned one gold in the 100 meters at the 1984 Olympics and three more in the 4 × 100 meter relay in 1984, 1988, and 1992.

- Lake Charles often hosts watercross competitions, a sport similar to motocross, except participants are on personal watercrafts or Jet Skis and navigate liquid tracks instead of those made of dirt.

- Basketball great Karl "the Mailman" Malone hails from Summerfield and first rose to stardom on the court while playing for Louisiana Tech, where he averaged 20.9 points per game. He then went on to play in the NBA, winning two MVP awards and retiring in 2004 with a 26.1 career scoring average.

- In 2022, Xavier University of Louisiana became the first historically Black college and university to win a National Association of Intercollegiate Athletics (NAIA) Competitive Cheer championship title.

MADE IN LA

Louisiana's agricultural outputs include:

- Soybeans
- Broiler chickens
- Rice
- Sugarcane
- Cattle and calves
- Corn
- Chicken eggs
- Cotton
- Sweet potatoes
- Louisiana is first in the country for crawfish production, yielding some 100 million pounds (45 million kg) each year.

Louisiana's industrial outputs include:

- Petroleum and coal products
- Chemical products
- Lumber and wood
- Transportation equipment
- Metal products

STARS ★ OF ★ THE ★ STATE

ELLEN DeGENERES

(b. 1958) Funnywoman and LGBTQ+ advocate DeGeneres was born and raised in Metairie, where she dreamed of becoming a veterinarian and worked odd jobs as a waitress and a department store clerk. After cracking jokes at a public speaking event, DeGeneres discovered her knack for comedy, she eventually rose to fame, first in stand-up comedy, then in a sitcom, and finally with her eponymous talk show. After famously coming out as gay both on-screen and off in 1997, she became a hero among the LGBTQ+ community. Her talk show has won 64 Daytime Emmys and she's earned the Presidential Medal of Freedom, along with other honors.

MAINE

★ ★ ★

"I Direct"

★ ★ ★

CAPITAL: Augusta **BIRD:** Black-Capped Chickadee **NICKNAME:** Pine Tree State **ENTRY:** 1820

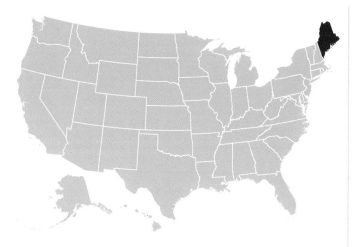

ME FACTS

- The population is 1,385,340.

- Maine was the 23rd state in the nation and is the 39th state in size.

- In addition to its oldest known inhabitants, the Mi'kmaq (now known as the Aroostook Band of Micmacs), Maine was home to the Houlton Band of Maliseet Indians, Passamaquoddy Tribe, and Penobscot Nation. All four nations remain federally recognized in the state.

- Born in Brewer in 1828, Joshua Lawrence Chamberlain became a Union hero during the Civil War. Stationed at Little Round Top in 1863, Chamberlain led a successful last-chance bayonet charge against Confederate soldiers to help turn the tide in the pivotal Battle of Gettysburg.

- From 1838 to 1839, Mainers and Canadians faced off over a northern boundary dispute in the Aroostook War. Also known as the Pork and Beans War for its inhabitants' diets, it was resolved without direct combat.

- Known for its lobsters and lighthouses, the state is also rich in blueberries, maple syrup, timber, and tourmaline. ▼

▶ STATE FLOWER

White Pinecone and Tassel

Pinus strobus, linnaeus

In 1895, Maine's legislature adopted the ubiquitous pine cone and tassel as the state flower, choosing it over the goldenrod and apple blossom.

1972

Born in 1931 in Bangor, Gerald Talbot was a leading civil rights leader. Instrumental in the passing of Maine's Fair Housing Bill and the Maine Human Rights Act, Talbot became the state's first Black legislator in 1972.

IN MAINE WE HAVE A SAYING THAT YOU DON'T SAY ANYTHING THAT DOESN'T IMPROVE ON SILENCE.

—Former Maine senator and U.S. secretary of state Edmund Muskie

- In 1775, a British sloop off the coast of Machias demanded lumber from the townspeople. When they refused, the sloop threatened to fire. In what became the first naval battle of the Revolutionary War, American captain Jeremiah O'Brien led a group of around 50 men to capture the British sloop H.M.S. *Margaretta*.

- Before Portuguese, Spanish, English, and French explorers arrived in the 16th century, Vikings may have landed in Maine. The first French settlement in Maine was in 1604 at Saint Croix Island. Over the next century, the British and French battled for the area until the British defeated their rivals in 1763.

- In 1851, while living in Brunswick, Harriet Beecher Stowe began the first of what would eventually number more than 40 newspaper installments of *Uncle Tom's Cabin*. Published as a two-volume book the following year, the work, which told the fictional tale of an enslaved man named Tom, quickly sold around 300,000 copies in its first year and greatly furthered northern abolitionist views.

- A New England tradition, today's clambakes are largely unchanged from 2,000 years ago: Participants dig a hole in the sand, and they line it with stones and wood for a fire. Once the fire has burned for several hours and the stones are hot enough, shellfish and vegetables are steamed in the pit between layers of seaweed.

- One popular dessert dates from the early 1800s and features an agricultural mainstay: potatoes. Potato doughnuts are made with mashed white potatoes or potato flour, which give them both density and moistness.

- Born in Rockland, Edna St. Vincent Millay was a poet and activist for women's rights. Millay, whose work often drew attention to feminism, female sexuality, and bisexuality, won the Pulitzer Prize in 1922.

- In 1912, L.L. Bean was founded, offering weatherproof apparel to the state's many outdoor enthusiasts. A private, family-owned company, L.L. Bean remains headquartered in Freeport. ▼

▶ **STORY OF** THE NAME Historians believe that the name "Maine" likely refers to the nautical term "mainland." ▪

STARS ★ OF ★ THE ★ STATE

BETTE DAVIS

(1908–1989) A critically acclaimed actress, Bette Davis created a thriving space for women in the previously male-dominated film industry. Born Ruth Davis in Massachusetts, Davis had strong ties to Maine: She spent summers there in her youth, became Ogunquit's first female lifeguard, and, after reaching stardom, kept an estate in Cape Elizabeth. Davis made her Broadway debut in 1929. This led to a Hollywood contract; however, Davis struggled to land substantive roles, as studios claimed she "lacked sex appeal." Despite this, Davis managed to win an Oscar for her role in the 1935 film *Dangerous* and began to challenge Warner Brothers for better roles and adequate pay. Critics labeled her difficult to work with, but by 1942 Davis was the highest paid woman in the country. Her work in *All About Eve* led to her eighth Academy Award nomination, and her 1962 film *Whatever Happened to Baby Jane?* remains a Hollywood classic. In 1977, Davis became the first woman to receive the American Film Institute's Lifetime Achievement Award. ▪

> ## MAINE IS A JOY IN THE SUMMER. BUT THE SOUL OF MAINE IS MORE APPARENT IN THE WINTER.
>
> —Author Paul Theroux

WEIRD BUT TRUE

- According to local lore, a sea serpent named Cassie lurks in the waters of Casco Bay.
- The Maine State Building was built in Chicago and shipped to Maine, piece by piece.
- One chocolatier in Scarborough displays a 1,700-pound (771 kg) moose made of chocolate.
- Maine was part of the Commonwealth of Massachusetts until it seceded in 1820.
- A "lost" British colony, founded in 1607 on the coast and known as Popham, was only rediscovered in 1994.
- Although lobsters are now considered a delicacy, they were so plentiful along the coast in the 1600s that they were used to feed prisoners.
- Brown bread is a popular type of dense and moist bread that comes in a can.
- One winter tradition is to make a dessert called "sugar on snow" by pouring boiling maple syrup onto snow and allowing it to cool.
- Maine is the only state in the U.S. with a one-syllable name.

HOT DOG!

Red snappers, a certain type of hot dog, are named for their color and "snap" when bitten into.

MISCELLANY

- People from Maine are called **Mainers**.
- **Moxie**, the official state soft drink, was invented locally. Made from gentian root, it is said to taste both sweet and bitter.
- **Hannibal Hamlin**, Abraham Lincoln's vice president, was from Paris Hill.
- The state mineral is **tourmaline**.
- Bangor claims to be the birthplace of the legendary folk hero **Paul Bunyan** and displays a 31-foot-tall (9.4 m) statue of him.

- The state berry is the **wild blueberry**, and the state dessert is blueberry pie.
- The state crustacean is, unsurprisingly, **the lobster**. The state harvests the majority of the lobster in the country.
- By size, Maine is almost as big as the other **five New England states** combined.
- **Wintergreen** is the state herb.
- The state tree is the **white pine**.
- Outside of Alaska, Maine has the largest **moose** population.

- The **whoopie pie**, the state's official treat, consists of two cookie-size rounds of chocolate cake with a white cream filling.
- The state fossil is *Pertica quadrifaria*.
- The **Thompson Ice House Harvesting Museum** preserves the tradition of harvesting ice from frozen ponds. Visitors can observe reenactments and participate.
- Maine produces 90 percent of the **toothpicks** in the country.

STORY OF THE ANIMAL

One of the most beloved breeds of cats in the United States (and around the world), the Maine coon is native to the state. Although historians know the breed existed by the early 1800s, no one is sure how the cats originally arrived in the state. In one legend, they descended from cats brought by Vikings exploring the New England coast. In another, Queen Marie Antoinette of France entrusted her longhaired cats to an America-bound ship captain, hoping to join them later. Either way, the large breed is well suited to the state—its long coats and tufted ears help keep it warm in the frigid winters. Friendly and good at mousing, it is also no surprise that the Maine coon has long been popular on local farms—in fact, the breed is the official state cat of Maine.

BY THE NUMBERS

3,000 THE NUMBER OF PEOPLE WHO TOOK PART IN THE PORTLAND RUM RIOTS OF 1855

1851 the year the Fryeburg Fair, a farm exposition, was first held

90% of Maine is covered by forest, which translates to 17.8 million acres (7.2 million ha) of trees.

24,000+ the state's estimated black bear population

44 pounds (20 kg): the weight to which American lobsters can grow

1947 the year of the Great Maine Fires, which destroyed more than 1,000 homes

47,000 the size in acres (19,020 ha) of Acadia National Park

15,000,000 TOURISTS VISIT THE STATE ANNUALLY.

65 the number of lighthouses in the state

400,000,000+ the number of copies sold of Mainer Stephen King's books

DESTINATION: MAINE

- Maine's most populated city, Portland is a mix of New England outdoor charm and artistic culture. The city is also a prime food destination: With more than 300 restaurants, some claim that it is the city with the second-most restaurants per capita.

- Established in 1919 as Lafayette National Park, Acadia National Park is one of the nation's 10 most visited national parks. The park got its start thanks to John D. Rockefeller, who donated 11,000 acres (4,452 ha) of land and oversaw the construction of a now famous network of carriage roads.

- Ogunquit, which takes its name from the Abenaki word for "beautiful place by the sea," gained popularity in the early 1900s as an artists' colony. Today, the resort town has a thriving LGBTQ+ community, and it celebrates its artistic roots with multiple galleries, festivals, and playhouses.

- The state is famous for the 65 lighthouses lining its coasts, all of which are rich in beauty and history (and—perhaps—ghosts). The most well-known is likely Portland Head Lighthouse, which was commissioned by George Washington in 1787. Owls Head Lighthouse, first built in 1825, is supposedly the country's most haunted lighthouse. And with its red-and-white stripes, the West Quoddy Head Lighthouse is not only one of the state's oldest, but also the most iconic.

- Maine's coast is also the only nesting site in the U.S. for Atlantic puffins. More than 4,000 of the black, white, and orange birds flock to the area each summer to raise their young. Tours along the coast and to Machias Seal Island let visitors observe the spectacle.

- At the Maine Lobster Festival in Rockland, participants enjoy oodles of lobster, parades, races, and the crowning of the Maine Sea Goddess.

- Established in 1844, Prospect's Fort Knox was built as a reaction to the area's vulnerable location during the War of 1812. The Fort garrisoned troops during the Civil War, including Maine's 20th regiment, and also during the Spanish-American War.

- Located on the Penobscot River, Bangor is known as the "Queen City of Maine." In addition to its culinary, cultural, and outdoor attractions, Maine's third largest city hosts multiple festivals and is the residence of famed horror author Stephen King.

▼ KENNEBUNKPORT

Maine's top beach destination, Kennebunkport, was settled in the 1600s as a shipbuilding town. Visitors can see the historic mansions built by sea captains, as well as partake in water activities such as whale-watching, sailing, fishing, kayaking, surfing, and more. The resort town is also popular in winter for its Christmas Prelude, which features parades, caroling, ice sculptures, and a Christmas tree made from lobster traps.

RECORD ★ SETTERS

In 1846, Maine became the first state to pass prohibition laws, making it illegal to manufacture, sell, or transport liquor.

SPORTING CHANCES

- On August 5, 1984, Cape Elizabeth native Joan Benoit was the gold medal winner in the first women's Olympic marathon.

- The state's ECHL ice hockey team, the Maine Mariners pay homage to the state in their logo: It features a lighthouse, the Dirigo star of Maine's motto, the abbreviation ME, and a pine tree.

- The Maine Black Bears are the athletic teams of the University of Maine. The school's football team has won 13 conference championships.

- Born and raised in Boothbay Harbor, Elle Logan is a three-time gold medal Olympic rower and two-time gold medal World Champion.

- A three-time Olympic gold medalist, Portland-born Ian Crocker set swimming records in the 50- and 100-meter butterfly, and in the 100-meter freestyle.

MADE IN ME

Maine's agricultural outputs include:

- Lobsters
- Eggs
- Dairy
- Potatoes
- Apples
- Blueberries
- Turkeys
- Maple products
- Hay
- Sweet corn

Maine's industrial outputs include:

- Paper products
- Aircraft parts
- Gas
- Electronic parts
- Chemicals
- Chemical woodpulp
- Laboratory reagents
- Facial tissues
- Immunological products
- Trailers and semi-trailers

▶ FIDDLEHEADIN'

Fiddleheads, a type of wild young fern considered a delicacy, have been collected by Mainers, colonists, and Native peoples for centuries. The tradition is known as fiddleheadin'.

STARS ★ OF ★ THE ★ STATE

HENRY WADSWORTH LONGFELLOW

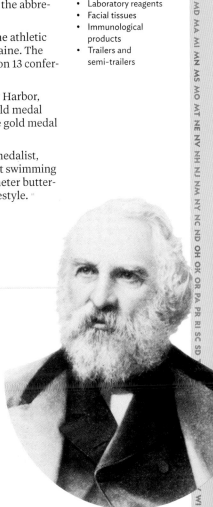

(1807–1882) Henry Wadsworth Longfellow was a celebrated poet who was among the first to gain widespread recognition for American poetry. Born in Portland (then still part of Massachusetts), Longfellow enjoyed a top education in literature and language. By 1842, his work *Ballads and Other Poems* had gained popularity across the nation, lauded for its romantic subjects and refined meters. In 1855, Longfellow's tale about a legendary Ojibwe chief, *The Song of Hiawatha*, became an immediate success. Similarly, his 1863 folk ballad "Paul Revere's Ride" appealed to national interests. In 1884, Longfellow became the first American poet to be memorialized in the Poet's Corner of London's Westminster Abbey.

MARIANA ISLANDS

CAPITAL: Saipan **FLOWER:** Plumeria **NICKNAME:** America's Best Kept Secret **ENTRY:** 1792

★ ★ ★ *America's Best Kept Secret* ★ ★ ★

MP FACTS

- The Northern Mariana Islands are located in Micronesia in the western Pacific Ocean.

- The total land area is 183.5 square miles (475 sq km).

- The population of all the islands is 47,329.

- Contact with the West began in 1521 when Portuguese explorer Ferdinand Magellan arrived during his circum-navigation of the world.

- Saipan played a key role during World War II. On June 15, 1944, U.S. forces entered the island, and a bloody, month-long battle with Japan ensued, killing tens of thousands before the American flag was raised in victory.

- The territory consists of 14 volcanic and coral islands.

- On August 6, 1945, the Enola Gay, an American B-29 bomber, took off from Tinian Island carrying a uranium bomb that it dropped on Hiroshima, Japan. ▼

▶ OFFICIAL BIRD

Mariana Fruit Dove
Ptilinopus roseicapilla

Endemic to the Northern Mariana Islands, the Mariana Fruit Dove is strikingly colorful with a bright green body, an orange belly, and a bright silver neck and chest.

1947

The Northern Mariana Islands have been part of the U.S. since 1947. Residents of the Northern Marianas voted to become a U.S. commonwealth in 1975.

> **INDIGENOUS PEOPLES AROUND THE WORLD ARE LONGTIME STEWARDS OF THE LAST REMNANTS OF WILDERNESS ON OUR PLANET.**
>
> —Chamorro eco-advocate Angelo Villagomez

- Some 43,400 people live on Saipan, the territory's capital. About 2,000 live on Tinian, and another 1,900 on Rota.

- The other islands—including Anatahan, Alamagan, Agrihan, Asuncion, Farallon de Medinilla, Farallon de Pajaros, Guguan, Maug Islands, Pagan, and Sarigan—are mostly uninhabited.

- The first settlers may have arrived by boat from Southeast Asia more than 3,500 years ago. These Indigenous people are known as the Chamorro.

- In 1565, the islands were claimed by the Spanish, who later named them after Mariana of Austria, the widow of Spain's King Philip IV.

- Spain sold the islands to Germany in 1899, but when the Germans were stripped of their overseas possessions after WWI, Japan took over.

- In 1978, the Northern Mariana Islands adopted their own constitution and local government—making it a commonwealth.

- Those born in the Northern Mariana Islands are considered citizens of the United States, but they can't vote in federal elections.

- One-third of the islands' residents are Filipino, with smaller populations of Chinese, Koreans, and other Pacific Islanders. About a quarter of the total population are Chamorro.

- About 90 percent of the population speaks a language other than English: Chamorro, Carolinian, Chinese, and Filipino are widely spoken.

- Average yearly temperatures on Saipan range between 79°F and 82°F (26°C and 28°C) and annual precipitation averages about 70 inches (178 cm). There are nine active volcanoes within the Northern Mariana Islands. ▪

◀ TAKE ME TO CHURCH

Roman Catholicism is the predominant religion on the islands, with members of other Christian denominations and Buddhists representing a significant minority.

▶ **STORY OF** THE DANCE Go to any ceremony in the Northern Mariana Islands and you are sure to see plenty of dancing, an important element of the culture. One of these dances is the *bailan pailitu*, or "stick dance," which involves dancers in traditional garb striking together thin sticks in rhythmic patterns. First performed by Indigenous Chamorro and Carolinians throughout the period of Spanish colonization, the stick dance remains a staple component in the islands' heritage and a source of pride. ▪

ANGELO VILLAGOMEZ

(b. 1978) A conservation leader born in a village on the island of Saipan, Villagomez is making it his mission to preserve his homeland and the oceans surrounding it. Through his work with the New Institute's Blue Nature Alliance, he led efforts to protect 6.95 million square miles (18 million sq km) of ocean, with the ultimate goal of protecting at least 30 percent of the ocean by 2030. He is a policy expert on global shark conservation and also studies the biodiversity in the Mariana Trench. A proud Chamorro, Villagomez advocates for social equity and encourages bringing Indigenous people into the conservation conversation. ▪

AL AK AS AZ AR CA CO CT DE FL GA GU HI ID IL IN IA KS KY LA ME MP MD MA MI MN MS MO MT NE NV NH NJ NM NY NC ND OH OK OR PA PR RI SC SD TN TX VI UT VT VA WA DC WV WI WY

- The island of Pagan was evacuated in 1981 after a volcanic eruption—and no one has lived there since.

- Saipan has the most consistent temperature on Earth. From 1927 to 1935, the lowest temperature recorded in Garapan, on Saipan, was 67.3°F (19.6°C) and the highest was 88.5°F (31.4°C) giving a range of only 21.2°F (11.8°C).

- Tinian is about the same size and shape as the island of Manhattan and has street names including Broadway, Eighth Avenue, and 86th Street.

- You can still see the pits where the atomic bombs were stored before being loaded into planes during World War II.

- Rota's Wedding Cake Mountain is said to resemble the tiered confection.

- A 2007 volcanic eruption on the island of Anatahan lasted nearly a year.

- The Mariana fruit bats help to repopulate plants in the area by spreading seeds in their poop.

- Graffiti from soldiers who fought in the Battle of Saipan can still be seen on the walls of a long-abandoned Japanese jail.

- Some believed that famed pilot Amelia Earhart did not crash into the ocean but was imprisoned on Saipan.

- At certain restaurants on Saipan, you can order Spam sushi.

- A plastic bag was found more than six miles (10,898 m) below the surface of the water off the Northern Mariana Islands, the deepest plastic debris ever found in the sea.

- A South Korean version of the reality show *Survivor* was filmed on the islands of Tinian and Rota.

RECORD ★ SETTERS

In 2009, Gregorio Kilili Camacho Sablan became the first person to represent the people of the Northern Mariana Islands in the U.S. Congress. Born on Saipan, Sablan's political career spans more than four decades.

MISCELLANY

- **Mount Tapochau,** Saipan's highest peak, tops out at 1,554 feet (474 m).

- The islands have their **own constitution,** part of which grants every person of Indigenous descent a homestead lot.

- On **Rota,** dubbed "The Friendly Island," it is customary to wave hello to anyone you pass by.

- In 2019, **487,000 tourists** traveled to the Northern Mariana Islands. Most visitors came from Japan, Korea, China, and Russia.

- Isley field, constructed in 1941 as a Japanese military airfield, later became **Saipan International Airport**.

- **Liberation Day**—the commemoration of the liberation of the islands from the Japanese as well as the release of the local population from U. S. internment camps—is celebrated on July 4 with parades and marching bands.

- The **cuisine** of the Northern Mariana Islands reflects Asian, American, and Spanish cultural influences. Red rice is a common dish for special occasions.

- The **Tinian Hot Pepper Festival** celebrates the island's famous hot pepper, the donne' sali.

- Rota is known for its **purple sweet potatoes**.

- Known locally as the **fanihi,** the Marianas flying fox is considered a gourmet delicacy.

- The star on the **Northern Mariana Islands flag** represents the U.S.'s protection over the commonwealth during WWII.

- There is also a gray pillar with a capstone on the flag—a nod to the **traditional pillars** used in building by the Chamorro people.

SAIPAN IS A PLEASANT ISLAND, WITH CALMING PATCHES OF BRIGHT GREEN VEGETATION AND BRILLIANT FLAME TREES.

—General Holland M. Smith, U.S. Marine Corps

BY THE NUMBERS

26 the weight in tons (23.6 t) of each latte shaft at the Rota Latte Stone Quarry. These megalithic stones were used as building supports by the ancient Chamorro people.

80% of Northern Marianas voters chose to make the islands a U.S. commonwealth in 1975.

800 the height in feet (244 m) of Suicide Cliff, which looms over Saipan and is the site where many Japanese civilians and soldiers jumped to their deaths rather than surrender to the American forces in the last days of the bloody battle there

45 THE DURATION IN MINUTES OF A FLIGHT FROM GUAM TO SAIPAN

57 different tree species grow within Saipan's botanical gardens, including the plumeria tree, which gives the islands their state flower.

46 the area in square miles (119 sq km) of Saipan, about the size of Disney World. It takes less than an hour to travel the island by car.

33 THE APPROXIMATE HEIGHT IN FEET (10 M) ABOVE SEA LEVEL OF SAIPAN'S STATUE OF THE ISLAND'S "SUGAR KING" HARUJI MATSUE, THE JAPANESE ENTREPRENEUR WHO ESTABLISHED THE SUGAR INDUSTRY ON THE ISLANDS IN THE EARLY 1920S

30 the height in feet (9 m) of the wooden cross carried by a group of Catholics on Saipan to the peak of Mount Tapochau as part of the island's Good Friday tradition

2000 B.C. the approximate year that ancient seafaring people journeyed to the Marianas from Southeast Asia in outrigger canoes

The first African American Marines to see combat in World War II served in Saipan. During the Battle of Saipan in 1944, some 800 U.S. troops unloaded food and ammunition from landing vehicles and delivered supplies to troops on the beach while under fire.

DESTINATION: NORTHERN MARIANA ISLANDS

- Remnants of World War II are still seen on many spots of the islands, including on Rota, where you can explore Tonga Cave, a large natural cavern that was used as the site of a makeshift hospital by the Japanese during wartime. It has also served as a place of refuge for residents during typhoons.

- Continue the history tour with a visit to the American Memorial on Saipan, a park marked by memorials in tribute to U.S. servicemen and Indigenous civilians who were killed in the battles between the United States and Japan in 1944.

The waters around the islands are home to five endangered whale species: blue whales, fin whales, humpback whales, sei whales, and sperm whales.

- Check out where the enormous Taga stones were once unearthed at Rota's Nieves Latte Stone Quarry, which is listed in the National Register of Historic Places. Though long abandoned, the quarry features the largest prehistoric megaliths in the Northern Mariana Islands, some of which are believed to be 1,000 years old.

- Take a (giant) step back in time by heading underground in the Kalabera Cave on Saipan. This subterranean spot was once used as a burial site, and remnants of the ancient culture remain here, including art on the walls drawn by Chamorro artists.

▲ PARADISE FOUND
Forbidden Island is a top snorkeling spot with breathtaking views.

- Since 1949, Catholics on Saipan have been worshiping at Mount Carmel Cathedral, the largest Catholic church in the Marianas. A standout landmark in the village of Chalan Kanoa, the cathedral's architecture is reflective of the Spanish influence on the area.

- Saipan's Grotto is a favorite spot among scuba divers, who flock to the collapsed cavern for a dip in the blue hole to catch glimpses of stingrays, clownfish, eels, nudibranchs, surgeonfish, parrotfish, white-tip sharks, and more underwater wonders.

- The Pacific WWII Maritime Heritage Trail is another magnet for divers. This underwater site features a bevy of Japanese and U.S. shipwrecks, assault vehicles, and aircraft wrecks.

- Shop for local fare and wares at the Garapan Street Market where vendors serve up street food, and live traditional music and dancers lend to the vibrant vibe.

▼ HOME RUN

Saipan's Little League team has made appearances at the Little League World Series in 1993, 2004, and 2006.

- Baseball became more popular during the Japanese occupation of the Northern Mariana Islands, when they organized military and civilian teams. Later, American soldiers kept the momentum going, eventually making baseball the islands' favorite sport.

- In 1969, Saipan hosted the first Micronesian Games (also known as the Micronesian Olympics), which ultimately became a quadrennial event including 10 countries, states, and territories.

- That year, the Northern Marianas' women's volleyball team won the islands' first gold at the Micronesian Games.

- Northern Mariana Islands athletes have since won several more medals at the Micronesian games, including double golds in the men's open water event at the 2018 event in Yap.

- In 2022, the Northern Mariana Islands hosted the Pacific Mini Games featuring 24 countries and territories from Oceania competing in nine Olympic sports, including baseball, badminton, beach volleyball, and golf.

- The Northern Mariana Islands are home to six golf courses, including two designed by golf star Greg Norman, which are both part of the Lao Lao Bay Resort.

- The 31-mile (50 k) Pika Bike Race has cyclists riding around the island of Tinian.

- In April, hundreds of runners compete in the Saipan Marathon, a big draw to the island for its scenic views along the course. ▪

MADE IN MP

Northern Mariana Islands' agricultural outputs include:

- Papayas
- Bananas
- Breadfruit
- Mangoes
- Copra (sun-dried or smoked coconut meat)
- Bok choy
- Eggs
- Pork
- Poultry

Northern Mariana Islands' industrial outputs include:

- Beauty products
- Scrap iron
- Electric batteries
- Jewelry
- Food and beverage products
- Scrap copper

SPORTING CHANCES

- The first known baseball game played on Saipan occurred in 1910, when Japanese students visiting the island played a game against the U.S. Marine Corps.

- Pro tennis player Colin Sinclair, a Pacific Games gold medalist, was born on Saipan and represents the Northern Mariana Islands on the international circuit.

STARS ★ OF ★ THE ★ TERRITORY

RAMONA V. MANGLONA

(b. 1967) Born on Saipan, Manglona left home at the age of 12 to pursue an education on the U.S. mainland, ultimately becoming the first in her family to graduate from a four-year college, and then law school. She then returned to the island to pursue her career, becoming the first Indigenous woman to pass the local bar exam. In 2011, President Barack Obama nominated Manglona to be a judge in the U.S. District Court for the Northern Mariana Islands, and in turn she became the first and only woman to hold that position for the commonwealth. ▪

MARYLAND

★ ★ ★

"Strong Deeds, Gentle Words"

★ ★ ★

CAPITAL: Annapolis **BIRD:** Baltimore Oriole **NICKNAME:** Old Line State **ENTRY:** 1788

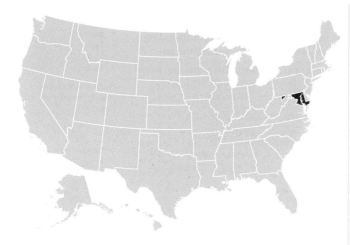

MD FACTS

- The population is 6,164,660.

- Maryland was the seventh state to join the Union and is the 42nd state in size.

- Perhaps most famous for its blue crabs, Maryland's natural resources also include coal, clay, and limestone.

- Before European explorers arrived, the region was inhabited by the Lenape, Nanticoke, Powhatan, Susquehannock, and Tutelo and Saponi. There are no federally recognized tribes there today.

- In 1608, famed English explorer Captain John Smith mapped the shoreline of the Chesapeake Bay, but it wasn't until 1632 that Maryland became a colony.

- In 1885, Baltimore's National Brewing Company began creating National Bohemian beer—also known as Natty Boh.

- The third largest estuary in the world, the Chesapeake Bay stretches 200 miles (322 km) from Havre de Grace down into Virginia. The bay produces around 500 million pounds (227 million kg) of seafood each year. It is also home to more than 3,600 species of plants and animals. ▼

▶ STATE FLOWER

Black-Eyed Susan
Rudbeckia hirta

Famed for its large, dark center and bright yellow petals, the flower matches the black and gold coloring of the state bird, insect, and cat.

1939

Old Bay Seasoning features a blend of 18 spices and is traditionally used to season crabs. Invented by a German immigrant in 1939, the spice has become so popular that it is now used to flavor beer, chips, and even ice cream.

NO STATE CAN MATCH THE BEAUTY OF THE CHESAPEAKE BAY, OUR BEACHES AND FARMS, OR THE MOUNTAINS OF WESTERN MARYLAND, THE PORT OF BALTIMORE, OR THE HISTORIC CHARM OF EVERY CORNER OF OUR STATE.

—Former governor Larry Hogan

- It wasn't until 1632 that Maryland became a colony. The charter was granted to Cecilius Calvert, the 2nd Lord Baltimore, who deployed his brother and about 200 colonists to settle the town of St. Mary's.

- During the War of 1812, Francis Scott Key watched Fort McHenry withstand attack. Key went on to pen "The Star-Spangled Banner," which was declared the national anthem in 1931.

- Born in Maryland around 1818, Frederick Douglass grew up enslaved and went on to become a preeminent abolitionist, publishing his own newspaper called *The North Star*, and serving as an advisor to President Abraham Lincoln.

- In 1906, Upton Sinclair, who was born in Baltimore, published his exposé of the meatpacking industry's exploitation of immigrant labor, titled *The Jungle*. The novel spurred changes around federal food-inspection laws.

- Baltimore native Thurgood Marshall successfully argued before the Supreme Court in *Brown v. Board of Education* that segregation in public schools was unconstitutional. Marshall became the first Black U.S. Supreme Court justice in 1967.

- Baltimore native John Waters is a filmmaker celebrated for his rebellious themes and use of camp, horror, and gross-out gags.

HARRIET TUBMAN

Harriet Tubman, born Amarinta Ross, grew up enslaved in Maryland. In 1849, she escaped to the free state of Pennsylvania, but was forced to leave behind her family. Over the next 10 years, she made around 13 trips back into Maryland, leading her friends, family, and approximately 70 more enslaved people to freedom. Tubman, who gained the nickname Moses for her role as a "conductor" on the Underground Railroad, went on to work as a spy, nurse, cook, and scout for the Union during the Civil War, eventually aiding in a raid that rescued more than 700 enslaved people.

STORY OF THE NAME As it was popular tradition for colonists to name new lands after presiding royals—often in an attempt to secure royal favor—Maryland was named after England's Queen Henrietta Maria (1609–1669), wife of King Charles I.

STARS ★ OF ★ THE ★ STATE

EDGAR ALLAN POE

(1809–1849) Edgar Allan Poe was a short-story author and poet famous for writing on topics dealing with mystery, horror, and science fiction. Born in Boston, Poe grew up suffering romantic heartbreak, familial death, and expulsion from the U.S. Military Academy at West Point. After settling in Baltimore, he began to write short stories and gained instant national fame after publishing his dark poem "The Raven" in 1845. Despite his critical successes, the author continued to meet with personal misfortune and suffered from alcoholism. He died in Baltimore in 1849, and he is still regarded as a genius of the macabre.

HOT FOOT!

It is tradition in Annapolis to celebrate the arrival of spring by burning socks.

> IT WAS BY A MARYLAND COLONEL IN THE YEAR 1777 THAT THE BRITISH RECEIVED, IN THE GALLANT DEFENSE OF AN IMPORTANT FORT, ONE OF THE FIRST LESSONS OF WHAT THEY WERE TO EXPECT FROM AMERICAN VALOR AND PATRIOTISM.
>
> —Marquis de Lafayette

▶ **STORY OF** THE CAKE About 12 miles (19 km) off of Maryland's coast is Smith Island, famous for its eponymous dessert: Smith Island Cake. The cake, which is made of six to 14 layers of yellow cake and chocolate fudge icing, may have arrived with the island's British, Welsh, and Cornish settlers in the early 1600s. It became tradition for wives to bake these long-lasting cakes for their husbands to take on oyster-harvesting trips. Today, it is Maryland's state dessert. ▪

WEIRD BUT TRUE

- Maryland's traditional white potato pie contains mashed potatoes instead of pumpkin or sweet potatoes.
- During the War of 1812, the town of St. Michaels tricked British barges into overshooting by hanging lanterns in the trees.
- Located in a cemetery in Baltimore, the tombstone of the inventor of the Ouija board is shaped like the game board.
- The wrecks of World War I–era wooden steamships in Mallows Bay have become a thriving marine habitat.
- The Baltimore Ravens, Maryland's NFL team, take their name from the famous Edgar Allan Poe poem.
- More than 50 duels were fought at the Bladensburg Dueling Grounds.
- Maryland's state drink is milk. ▪

RECORD ★ SETTERS

The first telegraph message was sent from Washington, D.C., to Baltimore, Maryland, by American inventor Samuel F.B. Morse in 1844.

MISCELLANY

- To some in Baltimore, a **"hon"** (short for "honey") refers to a specific type of working-class woman, often bedecked in a beehive hairstyle and cat's-eye glasses, from the late 1950s and early '60s.
- To satisfy the requirements of **pit beef**, a round roast must be cooked so that it is both medium rare and charred on the outer edges. It is then sliced thinly and plopped on a Kaiser roll with horseradish, mayo, and onions.
- Maryland's state cat is the **calico cat**.
- Baltimore's **Little Italy** is known for its strong Italian American heritage. The community features restaurants, bakeries, and a traditional Feast of Saint Anthony.
- A 200-year-old bar in Baltimore claims to have served **Edgar Allan Poe** his last drink.
- Maryland's state dinosaur is the **Astrodon johnstoni**, a sauropod from the early Cretaceous.
- When **William and Salie Utz** began their small potato chip brand in Pennsylvania in 1921, they found a devoted fan base in the Baltimore area. Today, Utz chips remain Baltimore favorites.
- Several now defunct **gold mines** are located in the state.
- Berlin has its own official dessert: the **peach dumpling**, a puff pastry folded around cooked peaches.
- **Skipjacks**, Maryland's state boats, are often used to dredge oysters from the Chesapeake.
- The state tree is the **white oak**.
- Some Baltimore bakeries still serve **smearcase**, a type of light cheesecake brought to the city by German immigrants in the 1800s.
- The **Patuxent river stone** is the state gem.
- The **Chesapeake Bay retriever**, the state dog, was originally bred by wealthy duck club owners along the Chesapeake Bay.
- Established in 1876, **Johns Hopkins University** remains a preeminent university.
- **Lacrosse** is the official state team sport.
- There are **6 libraries** on the main University of Maryland campus.
- Erected in Annapolis in 1779, the stately **Maryland State House** is the country's oldest state capitol in continuous legislative use.

BY THE NUMBERS

17.6 the length in miles (28.3 km) of the Chesapeake Bay Bridge Tunnel

10 to **20** million years ago, the Calvert Cliffs were formed.

2,632 the number of games played in an unbroken streak by baseball's "Iron Man," Cal Ripken, Jr.

300 the weight in pounds (136.1 kg) of the world's largest crab cake, made in Timonium

230 the length in feet (70 m) of the Wheaton Metro station escalator

11,684 THE LENGTH IN MILES (18,804 KM) OF THE CHESAPEAKE BAY'S SHORELINE

1850 the year the United States Naval Academy was founded in Annapolis

184.5 the length in miles (296.9 km) of the Chesapeake & Ohio Canal, a late 19th-century transportation system that stretches from Washington, D.C., to Cumberland, Maryland

$100,000,000 was the estimated destruction cost of the Great Baltimore Fire in 1904.

3,360 feet (1,024 m) is the elevation of Hoye Crest, Maryland's highest point.

◄ **HORSIN' AROUND**

Although visitors come to Assateague Island for beach camping, the main draw is the chance of seeing the island's wild horses. Technically "feral," these horses are the descendants of domesticated ancestors and have reverted to a wild state. According to local folklore, the horses' ancestors were the survivors of a Spanish shipwreck.

DESTINATION: MARYLAND

- Founded in 1729, Baltimore is Maryland's largest city, with more than 1.5 million inhabitants. The city is famous for its diverse population and culture. Historical sites include Fort McHenry, multiple places once haunted by Edgar Allan Poe, and the nation's first monument to George Washington. At Baltimore's Inner Harbor, visitors can climb aboard various historic ships from the 1800s, explore the Maryland Science Center, or tour the award-winning National Aquarium.

- Picturesque and rich in history, the capital Annapolis was settled in 1649. The city's location on the Chesapeake makes it a top destination for those wishing to sail, kayak, swim, or feast on crab. Annapolis also draws history buffs, who come for the U.S. Naval Academy, St. John's College, and historic homes.

- Built in 1902, the Ocean City Boardwalk is considered one of the best boardwalks in the country. In addition to rides, arcades, and open stretches of beach, Ocean City features a wide variety of local food, from Maryland crab cakes to saltwater taffy.

- On September 17, 1862, the Battle of Antietam became one of the bloodiest conflicts of the Civil War. As the Union rebuffed a Confederate invasion, the two sides suffered a total of more than 23,000 killed, wounded, or missing soldiers. Today, visitors can pay their respects at Antietam National Battlefield.

- Originally the Army Medical Museum established during the Civil War, the National Museum of Health and Medicine remains a repository of unusual specimens and historic collections. Guests can learn about the development of American medicine.

- Located in Laurel, Dinosaur Park is one of the most important dinosaur fossil sites in the eastern United States. Visitors can take part in the search for Cretaceous period fossils.

- The Bladensburg Battlefield marks the location of a disastrous battle during the War of 1812.

STARS ★ OF ★ THE ★ STATE

MATTHEW HENSON

(1866–1955) Born in Nanjemoy, Matthew Alexander Henson was raised by Black parents who struggled under the exploitative sharecropping system of Reconstruction-era America. After losing both parents, Henson began work as a cabin boy at 12 years old. Upon meeting Robert Peary in 1887, Henson quickly impressed the famed explorer and was hired to join expeditions to Nicaragua and Greenland. Henson became known for not only his survival skills, but his dedication to learning about, respecting, and employing the survival methods of local Inuit cultures in the Arctic. Armed with these abilities, Henson and Peary partnered to attempt to reach the North Pole. After seven failed attempts, the team succeeded in 1909, making Henson one of the first humans to stand at the North Pole. He received a Congressional Medal in 1944.

▲ MARYLAND MICHAEL
A native of Baltimore, swimmer Michael Phelps is the most decorated Olympian of all time with 23 gold, three silver, and two bronze medals.

MADE IN MD

Maryland's agricultural outputs include:

- Soybeans
- Chicken
- Wheat
- Corn
- Dairy
- Flowers
- Eggs
- Cattle hay
- Turkey

Maryland's industrial outputs include:

- Aircrafts and parts
- Gas
- Military products
- Machinery
- Zinc, nickel, and other metals
- Transportation equipment

SPORTING CHANCES

- Jousting, a medieval equestrian sport in which opponents attempt to knock each other from their mounts, has been popular in Maryland since colonial times. It remains the official state sport.

- Perhaps the most famous baseball player of all time, George Herman "Babe" Ruth was born in Baltimore in 1895. Known as the Sultan of Swat and the Great Bambino, Ruth was legendary for setting home run records.

- Major League Baseball's Orioles moved from St. Louis (where they were named the Browns) after the 1953 season. Once in Baltimore, the Orioles won World Series titles in 1966, 1970, 1983.

- Although they are considered a relatively young team, having been renamed from the Cleveland Browns in 1996, the Baltimore Ravens have already won two Super Bowl titles: XXXV and XLVII.

- Originally known as stickball, lacrosse was developed by various Algonquin peoples. The sport was soon adopted by European colonists and remains popular in Maryland today. The University of Maryland's Terrapins are regular national champions of the Division I collegiate athletic conference.

- Born in Russia and raised in an orphanage, Russian American Tatyana McFadden was paralyzed from the waist down due to spina bifida. After being adopted and raised in Maryland, McFadden went on to become a Paralympic champion with 17 total medals.

- Known for "the streak"—the most consecutive games played by any baseball player in history—Cal Ripken, Jr., played 21 seasons for the Baltimore Orioles. He was inducted into the Baseball Hall of Fame in 2007.

- Raised in Bethesda, swimmer Katie Ledecky is a three-time Olympian and 10-time Olympic medalist. At age 15, she was also the youngest athlete on the 2012 U.S. Olympic Swimming Team at her first Olympics.

RECORD ★ SETTERS

In 1811, the government began construction on the country's first national road, which would stretch from Baltimore to East St. Louis, Missouri.

MASSACHUSETTS

CAPITAL: Boston **FLOWER:** Mayflower **NICKNAME:** Bay State **ENTRY:** 1788

★ ★ ★ *"By the Sword We Seek Peace, but Peace Only Under Liberty"* ★ ★ ★

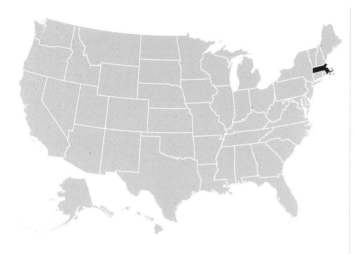

MA FACTS

- The population is 6,981,974.

- It was the sixth state admitted to the Union and is the 45th state in size.

- Around the year 1000, Norse explorer Leif Eriksson may have been the first European to explore the region.

- Numbering among the state's many great writers and poets are E. E. Cummings, Emily Dickinson, Louisa May Alcott, Phillis Wheatley, and Nathaniel Hawthorne.

- In addition to its rich colonial history, the state is famous for its seafood and desserts. Major industries include finance, technology, medicine, manufacturing, fishing, and tourism.

- In 1775, British soldiers planned to seize weapons and gunpowder stored in Concord. Paul Revere and others set off from Boston on the famous Midnight Ride to warn of the impending attack. As colonists and soldiers clashed, a shot was fired—though historians debate by whom—marking the Revolutionary War's beginning with the "shot heard 'round the world." ▼

▶ STATE BIRD
Black-Capped Chickadee
Poecile atricapillus

Named for its *chick-a-dee-dee-dee* calls, the state bird remains local throughout winter and is known for its cheery, active behavior.

1773

In 1773, colonists frustrated by taxes and lack of legislative representation boarded East India Company trade ships and tossed the cargo into the harbor in what is now known as the Boston Tea Party.

THE MALLARDS CONTINUE THEIR SEARCH, FLYING OVER BOSTON LANDMARKS SUCH AS BEACON HILL, THE MASSACHUSETTS STATE HOUSE, AND LOUISBURG SQUARE.

—Author Robert McCloskey, *Make Way for Ducklings*

- The area is thought to have been populated for around 10,000 years. Original inhabitants of the area included Wampanoag, Mohegan, and Mohican peoples. The Mashpee Wampanoag Tribe and Wampanoag Tribe of Gay Head (Aquinnah) remain the only federally recognized tribes.

- Massachusetts is one of the country's largest cranberry producers.

- In 1620, a group of Puritan pilgrims seeking religious freedom arrived on the *Mayflower* and founded the Plymouth Colony. Around 1,000 more Puritans arrived in 1630 and founded the Massachusetts Bay Colony. In 1691, the settlements merged.

- Relations between the colonists and Indigenous peoples deteriorated when the Wampanoag leader Wamsutta died after being forcefully held captive at Plymouth. In 1675, Wamsutta's brother Metacom (also known as King Philip) led his tribe and a coalition of allies to drive the colonists from New England. The conflict, now known as King Philip's War, lasted until Metacom's death in 1676.

- Indigenous groups often used pits and hot stones to bake navy beans with bear fat and maple syrup. European settlers adapted the dish, often using pork and molasses. The dish's popularity led to Boston's nickname: Beantown.

- The Salem witch trials were a series of accusations and persecutions centering around the belief that witches had invaded the small town of Salem. In 1692, the erratic behavior of two young girls sparked a yearlong bout of paranoia, which led to the imprisonment of more than 150 men and women and 20 executions.

In the early 1780s, Deborah Sampson disguised herself as a man, joined the military, and fought in the Revolutionary War.

- Born William Edward Burghardt Du Bois in Great Barrington in 1868, W. E. B. Du Bois co-founded the National Association for the Advancement of Colored People (NAACP). His works remain formative pieces on the roles and lives of Black Americans in society and their fight for equality.

- During the 19th century, the state became a haven for naturalists and philosophers. Among the most notable were Concord native Henry David Thoreau and Boston native Ralph Waldo Emerson, who together helped pioneer transcendentalist thought.

- In 2001, GLAD (GLBTQ Legal Advocates & Defenders) sued the state on behalf of all same-sex couples denied marriage licenses. Two years later in *Goodridge v. Department of Public Health*, the state ruled that the same laws and procedures should govern all marriage, regardless of sex.

STARS ★ OF ★ THE ★ STATE

SUSAN B. ANTHONY

(1820–1906) Susan B. Anthony was a women's suffrage activist and abolitionist who played an instrumental role in achieving women's right to vote. Born in Adams, Massachusetts, Anthony was raised Quaker with the belief that all are equal. After being rebuffed at an 1852 temperance meeting because of her gender, Anthony became dedicated to fighting for women's equality. Along with activist Elizabeth Cady Stanton, she organized the National Woman Suffrage Association in 1869. Over the next few decades, the pair traveled throughout the country to champion the cause, with Anthony even being arrested for casting a vote in the 1872 presidential election. Although she did not survive to see the passage of the 19th Amendment, her tireless efforts paved the road toward equality.

> ## MASSACHUSETTS HAS BEEN THE WHEEL WITHIN NEW ENGLAND, AND BOSTON THE WHEEL WITHIN MASSACHUSETTS.
>
> —Rev. F.B. Zincke, *Last Winter in the United States*

HOMETOWN PUP
Named for the city in which they were first bred, Boston terriers were the first purebred dog breed developed in the U.S.

WEIRD BUT TRUE

- "Masshole"—a negative term for an inhabitant of Massachusetts—is an official word in the *Oxford English Dictionary*.

- There is a state groundhog named Ms. G.

- There is a lake called Lake Chargoggagoggmanchauggagoggchaubunagungamaugg.

- Christmas was banned by the Puritans for an entire generation, beginning in the mid-1600s.

- It is illegal to have exploding golf balls.

- Salem's Satanic Temple's mission is to "encourage benevolence and empathy, reject tyrannical authority, advocate practical common sense, oppose injustice, and undertake noble pursuits."

- "Mary Had a Little Lamb" may have been based on a real local girl and her lamb.

DR. SEUSS
Born in Springfield, author and illustrator Theodor Seuss Geisel—commonly known as Dr. Seuss—is the official state children's author.

MISCELLANY

- People from Massachusetts are called **"Bay Staters."**

- The state colors are **blue, green, and cranberry**.

- Known colloquially as **Southie**, South Boston was historically home to a large Irish Catholic population and hosts one of the largest St. Patrick's Day parades in the country.

- The state cat is the **tabby**.

- In 1919, an exploded storage tank in Boston released more than two million gallons (8 million L) of molasses and killed 21 people in what is now known as the **Great Molasses Flood**.

- The state game bird is the **wild turkey**.

- The state fossil is **dinosaur tracks**, in honor of the enormous theropod tracks found in Granby.

- Famed American painter **Norman Rockwell** is the state artist.

- Massachusetts is believed to take its name from the **Algonquian** words for "at the great hill," which referred to the Blue Hills south of Boston.

- The state song is **"All Hail to Massachusetts."**

- The state dessert, **Boston cream pie**, is actually a yellow cake filled with custard or cream and topped with chocolate. It is believed to have been invented in 1856 by an Armenian French chef.

- Between 1880 and 1920, more than four million Italians immigrated to the United States. Boston became a **hub of Italian American culture**, and people continue to celebrate the heritage with food and festivals such as St. Anthony's Feast.

- **Johnny Appleseed**, a folk hero who supposedly spread apple seeds across New England and parts of the Midwest, is thought to be based on the real-life Bay Stater John Chapman, who made his living planting orchards.

- Built around 1637, the Fairbanks House in Dedham is the **oldest known timber frame house** still standing in North America.

RECORD ★ SETTERS
When she settled Taunton in 1637, Elizabeth Poole became the first woman on record to found a town in the Americas.

BY THE NUMBERS

342 chests of tea were thrown into **Boston Harbor as colonists protested tea taxes**

3,491 the height in feet (1,064 m) of Mount Greylock, the highest point

4 the number of U.S. presidents from Massachusetts: John Adams, John Quincy Adams, Calvin Coolidge, and John F. Kennedy

1983 THE YEAR THE FIRST COMPUTER VIRUS WAS DEMONSTRATED AT MIT

1930 the year chocolate chip cookies were invented at the Toll House Inn near Whitman

4,500+ the number of black bears

1781 THE YEAR ELIZABETH FREEMAN SUED FOR HER FREEDOM UNDER THE NEWLY CREATED BILL OF RIGHTS, MAKING HER THE FIRST ENSLAVED WOMAN TO BE FREED IN THE STATE

480 the width in feet (146 m) of the Cape Cod Canal

DESTINATION: MASSACHUSETTS

- Boston's 2.5-mile (4 km) Freedom Trail highlights 16 locations, such as Boston Common (founded in 1634 as the country's oldest park, and later home to antislavery meetings, Vietnam War protests, and civil rights rallies); Faneuil Hall, which was built in 1742 and served as a main meeting place of the Revolutionary War; and the gravesites of Paul Revere, Samuel Adams, and John Hancock.

- A one-time vacation destination for President John F. Kennedy, Cape Cod is famous for its laid-back lifestyle and local foods. The 65-mile (105 km) spit of land also has a robust LGBTQ+ community.

- Harvard is the oldest institution of higher education in the U.S. Established in Cambridge in 1636, the school has produced seven U.S. presidents, including John Adams, John Quincy Adams, Rutherford B. Hayes, Theodore Roosevelt, Franklin D. Roosevelt, John F. Kennedy, and Barack Obama. It is home to the largest academic library in the world.

- Founded in Boston in 1861, the Massachusetts Institute of Technology (MIT) soon developed into one of the world's top centers of scientific and technical research. Today, MIT continues to act as a scientific leader and is equipped with a nuclear reactor, various observatories, a wind tunnel, an artificial intelligence laboratory, and more.

- Settled in 1642, Martha's Vineyard developed a robust fishing and whaling industry. Accessible only by air or by sea, it has become a popular destination for beachgoers and boat enthusiasts.

▼ NANTUCKET

Visitors to Nantucket, located off the coast of Cape Cod, enjoy the island's pristine beaches and historic lighthouses. Outdoor and water activities are plentiful, as are various museums focusing on whaling, shipwrecks, and art.

COURAGE—JUDGMENT—INTEGRITY— DEDICATION—THESE ARE THE HISTORIC QUALITIES OF THE BAY COLONY AND THE BAY STATE.

—President John F. Kennedy

- A living museum, Plimoth Patuxet provides immersive re-creations of a Wampanoag village and colonial life at the Plymouth settlement.

- The site of the famed witch trials, Salem is a town rich in history and culture. Salem is at its most popular during the Halloween season, when almost a million visitors flock to numerous parades, tours, haunted houses, and balls.

- At Stellwagen Bank National Marine Sanctuary, humpback, sei, fin, pilot, and minke whales frolic alongside dolphins, porpoises, and seals. On top of excellent whale-watching, Stellwagen Bank offers bird-watching and fishing.

STORY OF THE ACCENT Famously unique and tricky to mimic, the Boston accent is notable for its "non-rhotic speech," which means that its speakers tend to drop the letter "r." Bostonians also draw out the letter "o" into "aw," and they have a habit of speaking quickly, which creates an accent completely unique to the region. Historians believe that this way of speaking is also a window into the past; the Boston accent likely descends from rustic British speech patterns brought to the New World by 17th-century settlers.

MADE IN MA

Massachusetts's agricultural outputs include:

- Dairy
- Cattle
- Flowers
- Cranberries
- Hay
- Apples
- Sweet corn
- Seafood such as cod, flounder, lobster, and crab

Massachusetts's industrial outputs include:

- Mining such as sand, gravel, and stone
- Gold
- Medical instruments
- Machinery
- Electronic processors and controllers
- Artificial joints and parts
- Gold waste

SPORTING CHANCES

- In 1891, Springfield College instructor James Naismith was faced with the end of the fall sports season and a restless group of student athletes who now had nothing to play. Tasked with finding an indoor activity to fill the empty season, he invented basketball.

- The world's oldest annual marathon, the Boston Marathon is a 26-mile, 385-yard (42.2 km) race from Hopkinton to Boston. It was first held in 1897 and continues to be one of the world's most prestigious racing events. ▼

- Born in Ware, Arthur "Candy" Cummings was a Hall of Fame baseball pitcher who is believed to have invented the curveball.

- Fenway Park, the Red Sox stadium in Boston, has a rooftop vegetable garden.

- Needham native Aly Raisman is a six-time Olympic medal gymnast and two-time Olympian. She was also pivotal in exposing the sexual abuse that she and her teammates suffered at the hands of their team doctor.

- Born in East Brookfield in 1862, Cornelius "Connie Mack" McGillicuddy went on to become the longest-serving manager in baseball history.

- Known as the Boston Strong Boy, John L. Sullivan was one of the most popular heavyweight and bare-knuckle boxers of the 19th century.

▶ HOW 'BOUT THEM SOX

Founded in 1901, the Boston Red Sox have won nine World Series titles. They are also famous for their long-standing rivalry with the New York Yankees, which originated when baseball legend Babe Ruth was traded from the Red Sox to the Yankees in 1920.

BENJAMIN FRANKLIN (1706–1790)

Benjamin Franklin was a scientist, author, inventor, and Founding Father of the United States. Born in Boston, Franklin moved to Philadelphia and set himself up as a currency and newspaper printer. Franklin accumulated great wealth and he was able to retire as a gentleman of leisure. He began to publish his own works, entered politics, and developed an interest in science. Franklin attempted to prove that lightning is a form of electricity by tying a metal key to a kite string and flying the kite in a thunderstorm. In the 1760s, when tensions grew between colonists and the crown, Franklin first sought to aid reconciliation. When that failed, he joined the Continental Congress and helped draft the Declaration of Independence. Franklin's significant contributions in politics and science shaped the development and character of the United States, and he remains one of the most well-known figures in American history.

MICHIGAN

★ ★ ★

"If You Seek a Pleasant Peninsula, Look About You"

★ ★ ★

CAPITAL: Lansing **BIRD:** American Robin **NICKNAME:** Wolverine State **ENTRY:** 1837

MI FACTS

- With a population of about 10,034,113, Michigan is the 10th most populous state in the nation.

- Located in the Great Lakes and Midwest regions, Michigan is the 22nd largest state in the U.S.

- Researchers believe Native Americans began to settle in the western Great Lakes region as early as 8,000 B.C.

- Today, Michigan is home to 12 federally recognized and four state-recognized tribes.

- With more than 51,000 Native Americans living in Michigan, the state has one of the top 15 Indigenous populations in the country.

- The name is derived from the Chippewa word *Michigama*, meaning large lake.

- Michigan was part of New France for nearly a century, with the oldest European settlement being Sault Sainte Marie, founded in 1668.

- French explorer Étienne Brûlé paddled Lake Superior in 1620, becoming the first known European to reach Michigan.

▶ STATE FLOWER

Apple Blossom
Pyrus coronaria

Each spring, these sweet-smelling, delicate pink and white blooms burst in clusters from the branches of apple trees.

1925

In 1925, Traverse City's National Cherry Festival was launched to celebrate the area's abundant cherry crop. The eight-day event draws hundreds of thousands of people for festivities including concerts, local fare, and, of course, cherry sampling. ▼

▶ BY ANY OTHER NAME

There are currently no wolverines in the Wolverine State (although one was spotted in 2010). The most abundant mammals include white-tailed deer, cougars, bats, moose, rabbits, squirrels, coyotes, and wolves.

I NEVER HAD A DULL MOMENT AT DETROIT.

—Michigan-born aviator
Charles Lindbergh

- The state was later ruled by Great Britain before the U.S. captured the territory during the War of 1812.

- It is the only state in the U.S. that borders four of the five Great Lakes: Superior, Huron, Michigan, and Erie.

- With 11,000 additional lakes, 51,438 miles (82,781 km) of rivers, and more than 300 waterfalls, over 40 percent of Michigan is covered in water, more than any other state.

- It's made up of two peninsulas: the Upper Peninsula (the U.P.) being the northern part, bordered only by Wisconsin and three Great Lakes. The Lower Peninsula (the "mitten") to the south is bordered by Indiana, Ohio, and three Great Lakes.

- The Upper Peninsula is one of the coldest and snowiest areas in the U.S., with some 150- to 300-plus inches (381 to 762 cm) of snow a year.

- The two peninsulas are connected by the Mackinac Bridge, one of the longest suspension bridges in the world at five miles (8 km) long.

- With a population of approximately 620,376, Detroit is Michigan's largest city—and was the state's original capital from 1835 to 1847. ▪

▲ **STORY OF** THE MUSIC The Motown sound was born in Detroit, where Berry Gordy, Jr., opened his now famous recording studio in a modest home on Grand Boulevard in January of 1959. Motown Records soon became a launching pad for some of the world's most successful singers, from Diana Ross to Stevie Wonder to the Temptations to Marvin Gaye. With more than 100 top 10 hits and millions of records sold, Motown music has reached every corner of the world, but its roots firmly remain in Detroit. The original sound studio, dubbed "Hitsville U.S.A.,'" serves as a museum dedicated to the legendary Motown movement. ▪

STARS ★ OF ★ THE ★ STATE

ARETHA FRANKLIN

(1942–2018) In a career that spanned six decades, Franklin, "the Queen of Soul," sold more than 75 million records, won 18 Grammys, and is arguably one of the greatest singers and songwriters of all time. Raised in Detroit, Franklin honed her singing chops at New Bethel Baptist Church, where her father was a minister. Inspired by the gospel sound, Franklin's powerful voice lent itself to hits like "Respect," "Chain of Fools," and "Natural Woman," among many others. She sang at the inauguration of three U.S. presidents and in 1987 became the first woman inducted into the Rock & Roll Hall of Fame. ▪

There are 129 lighthouses along the shores of Michigan, more than any other state.

WEIRD BUT TRUE

- A border collie was trained to shoo away birds at a Michigan airport so planes could take off safely.

- A Farmington Hills company collected 690 pounds (313 kg) of dryer lint, setting a world record for the largest lint ball in 2019.

- Battle Creek, home to the Kellogg Company, is known as "Cereal City."

- A mail boat that delivers to freighters in the Great Lakes boasts the only floating zip code in the United States.

- Montague has the world's largest weather vane, standing taller than a four-story building with an arrow as long as an SUV.

- The term "Yooper"—referring to residents or natives of the Upper Peninsula (the U.P.)—was added to *Merriam-Webster Dictionary* in 2014.

- Detroit has issued its own form of currency, a $3 denomination known as the "Cheers."

- There have been reports of ships and planes disappearing as well as UFO sightings within the Lake Michigan Triangle.

- "Yooperlites"—partially molten rocks —have been found on the banks of Lake Superior.

- More than 40 magicians are buried in Colon's Lakeside Cemetery—more than any other cemetery in the world.

- You could take a class on "Surviving the Coming Zombie Apocalypse" at Michigan State University.

- Each June, Log Cabin Day is celebrated, a homage to preserving the wooden homes found throughout Michigan.

MISCELLANY

- Detroit is nicknamed **"Motor City."** The "big three" manufacturers, Ford, General Motors, and Chrysler, are still headquartered in the state.

- The Upper Peninsula's **copper rush** of the mid-1800s created more fortunes than the California gold rush.

- Some 30 **mastodon footprints**—the longest and most intact trackway of its kind— were unearthed near Saline.

- Stanton Township hosts **one of the largest Finnish populations** in the U.S.; nearby Hancock is also the home to Finlandia University (also known as F.U.).

- In 1866, Detroit pharmacist **James Vernon** created his own ginger ale, considered one of the nation's oldest sodas.

- **Holland** was founded by Dutch Americans in 1847. The town is known for its spring tulip festival and its Dutch windmill, the DeZwaan.

- Michigan is the only state that is made up of **two peninsulas**.

- **Chlorastrolite**, the state gem also known as the Isle Royale greenstone, is found in the Keweenaw Peninsula.

- **One of the world's largest cement manufacturing plants** is in Alpena.

- In 1974, **Gerald Ford** became the first— and so far only— U.S. president from Michigan. Although born in Nebraska, Ford grew up in Grand Rapids and attended the University of Michigan.

- Michigan has the third highest concentration of **electrical engineers** in the U.S.

- Martin Luther King, Jr., read an early version of his "I Have a Dream" speech during the **Detroit Walk to Freedom** on June 23, 1963—two months before the famed Lincoln Memorial speech.

- Local lore says that **Ann Arbor** was named after Ann Allen and Mary Ann Rumsey, the wives of the University's founders, John Allen and Elisha Walker Rumsey.

- The state reptile is the **painted turtle**.

- Michigan ranks sixth in the nation for **patent awards**.

- Grand Rapids' 24-foot (7.3 m) **Leonardo da Vinci horse**—called "Il Cavallo"—is the largest equestrian bronze sculpture in the Western Hemisphere.

▶ RARE BIRD

One of the rarest birds in North America nests only in Michigan (and adjacent parts of Wisconsin and Ontario). The gray-and-yellow Kirtland's warbler breeds in young jack pine forests. It has suffered from loss of habitat due to deforestation for decades, but recent conservation efforts spurred an impressive surge in the warbler's population, bumping the bird off the Endangered Species list.

BY THE NUMBERS

20 the number of chandeliers in Lansing's capitol building, each originally lit by gas

1,450,000 estimated number of trees in Ann Arbor, also known as "Treetown"

3 MINUTES 45 SECONDS the length of the world's largest toy lightsaber battle, featuring 3,889 participants during the first intermission of a Kalamazoo Wings hockey game

10.76 HEIGHT IN FEET (3.28 M) OF THE WORLD'S BIGGEST SNOWBALL, FORMED IN HOUGHTON

4 the number of counties (Iron, Dickinson, Gogebic, and Menominee) that are in the Central Time Zone. All others are in the Eastern Time Zone.

7,000 the size in acres (2,833 ha) of the world's largest limestone quarry, near Rogers City

4 THE NUMBER OF FLAGS THAT HAVE FLOWN OVER NILES, MICHIGAN: FRENCH, ENGLISH, SPANISH, AND AMERICAN

80% of North America's surface freshwater supply is contained in the Great Lakes.

12,000,000 the size in cubic feet (339,802 m³) of Detroit's Masonic Temple, the largest in the world, which houses a 4,000-seat auditorium

7 the weight in tons (6.4 t) of the 55-foot-tall (16.8 m) Cross in the Woods, in Indian River, one of the largest crucifixes in the world

112°F (44°C): the highest recorded temp in Michigan, in Mio, on July 13, 1936

-51°F (−46°C): THE ALL-TIME COLDEST TEMPERATURE IN MICHIGAN, IN VANDERBILT, ON FEBRUARY 9, 1934

DESTINATION: MICHIGAN

- Stretches of sandy beach sit in the shadows of soaring bluffs at Sleeping Bear Dunes National Lakeshore, hugging Lake Michigan in the Lower Peninsula. Scale to the top of the South Manitou Island Lighthouse to take in sweeping views of the surrounding lake and lush landscape.

- Among the many museums to take in while in Detroit, the Dossin Great Lakes Museum features a fascinating look at model ships. Then hit the 135-year-old Detroit Institute of Arts in midtown, an impressive collection of works spanning centuries. And the nearby Detroit Historical Museum offers a deep (and fascinating) dive into the city's layered past.

- Embrace the craft brew culture on Grand Rapids' Beer City Ale Trail, which boasts more than 80 breweries (and more craft beer per square mile than almost anywhere else on Earth). Brewery Vivant, housed in a historic former funeral home, is an especially lively spot.

> ## THERE IS A GENTLENESS IN MICHIGAN THAT YOU JUST CAN'T REPLICATE.
>
> —Former governor Jennifer Granholm

- A few hours south of Sleeping Bear, find the postcard-perfect city of Saugatuck, home to sandy beaches and vineyards. While there, take a trip on *Diane*, a hand-propelled ferry, across the Kalamazoo River. In operation since 1838, it's said to be the only remaining chain-driven ferry in the country.

STARS ★ OF ★ THE ★ STATE

HENRY FORD

(1863–1947) An American businessman and founder of the Ford Motor Company, Ford is credited with pioneering the mass production system that made cars affordable for many people. Born in Springwells Township in Wayne County, Ford constructed his first steam engine at 15 years old. He went on to become the chief engineer at Thomas Edison's Illuminating Company while tinkering with engines, ultimately designing the Model T, which he introduced in 1908. Because of Ford's assembly line system, more cars were created in less time and with less labor—achieving his goal of building "a car for the great multitude" and ultimately revolutionizing the auto industry.

RECORD ★ SETTERS

When Cora Reynolds Anderson was elected to the Michigan House of Representatives in 1925, she became not only the first woman from the state to ascend to the position, but the first Native American woman ever to serve in a state legislature.

Michigan's agricultural outputs include:

- Dairy
- Dry edible beans
- Eggs
- Wheat
- Floriculture
- Honey
- Hops

Michigan's industrial outputs include:

- Medical devices
- Cybersecurity
- Carbon fiber
- Aerospace
- Automotive manufacturing

SPORTING CHANCES

- There are four major league professional sports teams, all based in Detroit: the Tigers (MLB), the Lions (NFL), the Pistons (NBA), and the Red Wings (NHL).

- A star football player at Grand Rapids South High School, future president Gerald Ford went on to play at the University of Michigan—and was later recruited by the Detroit Lions and the Green Bay Packers.

- Basketball star Earvin "Magic" Johnson hails from Lansing and played at Michigan State before going on to win five NBA titles with the Los Angeles Lakers in the 1980s.

- Michigan has had medal winners in every Summer Olympics except 1896 and gold medalists in all but four Summer Olympics.

- University of Michigan's "The Big House" football stadium is the largest in the country, with 107,601 seats. ▽

- The real-life "Gipper"—Notre Dame's first All American football player made famous by a 1940 movie starring Ronald Reagan—was from the town of Laurium.

- The Detroit Skating Club in Bloomfield Township is a prominent training center for the world's best figure skaters; Tara Lipinski, who became the youngest female to win the gold medal at the Olympic Games in 1998, skated there.

- From 1968 to 1985, Muskegon hosted the World Snurfing Championships, a predecessor to snowboarding.

- In 2010, "The Big Chill at the Big House" hockey game between the University of Michigan and Michigan State University in Ann Arbor had a crowd of 104,173, the largest confirmed audience for a hockey match.

- In 2021, 18-year-old runner Hobbs Kessler of Ann Arbor broke a 55-year-old U.S. under-20 record in the 1500 meters; he also competed in the U.S. Olympic Trials that year and made it to the semifinals.

MINNESOTA

★ ★ ★
"Star of the North"
★ ★ ★

CAPITAL: St. Paul **BIRD:** Common Loon **NICKNAME:** North Star State **ENTRY:** 1858

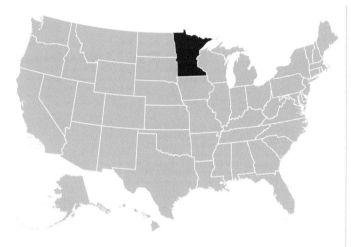

MN FACTS

- Minnesota is the 14th largest state in the United States.

- A small extension, known as the Northwest Angle, makes Minnesota the most northerly state of the lower 48.

- Archaeologists have traced human activity in the area to at least 9,000 or possibly 12,000 years ago.

- The Dakota tribe is credited for naming the state, drawing from the word *mnisota*, said to mean either "cloudy, muddy water" or "sky-tinted water."

- From the mid-1600s to the mid-1700s, the French claimed this region, before the U.S. acquired some of it through the Treaty of Paris in 1783 and the remaining area in the Louisiana Purchase in 1803.

- Its population ranks 21st in the country, with more than 5.7 million residents.

- Minneapolis and Saint Paul, are home to one of the highest concentrations of *Fortune* 500 companies in the country, including Target, Best Buy, General Mills, and Land O'Lakes. ▼

▶ **STATE FLOWER**
Pink and White Lady's Slipper
Cypripedium reginae

Also known as the showy lady's slipper, this pink-petaled flower grows mostly in Minnesota's swamps and woods.

1849

Minnesota's legal identity was created as the Minnesota Territory in 1849; it took another nine years for it to earn its statehood.

> **MINNESOTA IS A STATE OF PUBLIC-SPIRITED AND POLITE PEOPLE, WHERE YOU CAN GET A GOOD CAPPUCCINO AND EAT THAI FOOD AND FIND ANY BOOK YOU WANT AND YET LIVE ON A QUIET TREE-LINED STREET WITH A BACKYARD AND SEND YOUR KIDS TO PUBLIC SCHOOL.**
>
> —Garrison Keillor, host of *The Prairie Home Companion* radio show, which aired from 1974 to 2016

- In the 1850s, immigrants from Norway, Sweden, and Finland came to Minnesota in droves, helping the population to skyrocket.

- During the late 1800s, Minnesota was a world leader in farming, and Minneapolis led the world in flour production for five decades.

- Today, more than 26 million acres (10.5 million ha) of land—about half the state—is dedicated to farming.

- The port city of Duluth sits on the southwestern end of Lake Superior, the world's largest freshwater lake.

- Minnesota has 17.4 million acres (7 million ha) of forest land, or 22 percent of its total land area.

- At 2,301 feet (701 m), Eagle Mountain in Boundary Waters Canoe Area Wilderness is the highest point in Minnesota.

- The state's location in the upper Midwest lends itself to frigid winters and hot and humid summers.

- The lowest temperature ever recorded was –60°F (–51.1°C), in Tower, on February 2, 1996.

- The highest? 115°F (46°C), on July 29, 1917 in Beardsley.

- There are some 2,699 gray wolves living in Minnesota, the largest population outside of Alaska.

- Park Rapids' Lake Itasca is the primary source of the Mississippi River, which flows for 680 miles (1,094 km) in the state. ▽

▶ **STORY OF** THE NAME "The Gopher State," one of Minnesota's three official nicknames, has its origins in an 1858 political cartoon, which poked fun at state legislators who were pushing for a $5 million bill to build new railroads. The cartoonist, R.O. Sweeney, depicted the politicians as half-human, half-gopher, likely a rib to them for being a nuisance, as those animals were mostly viewed back then. The cartoon was widely circulated and forever linked Minnesota to gophers.

STARS ★ OF ★ THE ★ STATE

JUDY GARLAND

(1922–1969) Born Frances Ethel Gumm in Grand Rapids, Garland was the daughter of a vaudeville couple who owned a small theater. She was 13 when she signed a movie contract with MGM, and 16 when she landed the iconic role as Dorothy in the film *The Wizard of Oz*, for which she received a special Academy Award. Garland's legacy lasts in her hometown, which offers tours of her childhood home, a museum with an extensive collection of memorabilia, and two festivals honoring the actress.

▶ KEEPS THE DOCTOR AWAY

Next time you bite into a Honeycrisp apple, you've got a Minnesotan to thank. The winter-hardy fruit—a cross between the Macoun and the Honeygold—was first produced in 1960 as part of an apple-breeding program at the University of Minnesota.

WEIRD BUT TRUE

- Instead of "Duck, Duck, Goose," many Minnesotans play "Duck, Duck, Gray Duck."

- A museum in Rochester, Minnesota, hosts an annual creepy doll contest.

- "Spambassadors" show visitors around a museum devoted to Spam in Austin.

- St. Paul was originally called Pig's Eye.

- Northwest Angle is the only place in the United States besides Alaska that sits north of the 49th parallel, the geographic border dividing the U.S. from Canada.

- Minnesota has a state muffin, and it's blueberry.

- Lutefisk, a semi-translucent and gelatinous seafood dish, is a traditional delicacy in certain parts of the state.

- Iona Beach on Lake Superior is covered in smooth pink rocks that, in certain conditions, "sing" when tossed by the waves.

- There's a rare corpse flower at the University of Minnesota's conservatory; it smells like rotting meat when it blooms.

- According to local legend, those who step across the Mississippi at its source in Lake Itasca will live a long and happy life.

- A Lafayette woman holds the world record for the largest collection of cow-related items, at nearly 20,000 pieces.

- Each February, hearty golfers play a tournament on frozen Lake Gull.

- Embarrass, Sleepy Eye, and Ball Club are all towns in Minnesota. ■

- In 1900, the **Mesabi Iron Range** was the largest iron-mining area in the world.

- Today, nearly **75 percent of the iron ore produced in the United States** is mined in Minnesota.

- Between two and 10 billion pounds (0.9 to 4.5 billion kg) of manganese—used to make aluminum and steel, and found in batteries—is located in the **Cuyuna Range** near Emily.

- The *Mary Tyler Moore Show* was set in Minneapolis; today a bronze statue of the actress greets passersby on Nicollet Avenue in the city.

- At 60,000, the **Hmong population** in Minnesota is one of the largest in the country, with the majority living near St. Paul.

- Built in 1855, the **Father Louis Hennepin Bridge** in Minneapolis was the first bridge to span the Mississippi River.

- Minneapolis has a thriving drama scene, with **three century-old theater houses** on Hennepin Avenue: the Orpheum, the Pantages, and the State theaters. There is also the Guthrie Theater, which is the largest regional playhouse in the country.

- From 1999 to 2003, former professional wrestler **Jesse "The Body" Ventura** served as governor of Minnesota.

- The **Minneapolis Sculpture Garden** is the largest facility of its kind in the U.S. with more than 40 larger-than-life installments, including the famed "Spoonbridge & Cherry," a 50-foot-long (15.2 m) spoon holding a cherry.

- Nine Yankee Stadiums could fit inside Bloomington's **Mall of America**, which encompasses 4.2 million square feet (390,193 sq m).

- Over 30,000 Minnesotans are employed by the **state's forest products industry**.

▲ PAUL AND BABE

In Bemidji, there are giant replicas of Paul Bunyan and Babe the Blue Ox that are nearly as tall as a two-story building. The pair have been on the National Register of Historic Places since 1988.

BY THE NUMBERS

6 number of nationally designated recreation areas in Minnesota, including Voyageurs National Park, North County National Scenic Trail, and Pipestone National Monument

44,926 length in miles (72,301 km) of Minnesota's shoreline, all consisting of lakeshore

1952 the year of the first successful open-heart surgery, performed on a five-year-old girl by doctors at the University of Minnesota

12 DIAMETER IN FEET (3.7 M) OF THE WORLD'S LARGEST BALL OF TWINE ROLLED BY ONE MAN, WHICH IS ON DISPLAY IN DARWIN

21 number of endangered or threatened species with habitats in Minnesota, including the rusty patched bumble bee, the state bee

60 number of barns adorned with painted quilt squares around Caledonia, dubbed the "Heart of Quilt Country"

70 AVERAGE ANNUAL SNOWFALL IN INCHES (178 CM) ALONG THE LAKE SUPERIOR SNOW BELT. THE SOUTHWEST PART OF THE STATE RECEIVES A FAR LESS SNOWY 36 INCHES (91 CM) PER YEAR.

8 the total length in miles (13 km) of the skyway system in downtown Minneapolis, the world's largest continuous indoor network of pedestrian pathways

2,125.04 miles (3,420 km) covered in 24 hours on a snowmobile by Willie Ewing of Becker, a world record for driving the farthest distance on a snowmobile in one day

1,600,000 number of Scandinavian Americans living in Minnesota—more than a quarter of the state's entire population

AL AK AS AZ AR CA CO CT DE FL GA GU HI ID IL IN IA KS KY LA ME MP MD MA MI **MN** MS MO MT NE NV NH NJ NM NY NC ND OH OK OR PA RI SC SD TN TX VI UT VT VA DC WV WI WY

DESTINATION: MINNESOTA

- Voyageurs National Park in International Falls is one of a handful of water-based national parks in the continental U.S. Containing some 84,000 acres (33,994 ha) of water along the Minnesota and Canadian border, there are four major lakes and other waterways within the park. In the warmer months, many visitors stay in houseboats, a novel way to explore this unique area.

- Sip on "whiskey for Vikings" at Vikre Distillery, which serves up different interpretations of aquavit, a nod to the area's strong Scandinavian roots. Made with malted barley and aged in cognac barrels, Vikre's award-winning spirit is an interpretation of the ancient Norsemen's spirit of choice.

- Held each August, the Minnesota State Fair in St. Paul is one of the largest and best-attended events of its kind in North America, attracting two million visitors annually. Also known as the "Great Minnesota Get-Together," the fair is noted for its agricultural exhibits, fairway rides, fried food (think fried olives on a stick and Spam burgers), and major musical acts.

- At the intersection of 38th Street and Chicago Avenue in Minneapolis sits a memorial for George Floyd, whose murder sparked worldwide protests over the treatment of Black people and racial minorities during the summer of 2020. Now known as George Floyd Square, the area remains a gathering place for people to pay their respects and a space for art installations inspired by and dedicated to Floyd, including murals and sculptures.

- Let your curiosity for all things eagles take flight at the National Eagle Center. Located on the banks of the Mississippi River in Wabasha, this state-of-the-art center offers wild eagle viewing, interactive exhibits, and a glimpse at the resident eagles, who star in a live program.

⚠ LAND OF LAKES
Known as the Land of 10,000 Lakes, Minnesota has 14,380 lakes that are over 10 acres (4 ha).

STARS ★ OF ★ THE ★ STATE

PRINCE
(1958–2016) An international sensation with seven Grammys and more than 150 million records sold worldwide, Prince (born Prince Rogers Nelson in Minneapolis) was a proud Minnesotan. In 1977, he recorded his first album, *For You,* at the Sound 80 studios—now called Orfield Labs—in Minneapolis. He was known to pop into nightclubs and music venues around the city and play, and his famed film *Purple Rain* featured the Minnesota River. Later in his career, Prince built an estate in Chanhassen, which he named Paisley Park after one of his songs. The sprawling home, which sits on nine acres (3.6 ha) of land, is now a museum highlighting Prince's life and career, as well as a recording studio and concert venue.

SPORTING CHANCES

- Surfing in the winter, when the winds whip up bigger waves, is a popular pastime on Lake Superior.

- Thirteen of the 20 U.S. players who played in the famed "Miracle on Ice" hockey game during the 1980 Olympics were born in Minnesota, and nine of them attended the University of Minnesota.

- Minnesota has professional sports franchises in all the major sports leagues: the Twins (MLB); the Vikings (NFL); the Timberwolves (NBA); the Lynx (WNBA); the Wild (NHL); and the United (MLS).

- The Vikings were the first NFL team to appear in four Super Bowls (1970, 1974, 1975, and 1977), but they've never won.

- The Twins have won two World Series championships, in 1987 and 1991.

- Bloomington and Minneapolis are the farthest north latitude cities to ever host a World Series game.

- The common loon, the state bird, serves as the mascot for the Minnesota United Football Club.

- Minnesota is known as the "Hockey State" and is home to the U.S. Hockey Hall of Fame, located in Eveleth.

- Launched in 1999, the Minnesota Vixen is the longest continuously operating women's American football team.

- The Metrodome in Minneapolis is the only stadium in the country to host a World Series, a Super Bowl, and an NCAA Final Four Basketball Championship.

- The University of Minnesota's mascot, a gopher, is named Goldy.

- When the University of Minnesota plays the University of Wisconsin, they compete for Paul Bunyan's axe—a six-foot-long (1.8 m) wooden trophy in the shape of an axe.

- Minnesotans make up the most resident anglers in the lower 48 states, as they regularly cast lines in the 18,000 miles (28,968 km) of rivers and streams.

- Minnesotans have been competing in the Winter Olympics since 1920; that year hockey player Tony Conroy of St. Paul scored 10 goals against Switzerland, setting an Olympic record.

- Jessie Diggins (one of the first Americans to win gold in cross-country skiing) and Lindsey Vonn (the first American woman to win gold in downhill skiing) grew up in Afton and Burnsville, respectively.

- Cindy Nelson, a four-time Olympian and the first U.S. skier to win a downhill World Cup, in 1974, grew up skiing at the Lutsen Ski Area (now called Lutsen Mountains).

- In 1936, two Minnesota brothers created "Shipstads and Johnson Ice Follies," the first traveling ice skating show in the world. The show was eventually sold and became "Disney On Ice."

Minnesota's agricultural outputs include:

- Minnesota is the world's largest cultivated wild rice producer, producing more than seven million pounds (3.2 million kg) annually.
- Corn
- Soybeans
- Hay, wheat, and other grains
- Dairy
- Cattle and calves
- Pork
- Every year, Minnesota turkey farmers raise more than 40 million birds, consistently ranking the state number 1 in U.S. turkey production.

Minnesota's industrial outputs include:

- Mining (iron ore, granite, sand, gravel, peat)
- Manufacturing
- Energy production

RECORD ★ SETTERS

Between 2021 and 2022, Mark Vande Hei of Eden Prairie spent 355 days on the International Space Station, setting a record for the longest ever space flight by an American astronaut.

MISSISSIPPI

★ ★ ★

"By Valor and Arms"

★ ★ ★

CAPITAL: Jackson **FLOWER:** Magnolia **NICKNAME:** Magnolia State **ENTRY:** 1817

MS FACTS

- The population is 2,940,057.

- Mississippi was the 20th state in the nation and is the 31st state by size.

- Until the expansion of white colonists into the area, the region's main inhabitants were the Choctaw, Natchez, and Chickasaw. Only the Mississippi Band of Choctaw are federally recognized.

- In 1682, French explorers claimed the region. As it was already inhabited by the Natchez—and had been since around A.D. 700—tensions grew, especially in response to the British and French subjugation of both Natchez and African enslaved people.

- For the first half of the 19th century, Mississippi was the country's leading producer of cotton.

- Beginning in 1811, steamboats—designed to traverse shallow waters and move against currents using steam power—became the river's most successful form of transportation. Originally used for trade, the boats became gambling houses, racing vessels, and theaters. ▼

▶ STATE WATERFOWL

Wood Duck

Aix sponsa

Though the state bird is the mockingbird, the state also has an official waterfowl. Unlike many other ducks, the wood duck nests in tree holes.

1897

Born near Meridian in 1897, James "Jimmie" Rodgers was a renowned musician. Drawing largely from the blues, Rodgers incorporated a yodel and simplicity in his songs that earned him a reputation as the "father of country music."

> ## [THE MISSISSIPPI VALLEY IS] AS REPOSEFUL AS A DREAMLAND, NOTHING THIS-WORLDLY ABOUT IT ... NOTHING TO HANG A FRET OR A WORRY UPON.
>
> —Author Mark Twain

- In 1902, President Theodore Roosevelt took a hunting trip to Onward. There, members of his group located a black bear, tied it to a tree, and urged the president to shoot it. Roosevelt, viewing this as unsportsmanlike, refused. Although the bear was ultimately killed, the story still spread across the nation, delighting Americans. Soon, a toymaker in New York created a stuffed bear, dedicated it to the president, and (with Roosevelt's consent) called it a "Teddy Bear."

- In 1962, James Meredith became the first student to desegregate the University of Mississippi.

- The Mississippi Delta region was originally settled by Indigenous tribes such as the Natchez. It later became the site of white-owned plantations and their enslaved Black laborers. The Reconstruction period saw a population shift due to "white flight" and the arrival of Jewish, Chinese, Italian, and Syrian immigrants. The clashes and combinations of cultures created unique developments in food, customs, literature, and music, including the origins of the blues and rock and roll.

- The Stennis Space Center is NASA's largest rocket engine testing complex.

- Both a natural and a farmed resource, catfish have been a Mississippi dietary mainstay for centuries.

- The state ranks third in U.S. sweet potato production and second in acreage.

- Born in Clarksdale, "King of Soul" Sam Cooke combined gospel, pop, and rhythm and blues to create legendary songs such as "You Send Me" and "A Change Is Gonna Come."

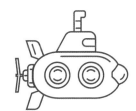

SINK ANOTHER ROUND

During Prohibition, a group of local men created a homemade submarine and used it to smuggle moonshine.

IDA B. WELLS-BARNETT

Born enslaved in Holly Springs in 1862, Wells was a preeminent journalist and activist. She played a pivotal role in the anti-lynching crusade, an effort to end the barbaric and widespread murders of Black people. Despite attacks on her offices and numerous death threats, Wells continued to report on and analyze lynching, sometimes going undercover to do so. Wells remained a passionate activist her entire life, helping to found the NAACP in 1909 and campaigning for women's suffrage in 1913.

STARS ★ OF ★ THE ★ STATE

OPRAH WINFREY

(b. 1954) Oprah Winfrey is a producer, actress, global media leader, and philanthropist. Born in Kosciusko, Winfrey overcame an extremely difficult childhood to become a local news anchor by the age of 19. In 1977, she made the switch to talk-show television, and by 1985 was the host of *The Oprah Winfrey Show*. A smash hit, the show reached more than 40 million viewers weekly and was licensed in 150 countries. Winfrey went on to act in multiple films, launch her own magazine, create a widely influential on-air book club, and founded the Oprah Winfrey Network (OWN). She also became a notable philanthropist, awarding hundreds of grants through the Oprah Winfrey Foundation and the Oprah Winfrey Leadership Academy Foundation for Girls in South Africa. Winfrey was awarded the Presidential Medal of Freedom in 2013.

Mississippi was the first state to approve Prohibition, which made it illegal for anyone to make, sell, or transport alcohol.

WEIRD BUT TRUE

- Found in the Delta, a Koolickle is a pickle marinated in Kool-Aid.
- In the early 1900s, Girls' Tomato Clubs taught young southern women how to can and preserve tomatoes.
- A camel named Douglas served with the local infantry during the Civil War.
- The city of Olive Branch is home to the largest bonsai nursery in the U.S.
- There are towns in Mississippi named Alligator, Mhoon Landing, and Panther Burn.
- Sports fans ring cowbells during Mississippi State games.
- Some people in the region put peanuts in their Coke.
- A chupacabra—a mythical monster—sighting turned out to be a coyote with mange. ▪

MISCELLANY

- The state has the largest percentage of population that identifies as **religious**.
- Though he is often associated with Tennessee, **Elvis Presley** was born in Tupelo in 1935.
- The state fossil is the **prehistoric whale**.
- **Mound Bayou**, a small town in the Delta, was originally founded in 1887 by freedmen Isaiah T. Montgomery and Benjamin T. Green as a haven for other formerly enslaved people.
- The state stone, **petrified wood**, is actually a fossil.
- Pioneering blues musician **Robert Johnson** was so talented that local rumors arose that he had "sold his soul to the Devil" in order to gain his otherworldly skills.
- The state song is **"Go, Mississippi."**
- The state reptile: the **American alligator**.

- **Tennessee Williams**, a playwright who won the Pulitzer Prize for *A Streetcar Named Desire*, was born in Columbus. ▲
- The state takes its name from the Mississippi River through a French derivation of an Anishinaabe name: **"Misi-ziibi,"** which means "Great River," which was turned into the French **"Messipi."**
- The city of Corinth is known for its local culinary creation: the **slugburger**. Made from ground beef and a starch, the slugburger is deep fried and takes its name from a slang term for its original cost: a nickel.
- The region features a variety of slow-cooked meats. **Smoked pulled pork** can be found with a variety of sweet or tangy sauces.
- People from MS are called **Mississippians**.
- Leland is known as the "birthplace" of **Kermit the Frog**.
- Found in the Mississippi Sound and nearby waters, the **bottlenose dolphin** is the state water mammal.
- In 1963, **Dr. James Hardy** and his team performed the first successful human lung transplant at University Hospital in Jackson.

◄ STORY OF THE SOUND

Birthed in the Mississippi Delta, the blues were created by enslaved Africans and their descendants. Enslaved singers and sharecroppers merged traditional West African chants and spirituals with revivalist hymns and work songs, innovating "blue notes" that were not on the standard scale. Notable artists such as Charley Patton, Bo Carter, and Carey Bell pioneered the sounds, performing solo and relying on guitars and harmonicas. In the early 1900s and beyond, legendary musicians such as B.B. King (pictured), Albert King, Eddie Boyd, Jessie Mae Hemphill, Robert Johnson, Jimmy Reed, and Otis Clay refined their own unique styles, sometimes adding piano or performing in groups. While the sounds morphed and eventually spread to Chicago, Detroit, and other cities, the meaning stayed the same: The blues were about sadness, longing, and deep emotion. Today, the Mississippi Blues Trail winds through the entirety of the state, featuring stops at the sites of iconic people and events. ▪

BY THE NUMBERS

87 mounds: the archaeological remains of a large Mississippian community first discovered at the Carson Mounds site

1.5 inches (3.8 cm): the average size of the southern devil scorpion

1848 the year the Mississippi School for the Blind, the country's first state-supported institution for blind people, was established

$243,000,000 WORTH OF MISSISSIPPI CATFISH SOLD IN 2021

148 years: the time that passed before the state officially ratified the 13th amendment, which had abolished slavery in 1865

66,000 men from Mississippi served in WWI.

16,461 the number of cases of yellow fever that occurred during the 1878 epidemic

2,350 miles (3,782 km): the length of the Mississippi River

1984 THE YEAR THE STATE PASSED THE 19TH AMENDMENT, WHICH HAD GRANTED WOMEN THE RIGHT TO VOTE IN 1920

- Created in 2011, the Mississippi Freedom Trail commemorates the sites of people and events that were instrumental in the ongoing fight for civil rights. The trail leads followers throughout the state to locations such as the site of Stokely Carmichael's "Black Power" speech.

- At the Natchez Trace Parkway, visitors can retrace a historic forest trail created by the Natchez and other Indigenous tribes that extends through Mississippi and other southeastern states for 444 miles (715 km).

- During the 1863 Battle of Vicksburg, Union general Ulysses S. Grant besieged the city for seven weeks before gaining control of the Mississippi River. Visitors to Vicksburg can learn more about the Civil War at Vicksburg National Military Park or the Old Court House Museum, or visit the antebellum McRaven home.

- Located on the Gulf of Mexico, the Gulf Coast is known for its plentiful beaches. The most popular set of beaches are located offshore on West Ship Island. Those looking for tranquility and quiet often head to the mainland's Pass Christian, while families seek out the water parks, fairgrounds, and casinos of Gulfport.

> ## THAT'S WHY I WANT TO CHANGE THINGS IN MISSISSIPPI. YOU DON'T RUN AWAY FROM PROBLEMS—YOU JUST FACE THEM.
>
> — Civil rights activist Fannie Lou Hamer

- The Great River Road, which traverses the length of Mississippi, follows the Mississippi River through 10 states and for 3,000 miles (4,828 km). Those who visit North America's second longest river might encounter otters, beavers, mountain lions, coyotes, hawks, eagles, and more.

- Jackson, the "City with Soul" features many stops along the state's Blues and Civil Rights Trails including the home of civil rights activist Medgar Evers, blues record labels, and more.

▲ BILOXI

Biloxi is known for its casinos, resorts, and golf championships. The city is also steeped in history: It was named for its earliest inhabitants, the Biloxi people; was home to Confederate president Jefferson Davis; and was the birthplace of ceramicist George E. Ohr.

STARS ★ OF ★ THE ★ STATE

CONWAY TWITTY

(1933–1993) Known for his resonant voice and songwriting skills, Conway Twitty was the preeminent country singer of the 1970s and '80s. Born Harold Lloyd Jenkins in Friars Point, Twitty was playing guitar by the age of four and had formed a band by age 10. In 1958, he catapulted to superstardom with his pop hit "It's Only Make Believe." His country roots and romantic ballads secured Twitty's status as a musical icon, earning him more than 50 number one hits such as "Hello Darlin'" and "After All the Good Is Gone." Twitty also made history with his duets with singer Loretta Lynn. He was inducted into the Country Music Hall of Fame in 1999.

MADE IN MS

Mississippi's agricultural outputs include:

- Chickens
- Eggs
- Cotton
- Catfish
- Soybeans
- Corn
- Cattle
- Timber
- Peaches
- Watermelons

Mississippi's industrial outputs include:

- Furniture production and upholstered products
- Oceangoing freighters and tankers
- Petroleum
- Electrical machinery
- Industrial machinery
- Paints and dyes
- Motor vehicles

SPORTING CHANCES

- Having earned All-American honors, former Ole Miss football player Michael Oher went on to play professionally in the NFL, winning Super Bowl XLVII with the Baltimore Ravens. Oher spent his early life in the foster care system and was periodically unhoused. His rise to athletic success was depicted in the Hollywood film *The Blind Side*. ▲

- Made up of 18 athletic teams representing Mississippi University, the Ole Miss Rebels—originally called the Mississippi Flood—first formed as a football team in 1893. The school's colors are navy blue and cardinal red, and the mascot is Tony the Landshark.

- Henry Armstrong, born Henry Jackson in Columbus, was the only professional boxer to hold world championship titles in three weight divisions at once.

- Born in Minter City, Lusia Harris-Stewart became a member of the first U.S. women's Olympic basketball team in 1976, and the following year became the first and only woman to be drafted by the NBA.

- Stickball, a forerunner of lacrosse that utilizes rackets, goal posts, and a soft ball, has been played by Choctaw people for hundreds of years.

- Born in Abbeville, Jennifer Gillom played and coached in the WNBA and was a member of the 1988 Olympic Gold Medal team in women's basketball. She has been inducted into both the Mississippi Sports Hall of Fame and the Women's Basketball Hall of Fame.

- Jacob Sanford "Jack" Cristil was a legendary sports broadcaster who served as the "Voice of the Bulldogs" at Mississippi State for 58 years. He was the 21-time winner of the Mississippi Broadcaster of the Year Award.

- Tailgating is an important tradition for Ole Miss sports fans. Fans gather (usually in a stadium parking lot) to cheer on their teams by grilling from the backs of their parked cars. ▪

RECORD ★ SETTERS

In 1870, Hiram Revels was elected to represent the state in the U.S. Senate, making him the country's first Black senator.

MISSOURI

★ ★ ★

"Let the Welfare of the People Be the Supreme Law"

★ ★ ★

CAPITAL: Jefferson City **FLOWER:** Hawthorn Blossom **NICKNAME:** Show-Me State **ENTRY:** 1821

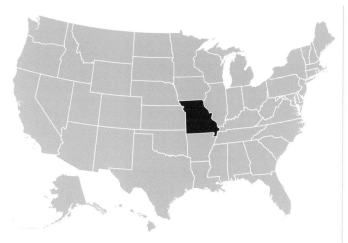

MO FACTS

- Covering 68,727 square miles (178,000 sq km), Missouri's size ranks 18th in the United States.

- Its population of 6,177,957 puts it as the 19th most populated state in the country.

- Warsaw, in the west central part of the state, holds the record for both the highest (118°F/47.7°C) and lowest (-40°F/-40°C) temperatures.

- Other than its neighbor Tennessee, Missouri is the only state to be bordered by eight different states.

- When it became a state in 1821, Missouri had a Native American population of around 20,000, with the most prominent tribes being the Kickapoo, Shawnee, Ioway, Otoe, Delaware, Niutachi, and Osage. However, by the 1830s, most Native Americans were forced to leave because of the Indian Removal Act.

- Missouri, named after the Missouri tribe, comes from the word *ouemessourita*, meaning "wooden canoe people," or "those who have dugout canoes."

- Missouri became a U.S. territory as a part of the Louisiana Purchase in 1803; it was admitted to the Union as a part of the Missouri Compromise in 1820, which granted Maine into the Union as a free state while allowing Missouri to enter without restrictions on slavery. The Missouri Compromise was ruled unconstitutional by the Supreme Court in 1857.

- In 1803, President Thomas Jefferson sent a secret message to Congress to procure $2,500 for what would become the Lewis and Clark expedition (1804–06). ◄

- In the early 1830s, Mormons migrated to the state seeking what they believed was the Garden of Eden. When violence broke out between Mormons and

▶ STATE BIRD

Eastern Bluebird
Sialia sialis

These blue-hued birds—said to be a symbol of happiness—can be spotted flying around the rolling Missouri countryside, especially during the spring.

1846

The 1846 lawsuit filed by Dred Scott, an enslaved man suing for his freedom (he lost in 1857), was one of the events that would lead to the Civil War.

FOR THY ELOQUENCE NEITHER CONVINCES NOR SATISFIES ME. I AM FROM MISSOURI. YOU HAVE GOT TO SHOW ME.

—Congressman Willard Duncan Vandiver, in an 1899 speech

non-Mormons, then governor Lilburn Boggs declared Mormons must be expelled from the state or "exterminated" if necessary. The order was upheld until 1976.

- A small herd of about 100 bison, the biggest mammal in North America, lives at Prairie State Park in Barton County.

- Today, 77 percent of the state's population identifies as Christian.

- Kansas City is the state's largest city (population: 509,297), with St. Louis second with some 286,578 residents.

- Farms cover about 63 percent of the state's total land area.

- Northwestern Missouri is the coldest and driest part of the state, and the climate becomes warmer and more humid moving farther toward the southeast.

- Ice storms, severe thunderstorms, flooding, and tornadoes are common in Missouri. The most destructive tornado to hit Missouri occurred in 1925 and stayed on the ground for more than three hours.

- Taum Sauk Mountain, in the St. Francois Mountains, is the state's highest

▲ GATEWAY ARCH

In 1804, the Lewis and Clark expedition set out from St. Louis to chart the Louisiana Territory, ultimately reaching the Pacific Ocean—sparking the city's nickname as the "Gateway to the West."

point at 1,772 feet (540 m). The lowest point is the St. Francis River at 230 feet (70 m) above sea level.

- More than 70 species of wild mammals live in Missouri, including opossums, woodchucks, beavers, coyotes, and bobcats.

- Missouri is split into four geographical regions: the Dissected Till Plains in the north; the Osage Plains in the west; the Ozark Plateau in the south; and the Mississippi Alluvial Plain in the southeast. ▪

STARS ★ OF ★ THE ★ STATE

LANGSTON HUGHES

(1902–1967)
James Mercer Langston Hughes, a Joplin-born poet, writer, and playwright, rose to prominence during the Harlem Renaissance, as his work honored the lives of Black people and spoke out against racial injustice. His works, such as *Jim Crow's Last Stand* and *Montage of a Dream Deferred*, which inspired early civil rights activists, made him one of the country's most significant writers of the 20th century. ▪

St. Louis's Anheuser-Busch, the maker of Budweiser beer, boasts the largest beer-producing plant in the country.

WEIRD BUT TRUE

- An 1812 earthquake near New Madrid caused the Mississippi River to run backward for several hours.

- The southeastern corner of Missouri is called the Bootheel, based on its distinct shape.

- Separate fires destroyed both the first and second capitol buildings in Jefferson City, in 1837 and 1911, respectively.

- A statewide referendum passed by Missouri voters on November 3, 1998, made it illegal to wrestle a bear.

- The putty-like substance on the roots of the Adam and Eve orchid, a wildflower that grows in Missouri, was used by the Native Americans as glue.

- The largest-ever game of Duck, Duck, Goose was played by 2,135 people in Rogersville in 2011.

- A Joplin pet food company celebrated its 10th anniversary by baking the world's biggest dog biscuit, which weighed as much as a black bear.

- No U.S. president is allowed inside the Gateway Arch due to security concerns.

▶ **STORY OF** THE MUSIC While the origins of blues music can't be pinpointed to an exact location, St. Louis has a large presence in the history of the genre. The city produced several musical stars, starting with Scott Joplin, who moved to the city in 1901 and popularized ragtime music, from which the blues evolved. In 1914, W.C. Handy was inspired to write "St. Louis Blues," which became one of the most popular blues songs in history, and the strains of piano, brass, and guitar could be heard in the city on any given evening. Over a century later, blues remains as ingrained in the culture of St. Louis as its famed barbecue. The National Blues Museum in downtown St. Louis tells the story of the blues from its origins to the still thriving genre that it is today.

MISCELLANY

- The **Underground Railroad** operated in Missouri in the 1840s and 1850s.

- The founder of **Hallmark** started off selling greeting cards out of a shoebox in Kansas City.

- Before he became president, **Harry Truman** owned a haberdashery in Kansas City.

- **Mark Twain's boyhood home** is in Hannibal, now a national historic landmark.

- The **University of Missouri** was the first college in the world to grant a journalism degree.

- American outlaw **Jesse James** was born in Clay County in 1847.

- There are more than 200 fountains in Kansas City, known as the **City of Fountains**.

- Most of the world's **Norton grapes**—the state grape—come from Missouri.

- Main Street, U.S.A. attractions at the **Disney theme parks are inspired by** downtown **Marceline**, where Walt Disney spent many years of his childhood.

- Kansas City's Country Club Plaza, opened in 1922, was the country's **first suburban shopping district**.

- Called the **"Cave State,"** Missouri has more than 6,000 caves, which are home to several species of bats.

- Ste. Geneviève National Historical Park has three of the five remaining **poteaux-en-terre (post in ground) homes** in North America.

- In May 1927, pilot **Charles Lindbergh** flew from Long Island, New York, to Paris, France—the first nonstop solo transatlantic flight in history—on a plane named the *Spirit of St. Louis*. What was behind the name? It was in honor of the St. Louis–based businessman who funded the construction of the plane.

T.S. ELIOT

(1888–1965) The only Missouri-born citizen to win a Nobel Prize, Eliot hailed from St. Louis, and was a leader in the modernist poetry movement. The grandson of William Greenleaf Eliot, the founder of Washington University in St. Louis, the young Eliot was part of an aristocratic family that strongly valued academia. Eliot became a poet while attending Harvard University; his breakout work coming in 1922 with *The Waste Land*, which is arguably among the most famous English-language poems of the 20th century. In 1948, he was awarded the British Order of Merit and the Nobel Prize for Literature, and in 1950 won a Tony Award for his play *The Cocktail Party*. Eliot's childhood home, built in 1904 in St. Louis, is now a city landmark.

▲ **GIANT EYEBALL**
There's a giant eyeball on display at Laumeier Sculpture Park in St. Louis.

BY THE NUMBERS

1904 THE YEAR OF THE WORLD'S FAIR IN ST. LOUIS, ALSO KNOWN AS THE LOUISIANA PURCHASE EXPOSITION, WHICH BROUGHT AN INTERNATIONAL CROWD TO THE CITY FOR THE FIRST TIME

105 the age of Plattsburg Judge Albert R. Alexander when he retired, making him the oldest serving judge in history

15,000,000 the number of acres (6.1 million ha) of tallgrass that used to cover the state. Today, you can only see the grass—which can grow high enough to cover a horseback rider on a horse—in Prairie State Park.

12 FEET **6** INCHES the length (3.8 m) of the beard of Pike County's Valentine Tapley, who didn't shave from 1860 until he died in 1910 as a protest to Abraham Lincoln's presidency

67 the number of plant and animal species living in Missouri that are considered endangered, including the gray wolf and the cold-water crayfish

20 the height in feet (6 m) of the world's largest chess piece, found at the World Chess Hall of Fame in St. Louis

65,000 THE MAXIMUM NUMBER OF VISITORS WHO FLOCK TO BRANSON ON A GIVEN DAY. THE CITY IS CONSIDERED A "RUBBER TIRE" DESTINATION SINCE MOST PEOPLE ARRIVE VIA VEHICLES, RVS, AND TOUR BUSES.

6 the minimum height in feet (1.8 m) required to be a part of the famed Budweiser Clydesdale horses, which live in a brick and stained-glass stable on the 100-acre (40 ha) Anheuser-Busch Brewery complex in St. Louis

8 FEET **11.1** INCHES the height (2.72 m) of the world's tallest man, Robert Pershing Wadlow of Alton, Illinois, a suburb of St. Louis, Missouri

171

DESTINATION: MISSOURI

- Perched on the Lake of the Ozarks shoreline, Ha Ha Tonka State Park is packed with scenic splendor, from caves to cliffs and sinkholes to freshwater springs. Camping, hiking, fishing, and boating are popular activities among visitors.

- Four herds of wild horses roam throughout the 80,000 acres (32,374 ha) of Ozark National Scenic Riverways. Believed to be descendants of Depression-era horses whose farmers turned them loose when they couldn't afford to feed them, the elusive equines are federally protected.

- Springfield is recognized as the official "birthplace of Route 66." It also features the immersive Wonders of Wildlife National Museum & Aquarium, the Fantastic Caverns (a tram tour allows you a front-row view of the ancient underground formations), the acclaimed Dickerson Park Zoo, and more.

- Take a spin on the 240-mile (386 m) Katy Trail, a bike path spanning the state.

- Going to Kansas City? Don't miss out on sampling more than 100 barbecue restaurants, featuring the regional style of slowly smoked, dry-rubbed meat drizzled in tomato-molasses sauce that originated in the city in the early 20th century.

- The Bonne Terre Mine is a marvel: Once the world's largest producer of lead ore, it has since flooded and can now be taken in via boat, foot, or underwater. With 100 feet (30.5 m) of visibility, Bonne Terre's Billion Gallon Lake is a scuba diver's dream.

- Music fans flock to Branson, the "Live Entertainment Capital of the World," where there are more theater seats than in New York City's Broadway Theater district.

- Missouri's fertile ground lends itself to an impressive number of vineyards, seven of which are showcased on the 30-mile (48 km) Hermann Wine Trail near the center of the lush Missouri Rhineland.

- In St. Louis, the must-see sites include the Old Courthouse, the historic Old Cathedral, Busch Stadium, and, of course, Gateway Arch National Park.

STARS ★ OF ★ THE ★ STATE

MAYA ANGELOU (1928–2014)
Born Marguerite Johnson in St. Louis, Angelou was an author, poet, historian, songwriter, playwright, dancer, stage and screen producer, director, performer, singer, and civil rights activist. Famous for writing seven autobiographies, most notably the best-selling *I Know Why the Caged Bird Sings*, she spoke at the inauguration of President Bill Clinton in 1993 and received the Presidential Medal of Freedom in 2010. Also a documentarian and filmmaker, Angelou is considered Hollywood's first Black woman director, and the Maya Angelou quarter, issued in 2022, is the first U.S. coin honoring a Black woman. Her birthplace in the Compton Hill neighborhood is a city landmark.

RECORD ★ SETTERS

In 1873, educator Susan Elizabeth Blow opened the first public kindergarten in the U.S. in St. Louis.

SPORTING CHANCES

- There are several major pro sports teams based in Missouri: the St. Louis Rams and the Kansas City Chiefs (NFL); the Kansas City Royals and the St. Louis Cardinals (MLB); the St. Louis Blues (NHL); and Sporting Kansas City (MLS).

- The Kansas City Chiefs won the Super Bowl in 1970 and 2020.

- The scoreboard at Arrowhead Stadium in Kansas City was the first to transmit instant replay.

- Collectively, the Royals and the Cardinals have made more than 20 World Series appearances.

- In 1944, two major league baseball teams from St. Louis—the Cardinals and the now defunct Browns—played each other in the World Series, dubbed the "Streetcar Series." The Cardinals won in six games.

- It's said that the University of Missouri's mascot was named for members of a militia known as the Tigers, formed to protect Columbia during the Civil War.

- St. Louis baseball star Timothy "Ted" Sullivan started the nation's first "farm system" for developing players. He's also credited with inventing the term "fans" (short for fanatic), based on his experience in Missouri.

- In 2013, Missouri State student-athlete Emily Beaver set the Guinness World Record for the fastest mile jogging while juggling three objects. Her time? 5:58.17.

- St. Louis was the site of the 1904 Summer Olympics, the first time the games took place in the U.S. They were held in tandem with the Louisiana Purchase Exposition, also known as the 1904 World's Fair.

- In 1984, Central Missouri became the first school in NCAA history to win national titles in the same year for both men's and women's basketball, a feat matched only by the University of Connecticut.

- The Kansas City Royals derive their name from a livestock show that the city has held since 1899.

- Gold medalists from the state include boxing brothers Leon and Michael Spinks (1976); tennis star Ken Flach (1988); and sprinter Janie Wagstaff, who was on the winning 4 × 100 meter relay in 1992.

▼ SO MANY MEDALS

Steve Cash of Overland, whose right leg was amputated due to osteosarcoma at age three, is a four-time Paralympian (2006, 2010, 2014, 2018) in sled hockey, earning three golds and one bronze.

MADE IN MO

Missouri's agricultural outputs include:

- Soybean
- Corn
- Cattle and calves
- Hogs
- Broiler chickens
- Chicken eggs
- Cotton

Missouri's industrial outputs include:

- Missouri is the top producer of mined lead in the United States, and it's mainly used in car batteries.
- Limestone
- Copper
- Silver
- Zinc
- Food, beverage, and tobacco products

MONTANA

★ ★ ★
"Oro y Plata"
(Spanish for "Gold and Silver")
★ ★ ★

CAPITAL: Helena **BIRD:** Western Meadowlark **NICKNAME:** Treasure State **ENTRY:** 1889

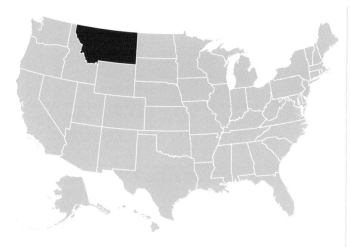

MT FACTS

- The population is 1,122,867.

- The 41st state to join the nation, Montana is the fourth largest in size.

- Before settlement by white explorers, the region was home to many Indigenous people. Today, there are seven federally recognized state tribes—the Blackfeet, Annishinabe Ne-i-yah-wahk (Chippewa-Cree), Confederated Séliš-Ktunaxa (Salish-Kutenai), Apsáalooke, Nakoda A'aninin, Nakoda Dakota, and Tsetsehesestahase Sotaahe—as well as the state-recognized Anishinaabe & Métis (Little Shell Chippewa Tribe).

- In 1876, as white settlers moved farther westward, the government demanded that all Sioux relocate to designated reservations. Under resistance leaders such as Tatanka Iyotake (Sitting Bull) and Tasunke Witco (Crazy Horse), alliances of Lakota Sioux, Northern Cheyenne, and Arapaho tribes refused to cede their lands.

- The state is known for its wide-open land and ranching lifestyle, but it is also a host to the finance, government, and trade industries. ▼

▶ STATE FLOWER

Bitterroot
Lewisia rediviva

For centuries, various Indigenous nations used this brightly colored plant for both trade and food, cooking it into dishes with berries or meat.

1864

From as early as 1864, prospectors unearthed gold, silver, and copper in Butte, earning Montana its nickname of the "Treasure State."

I AM IN LOVE WITH MONTANA. FOR OTHER STATES I HAVE ADMIRATION, RESPECT, RECOGNITION, EVEN SOME AFFECTION, BUT WITH MONTANA IT IS LOVE.

—Author John Steinbeck

- Lieutenant Colonel George Armstrong Custer attacked Tatanka Iyotake and his followers, who had gathered at the Little Bighorn River to celebrate the Sun Dance ceremony. Led by Tasunke Witco and inspired by Tatanka Iyotake's previous visions, the tribes defended themselves and destroyed Custer's battalion in what came to be known as the Battle of Little Bighorn, or Custer's Last Stand. ▶

- The rich grasslands and wide-open plains have drawn cowboys and cattle ranchers since the early 1800s. As new settlers poured into the area, the beef industry began to boom. Texan cattle operators drove their longhorn cattle up to Montana to feed, spurring the state's age of the open range.

- In 1912, a group of Hutterites—a religious group of the Protestant Reformation—established Spring Creek Colony. Today, they continue to practice their religion communally, living in rural colonies of 80 to 150 people.

- In the late 1800s, organizations meant to evict Chinese citizens sprang up in Butte, culminating in an anti-Chinese boycott. In response, immigrants Hum Fay, Quon Loy, and Dr. Huie Pock successfully won their suit against the discriminatory boycotts.

- High populations of beavers in Montana drew mountain men and trappers to the territory in the 1800s after the availability of beaver fur in the eastern regions had diminished due to over-hunting and land clearing. With high consumer demand for beaver fur hats, fur trading posts began to pop up across Montana.

- Venerated for his propensity to embrace the strange in unconventional projects such as *Eraserhead*, *Twin Peaks*, and *Mulholland Drive*, director David Lynch was born in Missoula in 1946.

- Though he was born in Ohio, billionaire Ted Turner makes his home at one of his four Montana ranches. A media owner known for his creation of TBS, CNN, Cartoon Network, and more, Turner is also an influential philanthropist devoted to fighting climate change and preserving the American West. ▪

STARS ★ OF ★ THE ★ STATE

GARY COOPER (1901–1961)

Gary Cooper was a popular actor of Hollywood's Golden Age, known for portraying the everyman hero. Born Frank James Cooper in Helena, he grew up as the son of a state supreme court justice. At the age of 23, Cooper left for Hollywood, intending to make a career as an illustrator. However, he instead found work as a stunt rider and cowboy extra. Cooper's big break came in 1929's *The Virginian*, and he went on to star in films such as *Morocco*, *Sergeant York*, and *High Noon*. Cooper became a beloved film star, known for his strong presence and roles as a brave-but-reluctant hero whose actions always reinforced his upright morals. Cooper won the Oscar for best actor in 1942, and was awarded the Special Academy Award for his career in 1961. ▪

MOOOVE OVER
Montana has more cows than people.

WEIRD BUT TRUE

- There is a state Cowboy Hall of Fame.
- A formation of rocks near Whitehall known as the Ringing Rocks gives off musical tones when struck.
- A glacier located in Custer National Forest is filled with millions of grasshoppers and locusts that have been frozen for centuries.
- A local dish called sheepherder hors d'oeuvres features saltine crackers topped with onion, cheese, and orange slices.
- In 2001, scientists discovered a 77-million-year-old mummified dinosaur, now known as Leonardo.
- When a fire burned most of the town of Havre, businesses decided to temporarily move underground—literally. Featuring a former opium den, restaurants, and more, the historical Havre Beneath the Streets can still be visited today.

△ TOUGH CROWD
In order to get their products certified as "bear-resistant," companies can send products to be "tested" by bears at Montana's Grizzly and Wolf Discovery Center.

BUT IF THERE BE NO PLACE FOR WILD BISON IN ALL OF MONTANA, THEN SURELY WE HAVE CROSSED A LINE BETWEEN THE LAST BEST PLACE AND THE ONCE BEST PLACE.

—Journalist Jim Bailey

◁ NOT A DOG
Sometimes called the poodle cat, the Selkirk Rex cat breed was developed in Montana.

MISCELLANY

- People from Montana are called **Montanans**.
- The state animal is the **grizzly bear**.
- There is a **state song**, a **state ballad**, and a **state lullaby**.
- The **Roe River** is the shortest river in the U.S., and one of the shortest in the world.
- **Flathead cherries** are a regional favorite.
- **Yogo sapphires**, known for their cornflower blue hue, can be found only in Montana.
- **"Our Lady of the Rockies"** is a 90-foot (27 m) statue of the Virgin Mary that overlooks Butte.
- The **mourning cloak butterfly** is one of the first butterflies to emerge in spring.
- Because **white buffalo** are considered sacred to several Indigenous groups, a white calf born in 1933 became a local symbol of conservation and recovery.
- The state is home to the **highest number of mammal species** in the United States.
- The state fossil is the **duck-billed dinosaur**.
- Helena native **Norman Holter** received a patent for the first heart monitor in 1965.
- According to legend, a rancher at **Fort Keogh** recorded a snowflake 15 inches (38 cm) wide and 8 inches (20 cm) thick in 1887.
- Montana's name is derived from the Spanish word for mountain, **montaña**.
- **Huckleberries** are frequently used in pies, pastries, and jams in Montana.
- **Montana agate** and **sapphire** are the state gemstones.
- The state grass is **bluebunch wheatgrass**.
- A breakfast food made from roasted wheat is known as **Cream of the West**.
- Montana has a state soil: the **Scobey series**.

RECORD ★ SETTERS
Founded in Butte in 1911, the country's oldest continuously running Chinese restaurant got its start as an infamous gambling den.

BY THE NUMBERS

12,799 FEET (3,901 M): THE ELEVATION OF GRANITE PEAK, THE HIGHEST POINT

28 million acres (11,331,198 ha): the vast expanse of state public lands

20 miles an hour (32 kph): the speed at which male bighorn rams can charge

21,026 the length in feet (6,409 m) of Fort Peck dam, located on the Missouri River

3.5 the width in miles (5.6 km) of a waterfall that existed some 10,000 years ago where Missoula is today

2,000 years: the approximate age of the state's oldest pictograph art, located at Bear Gulch

103°F (57.2°C): THE TEMPERATURE VARIATION EXPERIENCED OVER ONE DAY IN LOMA IN 1972. THE LOW WAS −54°F (−47.7°C) AND THE HIGH WAS 49°F (9.4°C).

48TH the rank in population density in the U.S.

$40,000,000 worth of silver uncovered during a blast at Granite Mine in 1875

An antiwar advocate and women's rights activist, Montana's Jeannette Rankin became the first woman to hold a U.S. federal government position in 1916.

DESTINATION: MONTANA

- Visitors flock to Glacier National Park for the incredible scenery, robust wildlife, and outdoor activities. The most popular destination is Going-to-the-Sun Road, a 50-mile (80.5 km) highway that bisects the park and offers spectacular views. Hikers enjoy the Highline Trail, a popular route that reaches dizzying heights.

- Helena was founded in 1864 as a mining town. Today, the city attracts fans of the outdoors for its location and picturesque views of Mt. Helena and Mt. Ascension. Helena also offers fine local dining, architecture, and history; it is home to five breweries, immersive wagon ride dinners, the classical capitol building, and the Gothic-style Cathedral of St. Helena.

- Although the majority of Yellowstone National Park is in Wyoming, 3 percent of its 3,472 square miles (8,992 sq km) and three of its five entrances are in MT. At the north entrance near Gardiner, the 1903 Roosevelt Arch marks the park's original access point. Near Cooke City, the northeast entrance leads to the Lamar Valley. And the west entrance, located near the town of West Yellowstone, is the busiest, offering premium access to the park's most famous geysers.

- In 1805, during their expedition to explore the newly acquired Louisiana Purchase, Meriwether Lewis and William Clark covered more territory here than in any other state. The expedition encountered buffalo and grizzly bears, charted parts of the Marias and Missouri Rivers, and stopped at a rock formation known as Pompey's Pillar, where William Clark carved his name into the stone, where it is still legible today.

- Local stops along the Lewis and Clark Trail include the Gates of the Mountains, a set of jutting cliffs so named by Lewis; Bozeman Pass, a mountain crossing located and recommended by Shoshone explorer Sacagawea; and more.

- The Grizzly & Wolf Discovery Center, located in West Yellowstone, is a nonprofit research center dedicated to wildlife conservation and public education. The center offers educational programs where visitors can view and learn more about the animals.

- With more than 5,800 acres (2,347 ha) of skiable land, Big Sky Resort is one of the largest skiing resorts in the U.S. Big Sky also offers a multitude of warm-weather activities such as white-water rafting, hiking, mountain biking, and fishing. ▪

▲ **STORY OF** THE PARK Known as the "crown of the continent," Glacier National Park covers around a million acres (404,686 ha) of wilderness. Formed by prehistoric glaciers, the park is an expanse of mountain ranges, alpine meadows, forests, and lakes, as well as 25 active glaciers that move and shrink. Evidence suggests that in addition to being home to abundant wildlife—including wolves, mountain goats, grizzly bears, mountain lions, and more than 300 species of birds—the park has been inhabited by humans for more than 10,000 years. In the 18th and 19th centuries, American settlers poured into the region to strike their fortunes in mining or beaver trapping. By the early 20th century, the region had become known less for its monetary value and more for its pristine wilderness and unparalleled beauty; it was established as the nation's 10th national park on May 11, 1910. ▪

SPORTING CHANCES

- ⚠ Mutton bustin' is a sport similar to bull riding where children ride or race sheep.

- Born in Billings, Dave McNally was a pitcher for the Baltimore Orioles who won 22 games in one season. *Sports Illustrated* has called him Montana's greatest athlete.

- Billings native Dan Mortensen is a legendary saddle bronc rodeo rider. He won six saddle bronc riding world championships, and in 1997 became the all-around world champion.

- Known for its world-class fly fishing, a fishing technique named for the insect-like lures used, Montana is also home to the International Federation of Fly Fishers in Livingston.

- Figure skater and Great Falls native Scott Davis secured the U.S. figure skating championship in both 1993 and 1994.

- Considered one of the greatest riflemen in the history of the United States, Lones Wigger, Jr., was a two-time Olympic champion.

- In 1902, 10 girls formed the Fort Shaw Indian Girls' Basketball Team.

- Born in Deer Lodge, Phil Jackson is a former NBA player and coach. As a player, Jackson won championships in 1970 and 1973. However, he is best known for his role as a coach, where he led his teams to a record-breaking 11 NBA championships.

- Born in Helena, Pat Donovan played for the NFL's Dallas Cowboys. He was named Montana's fourth greatest athlete by *Sports Illustrated*.

- Denise Curry is a Women's Basketball Hall of Fame member. Born in Fort Benton, she went on to win gold medals at the 1979 World Championships, 1983 Pan American Games, and 1984 Olympics.

- Born in Montana City, Scot Schmidt is an extreme skier known for his role in pioneering the sport of freeskiing. Schmidt became famous for his daring jumps and for tackling enormous mountains.

- Bozeman resident Conrad Anker is one of the world's greatest alpinists and mountaineers. In addition to three Mount Everest summits, Anker claimed first summits of six mountains across the world.

MADE IN MT

Montana's agricultural outputs include:

- Wheat
- Beef and veal
- Other grain products
- Animal feed
- Lentils
- Chickpeas
- Malt

Montana's industrial outputs include:

- Cigarettes
- Coal
- Copper
- Metal waste
- Machinery
- Civilian aircraft
- Plasma
- Silicon
- Lasers

STARS ★ OF ★ THE ★ STATE

EVEL KNIEVEL

(1938–2007) Born Robert Craig Knievel in Butte in 1938, Knievel's youth was marked by several run-ins with the law. (According to legend, it may even have been these cops who first gave Knievel his new name, dubbing him "evil Knievel.") After joining a stunt riding troupe in the 1960s, Knievel began a solo career which established him as a legendary daredevil famous across the U.S. for his death-defying motorcycle stunts. Instantly recognizable in his Americana-themed jumpsuits, Knievel performed more than 300 stunts, including a leap over the fountains at Caesars Palace in Las Vegas and a jump over 14 Greyhound buses in Ohio. Knievel died in 2007 at the age of 69.

NEBRASKA

★ ★ ★

"Equality Before the Law"

★ ★ ★

CAPITAL: Lincoln **BIRD:** Western Meadowlark **NICKNAME:** Cornhusker State **ENTRY:** 1867

NE FACTS

- The population is 1,967,923.

- Nebraska is the 15th largest state and was the 37th state to join the nation.

- The state is famed for its wide-open spaces. Major industries include finance, insurance, health care, and military and defense.

- Born William Frederick Cody, frontier soldier-turned-showman Buffalo Bill Cody staged the first showing of his soon-to-be-legendary (and infamous) Wild West show in Omaha in 1883.

- Born in Omaha in 1913, Gerald Ford served in the Navy as lieutenant commander during WWII. He was elected to Congress in 1948 and became the 38th president of the United States in 1974.

- The U.S. government established Fort Atkinson in 1820. The area became a popular route for the fur trade, and the fort remains a historical state park.

- Known for its pioneering history, today Omaha has become a top destination for festivals such as the Nebraska Balloon and Wine Festival, Cinco de Mayo, the Farnam Festival, and many more. ▼

▶ STATE FLOWER

Goldenrod
Solidago

Established as the state flower in 1895, goldenrod is a genus of more than 100 species of flowers known for their sunshine hue.

1898

Also known as the Trans-Mississippi and International Exposition, Omaha hosted a world's fair in 1898 that drew some 2.6 million visitors.

MY FIRST YEARS WERE SPENT LIVING JUST AS MY FOREFATHERS HAD LIVED—ROAMING THE GREEN, ROLLING HILLS OF WHAT ARE NOW THE STATES OF SOUTH DAKOTA AND NEBRASKA.

—Ponca chief Standing Bear

- In 1863, a farmer filed the first homestead claim for a plot of Nebraska land. The Homestead Act had been signed into law the year before by President Lincoln to encourage settlement of the western frontier.

- In 1877, after the U.S. government evicted the Ponca people from Nebraska, Chief Standing Bear successfully asserted his right to return to bury his son in *Standing Bear v. Crook*, becoming one of the first Indigenous people to be granted civil rights under U.S. law.

- Original inhabitants included the Hinono'eino (Arapaho), Cheyenne, Kansa, Lakota and Dakota, Missouria, Omaha, Otoe, Pawnee, and Ponca. Today, federally recognized nations include the Omaha, Ho-Chungra (Winnebago), Ponca, and Santee Sioux.

- A University of Nebraska military science instructor, John J. Pershing went on to command the American troops deployed to Europe in World War I. Pershing later served as U.S. Army chief of staff for three years.

- The popular Runza sandwich is a pocket-like dough bun stuffed with beef, onions, and cabbage.

- In 1923, Willa Cather received a Pulitzer Prize for her depiction of wholesome Nebraskan frontier life in the novel *One of Ours*.

- According to Nebraska lore, the Reuben sandwich was invented in 1925 by an Omaha grocer named Reuben Kulakofsky to feed a peckish group of late-night poker players.

- In the summer of 1931, hordes of grasshoppers decimated crops across the state.

- In 1948, Offutt Air Force Base became home to the Strategic Air Command (SAC). After SAC was decommissioned in 1992, U.S. Strategic Command (USSTRATCOM) was created in its stead.

▲ BUFFALO SOLDIERS

During the Civil War, some 10 percent of Union soldiers were Black volunteers. Upon the war's end, the government established its first Black regular regiments, one of which was at Fort Robinson. According to legend, these men—who served at the country's frontiers and acted as some of the first park rangers—became known as "Buffalo Soldiers" because of nicknames given by local Indigenous peoples.

STARS ★ OF ★ THE ★ STATE

JOHNNY CARSON

(1925–2005) An icon of late-night television, famed comedian Johnny Carson got his start in Nebraska. Born in Iowa in 1925, Carson relocated to attend the University of Nebraska following his Navy service during World War II. While there, Carson studied theater and began working for various radio stations. In the early 1950s, he moved to Los Angeles and soon helmed his own show, *The Johnny Carson Show*. In 1962, he began his 30-year stint as the host of *The Tonight Show*, where he influenced the course of American talk shows. He was awarded the Presidential Medal of Freedom in 1992. ▪

- Located in Alliance, a replica of Stonehenge is built entirely out of cars.
- Developed in Hastings, Kool-Aid is the official state soft drink.
- In 2018, Nebraska changed its tourism slogan to "Honestly, it's not for everyone."
- Taylor is populated in part by its "Villagers": life-size, black-and-white cutouts depicting residents through the decades.
- Plainview's Klown Doll Museum showcases more than 7,000 clown-themed items.
- Found in Boys Town, the world's largest ball of stamps is made of some four million canceled stamps.
- Omaha features a 13-foot (4 m) statue of a giant fork twirling spaghetti.
- A Cheese Frenchee = a deep-fried grilled cheese sandwich.

◢ BEACH, PLEASE

Central Nebraska has the largest spread of sand dunes in North America.

- Fans of the University of Nebraska's football team, the Cornhuskers, often wear corn-shaped foam hats to games.
- The popular drink "red beer" is beer mixed with tomato juice.
- In 1902, several reputable citizens in Alma reported being haunted by a ghostly woman clothed in black, whose origin remains a mystery.
- A company in Omaha offers storm-chasing tours, during which they follow severe weather such as tornadoes or hurricanes.

RECORD ★ SETTERS

In 1867, Congress overrode President Andrew Johnson, making Nebraska the only state to be admitted to the Union despite a presidential veto.

◢ PASS THE BUTTER

Butter sculpting, a local tradition, often involves carving life-size statues of people and animals out of butter.

MISCELLANY

- People from Nebraska are called "Nebraskans."
- Civil rights leader **Malcolm X** was born Malcolm Little in Omaha in 1925.
- Nebraska comes from the Oto word for **"flat water."**

- The state fish is the **channel catfish**.
- **Blue chalcedony** is the state gemstone.
- Nebraska has a state grass: **little bluestem**.
- The state rock is **prairie agate**.
- **Abundant natural resources** include the High Plains Aquifer,

corn, gas, oil, as well as some 385 soil series, some of which are naturally fertile for crops, and others of which are used for grazing.

- The state beverage is **milk**.
- **Mammoth** is the state fossil.

BY THE NUMBERS

100

MILES (161 KM):
THE DISTANCE A
VISITOR CAN SEE
FROM THE TOP OF
SCOTTS BLUFF

9,000,000+ THE NUMBER OF IRRIGATED
ACRES (3.6 MILLION HA) OF
LAND IN NEBRASKA

2.49
miles (4 km): the width
of the damage path left
by the Hallam tornado
in 2004

310 the length in miles
(500 km) of the
Platte River

6,000
years: how long it would take to naturally
refill the Ogallala Aquifer if it were drained

$200,000
THE VALUE OF GOLD
THAT TRAVELED
ALONG THE HISTORIC
385-GOLD RUSH BYWAY
DURING ITS HEYDAY

25 FEET **7** INCHES (4.4 m) the length of Archie, the
biggest mammoth fossil in the
world, discovered in Lincoln County

1874 the year Nebraskans
caught a glimpse of
Coggia's comet

60 miles an hour (98 kph): the speed at which
Pronghorn antelopes can run

In 1872, Nebraska became the first state to celebrate the holiday of Arbor Day by planting more than one million trees.

DESTINATION: NEBRASKA

- Omaha is home to a zoo, historic district, children's museum, a pedestrian bridge, and some of the world's largest locomotives.

- An iconic western landmark, Chimney Rock's ash, clay, and sandstone spire served to guide pioneers along the Oregon, California, and Mormon trails.

- Lincoln's many sights include Pioneers Park Nature Center, the state's capitol, and the Historic Haymarket District, as well as museums on roller skating, quilts, tractors, and more.

- Described as the "Pompeii of prehistoric animals," the 360-acre (146 ha) Ashfall Fossil Beds feature preserved fossil sites and ongoing archaeological digs.

- Campers, hikers, and picnickers will adore Indian Cave State Park, a park along the Missouri River known for its sandstone cave.

- The 800-foot-high (244 m) Scotts Bluff is a designated national monument that covers 3,000 acres (1,214 ha) of wilderness and is home to animals such as black-tailed prairie dogs, coyotes, and mule deer.

- Between late winter and early spring, some one million sandhill cranes stop in the Platte River Valley as part of their migration.

- Visitors to the University of Nebraska–Lincoln should be sure to check out the Dairy Store, where UNL student food scientists experiment with ice cream flavors daily.

- Since 1988, Dannebrog has celebrated Grundlovsfest, a Danish heritage festival featuring Danish pancakes, horse and buggy rides, a quilt show, a beer garden, and more.

- Each June, the National Pony Express Association begins their "re-ride," a 10-day re-creation of the Pony Express that begins in Missouri, moves through Nebraska, and ends in California.

- With a Pony Express station, turn-of-the-20th-century automobiles, and Buffalo Bill's saddle, Harold Warp Pioneer Village in Minden is an ode to Americana.

- Nearly driven to extinction by ranchers and hunters in the late 1800s, bison have made a comeback thanks to places like Fort Niobrara National Wildlife Refuge. Visitors can also see elk, deer, and more than 230 species of birds. •

▶ **STORY OF** LIFE ON THE PRAIRIE In 1862, to encourage Americans to settle newly acquired frontier lands, the government passed the Homestead Act. Under this act, American citizens and soon-to-be citizens could claim 160 acres (64.7 ha) of prairie and pay only the filing fee if they committed to farming it for five years. But the offer came with an undisclosed caveat: Life would be hard. Sod busters, as settlers came to be called, built their homes from tightly packed soil. People burned dried cow dung for fuel. Communities were isolated, and cultural differences between immigrants added difficulty. But settlers endured the hardships to form long-lasting communities that led to the Nebraska of today. •

> **WE WERE AT SEA—THERE IS NO OTHER ADEQUATE EXPRESSION—ON THE PLAINS OF NEBRASKA.**
>
> —Author Robert Louis Stevenson

HENRY FONDA

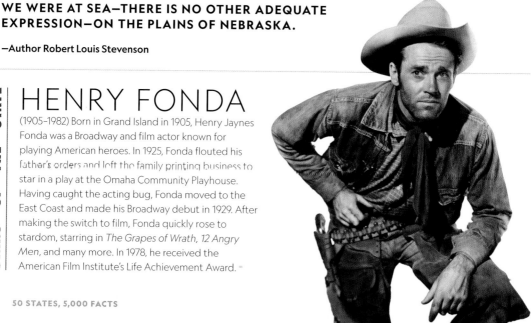

(1905–1982) Born in Grand Island in 1905, Henry Jaynes Fonda was a Broadway and film actor known for playing American heroes. In 1925, Fonda flouted his father's orders and left the family printing business to star in a play at the Omaha Community Playhouse. Having caught the acting bug, Fonda moved to the East Coast and made his Broadway debut in 1929. After making the switch to film, Fonda quickly rose to stardom, starring in *The Grapes of Wrath*, *12 Angry Men*, and many more. In 1978, he received the American Film Institute's Life Achievement Award. •

▲ REACH FOR THE STARS

Known as "Astro Clay," Clayton Anderson became Nebraska's first astronaut in 1998. He encourages others to never give up, citing that he himself applied to NASA 15 times before being accepted.

MADE IN NE

Nebraska's agricultural outputs include:

- Soybeans
- Corn
- Beef
- Grain products
- Sorghum
- Wheat
- Pork

Nebraska's industrial outputs include:

- Manufactured food products
- Gas
- Farming equipment
- Medications
- Insecticide
- Veterinary vaccines
- Fungicide

SPORTING CHANCES

- The youngest player to enter the Pro Football Hall of Fame, Gale Sayers grew up in Omaha. In addition to speed and evasion skills, Sayers is known for the depiction of his friendship with fellow player Brian Piccolo in the 1971 television movie *Brian's Song*.

- Born in Elba in 1887, Grover Cleveland "Pete" Alexander pitched for the Philadelphia Phillies, the Chicago Cubs, and the St. Louis Cardinals. He was known for his tricky, hard-to-hit pitches.

- Professional boxer and heavyweight champion Max Baer was a bright spot for many during the hard years of the Depression. Born in Omaha in 1909, he went on to also star in movies such as *The Prizefighter and the Lady*.

- Olympic wrestler, gold medalist, and National Wrestling Hall of Famer Rulon Gardner graduated from the University of Nebraska.

- Omaha native Bob Gibson briefly toured with the Harlem Globetrotters, but he signed with the St. Louis Cardinals as a pitcher in 1957. Famously, in a stretch of 95 consecutive innings, Gibson allowed only two runs.

- Originally called the Royals, minor league baseball team the Omaha Storm Chasers got their new name during a "name the team" contest in 2010.

- On top of being awarded 1995 Co-National Player of the Year, competing in the Olympics, and holding the University of Nebraska record for most kills in a four-set match, volleyball player Allison Weston is one of just seven UN players to have her jersey number retired.

- Established in Burwell in 1921, Nebraska's Big Rodeo was instrumental in gaining recognition for rodeo as a sport.

- Though the University of Nebraska athletic teams were originally known as the Old Gold Knights, they have been the Cornhuskers—often shortened to the Huskers—since 1902. Their mascots are now Herbie Husker and Lil' Red, though past iterations have included Corncob Man and Mr. Cornhead.

- UNL's Memorial Stadium can seat more than 85,000 fans, and in 2009 celebrated its 300th consecutive sold-out game.

NEVADA

★ ★ ★

"All for Our Country"

★ ★ ★

CAPITAL: Carson City **BIRD:** Mountain Bluebird **NICKNAME:** Silver State **ENTRY:** 1864

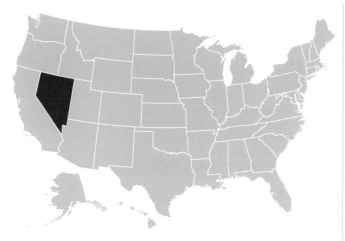

NV FACTS

- The seventh largest of the 50 states, but with a population of 3.2 million (28.7 people per square mile/11 per sq km), Nevada is one of the most sparsely populated.

- Federal or tribal land covers 87 percent of the state.

- Nevada is the driest state in the country in terms of annual average precipitation, which is only 10.2 inches (26 cm).

- The state's highest point, Boundary Peak, rises up to approximately 13,140 feet (4,005 m).

- Nevada ranks as the third-most seismically active state in the U.S.; there are several small earthquakes every day.

- The word "Tahoe" is a mispronunciation of the Washoe words for "the lake" (*Da ow*).

- Lake Tahoe, North America's largest alpine lake, is as deep as the Empire State Building is tall.

- Nevada has some 300 mountain ranges. The number of peaks that rise above 10,000 feet (3,048 m) is 134. ▼

▶ STATE FLOWER

Sagebrush
Artemisia tridentata

Big sagebrush can be spotted growing in the Nevada desert. True to its name, the grayish-green bush can grow to be up to 12 feet (3.7 m) tall in some spots.

1864

In 1864, Nevada became the second of two states added to the Union during the Civil War (the first being West Virginia) and became known as the "Battle Born State" as a result.

WHAT HAPPENS HERE, ONLY HAPPENS HERE.

—Las Vegas slogan

- Native American tribes, including the Washoe, Northern Paiute, Southern Paiute, and Western Shoshone have inhabited the area for thousands of years.

- The area was claimed by Spain in 1519 and later by Mexico in 1821. In 1848, the territory was ceded to the U.S. in the Treaty of Guadalupe Hidalgo.

- Mormon settlers were the first permanent non-Native residents, inhabiting the area now known as Genoa, where they built a trading post in 1851.

- The discovery of silver at the Comstock Lode mine brought an onslaught of settlers, sparking the creation of the Nevada Territory in 1861.

- Some 30 miles (48 km) southeast of Las Vegas, the Hoover Dam is the highest concrete arch dam in the United States at 726 feet (221 m) and was once the tallest in the world.

- Nearly 10,000-year-old petroglyphs, the oldest known rock art in North America, have been discovered outside of Reno.

- Today, 66 percent of residents are Christian (25 percent are Catholic), with 4 percent to 5 percent registered as Mormon.

▲ **STORY OF** THE FLAG It took some time to perfect the state flag—86 years to be exact. The flag's design has changed four times since 1905, most recently in 1991, after a Nevada legislative researcher discovered a clerical error from a 1929 bill approving a design for the flag. The problem? The word "Nevada" was set in the wrong place—it was somewhat oddly arranged around the silver star instead of below the sagebrush wreath. So the state legislature passed a new bill, this time moving the state's name beneath the star. It hasn't been touched since. ▪

- Following the 2018 midterm elections, Nevada became the first state in the U.S. with a female-majority legislature, with women holding 51 percent of the seats.

- Hoover Dam created Lake Mead, the nation's largest human-made reservoir, capable of holding some 28.9 million acre-feet of water (an acre-foot is equivalent to about 326,000 gallons [1.2 million L]). ▪

STARS ★ OF ★ THE ★ STATE

ANDRE AGASSI

(b. 1970) It's said that Las Vegas–born Agassi was serving a tennis ball by the age of two; by 17, he had won his first professional tournament. Known for his flashy fashion and charisma on the court, Agassi went on to win eight Grand Slam titles as well as a "career Grand Slam"— coming in first at least once in each of the four major tennis tournaments: Wimbledon, the Australian Open, the French Open, and the U.S. Open. Upon his retirement in 2006, Agassi and his wife, fellow tennis pro Steffi Graf, settled in Las Vegas, where he has a private nonprofit funding youth education. ▪

187

◀ TESTING GROUNDS

A vast portion of the Mojave Desert, 1,350 square miles (3,496 sq km), is designated as nuclear testing grounds and are legally uninhabitable.

Nevada was the first state to ratify the 15th Amendment to the U.S. Constitution, prohibiting the states and federal government from denying a citizen the right to vote based on "race, color, or previous condition of servitude."

WEIRD BUT TRUE

- In Death Valley, the kangaroo rat can live its entire life without drinking a drop of liquid.

- In the late 1800s, camels hauled salt and mining supplies in Virginia City.

- Reno is farther west than Los Angeles.

- A bathroom in a Las Vegas casino showcases a section of the Berlin Wall.

- Called the country's scariest motel, Tonopah's Clown Motel is located next to an old cemetery and is said to be haunted.

- The eight-foot-tall (2.4 m) bronze "toilet paper hero" statue outside of the Hoover Dam honors Alabam, a man who cleaned outhouses during the construction of the dam.

- Nevada is home to the micronation Molossia, located on 11 acres (4.5 ha) of land near Virginia City. Although not recognized by any government, it has its own post office, national bank, and space program.

- Modeled after the Pantheon of Rome, the Pershing County Courthouse is believed to be the only functioning round courthouse in the nation.

- After many reports of alien sightings along a stretch of State Route 375 between Las Vegas and Tonopah, the state renamed it Extraterrestrial Highway. ▼

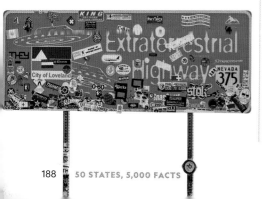

▲ HOLD YOUR HORSES

Some 43,000 wild horses roam throughout the state, with many concentrated in the Virginia Range between Virginia City and Reno.

MISCELLANY

- According to locals, the official pronunciation of the state is **Ne-VAD-uh** (with the second syllable rhyming with "mad") is the standard pronunciation, not Ne-VAH-duh (second syllable rhymes with "spa").

- In the 1930s, **Carson City** had a population of just 1,500 and billed itself as "America's Smallest Capital." Today, it has some 55,000 residents.

- The **coldest temperature** recorded in the state was -50°F (-45.5°C) in San Jacinto.

- The **hottest temperature** recorded in the state was 125°F

(51.6°C) in Laughlin, which is one of Nevada's lowest points at 605 feet (184 m) above sea level. Only two other places have recorded higher temperatures: Lake Havasu, Arizona (128°F/53.3°C) and Death Valley in California (134°F/56.6°C).

- The **cui-ui**, an endangered sucker fish that can live for 40 years, is endemic to Pyramid Lake near Reno.

- The **ichthyosaur** is the official state fossil.

- At some 6,500 feet (1,981 m), Lake Tahoe's **Rubicon Trail Lighthouse** has the highest elevation of any lighthouse in the country.

- The only scenic byway in the country that lies entirely within a tribal reservation winds through the **Pyramid Lake Indian Reservation**.

- Some 40 cars, vans, and trucks are on display in various artistic arrangements at the **International Car Forest** of the Last Church, just outside the town of Goldfield.

- One of the world's **oldest bristlecone pine trees**—estimated between 4,700 and 5,000 years old—grows in Great Basin National Park.

- Until 1903, Las Vegas was spelled **"Los Vegas"** to avoid confusion with Las Vegas, New Mexico.

Las Vegas

42,000,000+

visitors travel to Las Vegas each year

30 the height in stories of the Luxor Hotel and Casino, which features the brightest spotlight in the world atop its famed pyramid

150,000

HOTEL ROOMS ARE AVAILABLE IN VEGAS, MORE THAN ANY OTHER MAJOR CITY.

1930 the year the Pair-O-Dice Club— the first casino in Las Vegas— opened, one year before the state's legalization of gambling

288 THE NUMBER OF YEARS IT WOULD TAKE A PERSON TO SPEND ONE NIGHT IN EVERY HOTEL ROOM ON THE STRIP

$1 the cost to trademark the tourism slogan, "What Happens Here, Stays Here," which later evolved to "What Happens Here, Only Happens Here."

1,149 THE HEIGHT IN FEET (350 M) OF THE STRATOSPHERE, THE TALLEST FREESTANDING OBSERVATION TOWER IN THE UNITED STATES

50 the weight in tons (45 t) of the bronze lion outside MGM Grand, said to be the largest bronze sculpture in the Western Hemisphere

$13.4 billion: Nevada's annual casino revenues

15 LENGTH IN MILES (24 KM) OF NEON TUBES ON THE VEGAS STRIP, ALONG WITH 9,900,000 LIGHT BULBS

- Las Vegas has a little (or a lot) of something for everyone: From legendary nightlife to star-studded shows to swanky hotels and nonstop shopping, there's no lack of entertainment at any time of the day—or night.

- Seeking a bit of downtime while in Vegas? Hit Red Rock Canyon National Conservation Area, about 25 miles (40 km) west of the Strip. With a one-way 13-mile (21 km) scenic drive, hiking, and trails, it's a quiet place to get away from it all.

- Nevada's 600-odd ghost towns offer a glimpse into the past, when prospectors created pop-up settlements as they hit the nearby mines in the hopes of striking it rich. The dry climate has helped preserve some structures dating back 100 years.

- You can't enter Area 51, a top secret area of Nellis Air Force Range and Nevada Test and Training Range rumored to have housed the development of the first Stealth aircraft and alien UFO research facilities, but a drive down the nearby Extraterrestrial Highway offers plenty of alien-themed roadside stops.

- Death Valley National Park may mostly occupy California, but parts of this vast desert spill into western Nevada. A visit there in spring reveals spectacular wildflower blooms.

- The state's other national park, Great Basin, is in the eastern part of the state near Utah. There are 40 known caves to explore during the day; hit the park at night for prime stargazing.

▼ FLY GEYSER

Southwest of the Black Rock Desert is a six-foot-tall (1.8 m) brightly colored mound that spews boiling water in the air. Known as the Fly Geyser, this otherworldly landmark was closed to the public for two decades until the Burning Man Project bought the land and made it accessible to all. Today, Fly Geyser is a centerpiece of the Burning Man event, an annual nine-day gathering of thousands in the Black Rock Desert marked by spontaneous musical performances, elaborate costumes, huge art installations, and plenty of partying.

- Known as the "biggest little city in the world," Reno is home to several museums, such as the National Automobile Museum and the Nevada Museum of Art, as well as a pleasant river walk along the Truckee, lined with restaurants and galleries.

- Perched 5,000 feet (1,524 m) above sea level, Elko's Cowboy Country showcases the American West, complete with a cowboy museum and vast wilderness to explore. ▪

STARS ★ OF ★ THE ★ STATE

CARRIE DANN

(around 1932–2021) A Native American land rights activist, rancher, and leader of the Western Shoshone Nation, Dann dedicated her life's work to protecting ownership of ancestral lands in central Nevada. Born in Crescent Valley and raised on her father's 800-acre (324 ha) ranch, she and her sister Mary (who passed away in 2005) protested against the U.S. government to defend Indigenous land rights. Today, a collection in the Nevada Museum of Art features artwork reflecting the Dann sisters' activism. ▪

MAN, I REALLY LIKE VEGAS.

—Singer and actor Elvis Presley

SPORTING CHANCES

- Las Vegas is home to three major league professional teams: the Vegas Golden Knights (NHL), the Las Vegas Raiders (NFL), and the Las Vegas Aces (WNBA).

- Las Vegas also hosts several minor league teams, including those in baseball and soccer.

- The state-of-the-art Allegiant Stadium, home base for the Raiders and UNLV's football team, features a 93-foot-tall (28 m) eternal flame built in honor of former Raiders owner Al Davis.

- Allegiant Stadium is the host site for Super Bowl LVIII in 2024.

- In 1950, University of Nevada punter Pat Brady recorded the longest punt in NCAA history when he booted the ball 99 yards (90.5 m) in a game against Loyola of Los Angeles.

- In 1990, UNLV won the men's NCAA national basketball title over Duke by 30 points, the largest margin of victory ever in the national title game.

- The World Series of Poker launched in 1970 at the Horseshoe Casino.

- University of Nevada's athletic teams were originally known as the Sagebrushers, named after Nevada's state flower. They later switched to the Wolf Pack.

- In 2021, Carson City native Krysta Palmer, who competed for the University of Nevada, Reno, won an Olympic bronze medal in women's 3-meter springboard diving, becoming the first American woman in 33 years to medal in the event.

- In 1910, boxers Jack Johnson and James Jeffries squared off in the ring in Reno to contest the world heavyweight crown in what was then billed as "The Fight of the Century." (Johnson won.)

- The land speed record was set in the Black Rock Desert when the ThrustSSC supersonic car clocked 763.035 miles an hour (1,228 kph), becoming the first car to break the sound barrier.

- Thousands of runners hit the Strip at night for the annual Rock and Roll Las Vegas marathon and half-marathon, which takes place downtown.

- Pro baseball player Bryce Harper grew up in Las Vegas and briefly attended the College of Southern Nevada before being drafted by the Washington Nationals in 2010.

- In 2006, Jamie Gold took home $12 million for winning the World Series of Poker, the biggest earnings to date.

- The National Bowling Stadium in Reno, which has been called the "Taj Mahal of Tenpins," features 78 lanes.

- In 2014, David Wise became the first person born and raised in Reno to win a gold medal in the Olympics, which he secured in the men's freeski half-pipe. He won another gold in 2018 and a silver in 2022.

MADE IN NV

Nevada's agricultural outputs include:

- Cattle and calves
- Dairy products
- Hay
- Chicken eggs
- Onions
- Hogs

Nevada's industrial outputs include:

- Metal manufacturing
- Computer and electronic products
- Electrical equipment
- Gold, silver, and copper production
- Lithium, iron, and molybdenum

RECORD ★ SETTERS

In 1978, Marie McMillan set the record for the fastest flight by a female pilot from Fresno, California, to Las Vegas. McMillan, who lived in Las Vegas, would go on to set 656 records, the most in the world by any female pilot.

NEW HAMPSHIRE

CAPITAL: Concord **FLOWER:** Purple Lilac **NICKNAME:** Granite State **ENTRY:** 1788

★ ★ ★ *"Live Free or Die"* ★ ★ ★

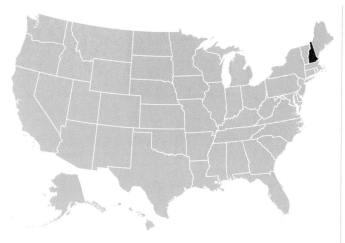

NH FACTS

- With a population of 1.4 million, New Hampshire is the 10th least populous state in the nation.

- It's the seventh smallest by area, covering 9,304 square miles (24,097 sq km), including 9,027 square miles (23,380 sq km) of land and 277 square miles (717 sq km) of inland water.

- Known as the Granite State for its many granite formations and quarries, New Hampshire has three other nicknames: Mother of Rivers, the White Mountain State, and Switzerland of America.

- Before French and English explorers arrived in the 1500s, Native American tribes, including the Abenaki and the Pennacook, lived on the land for thousands of years.

- Each year, the state's maple industry produces some 150,000 gallons (567,811 L) of maple syrup.

- At 6,288 feet (1,917 m), Mount Washington is the highest peak in the northeastern U.S. ▼

▶ STATE BIRD

Purple Finch
Haemorhous purpureus

These finches flit around New Hampshire during all seasons. Only males are purple; females are mostly brown.

1788

In 1788, New Hampshire, one of the 13 original colonies, became the ninth state to ratify the U.S. Constitution.

> THANKS TO THE MORNING LIGHT, THANKS TO THE FOAMING SEA, TO THE UPLANDS OF NEW HAMPSHIRE, TO THE GREEN-HAIRED FOREST FREE

—Poet Ralph Waldo Emerson

▶ **SPLAT!**
The first known paintball game was played on June 7, 1981, in the New Hampshire woods.

- The first-in-the-nation presidential primary election is held in New Hampshire every four years. (Until the 1992 elections, no candidate had ever won the U.S. presidency without first winning in the state.)

- New Hampshire is home to the nation's first wind farm, on Crotched Mountain in the southern part of the state. Constructed in 1980, it consists of 20 wind turbines.

- Residents are referred to as "Granite Staters."

- The state uses its original constitution, ratified in 1784. It's the second oldest continuously used constitution in the country.

- New Hampshire has 1,300 lakes or ponds and about 40 rivers with a total mileage of about 41,800 miles (67,271 km).

- All told, some 500 species of vertebrate animals call New Hampshire home. The count includes mammals such as eastern red bats, raccoons, moose, and the state mammal, white-tailed deer. There are also amphibians, like red-spotted newts, fish such as brook trout, and several types of birds, like great horned owls and hairy woodpeckers. ▪

▶ **STORY OF** THE MOTTO On July 31, 1809, New Hampshire native John Stark, a hero of the Revolutionary War, planned to make a toast at a celebration for the anniversary of the battle of Bennington in Vermont. The story goes that Stark, then 81, fell ill and couldn't attend the event, but sent a toast to be read by a counterpart. Part of that toast? The line "Live free or die: Death is not the worst of evils," believed to have been a take from the French phrase *Vivre libre ou mourir*. The brashness of the line resonated with the audience—and eventually, the entire state. It was adopted as the official motto in 1945. ▪

▲ **WE HOLD THESE TRUTHS ...**
New Hampshire delegates were the first to sign the Declaration of Independence in 1776.

STARS ★ OF ★ THE ★ STATE

ROBERT FROST
(1874–1963) Frost, the highly celebrated poet who grew up in Lawrence, once taught at Pinkerton Academy in Derry while dabbling in his own fledgling writing career. When he sold his family's farm to move to London and pursue poetry, he began to see success. Frost eventually made his way back to the state, settling in Franconia. It was during this period that he wrote *New Hampshire*, a collection of poems that included his observations about the state, for which he won the 1924 Pulitzer Prize for poetry. Frost also served as a poet-in-residence at Dartmouth College in Hanover. Today, his Franconia home doubles as a museum dedicated to the poet. ▪

Chutters candy store in Littleton boasts the longest candy counter on the planet, a 112-foot-long (34 m) display of sweets stored in old-fashioned glass jars.

WEIRD BUT TRUE

- A standout landmark and state symbol, the "Old Man of the Mountain" rock formation in Franconia Notch—named for being distinctly shaped like a man's profile—collapsed in 2003, despite valiant efforts to save the 40-foot-tall (12 m) anthropomorphic cliff. Today, the Old Man's profile remains on the state quarter.

- Russian salad dressing was invented in New Hampshire, not Russia.

- There are two drowned ancient forests in Rye; at low tide you can spot seaweed-covered cedar and pine stumps dating back thousands of years.

- There's an empty gorilla cage, an elephant enclosure, and a building in the shape of a shoe at Benson Park in Hudson, the site of a former zoo that operated there from 1924 to 1987.

- In 1941, the entire town of Hill was relocated to accommodate the construction of a dam.

- A Cold War–era rocket, the type that once sent astronauts to space, is on display in Warren.

- An eatery in Concord once made the world's largest meatball, weighing in at 222.5 pounds (101 kg).

- The ghost town of Monson, which was incorporated in 1746 and abandoned in 1770, is now a park.

- In 1961, a Portsmouth couple claimed to be abducted by extraterrestrials and taken into a UFO—the first known story of an alien kidnapping in the country.

▶ UNCLE SAM

The childhood home of "Uncle Sam" Wilson, the real-life inspiration for the classic American icon, is located in Mason.

MISCELLANY

- **Franklin Pierce**, the 14th president, was the first and only president from New Hampshire.

- **Franklin Pierce University** in Rindge, founded in 1962, is named after the former president.

- **Christa McAuliffe**, the first American civilian selected to go into space, hailed from Concord.

- There's an eight-foot-tall (2.4 m) statue of a laughing man's face on the campus of **Saint Anselm College**.

- **Frankenstein Cliff** near Jackson is named for a landscape painter, not the fictional monster.

- The state fruit is **the pumpkin**.

- The first permanent **potato patches** in North America were established in 1719, most likely near Londonderry, by Scotch-Irish immigrants.

- When the **Treaty of Portsmouth** was signed in September 1905 to end the Russo-Japanese War, New Hampshire became the only state to have hosted the formal conclusion of a foreign war.

- The Mount Washington Hotel was the site of the **Bretton Woods Conference**. The conference resulted in the creation of the International Monetary Fund (IMF) and the International Bank for Reconstruction and Development (IBRD).

- The country's first free—meaning tax-supported—**public library** was established in 1833 in Peterborough.

- In 2012, a New Hampshire man named **Vermin Supreme** ran for U.S. president on a platform of "free ponies and mandatory tooth brushing" for everyone. He received 833 votes.

- New Hampshire is one of five states with **no sales tax**.

- St. John's Episcopal Church in Portsmouth is home to the **Brattle Organ**, the oldest still-in-use pipe organ in the U.S.

- In 1938, **Cannon Mountain ski resort** opened North America's first aerial passenger tramway.

- The 1995 film **Jumanji**, starring Robin Williams, was filmed on location in Keene.

- New Hampshire is the only state that **does not have a law requiring adults to wear seat belts** while in a car. Kids are required to buckle up.

BY THE NUMBERS

10 the width in feet (3 m) of Becky's Garden Island on Lake Winnipesaukee, where a mini house sits

43 the wingspan in inches (1 m) of the barred owl, which is native to New Hampshire

30,581 THE NUMBER OF JACK-O'-LANTERNS ON DISPLAY AT A 2013 HALLOWEEN FESTIVAL IN KEENE, A WORLD RECORD

231 miles an hour (372 kph), the speed of one of the highest wind gusts ever recorded on Earth, captured on Mount Washington in 1934

460 THE LENGTH IN FEET (140 M) OF THE CORNISH-WINDSOR COVERED BRIDGE, THE LONGEST WOODEN COVERED BRIDGE IN THE U.S. AND THE LONGEST TWO-SPAN COVERED BRIDGE IN THE WORLD

396 the number of canoes and kayaks that took off at once in Laconia's Endicott Rock Park in 2014, the largest simultaneous launch of its kind

81% of the state is covered in forest, making it the second most forested state in the U.S.

339 the number of people who made bouquets simultaneously in Newport in 2019, setting a world record

13 the length in miles (21 km) of New Hampshire's coastline, the shortest of all coastal states

1793 the year New Boston's Molly Stark cannon was cast. Fired off every 4th of July, it's thought to be the oldest still-in-use cannon in the U.S.

182 the maximum depth in feet (56 m) of Newfound Lake, one of New Hampshire's deepest and said to be one of the cleanest lakes in the world

- Each winter, Sutton's Kezar Lake hosts an annual ice harvest, a traditional task of collecting surface ice for storage—in this case, for ice cream in the summer at nearby Muster Field Farm. Guests can watch the ice loaded out onto wagons and also check out antique Ford Model T snowmobiles, maintained by a local club.

- During the cold months, a crew in North Woodstock spends some 4,000 hours creating a giant fortress, tunnels, slides, and more out of 25 million pounds (11.3 million kg) of ice—all illuminated by twinkling LED lights at night.

- Downtown Portsmouth offers a charming small-town vibe with several restaurants, historic homes, and museums, including the Strawbery Banke Museum, featuring the oldest neighborhood in the state settled by Europeans; buildings there were constructed between the 1600s and the 1800s.

RECORD ★ SETTERS

On May 5, 1961, Derry-born Alan Shepard became the first American in space. The Pinkerton Academy graduate spent 15 minutes flying in the Mercury capsule named Freedom 7 before a safe return to Earth.

11,926,000

THE ESTIMATED WEIGHT IN POUNDS (5.4 MILLION KG) OF THE MADISON BOULDER, THOUGHT TO BE THE LARGEST GLACIAL DEPOSIT OF ITS KIND IN NORTH AMERICA

▲ LEAF PEEPERS DELIGHT

Fall foliage is ubiquitous in New Hampshire; the Kancamagus Highway, a 34.5-mile (55.5 km) scenic drive along NH Rt. 112 between Bath and Conway, is a go-to spot for leaf lovers.

- In the summer, water lovers flock to the banks of Lake Winnipesaukee, tucked in the foothills of the White Mountains. Hop on a boat or kayak and paddle around to explore the 365 islands on the lake (274 of which are habitable), or try waterskiing or wakeboarding in the mostly tranquil waters.

- Not too far from Portsmouth is the sprawling Wentworth by the Sea Historic Hotel in New Castle. Once abandoned and condemned, it was restored to its former glory in the early 2000s and is now one of the state's most luxurious resorts.

- Follow the Wine, Cheese, and Chocolate Trail and indulge in some of the finest wineries, creameries, and sweets shops across the state.

MADE IN NH

New Hampshire's agricultural outputs include:

- Dairy products
- Chicken eggs
- Turkeys
- Apples
- Cattle and calves
- Maple products
- Sweet corn
- Hay

New Hampshire's industrial outputs include:

- Computer and electronic products
- Fabricated metal products
- Machinery
- Electrical equipment and appliances
- Food, beverage, and tobacco products
- Plastics and rubber products
- Chemicals

SPORTING CHANCES

- The state has no major professional sports teams, but there is one minor league baseball team: the New Hampshire Fisher Cats.

- From 2001 to 2015, the Manchester Monarchs were part of the American Hockey League as a minor-pro affiliate of the NHL's Los Angeles Kings, before moving to Ontario.

- Loudon's New Hampshire Motor Speedway—known as the "Magic Mile"—is New England's only stop on the NASCAR Monster Energy circuit.

- Skiing is the official state sport; there are several ski resorts to choose from, including the top-rated Bretton Woods.

- Bretton Woods boasts the state's first eight-passenger gondola, traveling at a speed of 1,200 feet (366 m) per minute.

- Olympians hailing from New Hampshire include swimmer Jenny Thompson, a five-time gold medalist from Dover, and Tessa Gobbo, a gold-medalist rower from Chesterfield.

- Every October, the town of Goffstown holds the Giant Pumpkin Regatta, an event where people race down the Piscataquog River in carved-out, supersize gourds.

- Waterville Valley Resort has served as the site for the U.S. Freestyle National Championships skiing event.

- In 2013, New Hampshire became one of the first states to offer bass fishing as a high school sport.

- Olympic downhill skier Bode Miller grew up in Franconia; fellow champion skier Mikaela Shiffrin lived in Lyme for a portion of her youth.

- Slalom, tricks, and jumping waterskiing competitions are held in Wolfeboro's Back Bay, including the annual state championships.

- The challenging Mount Washington Road Race in Gorham draws some 1,300 runners annually to scale the 7.6-mile (12.2 km) Mt. Washington Auto Road.

SARAH JOSEPHA HALE

(1788–1879) Next time you hear the tune "Mary Had a Little Lamb," you have Hale to thank. The Newport-born writer and editor—one of the first female American novelists—is perhaps best remembered for writing the famous children's ditty, which was originally penned as a nursery rhyme, in 1830. A widowed mother of five, Hale turned to writing to support her family. She is also credited with helping to establish Thanksgiving as a national holiday.

NEW JERSEY

★ ★ ★
"Liberty and Prosperity"
★ ★ ★

CAPITAL: Trenton **FLOWER:** Violet **NICKNAME:** Garden State **ENTRY:** 1787

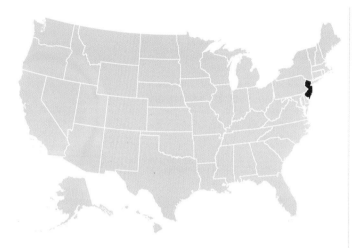

NJ FACTS

- The population is 9,261,699.
- Major economic areas and industries include life sciences, IT, finance, pharmaceuticals, and manufacturing.
- Natural resources include granite, sand, gravel, clams, woodlands, and water.
- Original inhabitants included the Unami, the Minisink, and the Unalachtigo. As a result of forced relocation to states such as Oklahoma, there are no federally recognized tribes today.
- In 1609, explorer Henry Hudson claimed the area for Holland, calling it New Netherlands. In 1664, the British captured the region, titling it New Jersey.
- In 1698, Alexander Laird emigrated from Scotland to Monmouth County. He began making applejack, a liquor made from apples, and established a distillery in 1717. The liquor was one of the first spirits produced in America.
- The country's fourth-oldest college, Princeton University was chartered in 1746 in Elizabeth. Over the next two centuries, the university added new schools, a chapel, and a graduate school; it opened its doors to women in 1969. Today, Princeton continually ranks among the top schools in the world.
- According to legend, the iconic saltwater taffy candy can be traced to confectioner Joseph Fralinger, who marketed the treat as an Atlantic City boardwalk souvenir.
- In 1876, inventor and businessman Thomas Edison created the world's first machine shop and industrial research laboratory in Menlo Park.
- Grammy and Academy Award–winning cultural icon Frank Sinatra got his start singing with a local group in Hoboken. ◀

▶ STATE BIRD

American Goldfinch
Spinus tristis

Declared the state bird in 1935, the male American goldfinch is known for its striking yellow feathers, while the female has more subtle shades.

1787

The country's fifth smallest state became the nation's third state in 1787.

NEW JERSEY FOR ME IS SO ALIVE WITH HISTORY. IT'S OLD, DYNAMIC, AFRICAN AMERICAN, LATINO.

—Author Junot Díaz

◀**SOMETHING IN THE WATER**
A series of 1916 shark attacks along the Jersey Shore was the inspiration for *Jaws*.

- In 1776, George Washington's army crossed the Delaware River to defeat a battalion of soldiers at the Battle of Trenton. The win gave the Continental Army a necessary boost of morale that would inspire them in battles to come.

- In 1777, a man named Oliver Cromwell was one of the few Black Revolutionary soldiers allowed to help support the cause when he enlisted in the Second New Jersey Continental Regiment.

- In 1858, the bones that fossil enthusiast William Parker Foulke discovered led to the assemblage of one of the most complete dinosaur skeletons to be found at the time. Today, *Hadrosaurus foulkii* remains the state dinosaur.

- In 1950, construction began on the $225 million New Jersey Turnpike.

- Thanks in part to programs like *The Sopranos*, New Jersey culture is often associated with its large population of Italian Americans. However, the state is also home to many other groups, including Irish Americans, Quakers, German Americans, and Black Americans. ▪

▲**STORY OF** THE BOARDWALK While Atlantic City is sometimes known as a miniature Sin City for its casinos, the boardwalk saw a different kind of sin in the 1920s. In 1929—amidst brazen flouting of the country's Prohibition laws—various crime leaders descended on the city for a summit meeting. Local crime boss Enoch Lewis "Nucky" Johnson hosted famed figures from Chicago and New York, such as the Masseria family, the D'Aquila family, and Al Capone himself. As its participants came to agreements dictating who was allowed to do business where, the conference became the birthplace of American "organized" crime. ▪

STARS ★ OF ★ THE ★ STATE

BRUCE SPRINGSTEEN

(b. 1949) Born to an Irish and Italian family in Long Branch, Bruce Springsteen is a singer and songwriter. Known as "The Boss," Springsteen's music sets lyrics that sympathize with the working-class American and explore social commentary around events such as the Vietnam War or the AIDS epidemic against a backdrop of guitar-dominated rock and folk-inspired melodies. The artist is renowned for his rough baritone vocals as well as smash hits such as "Born to Run," "Born in the U.S.A.," and "Dancing in the Dark." Springsteen's albums have sold more than 65 million copies in just the U.S., and he has won 20 Grammys, an Academy Award, and was awarded the Presidential Medal of Freedom in 2016. ▪

GENIUS!
Albert Einstein lived in Princeton and worked at the university.

Born in Rutherford in 1883, William Carlos Williams helped give rise to poetry dedicated to everyday life. Using energetic and often clipped wording—occasionally titled with the Spanish of his Puerto Rican heritage—to depict simple and intimate moments, Williams created a uniquely American form of poetry that would help to inspire the beat generation. He was awarded the Pulitzer Prize posthumously in 1963.

RECORD ★ SETTERS

The first brewery in the country was opened in Hoboken around 1641 by Dutch brewmaster Aret Teunissen Van Putten.

WEIRD BUT TRUE

- There is a floating hot dog stand on the Delaware River.

- Scientists found a 90-million-year-old tick preserved in amber in a vacant lot in Sayreville.

- One creamery in the state has made ham-flavored ice cream.

- A museum in Sterling Hill is dedicated solely to fluorescent rocks.

- A restaurant in Jersey City has served burgers made from yak, kangaroo, alligator, and camel.

- Margate is home to a six-story-high statue of an elephant named Lucy.

- There is a collection of death masks—casts taken of a person's face after they have died—at Princeton.

MISCELLANY

- The **famous duel** in which Aaron Burr fatally shot Alexander Hamilton happened in Weehawken.

- The state fish is the **brook trout**.

- A *War of the Worlds* **monument** exists in Grovers Mill, the site of the fictional alien invasion in Orson Welles's 1938 radio story.

- New Jersey's state fruit is the **highbush blueberry**.

- The state animal is the **horse**.

- The **first drive-in** theater was patented in Camden.

- **Captain Kidd** may have buried his treasure along the state's coastline.

- The **bog turtle** is the state reptile.

- A New Jersey "**sloppy joe**" refers to a double-decker sandwich made with deli meats, cheese, sauerkraut, and Russian dressing.

- **William Alexander "Bud" Abbott**, of Abbott and Costello, was born in Asbury Park.

- The state is named for the **English Channel island** of Jersey.

- The state butterfly is the **black swallowtail**.

- People from New Jersey are called **New Jerseyites** or **New Jerseyans**.

- **Jersey blue and buff** are the state colors.

- The **world's first boardwalk** was constructed in Atlantic City in 1870.

- A diner in Clinton offers a 50-pound (23 kg) **Mt. Olympus burger**.

STARS ★ OF ★ THE ★ STATE

WHITNEY HOUSTON

(1963–2012) Whitney Houston achieved record-setting superstardom thanks to her powerful vocals, captivating performances, and smash dance hits. Born in Newark in 1963, Houston grew up in a musical family that included notable vocalists Dionne Warwick, Dee Dee Warwick, and Cissy Houston. Houston's first album debuted in 1985 and scored three consecutive number one singles and a Grammy for "Saving All My Love for You." Two years later, she became the first woman to enter the *Billboard* chart at number one. In 1992, Houston made her acting debut in *The Bodyguard*. She went on to sell more than 200 million albums, videos, and singles. She won two Emmys, six Grammys, and countless other awards. She passed away in 2012 and was inducted into the Rock & Roll Hall of Fame in 2020.

BY THE NUMBERS

1,803 THE HEIGHT IN FEET (550 M) OF HIGH POINT PEAK, THE APTLY NAMED HIGHEST POINT

122 miles (196 km): the length of the New Jersey Turnpike

1855 the year New Jersey–born Grover Cleveland became president

144,000,000+ the number of records sold by the band Bon Jovi, led by Perth Amboy native Jon Bon Jovi

100 the number of battles fought in New Jersey during the American Revolution

834 PEOPLE AT THE JEWISH CENTER OF PRINCETON SET A WORLD RECORD IN 2012 FOR THE MOST PEOPLE LIGHTING MENORAHS AT THE SAME TIME.

1919 THE YEAR THE FIRST PASSENGER FLIGHT IN AMERICAN HISTORY WAS FLOWN FROM NEW YORK CITY TO ATLANTIC CITY

9,800+ FAMILY-OWNED FARMS EXIST IN THE STATE.

70,000 the size in acres (28,328 ha) of the Delaware Water Gap National Recreation Area

△ CAPE MAY
Travelers seeking a quieter atmosphere turn to Cape May, where picturesque Victorian-style resorts line the beaches.

DESTINATION: NEW JERSEY

- To keep sand from infiltrating the hotels and stores along Atlantic City's coast, an 1870 businessman had an unusual proposition: a walkway made of wooden boards. Today, Atlantic City draws some 27 million visitors a year to its casinos, bars, high-end restaurants, and easy access to sandy beaches.

- For nearly a century, Hoboken has hosted a version of a 600-year-old Italian festival known as the Feast of the Madonna Dei Martiri.

MULTIPLE LOCATIONS OF THE UNDERGROUND RAILROAD, AN ESCAPE NETWORK AIMED TO HELP FLEEING ENSLAVED PEOPLE, WERE ESTABLISHED IN NEW JERSEY PRIOR TO THE CIVIL WAR.

- Just a 30-minute drive from Atlantic City, Ocean City is a family-friendly alternative. As a dry town—meaning there is no alcohol sold within its limits—it switches the focus to boardwalk rides water parks, and outdoor activities like parasailing.

- In Cape May, visitors can stroll through aquariums and museums, tour historic lighthouses, play rounds of golf, or visit a local brewery.

- Now located off Camden, the U.S.S. *New Jersey* is the most decorated battleship in U.S. history. Designed in 1938, the battleship launched on the first anniversary of the Pearl Harbor attacks and went on to fight in history's two largest naval battles.

- Set across from the Manhattan skyline in Jersey City, Ellis Island, and the Statue of Liberty, Liberty State Park covers 1,212 acres (491 ha) of public space. Close by is the Liberty Science Center, full of family-friendly interactive exhibits that let kids climb rock gyms, explore mazes, and observe unusual animals.

- At the Trenton Pork Roll Festival, festival goers celebrate an iconic state food.

- In October, Wildwood hosts the Race of Gentleman, a celebration of vintage vehicles that includes beach races, bonfires, and more.

- Covering 22 percent of the state's land, the Pine Barrens attracts outdoor enthusiasts to its campgrounds and hiking and cycling trails. It also appeals to fans of the spooky: According to legend, the Pine Barrens are roamed by a bizarre creature known as the Jersey Devil.

RECORD ★ SETTERS

Les Paul invented one of the first solid body electric guitars in Mahwah in 1940 with the creation of "The Log."

SPORTING CHANCES

- Martin Brodeur (Canada) of the New Jersey Devils is one of two goalies to record 48 wins in a National Hockey League season, a league record.

- Raised in Delran, Carli Lloyd is a four-time Olympian soccer player and two-time FIFA Women's World Cup champion. Lloyd is the all-time leading scorer in U.S. Women's National Team Olympic history.

- Born in Newark in 1972, Shaquille "Shaq" O'Neal is considered one of the greatest basketball players of all time. After winning the Olympic gold medal with his team in 1996, Shaq joined the Los Angeles Lakers, going on to become league MVP in 2000 and leading the team to three championships.

- In 1846, Hoboken's Elysian Fields hosted the first officially organized baseball game (using mostly familiar modernized rules) in history.

- East Brunswick native Heather O'Reilly is a three-time Olympic gold medalist in soccer and a 2015 Women's World Cup champion.

EVERYTHING IS LEGAL IN NEW JERSEY.

—Alexander Hamilton, in *Hamilton* by Lin-Manuel Miranda

- In 2014 at Old Bridge Township Raceway Park in Englishtown, Erica Enders-Stevens broke the speed record for the 440-yard (402 m) race for the National Hot Rod Association in a Pro Stock car class.

- Despite being located in East Rutherford, MetLife Stadium is home to NFL teams the New York Giants and New York Jets.

- Born Arnold Raymond Cream in Merchantville to Barbadian immigrants in 1914, Jersey Joe Walcott was a world heavyweight champ.

- Thanks to the university's black and orange colors, Princeton's sports mascot has been the tiger since 1882.

- Born in Vineland, Mike Trout is considered one of the best all-around baseball players of the 21st century, holding three American League MVP trophies.

MADE IN NJ

New Jersey's agricultural outputs include:

- Blueberries
- Tomatoes
- Apples
- Bell peppers
- Peaches
- Horses
- Dairy
- Eggs
- Greenhouse and nursery products

New Jersey's industrial outputs include:

- Palladium
- Petroleum
- Metal waste
- Cell phones

STARS ★ OF ★ THE ★ STATE

PAUL ROBESON

(1898–1976) Born in Princeton in 1898, Paul Robeson was an actor, athlete, singer, and civil rights advocate. Internationally famed for his performance in the titular role in *Othello* and for his robust singing in Broadway's *Show Boat*, Robeson was later accused by the House Un-American Activities Committee (HUAC) of being a communist when he spoke out against the treatment of Black people in the Army and across the country. Despite the discrimination he faced, Robeson persevered, meeting with Albert Einstein to discuss peace strategies and continuing to sing at Carnegie Hall. Robeson passed away at age 77.

NEW MEXICO

★ ★ ★

"It Grows as It Goes"

★ ★ ★

CAPITAL: Santa Fe **BIRD:** Greater Roadrunner **NICKNAME:** Land of Enchantment **ENTRY:** 1912

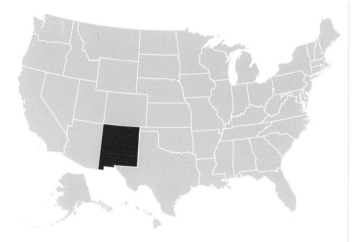

NM FACTS

- The population is 2,113,344.

- Primary industries include oil, gas, mining, and coal.

- The state's official cookie is the biscochito: a flaky, cinnamon- and anise-flavored treat first introduced by Spanish colonizers in the 16th century.

- Annie Dodge Wauneka devoted herself to increasing access to public health and became the first Indigenous person to receive the Presidential Medal of Freedom.

- Around the 15th century, different groups of Athabascan-speaking Diné (Navajo and Apache) arrived in the region, where they farmed corn and created ceramics.

- New Mexico was the 47th state to join the Union and is the fifth largest.

- Some 120 years after hundreds of Chicanos were forcibly displaced as a result of the Treaty of Guadalupe Hidalgo, activist Reies López Tijerina (at left) led a movement to demand the restoration of confiscated lands. ▼

▶ STATE FLOWER

Yucca
Yucca spp.

The plant was prized by American settlers both for its edible parts and for its use as a shampoo and soap.

1610

Originally built in 1610, Santa Fe's San Miguel Chapel is the oldest church in the continental U.S.

WHEN I GOT TO NEW MEXICO THAT WAS MINE. AS SOON AS I SAW IT, THAT WAS MY COUNTRY. I'D NEVER SEEN ANYTHING LIKE IT BEFORE, BUT IT FITTED TO ME EXACTLY. IT'S SOMETHING THAT'S IN THE AIR, IT'S JUST DIFFERENT. THE SKY IS DIFFERENT, THE STARS ARE DIFFERENT, THE WIND IS DIFFERENT.

—Painter Georgia O'Keeffe

- The Navajo Nation is the largest Indigenous tribe in the country, with more than one-third of its members residing in New Mexico.

- The Clovis people may have arrived some 12,000 years ago. Over time, three distinct cultures emerged: the ancestral Puebloan, Mogollon, and Hohokam.

- In addition to several Diné nations, the state remains home to 19 other federally recognized tribes. There are eight Indigenous languages spoken throughout the region.

- Natural resources include perlite glass, potash, oil, coal, and copper.

- Spain founded Santa Fe in 1610, making it the third oldest U.S. city founded by European colonists.

- Under Spanish colonization one Tewa Pueblo leader known as Popé led a revolt that successfully drove the colonists from the area.

- Two years after the Treaty of Guadalupe Hidalgo in 1848 the New Mexico area was admitted as a free territory as part of the Compromise of 1850.

- Bill Gates and Paul Allen founded Microsoft in Albuquerque on April 4, 1974. ▪

▲ **STORY OF** THE STONE Turquoise, which can be found throughout the region, has been mined since at least the sixth century by ancestral Puebloan peoples. Considered sacred, the gem has been sculpted into beads and statues by Indigenous nations across the area, from the Pueblo to the Navajo to the Apache. Today, turquoise sits at the intersection between commerce and culture, featuring in fine jewelry work and also being worn as a protective talisman. ▪

STARS ★ OF ★ THE ★ STATE

GEORGIA O'KEEFFE

(1887–1986) A master of modernist art, Georgia O'Keeffe is perhaps best known for her portrayals of the Southwestern landscape and intimate depictions of natural subjects. Born in Wisconsin in 1887, O'Keeffe studied in Chicago and New York, quickly gaining attention for her abstract pieces. A member of the National Women's Party, O'Keeffe rejected categorizations of her work as innately feminine or sexual, fighting instead for recognition of each piece on its own merit, regardless of her gender. In 1929, O'Keeffe began to spend much of her time painting in New Mexico before permanently moving to Ghost Ranch in 1949. Her works captured the state's limitless sky and vast desert, often juxtaposing the sharper organic forms of bleached animal skulls with softer floral elements. Today, O'Keeffe is regarded as one of the greatest modernist painters of all time and an icon of American art. ▪

⚠ SSSSSSSSS

There is a museum in Albuquerque devoted entirely to rattlesnakes.

- The official state question—red or green?—is in reference to chili type preference.

- The piñon pine tree is the official state tree. Its wood has an earthy, smoky scent and it produces a nut consumed by humans and wildlife alike.

- A local flower, the chocolate daisy, gives off a chocolatey scent.

- One custard shop in Las Cruces serves a Green Chile Sundae …

- … and a vineyard in Hatch Valley makes hatch chili wine.

- When driven over at the right speed, car tires play "America the Beautiful" as they traverse a certain stretch of highway in the state.

- In Santa Fe there is an 82-foot-long (25 m) sculpture of a blue whale made of recycled plastic.

- Each fall, Santa Fe holds a festival where residents purge their sadness and gloom by burning an effigy of a character called "Zozobra."

- New Mexico State University has an institute devoted to researching chili peppers.

- Each holiday season, the city of Albuquerque puts up a snowman made of tumbleweeds.

- At the Great American Duck Race in Deming, festivalgoers can race ducks, compete in a tortilla toss, and watch a duck parade.

I AM HAPPIER AT MY RANCH IN THE MIDDLE OF NOWHERE WATCHING A BUG CARRY LEAVES ACROSS THE GRASS, LISTENING TO SILENCE, RIDING MY HORSE, AND BEING IN OPEN SPACE.

—Fashion designer Tom Ford

⚠ TSÉ BIT' A'Í

Given its spiritual and cultural significance to the Diné, the volcanic rock landmark known as Tsé Bit' A'í (or Shiprock Peak) is off-limits to hiking or climbing.

- People from New Mexico are called **New Mexicans**.

- The state aircraft is the **hot-air balloon**.

- The state animal is the **black bear**.

- The state colors are **red and yellow**.

- *Coelophysis* is the state's fossil.

- When Confederate forces invaded the New Mexico territory in 1862, Union troops turned them back at Glorieta Pass, known as the **"Gettysburg of the West."**

- **Posole** was first cooked by Indigenous Mesoamericans.

- The state possibly took its name from the Aztec word meaning **"place of [the god] Mexitli."**

- **Pueblo bread** is a soft, fluffy delight that's cooked in traditional *hornos* (outdoor ovens).

- The state's official butterfly is the **Sandia hairstreak**.

- The **New Mexico spadefoot toad** is the state amphibian.

In 1945, the world's first atomic bomb was detonated at testing grounds at Trinity Site, now designated a national historic landmark.

BY THE NUMBERS

1948 the year Indigenous Americans won the right to vote in New Mexico

27 the number of radio antennas at the Very Large Array, a radio observatory located outside Socorro

13,161 the height in feet (4,011 m) of Wheeler Peak, the state's highest point

1,604 FEET (489 M): THE DEPTH OF LECHUGUILLA LIMESTONE CAVE

60,000 YEARS AGO: THE LAST ERUPTION OF THE CAPULIN VOLCANO

119 caves make up Carlsbad Caverns, a series formed over millions of years.

$10,000,000 the cost of the Gadsden Purchase, which integrated 29,670 square miles (76,845 sq km) of Mexican land into New Mexico and Arizona

▶ SIMMER DOWN

Eaten regularly across the state and often served at saint's day feasts, posole is a stew made with either red or green chilies (*rojo* or *verde*) and filled with simmered meats and white corn or hominy.

DESTINATION: NEW MEXICO

- Santa Fe's unique blend of cultures and stunning natural settings make it a place like no other. Whether visitors wish to peruse the wares of local artisans, sample food inspired by Indigenous tradition, or enjoy the desert vistas on horseback, there is something for everyone.

- Located in Alamogordo, the New Mexico Museum of Space History showcases the state's important role in space exploration.

- Home to multiple Dark Sky Parks, the state has some of the best locations for stargazing. At places like Capulin Volcano National Monument or Clayton Lake State Park, visitors can see an abundance of stars.

- In 1947, an unidentified flying object crashed to the ground in Roswell. Locals claimed the vehicle was a flying saucer. Eventually, the truth came out: It wasn't an alien visit but a government cover-up of secret technology known as Project Mogul. Regardless, the town's status as a UFO landing pad persists. Visitors can enjoy alien-themed restaurants and souvenirs and visit a UFO museum.

- Bandelier National Monument encompasses petroglyphs and dwellings from the past 11,000 years. The Main Loop and Tsankawi trails pass through alcoves and dwellings created by the ancestral

In 1928, Octaviano Larrazolo of New Mexico became the first Latino to be elected to the United States Senate.

Puebloans, while Falls Trail and Cerro Grande lead visitors to waterfalls and through forests.

- In Nageezi, Chaco Canyon is a testament to the ingenuity and complexity of the ancestral Puebloan culture. Featuring enormous stone Great Houses often oriented in important astronomical directions, the area is the greatest archaeological site dedicated to the Chacoan peoples.

- Fans of nature or history shouldn't miss the Cumbres & Toltec Scenic Railroad, a historic steam-powered railroad route that winds up mountains and over wooden bridges through the Toltec Gorge.

- After prospectors discovered silver in the area in 1870, the town of Shakespeare (originally called Ralston) sprang up to accommodate the influx of miners. Just 23 years later, a depression caused the mines to close, leaving the town abandoned. Visitors can still see the Shakespeare ghost town today.

- Built between 1877 and 1881, Santa Fe's Loretto Chapel is the site of an alleged miracle. Constructed by an unknown architect, the chapel contains an architectural feat: a double spiraling staircase with no visible supports. Some believe that the preternaturally skilled architect may have been St. Joseph.

- Billy the Kid, one of the West's most infamous outlaws, met his end near Fort Sumner. Legend (likely apocryphal) has it that the gunman killed 21 men before being captured and sentenced in Mesilla. However, the outlaw escaped, remaining at large for more than two months before being shot and killed at a local ranch. His grave is at Fort Sumner.

- Albuquerque is home to the International Balloon Fiesta.

During WWII, 29 Diné men from the state's Navajo reservation underwent intensive military and code training to become code talkers. They devised an invaluable code based on Diné vocabulary and a specially created alphabet, sending more than 800 messages without error. All together, some 420 Navajo code talkers served during the war.

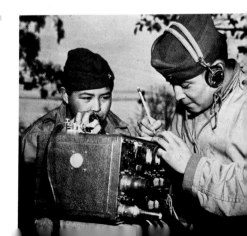

SPORTING CHANCES

- Born in Santa Rita in 1922, Ralph Kiner served in the military for three years during WWII before joining the Pittsburgh Pirates in 1946. He quickly led the National League in home runs and was inducted into the Baseball Hall of Fame in 1975.

- The state does not have a professional sports team.

- Located in Albuquerque, Duke City BMX is the country's largest covered bicycle motocross facility.

- Born in 1939 in Albuquerque, Al Unser is considered one of the most successful race car drivers in the Indianapolis 500. Over the course of his career, he took four first-place finishes and 11 other top-10 finishes.

- Ray Birmingham, head coach of the University of New Mexico baseball team, was inducted into the National Junior College Athletic Association Baseball Coaches Hall of Fame in 2011 and the New Mexico Sports Hall of Fame in 2015.

- Raised in Jal, golfer Kathy Whitworth holds the most tournament victories by a professional: 88 victories over a span of 23 years.

- A popular local sport for all ages is sledding on the dunes of White Sands National Park.

- Everett Bowman, from Hope, was a two-time champion cowboy who also held rodeo victories in steer wrestling, calf roping, and steer roping. He was inducted into the ProRodeo Hall of Fame in 1979.

- Located in Albuquerque, Ross Anderson is an Indigenous speed skier who holds the record for fastest American time: 154.06 miles an hour (247.93 kph).

- The University of New Mexico's athletic colors, silver and cherry, were chosen to represent the Sandia Mountains and the Rio Grande River.

STARS ★ OF ★ THE ★ STATE

NANCY LOPEZ

(b. 1957) One of the world's preeminent golfers, Nancy Lopez was born in California in 1957 but spent her childhood in Roswell. She began playing golf at just eight years old, and left college to become a professional golfer in 1977. Her career saw immediate success, and she was named the Ladies Professional Golf Association (LPGA) Rookie of the Year and Player of the Year in 1978. She won the LPGA championship in the same year and secured the Vare Trophy both that year and the next. Lopez went on to win many more events, and in 2004 became the first woman to receive the Francis Ouimet Award for Lifelong Contributions to Golf.

NEW YORK

★ ★ ★
"Excelsior"
★ ★ ★

CAPITAL: Albany **BIRD:** Bluebird **NICKNAME:** Empire State **ENTRY:** 1778

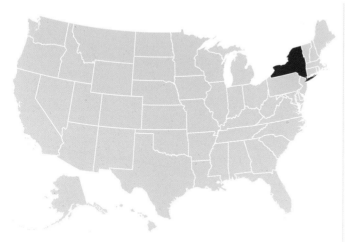

NY FACTS

- New York is the fourth most populous, the 30th largest in area, and the eighth most densely populated of the 50 states of the United States.

- New York City is the most populous city in the U.S., and the New York metropolitan area is one of the most populous in the world.

- It is the only state that borders both the Atlantic Ocean and the Great Lakes.

- The first people arrived in New York around 10,000 B.C. Their descendants included Native American tribes such as the Mohawk, Cayuga, Oneida, and Seneca.

- New York City served as the nation's first capital for one year. (The capital moved to Washington, D.C., in 1790.)

- In 1789, George Washington was sworn in as president at Federal Hall on Wall Street.

- Between the late 1800s to the 1950s, millions of immigrants passed through Ellis Island in New York Harbor to become U.S. citizens. It's estimated that as many as four in 10 Americans can trace at least one ancestor to this migration.

▶ STATE FLOWER
Rose
Rosa

New York doesn't discriminate when it comes to its favorite flower; any rose in any color is considered the official bloom.

1886

The Statue of Liberty, a gift from France, was erected in 1886 on what is now called Liberty Island. ▼

THE CITY SEEN FROM THE QUEENSBORO BRIDGE IS ALWAYS THE CITY SEEN FOR THE FIRST TIME, IN ITS FIRST WILD PROMISE OF ALL THE MYSTERY AND THE BEAUTY IN THE WORLD.

—Author F. Scott Fitzgerald, *The Great Gatsby*

- The European settlement of New York was led by the Dutch, settling along the Hudson River in 1624. They established the colony of New Amsterdam on the island of Manhattan.
- Once the British took control of the area in 1664, it was renamed New York, after the British Duke of York.
- Four New York governors were eventually elected president of the U.S.: Grover Cleveland, Theodore Roosevelt, Franklin D. Roosevelt, and Martin Van Buren.
- Albany became the capital of the state in 1797.
- Adirondack Park encompasses 6 million acres (2.4 million ha), with 30,000 rivers and streams, and 3,000 lakes and ponds.
- Covering about 68 square miles (175 sq km) and measuring 618 feet (188 m) deep, Seneca Lake is the largest and the deepest of the Finger Lakes.
- Niagara Falls, one of the most famous waterfalls in the world, is located on the border of Ontario, Canada, and New York, United States.
- Experts believe that New York's 11 Finger Lakes were formed more than two million years ago during the Ice Age, by glaciers that carved crevices into the land. The ice melted, leaving the lakes behind.
- Located within the Adirondack Mountains, Mount Marcy, at 5,344 feet (1,629 m), is the state's tallest peak.
- More than 60 varieties of grapes are grown in New York, making it the country's third largest wine-producing state.

STORY OF THE DRINK Just call the martini the toast of the town. After all, the classic cocktail is said to have been first crafted at the Knickerbocker Hotel in Times Square in 1912. The story goes that hotel bartender Martini di Arma di Taggia served business magnate and bar regular John D. Rockefeller a drink made from dry gin and vermouth. Rockefeller loved the concoction and continued to order it, naming it "Martini" after the man who mixed it.

STARS ★ OF ★ THE ★ STATE

BILLIE HOLIDAY
(1915–1959) One of the greatest jazz and blues singers of the 1930s and '40s, Holiday was born in Philadelphia but moved to Harlem as a teenager. There, she was discovered by a producer while singing in a jazz club, soon achieving star status as "Lady Day." Known for her emotional and expressive vocals, Holiday performed hits like "God Bless the Child" and "Strange Fruit" at New York City clubs including Café Society and Ebony, while also enjoying success on the road and throughout Europe. Her final performance was at the Phoenix in Manhattan's Lower East Side—months later, she succumbed to her long battle with drug and alcohol addiction.

WEIRD BUT TRUE

- The Empire State Building has its own zip code.

- Perforated toilet paper was invented in Albany.

- There's a museum for drain tiles in Geneva.

- Before the Brooklyn Bridge opened to the public, a parade of 21 elephants crossed the bridge to demonstrate that the bridge was safe and ready for use.

- Legend says that anyone who enters the cave of the evil spirit beside Niagara Falls will be cursed with bad luck.

- Immigrants to Ellis Island were often served ice cream as part of their first American meal.

- There's a mini tropical rainforest inside a midtown Manhattan office building.

- A library book checked out by George Washington was returned to a New York City library 221 years late.

- It's illegal to keep a rooster, goose, duck, or turkey as a pet in New York City—but hens are OK.

- In Oneida, there's a tiny church in the middle of a large pond that fits three people.

- You can visit a 100-year-old shipwreck on Fire Island; the wreckage was unearthed by Hurricane Sandy in 2012.

- Albert Einstein's eyeballs are said to be stored in a New York City safety deposit box.

▲ WINGS UP

The original Buffalo wings were invented in the city of Buffalo at the Anchor Bar.

MISCELLANY

- ▲ There are nearly 60 species of **wild orchids** native to NY.

- Weighing in at 800 pounds (363 kg), the **Moon weather vane** on top of the Delaware & Hudson Railroad building in Albany is the largest working weather vane in North America.

- Dating back to early 1658, Montauk's **Deep Hollow Ranch** bills itself as the oldest working cattle ranch in the country.

- Opened in 1830, the **Mohawk and Hudson River Railroad**, which ran between Albany and Schenectady, was the first passenger railroad in the U.S.

- Broadway was originally an Algonquin Indian trade route known as the **Wiechquaekeck Trail**.

- **Niagara Reservation** was the first state park in the U.S.

- **English muffins** originated in New York, not England.

- There are 17 steps approaching the western entrance of **Albany's state capitol building**, along with 77 steps approaching its eastern entrance—honoring the year 1777, when New York's current state government replaced the colonial system.

- On December 10, 1995, some 34 inches (86 cm) of snow fell in **Buffalo**, a record amount for the city.

In 2012, Grace Meng became the first Asian American elected to Congress from New York. In 2004, her father, Jimmy Meng, was the first Asian American to win election to the state legislature.

BY THE NUMBERS New York City

1905 the year New York City's first pizzeria, Lombardi's, opened

125 combined length in miles (200 km) of bookshelves in the city's largest public library

100 HOURS: THE AMOUNT OF TIME THE AVERAGE DRIVER IN NEW YORK CITY SPENDS PER YEAR LOOKING FOR A PARKING SPOT

665 the length in miles (1,070 km) of subway track throughout the city, connecting 472 subway stations

7 the number of spikes on the crown of the Statue of Liberty, representing the seven oceans and the seven continents of the world

200 approximate number of languages spoken in New York City

$2.75 average cost of a single New York City subway ride

40 the average commute in minutes for New Yorkers, which is about 14 minutes longer than the national average

48 size in acres (19.4 ha) of Grand Central Terminal, the world's largest railway station, which has 44 platforms

◄ PLAY BALL

At one time, New York had three baseball teams: the Yankees, Giants, and the Brooklyn Dodgers. (The latter two moved to the West Coast in 1957.)

DESTINATION: NEW YORK

- From the Top of the Rock (that's the observatory on top of Rockefeller Center) to the sleek, futuristic underground transportation hub and shopping mall known as the Oculus, New York City covers it all. Check out the Vessel in Hudson Yards, a spiraling, soaring landmark that offers stunning views of the city.

ONE WORLD TRADE CENTER, THE TALLEST BUILDING IN THE WESTERN HEMISPHERE, WHICH WAS COMPLETED IN 2014, STANDS 1,776 FEET (541 M) HIGH.

- Nestled in the Adirondack Mountains, the Lake Placid Olympic Museum showcases the events of and artifacts from two Winter Games held there. While in the area, sample some of the regional wine and craft beer at the many local wineries and breweries.

- More than 3,100 tons (2,812 t) of water flows over the edge of Niagara Falls every second. Head to the northwestern reaches of New York to see the falls for yourself. A Maid of the Mist ride gets you an up-close-and-personal view; just be prepared to get a bit wet.

- Some 36 percent of Catskill Park's 700,000-plus acres (283,280 ha) are federally designated as "forever wild," so there's no lack of wide-open spaces. Skiing and snowboarding are popular activities in the winter (Belleayre Mountain's ski resort is one of the largest in the area), while summer is a draw for hikers, bikers, and boaters.

- Quaint towns, charming wineries, and lush landscapes welcome visitors to the Finger Lakes region. Ithaca, home to both Cornell University and Ithaca College, is one of those towns, with the added bonus of spectacular state parks. Head there in the fall for gorgeous fall foliage.

- Syracuse is more than a university town. The I.M. Pei–designed Everson Museum of Art houses 10,000 works of art including one of the largest holdings of international ceramics in the nation. Love sports? See the Orange play football or basketball at the JMA Wireless Dome, the largest dome structure on any college campus in the country.

- The state's third-most populated city, Rochester has a metropolitan vibe without the hustle-and-bustle of New York City. Families flock to the Strong National Museum of Play, while flower lovers will revel in the world's largest lilac collection at Highland Park Conservatory.

- Head "out east" to Montauk, Long Island's easternmost point. Known for its pristine beaches and lobster rolls, it's also the site of New York's oldest lighthouse, completed in 1796. ▼

RECORD ★ SETTERS

Stretching 85 miles (137 km) between the Rondout Reservoir in Ulster County to the Hillview Reservoir in Yonkers, the Delaware Aqueduct is the world's longest continuous tunnel. It provides more than 1 billion gallons (3.8 billion L) of water each day to more than 9.6 million New Yorkers.

△ HITTING THE STREETS
Each autumn, more than 50,000 runners hit the streets of all five boroughs for the famed New York City Marathon.

MADE IN NY

New York's agricultural outputs include:

- Milk
- Corn for grain
- Hay
- Cattle and calves
- Apples
- Floriculture
- Cabbage
- Sweet corn
- Potatoes
- Tomatoes
- Grapes

New York's industrial outputs include:

- Machinery
- Computer and electronic products
- Transportation equipment
- Chemicals
- Paper
- Plastics and rubber

SPORTING CHANCES

- In 1962, the Mets arrived, and they've played at Citi Field in Queens since 2009.

- The Yankees have played in 40 World Series, winning 27, the most championship appearances and most victories by any pro team.

- There are two NBA teams: the New York Knicks and the Brooklyn Nets, plus the WNBA's New York Liberty.

- The NFL's New York Giants and New York Jets both play at MetLife Stadium (in New Jersey), but only play each other every four years.

- The Buffalo Bills are the only team to appear in and lose in four straight Super Bowls.

- There are also two pro hockey teams (the Rangers and the Islanders), plus two soccer teams (New York Red Bulls and New York City FC).

- The Rangers are nicknamed the "Broadway Blueshirts."

- Madison Square Garden, now home to the Knicks and the Rangers, originally launched in 1879 as a circus venue. The building used today opened in 1968, and it was refurbished in 2013.

- Saratoga Race Course is one of the oldest major sports venues in America. Its first thoroughbred race dates back to 1847.

- Lake Placid hosted the Winter Olympics twice: in 1932 and 1980.

- The National Baseball Hall of Fame is located in Cooperstown.

JENNIFER LOPEZ (b. 1969)

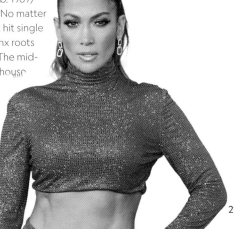

"No matter where I go I know where I came from," sings Lopez in her 2002 hit single "Jenny from the Block." Indeed, "J Lo" has held tight to her Bronx roots despite rising to mega-fame as a singer, dancer, and actress. The middle child of Puerto Rican parents, Lopez grew up in a modest house in the Castle Hill neighborhood, where she took dancing and singing lessons. She eventually landed a coveted "Fly Girl" gig on the hit show *In Living Color*, which launched her career, first as a dancer and later as an actress, singer, producer, and designer. Considered one of the most influential stars of all time, Lopez's net worth is estimated to be about $400 million.

NORTH CAROLINA

CAPITAL: Raleigh **BIRD:** Northern Cardinal **NICKNAME:** Tar Heel State **ENTRY:** 1789

★ ★ ★ *"To be, rather than to seem"* ★ ★ ★

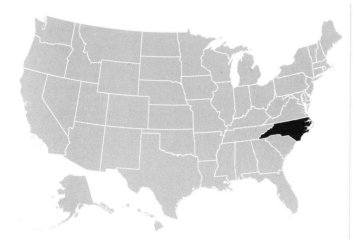

NC FACTS

- The population is 10,698,973.

- Major industries include aerospace, aviation, and defense; the automotive industry; as well as biotechnology and pharmaceuticals.

- North Carolina was the 12th state and is the 29th state in size.

- Natural resources include timber, fish, meat, clay, and minerals.

- The region's original inhabitants include the Catawba, Ani-Yun-Wiya (Cherokee), Muscogee (Creek), Hatteras (Croatan), Tuscarora, Yésah (Tutelo), Saponi, Cheraw, Waccamaw, and Chicora.

- In 1669, the local governors enlisted British philosopher John Locke to create the Fundamental Constitutions of Carolina, a model of government for the colony.

- Dolley Madison, the fourth first lady of the United States was born in Guilford County in 1768.

- During the Civil War, North Carolina was the second-to-last southern state to secede.

▶ STATE FLOWER
Dogwood
Genus *Cornus*

One of the most common trees found across the state, the dogwood has blooms that are usually a soft white or pink.

1926

Born in Mount Airy in 1926, Andy Griffith was an actor known for playing folksy, charming characters in shows such as *The Andy Griffith Show* and *Matlock*. He was also a notable singer, winning a Grammy in 1997 for his southern gospel music. ▼

IF WE ALL WORKED ON THE ASSUMPTION THAT WHAT IS ACCEPTED AS TRUE IS REALLY TRUE, THERE WOULD BE LITTLE HOPE OF ADVANCE.

—Inventor and aviator Orville Wright

- In 1808, after graduating from Princeton, Black American John Chavis opened his own school in North Carolina. The school taught white students during the day and Black students at night.

- Famed hunter and American folk figure Daniel Boone served as a ranger in North Carolina.

- Thelonious Monk, one of the greatest jazz musicians of all time, was born in Rocky Mount in 1917.

- Born in Stony Fork Township, Arthel Lane "Doc" Watson was a folk musician whose bluegrass stylings remain influential in country music today. Beloved for his finger speed and precision and flat-picking skills, Watson was instrumental in gaining national recognition for folk music in the 1960s.

- In 1960, four young Black students sat themselves at the whites-only segregated counter of the Greensboro Woolworth's. This act marked the beginning of one of the country's most famous sit-ins, during which the four men—known as the Greensboro Four—remained seated to protest segregation and racial discrimination.

- Clogging, the state folk dance, consists of foot-based movements such as shuffles, taps, and buck dancing.

- The Venus flytrap is the official state carnivorous plant. ▪

▶ **STORY OF** THE SOUND Though it has come to be an instrument deeply associated with the American South, the banjo's roots stretch back to sub-Saharan Africa, where stringed instruments have been played for centuries. Transported to the Americas by enslaved Africans, the instrument is mentioned in the journal of a visitor to the North Carolina region in 1787. By 1847, the banjo often accompanied the fiddle, and soon gained popularity in the Appalachian region, where musicians made their own instruments from groundhog skins. Already a local mainstay, the banjo became nationally popular thanks to artists such as Gus Cannon, Etta Baker, and Earl Scruggs, who made the banjo's stylings essential to jug band music, blues, and bluegrass, respectively. ▪

STARS ★ OF ★ THE ★ STATE

NINA SIMONE
(1933–2003) Born Eunice Kathleen Waymon in Tryon in 1933, Nina Simone was an iconic musician and an influential activist. Though Simone displayed exceptional piano skills from an early age, she also faced constant prejudice and racial discrimination. Both her innate musical abilities and the discrimination she encountered changed her art. Not long after Simone achieved success in the 1950s with her smash hit "I Loves You, Porgy," she began using her songwriting to cast a spotlight on the violence against Black people that was sweeping the nation with songs such as "Mississippi Goddam." Though Simone faced radical backlash from many white listeners, her music inspired countless activists and became a revolutionary force that lingers today. ▪

217

> **I HAVE KNOWN MORE COLORFUL NORTH CAROLINA POLITICAL FIGURES THAN I HAVE COLORLESS ONES.**
>
> —Former senator Jesse Helms

WEIRD BUT TRUE

- Because of a type of algae, oysters off the coast of North Carolina turn a shade of green-blue.
- Local Ridgeway cantaloupes were once shipped to New York City and Washington, D.C., as delicacies.
- Lake Norman has its own cryptid: "Normie" the lake monster.
- In 2006, thousands of bags of chips washed ashore after they fell off a nearby ship.
- So many purple martins roost on a bridge in Manns Harbor during their migration that the speed limit is lowered from July through August.
- The rare blue ghost fireflies, which are found in Asheville, glow blue.
- A museum in Durham is dedicated to tubas. ▼

▲ SECRET SQUIRREL?

Brevard is famous for its white squirrels—which are actually eastern gray squirrels with a pigment mutation.

MISCELLANY

- People from North Carolina are called **North Carolinians**.
- There are two state berries (the **strawberry** and the **blueberry**), and one state fruit (the **Scuppernong grape**).
- The state beverage is **milk**.
- **High Point** is known as the "Furniture Capital of America."
- Located on Roanoke Island, the **oldest grape vine** in the U.S. is also called the "Mother Vine."
- **Red** and **blue** are the state colors.
- **Pig pickin'**, the name for a get-together involving the cooking of a whole pig over coals, is super popular.
- Other **staples of a pig pickin'**? Macaroni and potato salad, baked beans, and a pig pickin' cake: a vanilla cake flavored with mandarin oranges.
- **Emerald** is the official precious stone.

- The Great Smoky Mountains are home to **1,500 black bears**.
- In 1996, salvagers discovered the wreck of the *Queen Anne's Revenge*, the ship of notorious pirate Blackbeard.
- The state horse is the **Colonial Spanish mustang**.
- **Gold** is the state mineral.
- Known for its hunting skills, the **Plott hound** is the state dog.
- The art at **Paint Rock** is estimated to be 5,000 years old.
- Lighter than its northern counterparts, **Hatteras-style clam chowder** relies on a simple, clear broth as its base.
- The **marbled salamander** is the official state salamander.

- Charlotte native **Charles Duke** became the 10th person to walk on the moon.
- North Carolina gets its name from **Britain's King Charles I**, who gifted it to the Lords Proprietors on the condition they name it after him. (*Carolus* is the Latin word for Charles.)
- The state's nickname —the **"Tar Heel State"**—comes from its abundant pine trees, which are used to make tar and pitch.
- Since 1917, **Cheerwine**, a cherry soda created in Salisbury, has been an iconic beverage across much of the South.
- Until the California Gold Rush, North Carolina was the country's main **gold supplier**.

THE STATE IS KNOWN AS THE "PIG PICKIN' CAPITAL OF THE WORLD."

RECORD ★ SETTERS

On April 12, 1776, the North Carolina colony became the first to call for freedom from the rule of Britain.

BY THE NUMBERS

1712 THE YEAR NORTH AND SOUTH CAROLINA SPLIT, AS THE COLONY WAS BELIEVED TO HAVE GROWN TOO LARGE TO FUNCTION UNDER A SINGLE GOVERNOR

1859 the year Abigail Carter of Clinton designed and created a pair of overalls, going on to become the country's first manufacturer of overalls

250 steps lead to the top of the Cape Hatteras Lighthouse.

6,684 feet (2,037 m): the height of the highest point in the Appalachian Mountains, Mount Mitchell

41 DAYS 7 HOURS 39 MINUTES the record time for hiking the Appalachian trail set by Karel Sabbe

531,286 THE SIZE IN ACRES (215,004 HA) OF NANTAHALA NATIONAL FOREST

1781 the year a civil war, known as the Tory War, between Tory loyalists and revolutionary Whigs, began

2+ number of presidents from the state (James K. Polk and Andrew Johnson). Andrew Jackson was from somewhere near the border between the Carolinas.

DESTINATION: NORTH CAROLINA

- Charlotte is a multicultural city that combines outdoor adventure with a wide variety of urban attractions. A perfect jumping-off point for a day on Lake Norman or Lake Wylie, the city also boasts the Discovery Place science museum, Billy Graham Library, Carowinds amusement park, and more.

- Located in Asheville, the Biltmore Estate is the country's largest home. Visitors to the site—built by businessman George Vanderbilt in the late 1800s—can tour the preserved estate.

- More than just the site where the Wright Brothers made aviation history, the Outer Banks (also known as OBX) is a famed vacation spot featuring more than 100 miles (161 km) of shoreline.

▼ SCENIC ROUTE

Whether through the changing colors of fall or under the thick blue skies of summer, the Blue Ridge Parkway offers drivers stunning views of the Appalachian Mountains. Visitors can stop in the highlands region to fish for trout or hike through wildflowers, visit art galleries in numerous small towns, stop at the spring Budbreak Wine and Craft Beer Festival in Mount Airy, or roam the entire 469 miles (755 km) of the parkway, which winds through the entirety of the state.

In 1903, Wilbur and Orville Wright achieved the first powered and sustained airplane flight with a pilot, paving the way for aviation.

- With more than 250 waterfalls in the state, hikers of all skill levels and ages can find something to enjoy. Great for families, Dry Falls includes a trail that meanders behind the falls, while French Broad Falls includes pools perfect for swimming, and Sliding Rock offers a natural water slide.

- In the winter, the mountainous state offers up plentiful skiing and snowboarding opportunities. Most snow bunnies head to Banner Elk, which acts as a base for both the largest ski area—Sugar Mountain—and Beech Mountain.

- First established as a settlement in 1785, Asheville has long been a beacon for explorers and artists, thanks to its picturesque rolling hills.

- Founded in Durham in 1966, Duke University's Duke Lemur Center is the world's largest lemur sanctuary.

- In 1587, some 115 British settlers arrived at Roanoke Island. John White, the governor, sailed back to England to retrieve more supplies. After a delay, he returned in 1590—to discover that the colonists had vanished. The lost colony remains an enduring part of American mythology.

- Launched in 1940, the battleship *North Carolina* earned 15 gold stars over the course of WWII. Visitors can take behind-the-scenes tours.

- Fans of livermush—a square patty of fried pork liver—should head to Marion's Livermush Festival for unlimited snacking.

MADE IN NC

North Carolina's agricultural outputs include:

- Tobacco
- Pork
- Chicken
- Cotton
- Soybeans
- Animal feed
- Other plant products

North Carolina's industrial outputs include:

- Civilian aircraft parts
- Medical products and equipment
- Defense weaponry
- Vaccines

SPORTING CHANCES

- Born in Akron, Ohio, Stephen Curry wowed the nation when he led Davidson College to the Elite Eight. He quickly became known for his three-point shot and was drafted by the NBA in 2009.

- Originally the Bobcats, the Charlotte Hornets NBA team was first owned by Robert L. Johnson, the first Black franchise majority owner in a major sports league.

- The mascot of the Carolina Panthers NFL team is a black jaguar named Sir Purr.

- In addition to its many races, the Charlotte Motor Speedway is famous for its camping.

- Born in Norlina, Stephanie Wheeler is a two-time Paralympic gold medalist as a member of the women's wheelchair basketball team.

- Charlotte is home to the NASCAR Hall of Fame.

- Stock car racing is the official state sport.

- Shelby, birthplace of Pro Football Hall of Famer Bobby Bell, celebrated Bobby Bell Day on August 28, 2021.

CAROLINA! CAROLINA! HEAVEN'S BLESSINGS ATTEND HER!

WHILE WE LIVE WE WILL CHERISH, PROTECT AND DEFEND HER.

—from "The Old North State," official state song

BIG TEN
Murphy is home to the world's largest set of the Ten Commandments.

STARS ★ OF ★ THE ★ STATE

THE EARNHARDTS

Dale Earnhardt, Sr., (1951–2001) was a legendary stock car racer known for his aggressive driving style (which earned him the nickname "The Intimidator") and numerous wins. Born in Kannapolis, Earnhardt, Sr., debuted at the NASCAR Winston cup in 1975, going on to secure Rookie of the Year in 1979. He won three titles consecutively on three occasions, and 76 victories in total, including 34 at the Daytona International Speedway. His son, Dale Earnhardt, Jr. (b. 1974), has continued the family tradition, becoming a fan favorite in the racing world. Though mostly retired, Earnhardt, Jr., has gone on to found JR Motorsports.

NORTH DAKOTA

CAPITAL: Bismarck **FLOWER:** Wild Prairie Rose **NICKNAME:** Peace Garden State **ENTRY:** 1889

★ ★ ★ *"Liberty and Union Now and Forever, One and Inseparable"* ★ ★ ★

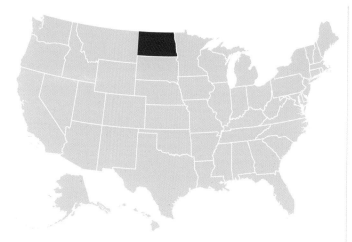

ND FACTS

- With a population of 779,261, North Dakota is the 47th most populous state. Its area of 70,704 square miles (183,123 sq km) ranks it as the 17th largest.

- Original inhabitants include Native Americans such as the Mandan, Lakota and Dakota Sioux, Chippewa, Hidatsa, Assiniboine (Nakoda), and Arikara.

- Pierre Gaultier de Varennes et de La Vérendrye was the first European to arrive in the area in 1738, leading the French to control the area until Spain and England took over.

- In 1803, the land was acquired by the U.S. as part of the Louisiana Purchase, creating the Dakota Territory.

- The Red River forms the eastern border of the state, with the Red River Valley extending 30 to 40 miles (48 to 64 km) on either side of the river. This region is a major producer of red potatoes.

- Theodore Roosevelt National Park in Medora is the only U.S. national park named after a person. ▼

▶ **STATE BIRD**
Western Meadowlark
Sturnella neglecta

North Dakota's native grasslands are home to these yellow-bellied birds, which fill the air with their flute-like songs.

1889

North and South Dakota were a single territory until the year 1889, when President Benjamin Harrison signed statehood proclamations for both and they were admitted as the 39th and 40th states, respectively.

I WOULD NOT HAVE BEEN PRESIDENT IF IT HAD NOT BEEN FOR MY EXPERIENCES IN NORTH DAKOTA.

—President Theodore Roosevelt

- In 1947 and in 1989, there were attempts to drop the word "North" from the state name; both resolutions were defeated by the legislature.

- Spanning 307,000 acres (124,238 ha) with a shoreline of 1,320 miles (2,124 km), Lake Sakakawea, created in 1954 by the construction of the Garrison Dam on the Missouri River, is one of the largest artificial reservoirs in the country. It's located about 75 miles (121 km) northwest of Bismarck.

- The top three most populated cities are Fargo (131,444), Bismarck (74,445), and Grand Forks (58,692).

- The state's highest point is White Butte in the southwestern corner of the state, standing at 3,506 feet (1,068 m) above sea level. The lowest? The far northeastern section of the Red River, at 750 feet (229 m) above sea level.

- Covering over one million acres (405,000 ha), Little Missouri National Grasslands is the largest grassland in the U.S. and one of three grasslands in the state.

- The average annual temperature ranges from 37°F (2.7°C) in the northern part of the state to 43°F (6.1°C) in the south, making it the coldest of the lower 48 states, on average.

- Ninety percent of the state's total land is devoted to farms and ranches.

- The highest recorded temperature was 121°F (49°C) in Steele, and the lowest −60°F (−51°C) in Parshall, both in 1936.

- The weather varies greatly throughout the state: The southwest part of the state is typically warmer than the northeast.

- The North Dakota State Mill and Elevator in Grand Forks is the only state-owned milling facility in the U.S.; it makes bread mix, flour, and pancake mix.

- North Dakota is home to 63 wildlife refuges, more than any other state, including Lostwood National Wildlife Refuge, which has more ducks than any other region in the lower 48 states.

STORY OF THE SONG "North Dakota, North Dakota, with thy prairies wide and free, all thy sons and daughters love thee, fairest state from sea to sea." These are the words of James Foley, a poet who spent his childhood in Bismarck and went on to become the unofficial poet laureate of the state. In 1926, Foley, then a widely published poet, was tapped by the Superintendent of Public Instruction to write lyrics for a song about North Dakota; he produced the "North Dakota Hymn" in return. It was eventually set to music and adopted as the official state song in 1947.

STARS ★ OF ★ THE ★ STATE

THEODORE ROOSEVELT

(1858–1919) "Teddy" Roosevelt first visited the badlands of the Little Missouri River Valley as a young assemblyman on a hunting trip from New York. He became so smitten by the state and its natural beauty that he bought land, spent a majority of his vacations, and owned a cattle ranch there, though he sold it off before becoming the president of the U.S. in 1901. Even as politics dominated his life, Roosevelt continued to visit the state where, as he said, "the romance of [his] life began," until just a few months before his death at the age of 60. Today, Theodore Roosevelt National Park honors the president and the land he loved.

WEIRD BUT TRUE

- In 2017, Buckets Blakes of the Harlem Globetrotters made a trick shot from the top of the tower of the State Capitol through a basketball hoop on the ground, 242 feet (74 m) below.

- The inventor of roll film for cameras was a North Dakotan. He suggested the camera company be named after northern Dakota and called Nodak. When he sold the patent, the new patent owner changed the first letter and called his company "Kodak."

- Thirty-eight-foot-tall (11.5 m) Salem Sue—the world's largest statue of a Holstein cow, in New Salem—can be seen from five miles (8 km) away.

- The state produces enough soybeans to make 483 billion crayons each year.

- Mr. Bubble Day is a state holiday, honoring North Dakotan Harold Schafer, who created the bath product in 1961.

- The town of Ruso has a population of one.

- Bismarck has the only asymmetrical capitol building in the U.S.

- Thorvold the Troll welcomes people to the Minot Visitor's Center.

- A massive, 3,591-pound (1,629 km) burger was eaten in Rutland in 1982. It was served to thousands.

MISCELLANY

- Dakota the Dinosaur, one of only six **mummified dinosaurs** worldwide, was found near Marmarth.

- Fargo is home to one of the world's **largest Microsoft field campuses,** employing some 1,600 team members.

- Nearly 500,000 acres (202,342 ha) of **sunflower fields** blanket the state.

- One-fifth of the population is employed in agriculture, and the state provides more than 90 percent of the nation's **canola and flaxseed**.

- North Dakota is the only state in the nation **without some form of voter registration**.

- The wood chipper featured in the **1996 movie** *Fargo* is on display at the Fargo-Moorhead visitor center.

- The aptly named Center, North Dakota, is the **geographical center of North America**—but there's a monument in the town of Rugby, some 145 miles (233 km) away, that claims the same distinction.

- North Dakota, along with Florida, has the **fewest number of earthquakes** in the country.

- North Dakota was one of the first states to allow **self-driving cars** on public roads.

- A partial skull of a **65-million-year-old** *Triceratops* fossil was unearthed in the Badlands.

- The state fossil is **Teredo-bored petrified wood**.

- Seventy-seven percent of North Dakotans affiliate with **Christian-based faith denominations**.

- Founded in 1885, Glencoe Sloan Memorial Presbyterian Church in Burleigh County is the **state's oldest church** that still holds services.

- North Dakota produces the **fifth largest amount of wind energy** in the U.S.

- Turtle Lake celebrates **Turtle Days**, a festival that includes turtle races.

RECORD ★ SETTERS

In 2017, Cara Mund of Bismarck became the first North Dakotan to be crowned Miss America. The Brown University grad aspires to be the first woman elected as governor of the state.

BY THE NUMBERS

5,220
the weight in pounds (2,368 kg) of French fries served at the 2015 French fry feed in Grand Forks. An annual event, the 2015 serving set a Guinness World Record.

26
the height in feet (8 m) of the world's largest buffalo monument, Dakota Thunder, a 60-ton (54.4 t) concrete giant that greets visitors to Jamestown

19
the height in stories of the state capitol building in Bismarck, one of only four tower-style capitols in the U.S.

400+
the number of free-roaming bison in Theodore Roosevelt National Park

30
the height in feet (9.6 m) of the Dala Horse in Minot, a replica of a Swedish toy reflecting the area's Scandinavian heritage

144
THE LENGTH IN MILES (232 KM) OF THE MAAH DAAH HEY TRAIL, A HORSEBACK RIDING, HIKING, AND BIKING TRAIL

1.8%
of North Dakota's land is forested.

351
billion: the amount in tons (318.4 billion t) of lignite in western North Dakota, the world's largest single deposit of its kind

726,000,000
bags of sunflower seeds can be filled by the amount of sunflowers grown in North Dakota each year.

1.5
million: the number of barrels of oil that have been produced in North Dakota in a single day

Opened in 1919, the Bank of North Dakota is a state-owned, state-run financial institution based in Bismarck, North Dakota. It is the only government-owned general-service bank in the United States.

DESTINATION: NORTH DAKOTA

- A symbol of unity between the U.S. and Canada, the International Peace Garden sits on the Canadian border in Dunseith and offers 2,339 manicured acres (947 ha) of lush greenery, wildflowers, freshwater lakes, waterfalls, and more in the Turtle Mountains. It was established in 1928 as a place "where people could share interests and celebrate friendship."

- Theodore Roosevelt once described the North Dakota Badlands as "so fantastically broken in form and so bizarre in color as to seem hardly properly to belong to this earth." See this dramatic scenery for yourself at Theodore Roosevelt National Park while hiking, taking a scenic drive, or strolling along the land at the Elkhorn Ranch site, where Roosevelt once lived.

- Follow the journey of the Corps of Discovery at the Lewis and Clark Interpretive Center in Washburn. Exhibits showcasing artifacts and art tell the complete story of this important expedition.

- The National Buffalo Museum in Jamestown shines the spotlight on the national mammal, which came close to extinction not too long ago. Bonus: There are two herds of bison living on the grounds.

- A state-of-the-art museum now sits on the site of the ancient Knife River Indian Village where Sacagawea first met Lewis and Clark. Visitors can learn about the culture of the Plains Indians and check out a reconstructed sacred structure called an earthlodge.

- Lions, and tigers, and bears, oh my: More than 600 animals, including moose, river otters, and more, can be spotted at the 90-acre (36 ha) Dakota Zoo in Bismarck.

- Fargo's Plains Art Museum is the largest art museum in the state, with some 4,000 works including traditional and contemporary Native American art, as well as artists of the 20th and 21st centuries from the Midwest and beyond. Nearby, the Fargo Air Museum has several historic—with many still flyable—planes on display, including a Wright Brothers' flier and an MQ-1 Predator unmanned aircraft.

- "Bonanza" farms ruled the prairies in the late 1800s, and today, Bonanzaville, USA, in West Fargo offers a re-creation of that time, with dozens of historic buildings including a log cabin, blacksmith shop, school, drugstore, general store, creamery, saloon, newspaper office, bank, barbershop, and more.

SACAGAWEA

(1788–circa 1812) During the fall of 1804, teenage Shoshone Indian Sacagawea lived in Awatixa Village on the Knife River with her husband, French Canadian trapper Toussaint Charbonneau. It was there that they met Meriwether Lewis and William Clark, who were leading the Corps of Discovery in a journey to the Pacific. The explorers took on Sacagawea (along with her husband and infant son) as a guide and interpreter, and she soon proved instrumental in their expedition as well as their survival, gathering edible plants along the route. In 2003, North Dakota gave a bronze statue of Sacagawea to National Statuary Hall in the U.S. Capitol Building, honoring her work as a "traveler and guide, a translator, a diplomat, and a wife and mother."

◀ ON ICE

The sport of curling in North Dakota traces back to 1901; today, the state has more than 10 competitive clubs and hosts major competitions, including the Collegiate Championships.

SPORTING CHANCES

- North Dakota has never had a major league professional sports team, but it is home to minor league baseball and hockey teams.

- In 1935, a Bismarck-based integrated baseball team called the Churchills won the National Baseball Congress semipro baseball tournament in Wichita, Kansas. Their star players included future Baseball Hall of Famers Satchel Paige and Hilton Smith.

- The name for the Bismarck Bucks, who play in the Champions Indoor Football League, was crowdsourced in a contest and announced live on TV.

- Before he played in the pros and coached the Chicago Bulls and Los Angeles Lakers to 11 NBA championships, Williston's Phil Jackson was a top player at the University of North Dakota.

- First played in 1966, the Potato Bowl football game was billed as a battle between two of the largest potato-growing regions in the U.S. (Idaho and the Red River Valley). The game has been played at the University of North Dakota ever since.

- A football powerhouse, North Dakota State has claimed nine NCAA Football Championship Subdivision (FCS) titles, making them the winningest team in the league.

- Thundar the Bison, North Dakota State's mascot, wasn't officially named until 1991, but the school athletes have been known as the "Bison" or the "Thundering Herd" since 1922.

- Roger Maris, a baseball legend whose MLB single-season home run record of 61 stood from 1961 to 1998, attended high school in Fargo.

- During her career, which spanned from 1978 to 2008, North Dakota State women's basketball coach Amy Ruley led the Bison to 671 wins, 10 conference titles, and five NCAA Division II titles.

- Rodeo is one of the most popular sports in the state and is competed on the professional, high school, and junior levels.

- Known as the "hockey twins," sisters Jocelyne and Monique Lamoureux of Grand Forks both played on Team U.S.A.'s gold-medal squad in the 2018 Pyeongchang games. Graduates of the University of North Dakota, they were the first set of twins ever to play women's ice hockey in the Olympics.

- Each January, anglers gather on the frozen surface of Six-Mile Bay in Devils Lake to compete for cash prizes in the DLVFD Ice Fishing Tournament, the largest ice contest of its kind in the state.

▼ SITTING BULL

The original burial site of Sitting Bull (Tatanka Iyotake), the famous Sioux chief, is in Fort Yates.

OHIO

★ ★ ★

"With God All Things Are Possible"

★ ★ ★

CAPITAL: Columbus **BIRD:** Northern Cardinal **NICKNAME:** Buckeye State **ENTRY:** 1803

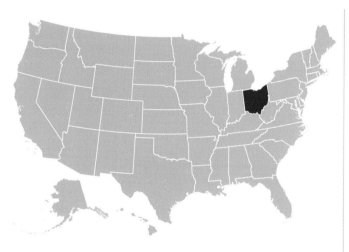

OH FACTS

- The population is 11,756,058.

- Natural resources include soil for agriculture, coal, gas, and rock salt.

- Original inhabitants of the area included the Erie, Kiikaapoa (Kickapoo), and Shawnee. Today, there are no federally recognized tribes in the state.

- As British colonists ventured into the area, tensions grew with the French, who also laid claim to the region. In 1756, hostilities escalated to the point of war. Preferring the few French settlers to incoming swarms of British, various Indigenous nations aligned themselves with the French, lending the conflict its name: the French and Indian War.

- The country's first airplane factory was established in Dayton in 1910 by Wilbur and Orville Wright, inventors of the first piloted airplane.

- The Ohio Women's Rights Convention, held in Akron in 1851, was a pivotal conference in the progress of women's equality. Among the participants—in addition to Susan B. Anthony, Elizabeth Cady Stanton, and Amelia Bloomer— was activist Sojourner Truth.

- The 17th state, it is the 35th state in size.

- A Cleveland native, Tracy Chapman is a singer and songwriter lauded for her rich vocals in songs such as "Fast Car" and "Give Me One Reason."

- Tecumseh, a Shawnee chief and orator who was born near present-day Xenia, advocated for an alliance among Indigenous nations to stave off invading colonists. During the War of 1812, Tecumseh allied with the British, leading a band of British and Indigenous fighters to capture Detroit. However, during a battle in 1813, Tecumseh was killed, leading to the dissolution of Indigenous resistance in the Ohio area.

▶ STATE FLOWER

Red Carnation
Dianthus caryophyllus

Designated in 1904, the red carnation was meant to honor the recently assassinated President McKinley, who often wore the blossom in his coat lapel.

1969

In 1969, Wapakoneta-born Neil Armstrong became the first person to walk on the moon. He first commanded Gemini 8 and then joined Apollo 11. A full-scale replica of the moon landing craft can be found in Warren.

IF I WERE GIVING A YOUNG MAN ADVICE AS TO HOW HE MIGHT SUCCEED IN LIFE, I WOULD SAY TO HIM, PICK OUT A GOOD FATHER AND MOTHER, AND BEGIN LIFE IN OHIO.

—Inventor and aviator Wilbur Wright

- According to lore, the buckeye candy was invented by Gail Tabor in the 1960s. The candies, consisting of smooth peanut butter balls dipped in chocolate to resemble the buckeye nuts of the official state tree, are an iconic local snack.

- Born in Cleveland in 1925, Paul Newman was an actor, director, and philanthropist. Famed on the screen for his piercing blue eyes, Newman himself preferred his philanthropy work, staunchly supporting gay rights and global disarmament. His organizations included Newman's Own, which has generated some $250 million for charity; the Scott Newman Center; and the Hole in the Wall Gang Camp.

- A free state, Ohio was home to abolitionist advocates such as Quakers and the Ohio Anti-Slavery Society, an abolitionist organization established in 1835. The state became a major hub of the nation's Underground Railroad network, with some 3,000 miles (4,828 km) of escape routes and safe homes.

- Top industries include automotive, steel, agriculture, aerospace, small appliances, and health care.

- Annie Oakley, renowned for her shooting accuracy, was born in Darke County in 1860.

- In 1970, students at Kent State University organized a protest against the Vietnam War. Clashes between protesters and police led the governor to deploy the Ohio National Guard, who opened fire when protesters threw rocks and debris at them. Four students were killed and nine more injured.

- Cincinnati chili is a meat-heavy, cinnamon-spiced chili served over cooked spaghetti noodles.

▶ **STORY OF** THE PRESIDENTIAL TOMBS Ohio has produced the second highest number of U.S. presidents, so it is perhaps no surprise that the state is home to some of the grandest presidential tombs. Buried in Cleveland, James Garfield—who was assassinated in 1881—is buried in a castle-like fortification replete with stained-glass windows in Lake View Cemetery. William Henry Harrison, in contrast, is buried in a simple tomb overlooking the Ohio River on Mount Nebo. Warren G. Harding's Harding Memorial evokes a more traditional approach with its neoclassical columns, but it's William McKinley who may have the grandest: Located in Canton, the enormous domed mausoleum can only be reached by climbing 108 steps.

STARS ★ OF ★ THE ★ STATE

TONI MORRISON (1931–2019)

Toni Morrison was an award-winning author whose works tended to focus on the experiences of Black women, pairing lyrical prose with folktale elements to create powerful and often devastating novels. Born Chloe Anthony Wofford in Lorain in 1931, she published her first novel, *The Bluest Eye*—an examination of Caucasian-centered beauty standards—in 1970. She went on to publish 10 more novels, as well as children's books and essays. In 1988, her novel *Beloved* received the Pulitzer Prize and was later adapted into a film. Morrison was awarded the Nobel Prize in 1993, the Coretta Scott King Award in 2005, and the Presidential Medal of Freedom in 2012.

▲ BIG PICNIC

A building in Newark was designed to look like a giant picnic basket.

WEIRD BUT TRUE

- At various farm fall events, kids can play in corn kernel pits instead of ball pits.

- Dublin's answer to Stonehenge is Cornhenge: a collection of corn statues installed in honor of Sam Frantz, the inventor of several hybrid corn species.

- Cornhenge is not to be confused with Zanesville's Vasehenge, an installation of 18 giant vases that celebrate the city's one-time status as the "Clay Capital of the U.S."

- Italian dictator Benito Mussolini once gifted a statue of Romulus and Remus to Cincinnati.

- An ice cream company headquartered in Columbus started a viral sensation when they released an everything bagel–flavored ice cream.

- In Lyndhurst, a 60-plus-year-old tradition involves an enormous seasonal art installation—known as Eggshelland—of thousands of brightly colored eggs for Easter.

- During the Tombstone Derby in Elmore, participants race in motorized caskets and coffins.

- One restaurant chain in Akron has hot dog buns signed by famous people, including Barack Obama, Burt Reynolds, Donald J. Trump, and others.

- Michigan and Ohio went to war during the Toledo War in 1835.

HELLO, CLEVELAND!

—*This Is Spinal Tap*, 1984

In 1872, Victoria Woodhull, a Homer native and women's suffrage leader, became the first woman to run for president of the United States.

MISCELLANY

- People from Ohio are called **Buckeyes** or Ohioans.

- The state amphibian is the **spotted salamander**.

- A **center of immigration** in the 20th century, the state is home to people of African, German, Italian, Jewish, Norwegian, Greek, Swiss, Polish, Lithuanian, Hungarian, Irish, and Czechoslovakian descent, among others.

- The name Ohio comes from the **Iroquois word for "good river."**

- The state fossil is the *Isotelus* **trilobite**, a type of giant marine arthropod.

- The **Cleveland Polish Boy** is a sandwich featuring a smoked sausage, coleslaw, fries, and barbecue sauce in a bun.

- The state reptile is the **black racer snake**.

- The state's only large-scale Civil War battle was fought in 1863 on **Buffington Island**.

- The state fruit is the **tomato**.

- **Tomato juice** is the state beverage.

▲ TOP DOC

Buckeye Lucile Petry Leone was the first woman to be appointed U.S. assistant surgeon general in 1949 and the first woman elected to the National Academy of Medicine in 1970.

- Though normally a steely gray, the state's gemstone, **Ohio flint**, comes in a variety of colors such as pink, red, yellow, blue, and more.

- The state is the setting for many **beloved American sitcoms and dramas**, including *The Drew Carey Show*, *3rd Rock from the Sun*, *WKRP in Cincinnati*, *Glee*, and many more.

- The Midwest used to be the site of large-scale wine production, as can still be seen in the ruins of the 1865 **Kelleys Island Wine Company**.

- Popular at breakfast are the German sausage patties known as **Goetta**, made of a blend of pork, beef, onion, oats, and spices.

BY THE NUMBERS

900 the weight in pounds (408 kg) of each of the world's largest drumsticks, located in Warren

12% of the state's population served during WWII

18,000 years: the age of the grooves left by glaciers in the limestone of Kelleys Island

110 miles (177 km): the length of the Ohio and Erie Canalway

210 the lowest depth in feet (64 m) of Lake Erie

12,000+ the number of roses grown at the Columbus Park of Roses

7 THE NUMBER OF U.S. PRESIDENTS BORN IN THE STATE: ULYSSES S. GRANT, RUTHERFORD B. HAYES, JAMES GARFIELD, BENJAMIN HARRISON, WILLIAM McKINLEY, WILLIAM H. TAFT, AND WARREN G. HARDING

1963 the year the Pro Football Hall of Fame was established in Canton

2 of those presidents were assassinated— President McKinley and President Garfield.

DESTINATION: OHIO

- Located in Sandusky and overlooking Lake Erie, Cedar Point is an amusement park with more than 150 years of history. Beginning as a public beach, the award-winning park launched its first ride in 1892 and is now home to multiple roller coasters and themed attractions. ▲

- Located on the Ohio River since 1788, Cincinnati is famed for its art museum, Great American Ball Park, and Zoo & Botanical Garden. History buffs are also drawn to the National Underground Railroad Freedom Center, the Cincinnati Museum Center, and the Cincinnati Reds Hall of Fame and Museum, while outdoor enthusiasts can stroll the many parks.

- Cleveland is perhaps best known for the Rock & Roll Hall of Fame, which opened amid much fanfare in 1995. Other top attractions include the West Side Market, multiple museums, the Great Lakes Science Center, and even the house used to film the holiday classic *A Christmas Story*.

- The state's border along Lake Erie features many beaches, including the scenic Kelleys Island State Park, the historic Main Street Beach, the family-friendly Lakeside Beach, and more.

- In northeastern Ohio, Amish Country is home to the largest community of Amish people in the world. Visitors can learn about the history and culture of these communities at the Amish & Mennonite Heritage Center in Millersburg, or dine at one of dozens of local restaurants.

- Inhabited for some 15,000 years, the region has been home to people since prehistoric times. Some evidence of this lies in the state's burial mounds. Shaped like a large snake with a curling tail, Serpent Mound was likely made by the Adena people more than 2,000 years ago (though other estimates place the date around A.D. 1,000).

- From the Cuyahoga Valley to the Hocking Valley, the state offers multiple scenic train routes in historic carriages.

- Fans of beverages should seek out Columbus's coffee trail and distillery trail. Other city sights include an arts district, the historic German Village, the science center, and the LEGOLAND Discovery Center.

- Located in Akron, Stan Hywet Hall is a historic home built by Goodyear Tire and Rubber Company co-founder F.A. Seiberling in 1915. The estate contains five buildings, 10 gardens, a conservatory, and more.

- Found only in parts of the eastern U.S. and Canada, a pawpaw is an oblong fruit that tastes like a cross between a banana and a mango. Too delicate and short-lived to ship, the fruit is best enjoyed locally, such as in gatherings like Albany's yearly Pawpaw Festival. ▪

STARS ★ OF ★ THE ★ STATE

CLARK GABLE

(1901–1960) Born William Clark Gable in Cadiz, Clark Gable was an iconic actor known as the "King of Hollywood." The son of an oil field worker, Gable dropped out of high school at 16 and traveled the country as an actor before landing in Los Angeles in the 1930s. Spotted by a producer while acting in a theater production, he signed with the Metro-Goldwyn-Mayer film company (MGM), quickly becoming known as a charming heartthrob. Though Gable won an Oscar for his role in the 1934 film *It Happened One Night*, he is perhaps best remembered for his turn as Rhett Butler in 1939's *Gone with the Wind*. ▪

SPORTING CHANCES

- Born in Akron, LeBron James is a celebrated basketball star. In 2004, at age 20, he became the youngest player ever to receive the Rookie of the Year Award.

- Columbus-born Simone Biles is considered one of the greatest gymnasts ever. She is the most decorated gymnast of all time with 34 Olympic and World Championship medals.

- In 1962, Cambridge native John Glenn became the first American to orbit Earth.

- Known as the "Golfer of the Millennium," Jack Nicklaus was born in Columbus in 1940. He holds 18 professional major championship titles.

- In 1869 in Cincinnati, the Cincinnati Red Stockings (now known as the Cincinnati Reds) defeated the Mansfield Independents in the first professional, paid baseball game.

- Spending close to $100 million on its athletics department each year, Ohio State University has 37 teams.

- Paul Brown, co-founder of the Cleveland Browns in 1946, is often credited with shaping the NFL into the league it is today thanks to his implementation of team and player statistical studies.

- Seating 102,780, Ohio State's stadium is the country's fourth largest on-campus facility.

- Over the years, the Cleveland Guardians have had many names: the Bluebirds, the Bronchos, the Naps, the Indians, and since 2021, the Guardians.

- Ohio University's bobcat mascot is named Rufus.

MADE IN OH

Ohio's agricultural outputs include:

- Soybeans
- Corn
- Animal feed
- Soybean meal
- Dairy
- Chicken eggs
- Pork
- Beef

Ohio's industrial outputs include:

- Civilian aircraft
- Motor vehicles
- Engines
- Cigarettes
- Medical instruments
- Road tractors

> ## IN NORTHEAST OHIO, NOTHING IS GIVEN. EVERYTHING IS EARNED. YOU WORK FOR WHAT YOU HAVE.
>
> —Pro basketball star LeBron James

◀ BUCKEYE BULLET

In 1936, Jesse Owens—who had previously set three track and field records within the span of an hour—won four gold Olympic medals. This incredible feat, which happened in Berlin under Adolf Hitler, flew in the face of Hitler's views on racial supremacy and served as a moral victory for those opposing him.

OKLAHOMA

★ ★ ★

"Work Conquers All"

★ ★ ★

CAPITAL: Oklahoma City **FLOWER:** Oklahoma Rose **NICKNAME:** Sooner State **ENTRY:** 1907

OK FACTS

- With a population of more than four million, Oklahoma ranks 28th in the U.S.

- The nation's 19th largest state, Oklahoma covers 69,899 square miles (181,048 sq km).

- The most populated city is Oklahoma City, with 694,800 residents. Tulsa and Norman are the next most populated.

- Some of the earliest inhabitants included the Jicarilla Apache, the Caddo, the Comanche, the Kiowa, the Osage, and the Wichita. ▼

- The state boasts the highest density of Indigenous languages. There are more than 40 distinct Native American languages spoken.

- In 1823, the Supreme Court ruled that Native Americans could not hold title to lands within the U.S. As a result, Native Americans were forced to leave their homelands to relocate to what's now Oklahoma—then called Indian Territory—an arduous and harrowing journey known as the Trail of Tears.

▶ **STATE BIRD**

Scissor-Tailed Flycatcher
Tyrannus forficatus

Designated in 1951, the scissor-tailed flycatcher was chosen as Oklahoma's state bird for its love of agriculture-harming insects such as wasps, moths, spiders, and, of course, flies.

1901

Oil was first discovered near Tulsa in 1901, and with a daily production exceeding 120,000 barrels, the city became known as the "Oil Capital of the World."

OKLAHOMA, WHERE THE WIND COMES SWEEPIN' DOWN THE PLAIN.

—Lyricist Oscar Hammerstein II, *Oklahoma!*

▶ **FAREWELL TO FREE PARKING**
The world's first parking meter, known as Park-O-Meter No. 1, was installed in the business district of Oklahoma City on July 16, 1935.

- The area was controlled by France and Spain between the 1600s and 1800s, when French emperor Napoleon Bonaparte acquired the land and later sold it as part of the Louisiana Territory.

- Water covers 1,220 square miles (3,170 sq km) of the state in lakes and ponds, not including rivers and streams.

- There are over 200 human-made lakes, more than any other state.

- Oklahoma has four mountain ranges: the Ozark Mountains, Ouachitas, Arbuckles, and Wichitas.

- Tornado Alley—the area of the U.S. where there is a high potential for tornado development—is centered near Oklahoma City. The annual average is 57 tornadoes. ▶

- Approximately 50 minor earthquakes occur in Oklahoma each year, but few are felt.

- Producing the fourth largest amount of natural gas in the nation, Oklahoma is home to 14 of the 100 largest natural gas fields in the country.

- Oklahoma produces more gypsum than any other state. It is the only state that produces iodine and one of seven states that produce helium. ▪

▶ **STORY OF** THE NICKNAME When the Oklahoma Territory was opened for settlement through land claims races—or land runs—tens of thousands made their way to the area in the hope of snagging some cheap land. Each race began with a pistol shot, and those who jumped the gun or entered the territory before the legal date and time were called Sooners. The nickname persisted, eventually being linked to an energetic, can-do spirit, and in 1908 the name became the mascot of the sports teams at the University of Oklahoma. ▪

STARS ★ OF ★ THE ★ STATE

GARTH BROOKS

(b. 1962) He's got friends in low places—and all over the world. Tulsa-born Brooks, who got his start singing in clubs while attending Oklahoma State University, is the top-selling solo artist in U.S. history with more than 157 million album sales. He launched into superstardom with his second album, *No Fences* (featuring his hits "Friends in Low Places" and "The Thunder Rolls"), which stayed atop the country charts for 23 weeks and sold more than 17 million copies. The first artist in history—in any genre—to have seven albums hit 10 million sales each, Brooks remains an international icon—and a charitable one, too. In 2021, he was awarded the George H.W. Bush Points of Light award for his philanthropic works, including with Teammates for Kids, a nonprofit that raises money for children in need. ▪

- 300 skeletons are on display at the Museum of Osteology in Oklahoma City, the only skeleton museum in the nation.

- Each April, Beaver hosts the World Championship Cow Chip Throwing Contest, a competition to see who can chuck dried cow manure the farthest.

- Oklahoma City is about the same distance from New York as it is to Los Angeles.

- Shopping carts were invented and used in Oklahoma before anywhere else in the world.

- Cimarron County is the only county in the U.S. that touches five states: Colorado, New Mexico, Texas, and Kansas (and Oklahoma, of course!).

- The official state meal is fried okra, squash, corn bread, barbecue pork, biscuits, sausage and gravy, grits, corn, strawberries, chicken-fried steak, pecan pie, and black-eyed peas.

- It's said that if you stand at the "Center of the Universe" landmark in Tulsa and make a noise, the sound is echoed back several times louder than it was made.

- There's a swimming pool shaped like the state of Oklahoma at the Governor's Mansion.

- Lamb testicles—aka "lamb fries"—are on the menu at a steakhouse in Oklahoma City.

- Cleveland, Orlando, Miami, Pittsburg, Chattanooga, Peoria, Burbank, and Fargo are all towns in Oklahoma. ▪

- During the 1930s, Oklahoma was plagued by devastating dust storms; the worst came on April 14, 1935, now known as "Black Sunday." As many as three million tons (2.7 million t) of topsoil blew off the Great Plains that day.

- So many residents left the plains for the West Coast to escape poverty brought on by the dust storms and the Great Depression that they became known as "Okies."

- The world's largest concrete totem pole reaches 90 feet (27 m) in Chelsea.

- The only skyscraper that famed architect Frank Lloyd Wright ever designed is the 19-story Price Tower in Bartlesville.

- Located within the "Bible Belt," Oklahoma is a religious state: 79 percent of residents are Christian, 18 percent are unaffiliated with any religion, and about 2 percent practice non-Christian religions.

- Stretching more than a mile long (6,565 feet, which equals 1.24 miles/2 km) and 147 feet (45 m) high, the Pensacola Dam, which holds back the waters of Grand Lake O' the Cherokee, is the longest multiple-arch dam in the world.

- About one in 12 residents of Oklahoma is a Native American—a higher percentage than in any other U.S. state.

- Five astronauts were born in Oklahoma.

- Oklahoma's state capitol building is the only capitol with an oil well directly underneath it.

- Enid, which has the third largest grain storage capacity in the world, is known as the Wheat Capital of the U.S.

- The world's largest deposit of alabaster is at Alabaster Caverns near Freedom.

- Tulsa's All Souls Unitarian Church, a megachurch, has weekly attendance topping 2,000.

- An Oklahoma City jewelry store recently displayed "The Heart of Oklahoma," a flawless 18.92-carat yellow diamond.

- One of the fastest wind speeds ever recorded on Earth, 318 miles an hour (512 kph), occurred in Moore during the 1999 Oklahoma City F5 tornado.

- Oklahomans collectively spend 3.5 million days hunting each year.

- A Tulsa woman is the only known person who has ever been hit with space trash.

- There are more than 400 banjos and other memorabilia on display at the American Banjo Museum in Oklahoma City.

- A herd of buffalo that descended from buffalo at the Bronx Zoo roam Wichita Mountains National Wildlife Refuge.

KRISTIN CHENOWETH

(b. 1968) From Broken Arrow to Broadway: Chenoweth's journey to a Tony Award–winning actress began in Oklahoma, where she sang gospel in churches, starred in school plays, and dabbled in beauty pageants, earning the title of Miss Oklahoma City University while she was a student there. She made her Broadway debut in 1997, and two years later won the Tony. In 2003, she played Glinda the Good Witch in the musical *Wicked*, picking up another Tony nomination. Chenoweth, who has also starred in movies and television shows, was inducted into the Oklahoma Hall of Fame in 2010 and into the Oklahoma Music Hall of Fame in 2011. ▪

BY THE NUMBERS

Route 66

2,238 LENGTH IN MILES (3,602 KM) OF THE ENTIRE ROUTE 66, WHICH PASSES THROUGH EIGHT STATES

9 width in feet (2.7 m) of the last remaining "ribbon road," a section of pavement laid in 1922

80 length in feet (24 m) of the Blue Whale in Catoosa, a historic landmark along Route 66 that's made of metal and cement

400 approximate number of miles (644 km) of Route 66 that are in Oklahoma, more than anywhere else

76 height in feet (23 m) of the Golden Driller statue in Tulsa along Route 66, which was adopted as a state monument in 1979

1946 THE YEAR SINGER NAT KING COLE HAD A HIT SINGLE WITH "(GET YOUR KICKS ON) ROUTE 66"

573 time, in hours, it took Cherokee citizen and Foyil-born Andy Payne to complete the 1928 Transcontinental Footrace, 2,400 miles (3,862 km) of which followed Route 66

650 NUMBER OF FLAVORED SODAS AT POPS 66 SODA RANCH, A ROADSIDE STOP IN ARCADIA

1924 the year businessman Cyrus Avery was appointed Oklahoma State Highway Commissioner, a position in which he designed Route 66

In 1907, Kate Barnard became the first woman in the U.S. elected to a state office; she served as Oklahoma Commissioner of Charities and Corrections for eight years. Today, a life-size bronze sculpture of "Miss Kate" sits on a bench in the state capitol building.

DESTINATION: OKLAHOMA

- Once a warehouse district, Bricktown in Oklahoma City is now a buzzing hub of bars, restaurants, and a one-mile (1.6 km) canal accessible by water taxi.

- Stretching 93 miles (150 km), the Wichita Mountain Scenic Byway passes through a wildlife refuge, where you can spot 50 species of mammal, including elk and bison. A side road takes you to the top of Mount Scott, a 2,464-foot (751 m) peak with views of the mountains and Lake Lawtonka below.

- At a height of 77 feet (23 m), Turner Falls is the gem of a park bearing the same name in the Arbuckle Mountains in Davis. From hiking trails to natural caves, the 1,500-acre (607 ha) park is a playground for outdoor enthusiasts.

- The 55-room Marland Mansion & Estate in Ponca City offers a glimpse into the opulence of the 1920s, when oil tycoon E.W. Marland built the sprawling home for $5.5 million. Known as the "Palace on the Prairie," the four-level home features Waterford crystal chandeliers, gold leaf-accented ceilings, and more intricate and luxurious details.

- Great Salt Plains State Park is the only place on Earth where you can dig up your own hourglass-shaped inclusions of selenite crystals. Located just north of Jet, the otherworldly, sparkling landscape (and the saltwater lake) are the remains of a prehistoric ocean that once covered the entire state.

▼ RIDE 'EM COWBOY

Oklahoma City's National Cowboy Museum houses more than 28,000 objects, including American Indian art and artifacts, and a replica of a 19th-century Western pioneer town.

SPORTING CHANCES

- Oklahoma City is home to an NBA team, the Thunder, as well as OKC Energy FC of the United Soccer League and one minor league baseball team.

- The Oklahoma University Sooners were playing football before Oklahoma became a state, with the first organized football game taking place in Oklahoma Territory in September 1895.

- Since the end of World War II, the Sooners have had more wins than any other school and the second-best winning percentage.

- In 1968, Tulsa's Madeline Manning Mims became the first American woman to win gold in the 800-meter race, setting an Olympic record in the process. ▼

- Bart Conner, who competed for the University of Oklahoma and won two gold medals at the 1984 Olympic Games, now runs the Bart Conner Gymnastics Academy in Norman, along with his wife, Romanian Olympic gold medalist Nadia Comăneci.

- Pulled by two white ponies, the University of Oklahoma's mascot, the Sooner Schooner, is a miniature version of the Conestoga wagon used by settlers of the state.

- After growing up in Commerce, Mickey Mantle went on to hit 536 home runs and win seven World Series with the New York Yankees. There are statues memorializing the "Commerce Comet," who died in 1995, in Commerce and Oklahoma City.

RECORD ★ SETTERS

In 1971, Patience Sewell Latting was elected as the mayor of Oklahoma City, making it the first large city to have a female mayor.

- Known for his diverse talent, Jim Thorpe is an Oklahoma legend: Born near Prague, in Indian Territory (now in Oklahoma) in 1888, he played professional football and baseball, and he won the decathlon and the pentathlon at the 1912 Olympic Games in Stockholm.

- An 18-foot (5.4 m) statue of 1996 Olympic gold medalist Shannon Miller stands in a park named in the gymnast's honor in her hometown of Edmond.

- Tulsa's Expo Square is the site of the annual U.S. National Arabian & Half-Arabian Championship Horse Show, considered one of the most prestigious Arabian horse shows in North America.

- The state is home to the National Softball Hall of Fame and Museum and the International Gymnastics Hall of Fame, as well as the National Wrestling Hall of Fame and Museum.

- The NCAA Women's College World Series has been held at the National Softball Hall of Fame Stadium every year since 1990, except for 1996. ▪

▶ HISTORY LESSON

Get your fill of Oklahoma history at the Museum of the Great Plains in Lawton, highlighting the various cultures that have inhabited the region since around 11,500 B.C. Nearby, Fort Sill National Historic Landmark and Museum showcases an active army fort dating back to 1869 and the gravesite of Apache chief Geronimo.

MADE IN OK

Oklahoma's agricultural outputs include:

- Rye
- Canola
- Beef
- Wheat

Oklahoma's industrial outputs include:

- Aerospace and defense
- Paper and packaging manufacturing
- Petroleum and coal products
- Beverage production
- Fertilizer manufacturing

▶ MILK IT

One million glasses of milk are produced every hour by Braum's Dairy in Tuttle.

OREGON

★ ★ ★

"She Flies With Her Own Wings"

★ ★ ★

CAPITAL: Salem **BIRD:** Western Meadowlark **NICKNAME:** Beaver State **ENTRY:** 1859

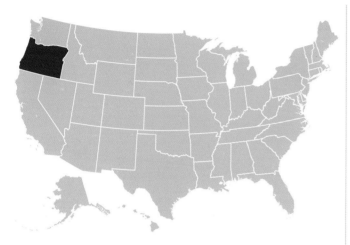

OR FACTS

- The population is 4,240,137.

- The 33rd state, Oregon is the 10th largest in size.

- Important industries include manufacturing, forestry, education, health, and government.

- Some Americans took a path out west in the 1840s that came to be known as the Oregon Trail. Pioneers traveled with wagons but rarely rode in them—most walked alongside for nearly the entire route to preserve their cattle. Not only was it slow-going— most wagon trains traveled about 16 miles (26 km) per day—it was highly dangerous.

- Oregon is a state devoted to the outdoors. From exploring the tide pools of the coast to skiing on Mount Hood, from hiking Multnomah Falls to horseback riding in the high desert, and from windsurfing the Columbia Gorge to rafting in Hells Canyon, Oregon has something for nature enthusiasts who love land, water, and sky—or all three. ▽

▶ STATE FLOWER

Oregon Grape
Mahonia aquifolium

Designated as the state flower in 1899, the Oregon grape plant blooms with sunny yellow flowers in the summer and berries in the fall.

1912

Harriet Redmond was a Black suffragist who helped Oregonian women gain the right to vote in 1912. She also fought against the Black exclusion laws that had begun to be set in place in 1844 and attempted to deny local residence to Black people.

ONE WAGON JUST PASSING ... WITH THE MOTTO, "ROOT, LITTLE HOG OR DIE" ... ON BOTH SIDES ... AND ON ANOTHER COVER IS WRITTEN, "BOUND FOR ORIGEN."

—Oregon Trail pioneer E.W. Conyers, May 25, 1852

▶ FERTILE GROUND

Natural resources include soil for agriculture, forests, water, and gemstones such as sunstone, opal, jade, and agate.

- Born sometime around 1840 in the Wallowa Valley area, In-mut-too-yah-lat-lat (Chief Joseph) was a chief of the Nimi'ipuu (Nez Perce) who attempted to lead his people toward Canada to escape persecution and the designated reservations created by the U.S. government.

- Thanks to the area's high population of beavers, John Jacob Astor's Pacific Fur Company at the eponymously named Fort Astoria became the region's first permanent American settlement in 1811.

- Among the 125 or so Indigenous nations native to the area were the Alsea, Bannock, Cayuse, Chetco, Chinook, Tlatskanai (Clatskanie), Coos, Taltushtuntede and Dakubetede (Galice and Applegate), Kalapuya, Klamath and Modoc, Molala, Multnomah, Nimi'ipuu (Nez Perce), and many more.

- In 1844, Robin Holmes, his wife Polly, and three of their children were enslaved and taken to Polk County by Nathanial Ford despite Oregon's status as a free territory. The Territorial Supreme Court ruled in Holmes's favor, both freeing his children and reaffirming that Oregon would be a free territory.

▲ GORGE-OUS!

Some 40 to 60 million years ago, volcanic activity began the eons-long formation of the Columbia River Gorge.

- The Corps of Discovery (now known as the Lewis and Clark expedition) sought the fabled Northwest Passage: a water route that would stretch from one coast of the country to the other, ending in Oregon. No such passage existed, but the expedition paved the way for westward expansion.

- *Portlandia* was a comedy sketch show that both celebrated and lampooned the city's affinity for activism and the coffee-drinking hipster stereotype. ▪

STARS ★ OF ★ THE ★ STATE

MATTHEW "MATT" GROENING

(b. 1954) Born in Portland in 1954, Matt Groening is a cartoonist best known for his creation of the smash-hit animated show *The Simpsons*. After attending Evergreen State College, Groening moved to Los Angeles, where he published his weekly cartoon strip *Life in Hell*. In 1989, after his comics attracted interest from television producers, Groening debuted a show featuring new characters on the Fox network. Not only did *The Simpsons* establish Fox as a major television network presence, it developed into a worldwide cultural phenomenon. The series, which continues to date, is the longest-running series on American television and has received 20 Emmy Awards. ▪

- Oregon has a state microbe: *Saccharomyces cerevisiae*, aka brewer's yeast.

- An Oregon-based ice cream shop has made flavors such as bone marrow and smoked cherries, fish sauce caramel with palm sugar, and dill pickle.

- An Oregon brewery made beer from microbes found in their brewmaster's beard.

- A Portland doughnut shop, Voodoo Doughnut, also performs wedding ceremonies.

- One Oregonian in Hillsboro lives in a restored airplane.

- There is a Portland city park situated on top of a dormant volcano.

- Popular across the state are mud runs: races where participants trudge through muddy courses. ▼

Covering some 2,384 acres (965 ha) of Malheur National Forest, a fungus known as the honey mushroom is the largest living organism on Earth.

- A Portland trend involves leaving tiny toy horses attached to iron rings. These rings were once used to secure real horses and carriages.

- Colossal Claude is the state's own local cryptid: a supposed sea creature that lives in the Columbia River.

- The Oregon Tourism Commission created a game based on the nostalgic classic, Oregon Trail. Only in this one, players pick whether to teach yoga, sample wines, and more.

- In Hood River, it is illegal to juggle without a license.

▲ HIGH TIMES

In 1998, the state legalized the medical use of marijuana, and in 2014, Measure 91 made the recreational use of cannabis legal as well.

MISCELLANY

- People from Oregon are called **Oregonians**.

- Oregon's state animal is the **beaver**.

- Different theories exist on the origin of the state's name: It may stem from a name jotted on a 1715 French map, or perhaps have to do with a British officer's 1765 claim that local peoples called a nearby river **"Ouragon."**

- The state beverage is **milk**.

- **Smith Rock State Park** is a premiere destination for rock climbing.

- There are **38,500 farms** in the state.

- According to one survey, **66% of**

Oregonians never use an umbrella, no matter the weather.

- Reedsport is the state capital of **chainsaw carving**.

- **Navy blue and gold** are the state colors.

- The state fossil is **Metasequoia**, an ancient type of redwood tree.

- The unofficial slogan of Portland is **"Keep Portland Weird!"**

- The state fruit, **the pear**, comes in four local varieties.

- Also known as heliolite, the **sunstone** is the state gem.

- The carpet used at **Portland International Airport (PDX)** has become a Portland icon.

- The state nut, the **hazelnut**, was originally called the filbert.

- The landscape of **central Oregon** is considered a high desert, and much of the terrain sits at an elevation of 4,000 feet (1,219 m) or more above sea level.

- The region has its own acronym: **PNW (Pacific Northwest)**.

- One of the most iconic flavors of Oregon is the **marionberry**. A cross in taste between a blackberry and a raspberry, the fruit is baked into pies and cobblers, cooked down into jam, whipped into ice cream and milkshakes, and even used to flavor vodkas and whiskeys.

BY THE NUMBERS

35 **NUMBER OF GLACIERS IN OREGON**

10,000 the number of rosebushes grown at the International Rose Test Garden in Portland

2,500 the approximate weight in pounds (1,134 kg) of an adult male Steller sea lion

99 percentage of all U.S. hazelnuts produced in the state

500,000 approximate number of settlers who arrived in the state via the Oregon Trail

12 **NUMBER OF BRIDGES THAT ARE WITHIN PORTLAND CITY LIMITS**

1971 **THE YEAR THAT PORTLAND HOSTED OREGON'S FIRST GAY PRIDE CELEBRATION**

1,500 the width in feet (457 m) of Willamette Falls

5,000,000 number of Christmas trees harvested annually in Oregon

▶ **STORY OF** THE SOUND Perhaps influenced by the muted weather, the young population, or the city's affinity for counterculture, Portland of the 1980s, '90s, and '00s became a haven for alternative and independent musicians. Chief among them may be Elliott Smith, whose mournful voice and soft melodies influenced indie rock for decades to come. Other artists such as the Decemberists embraced folk rock with their shanties and long-form songs relying on instruments such as accordions, violins, and even the theremin, while others still—such as Modest Mouse, the Shins, and the Dandy Warhols—turned to the yelping or husky vocals that became hallmarks of indie rock. ▪

DESTINATION: OREGON

- Situated in the state's high desert and surrounded by towering peaks, Bend is the perfect place to explore lava caves, ski, hike, raft, or simply watch the sun set.

- On top of its many bars, restaurants, thrift stores, and coffee shops, some of Portland's top attractions include Powell's Books and the Oregon Symphony. Fans of nature can explore Forest Park's 5,200 acres (2,104 ha).

- Reaching 11,239 feet (3,426 m) above sea level and capped by 11 glaciers, Mount Hood is the tallest mountain in the state. The dormant volcano's most recent eruption was a minor one in 1907.

- Some 150 miles (241 km) long, the Willamette Valley was formed over millions of years by volcanic activity and waterways. Around 12,000 years ago, a cataclysmic deluge of water flooded the area. Today the area contains more than 700 wineries.

- Visitors and locals alike spend their time windsurfing or paddleboarding on the Columbia River Gorge, hiking the cliffs and waterfalls, or relaxing with a beer at one of the local breweries.

OREGON IS AN INSPIRATION. WHETHER YOU COME TO IT, OR ARE BORN TO IT, YOU BECOME ENTRANCED BY OUR STATE'S BEAUTY, THE OPPORTUNITY SHE AFFORDS, AND THE INDEPENDENT SPIRIT OF HER CITIZENS.

—Tom McCall, governor's address to the 1973 Oregon Legislature

- Astoria offers a unique combination of coastal activities, history, and culture. Visitors interested in the city's past can check out local pioneer cemeteries or the Astoria Column, a monument to the Great Northern Railway.

- One of the most iconic brewpubs of the Pacific Northwest, McMenamins began in 1983 with a Portland brewery and has since expanded to 56 locations with a goal of preserving historic properties.

- Ashland welcomes thespians and film buffs to its annual Shakespeare festival and Ashland Independent Film Festival.

- Incorporated in 1880, Pendleton's Old West spirit lives on today. It is the original home of Pendleton Woolen Mills, now a company famous for their blankets and flannel shirts.

- Reaching depths of 1,943 feet (592 m), Crater Lake is the country's deepest lake and sits inside the 7,700-year-old caldera of a dormant volcano. The island at the center, Wizard Island, is a volcanic cinder cone. ▽

◀ FIRST GOLD

In 1984, Brightwood-raised Bill Johnson became the first American to win an Olympic gold medal in Alpine skiing.

MADE IN OR

Oregon's agricultural outputs include:

- Dungeness crab
- Grass seed
- Hazelnuts
- Pink shrimp
- Crops such as hops, potatoes, wheat
- Fruits such as cherries, apples, blackberries, and blueberries

Oregon's industrial outputs include:

- Computers and electronics
- Industrial machinery
- Chemicals
- Motor vehicles

SPORTING CHANCES

- The state's NBA team, the Portland Trailblazers, were named as a nod to the Lewis and Clark expedition.

- Roller Derby, a full-contact rollerskating game, is a popular local sport. Portland's Wheels of Justice team competes in the Women's Flat Track Derby Association and holds four world championship titles.

- Housed in McMinnville's Evergreen Aviation & Space Museum, the Spruce Goose is the world's largest wooden airplane. Designed by Howard Hughes as a troop transport vehicle for WWII in 1942, the plane only ever flew once.

- Nike, Inc., was founded in Beaverton in 1964 by Oregonians Bill Bowerman, a University of Oregon track and field coach who would go on to coach in the Olympics, and Phil Knight, one of Bowerman's track stars. In 1993, rival sporting footwear company Adidas moved its U.S. base to the state as well.

- Portland native Tonya Harding is a former competitive figure skater who became the first woman to land a triple-axel jump while in competition. Harding was implicated in 1994 in an assault on fellow competitor Nancy Kerrigan.

- First held in 1910, the Pendleton Roundup hosts one of the country's most popular rodeos, as well as parades, pageants, and the Indian Relay Race.

- Born in Milwaukie in 1910, Dorothy Stenzel was a stunt pilot who set world records first by flying for 56 inverted snap rolls, and then for flying 69 consecutive outside loops. ◾

RECORD ★ SETTERS

Oregonian Linus Pauling was the first—and remains the only—person to be awarded two undivided Nobel Prizes: the Nobel Prize in Chemistry and the Nobel Peace Prize.

STARS ★ OF ★ THE ★ STATE

HAZEL YING LEE

(1912–1944) In 1912, Hazel Ying Lee was born in Portland to parents who had immigrated from China. At the age of 19, Lee discovered her passion for flying when she sat in on a friend's piloting lessons at a local airstrip. After saving up money by working as an elevator operator, Lee soon had enough money to earn a license of her own, making her one of the first female Chinese Americans to earn a pilot's license. In 1943, Lee made further history when she joined the Women Airforce Service Pilots (WASP) and became the first Chinese American woman to fly for the U.S. military. Lee quickly became known for her quick thinking and ability to keep calm in tough situations, and she survived multiple emergency landings. However, despite her skills and patriotism, she often faced racial discrimination. In 1944, Lee died in the line of duty as the result of an aircraft collision. ◾

PENNSYLVANIA

CAPITAL: Harrisburg **FLOWER:** Mountain Laurel **NICKNAME:** Keystone State **ENTRY:** 1787

★ ★ ★ *"Virtue, Liberty, and Independence"* ★ ★ ★

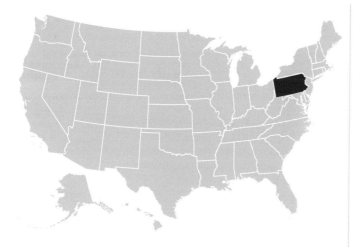

PA FACTS

- Pennsylvania stretches about 300 miles (480 km) from east to west and 160 miles (258 km) from north to south.

- It's ranked 33rd in the country in terms of area. Its population is 12,972,008.

- Philadelphia is the biggest city with a population of almost 1.6 million.

- Archaeologists have found artifacts indicating prehistoric people lived in Washington County as early as 16,000 years ago.

- Native American tribes, including the Lenape, Susquehannock, Erie, Seneca, and Oneida, lived on the land that's now Pennsylvania.

- In 1681, Englishman William Penn, a member the Quakers, founded the British colony of Pennsylvania.

- Philadelphia hosted the First Continental Congress in 1774, and the Second Continental Congress beginning in 1775. The latter produced the Declaration of Independence in 1776. ▼

▶ STATE BIRD

Ruffed Grouse
Bonasa umbellus

The non-migratory bird has long been a target for hunters, but recently its population is growing thanks to conservation efforts.

1863

In November 1863, President Abraham Lincoln gave his famous Gettysburg Address at Gettysburg National Cemetery.

> **THERE IS NOT A PITTSBURGH MAN WHO DID NOT EARN HIS SUCCESS THROUGH HIS DEEDS.**
>
> —President Theodore Roosevelt

◀ **MINT IT**

The Coinage Act of 1792 led to the opening of the first U.S. Mint, in Philadelphia. It remains open to this day.

- After being persecuted in England for his Quaker religion, William Penn was determined to make Pennsylvania a place where people could practice freedom of religion. This included a wave of Quakers, Mennonites, and Amish, who emigrated from Germany.

- The Battle of Gettysburg, which took place from July 1 to 3, 1863, ended the Confederacy's northern invasion.

- Pennsylvania is called the "Keystone State" because of its central location within the 13 original colonies, as well as the role it played in holding together the states of the new nation.

- On September 27, 1777, while Philadelphia was occupied by the British, Lancaster served as the nation's capital.

- Pennsylvania is one of the top states for coal mining.

- The Pocono Mountains, in the northeast, cover nearly 2,400 square miles (6,215 sq km), including 150 lakes and 170 ski trails.

- Pennsylvania was the second state to ratify the U.S. Constitution, which was drafted and signed in Independence Hall in 1787.

- The highest point is Mount Davis, which, at 3,213 feet (979 m) above sea level, is at a lower elevation than the lowest point in the entire state of Colorado.

- Covering 2,052 acres (830 ha), Fairmount Park in Philadelphia is the largest city park in the country.

- The United States' first daily newspaper, the *Pennsylvania Packet and Daily Advertiser*, was published in Philadelphia on September 21, 1784.

- There are almost 300 colleges, universities, and technical schools in the state, including the Penn State Main Campus in University Park, which has an enrollment of around 46,000.

- There are 55 colleges located within 20 miles (32 km) of Philadelphia alone, including the University of Pennsylvania, the oldest university in the country.

▶ **STORY OF** THE NAME Contrary to popular belief, William Penn didn't name the state for himself. Rather, the name was bestowed on the colony on March 4, 1681, by King Charles II, who named it after Penn's deceased father, Admiral Sir William Penn, to whom the king owed a debt. Penn did get to name the capital, Philadelphia; he combined the Greek words for love (*phileo*) and brother (*adelphos*), sparking the nickname of "the city of brotherly love."

STARS ★ OF ★ THE ★ STATE

GRACE KELLY

(1929–1982) Born in Philadelphia, Kelly spent her formative years in the city before going on to pursue acting—and eventually becoming royalty. In 1955, she won an Academy Award for her turn in *The Country Girl*; that year she also met the prince of Monaco at a photo session for *Paris Match*. The pair announced their engagement from her parents' Philly home in 1956 and later married in a lavish ceremony. "Princess Grace" became an international icon—remaining so even after her tragic death following a car accident in 1982. Today, Kelly's childhood home, recently restored by her son, Prince Albert II, is a state historical landmark.

The country's first drive-in gas station opened in Pittsburgh in 1913. On opening day, gas sold at 27 cents a gallon.

- The town of Bethlehem drops a giant Peeps chick at midnight to mark the new year.
- The giant Koontz coffee pot, a roadside attraction in Bedford County, stands 18 feet (5.5 m) tall and is big enough to hold more than 800,000 cups of coffee.
- The Eastern hellbender, a salamander that also goes by the names Allegheny alligator, devil dog, mud devil, and snot otter, is the state amphibian.
- During Prohibition, the Yuengling company created "near beers" with a low alcohol content, including the Yuengling Juvo, an energy drink made with cereal grains.

WEIRD BUT TRUE

- The state is home to the world's largest paint can (near Shippensburg) and the world's largest clothespin (in Philadelphia).
- Pennsylvania is misspelled on the Liberty Bell—it reads "Pensylvania" because the bell was manufactured before founders agreed on a common spelling for the state's name.
- A professor in Pittsburgh invented the smiley face emoticon in 1982.
- Before the Nittany Lion was made the official mascot, Penn State students rallied around Old Coaly, a mule used in the construction of Old Main, the university's administrative center, in the late 1800s.
- Benjamin Franklin went door-to-door in Philadelphia to raise money for street cleaning.
- In North Huntingdon there's a museum dedicated to the Big Mac, which was first created more than four decades ago in western Pennsylvania.
- Pennsylvania is known as the "snack food capital of the world" because of its many pretzel, chip, and chocolate factories.
- A mine beneath the abandoned town of Centralia has been on fire for more than 60 years.

MISCELLANY

- There are also **three official state locomotives**, two steam and one electric.
- Actor **Jimmy Stewart**, star of *It's a Wonderful Life*, was born in the town of Indiana, which now honors its famous son with a museum, a parade, a statue, and a yearly festival honoring that classic holiday film.
- Each August, tens of thousands of people attend the **Pittston Tomato Festival**, which celebrates the acres of the region dedicated to commercial tomato growing.
- Chester County's **Kennett Square** produces half of America's mushrooms.

- Lancaster's Central Market is one of the oldest continuously operating public **farmers markets** in the nation.
- Each December, thousands of people gather on the Delaware River in **Washington Crossing** to watch the reenactment of George Washington's 1776 Christmas night river crossing.
- **Leap-the-Dips** in Lakemont Park near Altoona was built in 1902, making it the oldest wooden roller coaster in the world.
- **Andrew Carnegie**, the steel magnate, co-founded his first steel company near Pittsburgh. He eventually sold his company for $480 million and later gave away more than $350 million.
- HBO's 2021 hit series *Mare of Easttown* starring Kate Winslet drew attention to the distinct **"Delco" accent** heard among many residents raised in or around Delaware County. Comedian Tina Fey, who grew up in Upper Darby, has also spoofed the accent on *Saturday Night Live*.

◀ **BIG DOG**
The Great Dane is the state dog of Pennsylvania.

BY THE NUMBERS

17,430,000
the number of people in the U.S. who eat at least five servings of Hershey's candy each month

6,000
weight in pounds (2,722 kg) of the statue atop the Pennsylvania State Capitol

3,819
the length in feet (1,164 m) of the Rockville Bridge over the Susquehanna River in Harrisburg. It's the longest stone arch bridge in the world.

200
NUMBER OF COVERED BRIDGES FOUND THROUGHOUT PENNSYLVANIA, THE MOST OF ANY STATE

444
the length in miles (715 km) of the Susquehanna River, the longest river on the East Coast

39%
accuracy of Punxsutawney Phil's winter prognostications; the famous groundhog makes an appearance from the town's square every February 2.

4,600,000
pounds (2.1 million kg) of fresh milk are processed on a yearly basis at the Penn State Berkey Creamery, the largest university creamery.

52°C
year-round temperature (11°C) inside the Indian Echo Caverns in Hummelstown

69.5
DEPTH IN FEET (21 M) OF DRAKE WELL IN TITUSVILLE, THE COUNTRY'S FIRST OIL WELL

- Get an up-close-and-personal view of pivotal pieces of the nation's history in downtown Philadelphia—all within walking distance. Snag a selfie with the Liberty Bell, an iconic symbol of American independence, on Market Street; check out where Benjamin Franklin toiled away at his printing press nearby; and then tour Independence Hall, where the Founding Fathers signed the Declaration of Independence.

- See where George Washington and other Founding Fathers attended services at Christ Church in Philadelphia. Built between 1727 and 1744, the structure features Georgian architecture and a baptismal font from the 1300s. The adjacent cemetery is also open to visitors; Benjamin Franklin and his wife, Deborah, are among the 1,400 buried there.

- Set in the woods of southwestern Pennsylvania, Fallingwater is one of eight Frank Lloyd Wright buildings in the U.S. that are on the UNESCO World Heritage list. But it's arguably his finest work: Created as a vacation home for the Kaufmann family, owners of Pittsburgh's largest department store at the time, the three-story abode was built by Wright over a waterfall. It has been open to the public since 1964.

- Situated on the banks of Lake Erie, Presque Isle State Park—a 3,200-acre (1,295 ha) sandy peninsula, is Pennsylvania's only coastline. The park draws some four million visitors a year.

▲ ANDYLAND

Andy Warhol was born in Pittsburgh in 1928; today the city hosts a seven-story museum dedicated to the artist who put pop art on the map, featuring thousands of works of Warhol's art.

STARS ★ OF ★ THE ★ STATE

MILTON HERSHEY

(1857–1945) Determined to make a career out of confections, Hershey, born on a farm in Derry Church, faced a series of failures before finding success with his Lancaster Caramel Company, which he sold for $1 million in 1900. He then turned his focus toward chocolate making, setting up a factory in his hometown (renamed "Hershey" in 1905), soon introducing Hershey's Kisses among other chocolate treats and amassing an impressive fortune. Hershey is known as much for his altruism as for his business acumen; he built schools, an amusement park, churches, recreational facilities, and housing for his employees. Today, Hershey's legacy lives on. His company is the biggest chocolate manufacturer in North America, and the Hershey's brand employs more than 18,000 people worldwide with an annual revenue of about $9 billion in 2022. ∎

SPORTING CHANCES

- The state is home to eight professional sports teams. They include the Philadelphia Phillies and Pittsburgh Pirates (MLB), Philadelphia 76ers (NBA), Philadelphia Eagles and Pittsburgh Steelers (NFL), the Philadelphia Flyers and Pittsburgh Penguins (NHL), and the Philadelphia Union (MLS).

- The Steelers have won six Super Bowls, including four in a six-year stretch (1975, 1976, 1979, 1980). The Eagles have won one Super Bowl, in 2018.

- During World War II, with many pro football players deployed, the Steelers and the Eagles merged to create the Steagles. Made up mostly of players who weren't able to serve in the war and coached by a pair of men who hated each other, the team managed to pull off a winning season.

- In the 1920s, Pottsville had a pro football team, the Maroons, which included several coal miners. They won the 1925 National Football League championship, but their title was taken away when it was discovered that the Maroons played in an unauthorized out-of-league game.

- NBA star Wilt Chamberlain's famous 100-point game was played in Hersheypark Arena on March 2, 1962.

- Penn State and the University of Pittsburgh are longtime athletic rivals; on the football field, Penn State has beat Pitt 53 times in 100 tries.

- During a 30-year span from 1894 to 1924, the University of Pennsylvania football team won seven national championships, making them one of the most successful college programs in history.

- Western Pennsylvania's strong Scottish heritage is celebrated at the annual Ligonier Highland Games, with competitions including heavy athletics, haggis hurling, and a keg toss.

- Golf in Western Pennsylvania dates to 1887 when Joseph Mickle Fox developed an eight-hole course in Foxburg after learning the sport at St. Andrews in Scotland.

- All 93,511 residents of Erie could fit into Penn State's Beaver Stadium, which has a seating capacity of 106,572.

- In the 1976 movie *Rocky*, the fictional boxer Rocky Balboa (played by Sylvester Stallone) ends his morning run with a jog up the steps of the Philadelphia Museum of Art. Every year, tens of thousands of people make the same trek up the 72 "Rocky Steps."

- Little League Baseball's first World Series was held in 1947 in Williamsport. A museum there showcases the past, present, and future of Little League.

- John Woodruff, a Black student from the University of Pittsburgh, won gold in track and field at the 1936 Berlin Olympics.

- Other gold medalists born in the state include Haverford-born Jean Shiley, who set a world record in the women's high jump at the 1932 Olympics.

- Each April, thousands of runners descend on the University of Pennsylvania's Franklin Field for the Penn Relays, an event which first kicked off in 1895.

MADE IN PA

Pennsylvania's agricultural outputs include:

- Mushrooms
- Beef cattle
- Hogs
- Chicken eggs and broilers
- Wheat
- Potatoes
- Oats
- Rye
- Barley

Pennsylvania's industrial outputs include:

- Pharmaceuticals
- Coal
- Liquefied propane
- Coal
- Palladium
- Precious metal compounds

RECORD ★ SETTERS

In 1942, Veronica Grace Boland became the first woman from Pennsylvania to serve in Congress. The Scranton-born Boland was in office for two months, completing the term of her late husband.

PUERTO RICO

★ ★ ★

"John Is His Name"

★ ★ ★

CAPITAL: San Juan **FLOWER:** Puerto Rican Hibiscus **NICKNAME:** Isle of Enchantment **ENTRY:** 1898

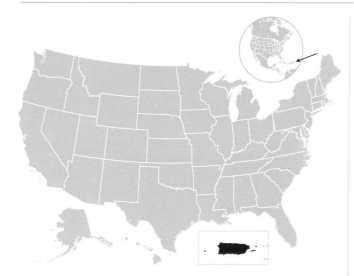

PR FACTS

- The island's population is 3,221,789.

- The archipelago is made up of several small islands located between the Caribbean Sea and the North Atlantic Ocean. The islands include the main island Puerto Rico, Vieques, Culebra, and Mona, as well as many small islets.

- Puerto Rico's economy relies on manufacturing, sugar, pharmaceuticals, the service industry, and coffee.

- Natural resources include seafood, minerals such as gold, copper, and silver, as well as clay and sand.

- Puerto Rico's official languages are Spanish and English.

- As a territory, Puerto Rico is under U.S. jurisdiction. Residents are granted U.S. citizenship and passports but cannot vote in presidential elections.

- The archipelago has been inhabited for at least 1,000 years by the Taíno culture. The Taíno often lived in agricultural community-based groups with complex governmental organizations. They developed sophisticated canoes for seafaring as well as localized arts such as weaving and carving.

- Christopher Columbus reached the islands in 1493. Fifteen years later, Juan Ponce de León conquered and colonized the islands, serving as the first governor.

- While locals consider themselves American, they often first and foremost consider themselves Puerto Rican (Boricua).

- One of the most influential pioneers of the U.S. LGBTQ+ civil rights movement was Sylvia Rivera, a New Yorker of Puerto Rican descent. As a transgender woman and an activist involved in the Stonewall Inn uprising of 1969, Rivera advocated for gay rights and transgender inclusion. ◀

▶ OFFICIAL BIRD

Puerto Rican Spindalis
Spindalis portoricensis

Known for its black-and-white striped head, this bird is small but mighty: To defend their nests, groups sometimes attack predators in what is known as "mobbing."

1873

For more than three centuries, the islands of Puerto Rico were cultivated by enslaved laborers of both Taíno and African descent. In 1873, after a prolonged push from the abolitionist movement, the Spanish National Assembly abolished slavery.

> **PUERTO RICANS, IT DOESN'T MATTER WHERE THEY LIVE, IT DOESN'T MATTER HOW LONG IT'S BEEN SINCE THEY VISITED THE ISLAND, THEIR HEARTS ARE THERE.**
>
> —Former governor Aníbal Acevedo Vilá

- In 1511, Taíno leader Agüeybaná II led a revolt against the Spanish.
- The U.S. took control of Puerto Rico as part of the 1898 Treaty of Paris.
- In 1917, the archipelago was granted its status as a territory—but it was not until 1952 that it could draft its own constitution and become an independently governed commonwealth.
- *Mofongo* is perhaps the most beloved and symbolic food. The dish combines local ingredients—such as plantains and pork cracklings—with the cooking techniques used to make West African *fufu* and a Spanish-inspired *sofrito* sauce.
- After locals were officially granted U.S. citizenship in the early 1900s, many families immigrated to New York City.
- Over time, these pockets of Boricua culture led to the Nuyorican literature movement: an intellectual boom of poets, writers, musicians, and artists.
- Born to a Puerto Rican family in New York, Alexandria Ocasio-Cortez was elected to Congress in 2018. She became the youngest woman and youngest Latina to serve. ∎

▲ **"KO-KEE"**

For centuries, the coqui frog has been a cultural symbol for the islands. Beloved for its tiny appearance and loud, song-like call— "ko-kee"—the frog features in local folklore, sayings, and art.

STORY OF THE SOUND Whether salsa first originated in Puerto Rico or Cuba is hotly debated, but certainly its popularity soared because of the Puerto Rican communities of New York. Arising from African, Spanish, and Indigenous musical traditions, salsa features fast-paced and upbeat rhythms, percussion instruments, and energetic, strong vocal work. It likely first appeared during the early 20th century, but it wasn't until the 1960s, when salsa became the favored dance music among New York Puerto Ricans, that it gained international fame. Today, salsa on the archipelago still features many original Indigenous instruments such as guiros. ∎

STARS ★ OF ★ THE ★ COMMONWEALTH

RITA MORENO

(b. 1931) Born Rosa Dolores Alverío in Humacao, Rita Morena is an actress, singer, and dancer. Moreno appeared in bit roles in musicals such as *The King and I* and *Singin' in the Rain*, but she gained prominence for her performance as Anita in *West Side Story* in 1961. Moreno received an Academy Award for her portrayal, going on to appear in numerous film and stage productions. She was awarded the Presidential Medal of Freedom in 2004 and has continued to act well into her 80s. ∎

RECORD ★ SETTERS

Located about 100 miles (161 km) northwest of Puerto Rico is the Milwaukee Depth, named after the first ship to sound it.

WEIRD BUT TRUE

- La Casa Estrecha, or the Narrow House, is a tiny structure only five feet (1.5 m) wide that serves as a home and an occasional art gallery.

- Although it is a U.S. territory, Puerto Rico competes as its own country in the Olympics.

- Mongoose are an invasive species in the area; they were originally brought in to curb the rat population.

- *Abyssobrotula galatheae* fish live at depths of 27,460 feet (8,370 m) in the Puerto Rico Trench.

Humans are generally not allowed on the small islet of Cayo Santiago, which is home to some 1,500 rhesus macaque monkeys.

MISCELLANY

- ▲ The critically endangered **Mona rhinoceros iguana** is found only on the Puerto Rican island of Mona.

- Puerto Rico means **"rich port" in Spanish**.

- **Locals are often referred to as Boricuas**, in reference to the original Taíno word for the islands: Boríkén.

- Puerto Rico has an **official coat of arms**.

- The national hymn is **"La Borinqueña."**

- On **Three Kings Day**, children leave out grass for the camels of the biblical three kings.

- The **U.S. dollar** is Puerto Rico's currency.

- A popular local **musical style, *plena*** became popular in the 1920s by mixing traditional African music with Spanish stylings.

- **No passport nor international phone plan** is needed for American travelers.

- The legal **drinking age is 18**.

- The **sweet piña colada**, famous with vacationers the world over, is the national drink.

- The **legend of the chupacabra**, a monstrous cryptid that supposedly survives by sucking the blood of goats, originated in Puerto Rico.

RECORD ★ SETTERS

Actor José Ferrer became the first Latino to receive an Academy Award for best actor in 1951 for his role in *Cyrano de Bergerac*.

BY THE NUMBERS

70 THE APPROXIMATE PERCENTAGE OF RUM IN THE CONTIGUOUS U.S. THAT COMES FROM PUERTO RICO

144 the number of islands, cays, and islets that make up the archipelago

4,390 the height in feet (1,338 m) of Cerro de Punta, the island's highest point

27,493 the depth in feet (8,380 m) of the Milwaukee Depth, which is located within the Puerto Rico Trench

6 MONTHS **THE LENGTH OF HURRICANE SEASON**

1,090 the length in miles (1,750 km) of the Puerto Rico Trench

1549 THE YEAR THE COCONUT TREE WAS INTRODUCED TO PUERTO RICO

60% of Puerto Rico's land is covered by mountains.

IN PUERTO RICO WE DANCE TO EVERYTHING.

—Rapper Bad Bunny

With more than 50 #1 Billboard Chart hits, singer Marc Anthony holds the Guinness World Record for most Premio Lo Nuestro awards (male).

DESTINATION: PUERTO RICO

- Old San Juan, the historic district of San Juan, has been continuously inhabited for some five centuries. A premier destination for foodies, the city is the birthplace of the piña colada and offers a range of dining experiences. Visitors can also stroll among the colorful colonial homes, the governor's mansion, the oldest cathedral in the U.S., and much more. ▲

- Castillo San Felipe del Morro—called El Morro—is an enormous 16th-century Spanish fort. Its nearby sister site, Castillo San Cristóbal, is the location where the first shots were fired during the Spanish-American War.

- El Yunque National Forest has the distinction of being the only U.S. tropical rainforest. Some 28,000 acres (11,331 ha), the area is home to many species of bats, birds, and reptiles, as well as rivers and scenic hiking routes.

- With over 300 miles (500 km) of coastline, it's hard to go wrong with beaches in Puerto Rico: Playa Flamenco is known for its white sands and calm turquoise waters; Cayo Icacos is beloved among boaters; Isla Verde boasts easy access to water sports.

- Several parts of Río Camuy Cave Park are accessible to the public.

- In early January, revelers descend upon San Juan for the San Sebastián Street Festival. Festivities feature parades, street music and concerts, dancing, and people dressed in themed attire.

- By day, Isla Vieques boasts popular, pristine beaches. At night, when the conditions are right at Mosquito Bay, the waters become bioluminescent, thanks to the phosphorescent presence of microscopic marine organisms known as dinoflagellates.

- One of the archipelago's best-known beaches since it hosted the World Surfing Championships in 1968, Rincón is famous among surfers.

- Carnival of Ponce is a local Catholic celebration similar to Mardi Gras or Carnival.

- Located in Cataño, Casa Bacardí is the world's largest premium rum distillery.

LIN-MANUEL MIRANDA

(b. 1980) Born in New York City to Puerto Rican parents, Lin-Manuel Miranda is a composer, actor, and lyricist. Miranda is perhaps best known for his work on Broadway, including the 11-time Tony Award–winning historical musical *Hamilton*, and four-time Tony Award–winning *In the Heights*, which shines a spotlight on the rich immigrant heritages that make up New York City. Miranda has also written original songs and contributed music and vocals to award-winning Disney films, such as *Moana* and *Encanto*. He has received numerous accolades and awards, including multiple Grammys, an Emmy, the Pulitzer Prize, as well as the 2015 MacArthur Foundation Award and the 2018 Kennedy Center Honors. Miranda has also dedicated himself to fundraising for the arts and for hurricane relief in Puerto Rico.

MADE IN PR

Puerto Rico's agricultural outputs include:

- Tobacco
- Coffee
- Pineapples
- Citrus
- Vegetables
- Chickens
- Cattle
- Pigs
- Sugar
- Plantains

Puerto Rico's industrial outputs include:

- Medication
- Insulin
- Medical equipment
- Petroleum
- Contact lenses
- Immunological products
- Clothing
- Chemicals

▲ ROBERTO CLEMENTE

Born in Carolina, Puerto Rico, Roberto Clemente began playing for the Brooklyn Dodgers in 1954, becoming one of the first Latino baseball icons in the country. Known for his batting skills, Clemente was the first Latino player to collect 3,000 hits. He died unexpectedly in a plane crash in 1972.

SPORTING CHANCES

- Baseball is the official sport.

- Gigi Fernández, an LGBTQ+ tennis champion from San Juan, has won 17 Grand Slam doubles championships and two Olympic gold medals for the U.S.

- In 2016, tennis champion and San Juan native Monica Puig won Puerto Rico its first Olympic gold medal.

- Since the World Surfing Championship was held in Rincón in 1968 (and again in 1988 and 2007), the archipelago has been a global surfing hot spot.

- In 1948, Río Piedras local Juan Evangelista Venegas won Puerto Rico's first medal at the Olympics when he earned bronze for bantamweight boxing.

- Located in San Juan, Hiram Bithorn Stadium was named for the first Boricua major league baseball player.

- Puerto Rico's basketball team does not compete as part of the NBA but in FIBA, the International Basketball Federation.

- Olympic-level skateboarder Emanuel "Manny" Santiago is known as "Manny Slays All" for his fearless approach to tricks.

- At the age of 17, Wilfred Benítez became the world's youngest boxer to win a World Boxing Championship.

- Scuba divers at Mona Island might encounter whales, sharks, and turtles.

- Snorkeling is a popular sport on the archipelago thanks to its numerous inlets, cays, and mangrove trees.

- Born in San Juan, Jonny Moseley became the first Puerto Rican to become a member of the U.S. ski team. He won an Olympic gold medal in 1998.

> **PUERTO RICO IS A HALFWAY POINT BETWEEN MY SPANISH HERITAGE AND MY AMERICAN IMMIGRANT IDENTITY ... IT IS A PLACE THAT I FEEL LIKE I BELONG.**
>
> —Chef José Andrés

RHODE ISLAND

★★★
"Hope"
★★★

CAPITAL: Providence **FLOWER:** Violet **NICKNAME:** Ocean State **ENTRY:** 1790

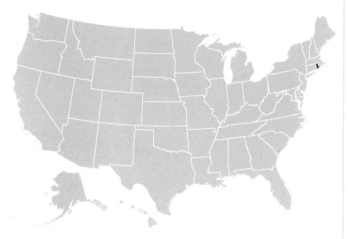

RI FACTS

- The population is 1,093,734.
- The 13th state to join the Union, Rhode Island is the smallest in area.
- On top of being known for its ocean-based industries and tourism, the state relies on health care, manufacturing, finance, and education.
- The state's natural resources include seafood, timber, and fertile soil.
- Original inhabitants included the Narragansett, Niantic, and the Wampanoag. Today only the Narragansett are federally recognized, though the state is also home to the Pauquunaukit (Pokanoket).
- Smithfield native Elizabeth Buffum Chace was an ardent suffragist and abolitionist. Chace went on to found organizations such as the Association for the Advancement of Women and the Rhode Island Woman Suffrage Association.
- Known as the "father of the American factory system," Samuel Slater kickstarted the country's cotton industry. Slater created a slew of American textile mills beginning with one on Blackstone River in 1790.

▶ **STATE BIRD**
Rhode Island Red
Gallus gallus domesticus

Developed in the state in the late 1800s, this breed of chicken is known for its rusty coloring and prolific egg-laying.

1877

Founded by Helen Adelia Rowe Metcalf in 1877, the Rhode Island School of Design (RISD) was one of the country's first independent art colleges. Today, the school is considered one of the most influential places of learning for art and design students. ▼

RHODE ISLAND, OH, RHODE ISLAND SURROUNDED BY THE SEA. SOME PEOPLE ROAM THE EARTH FOR HOME; RHODE ISLAND'S IT FOR ME!

—from "Rhode Island It's for Me," the state song

- During the 1880s, Newport saw an incredible influx of wealth—thanks to the creation of sumptuous vacation homes for some of the country's wealthiest citizens. These American businessmen were often referred to as robber barons for their cutthroat and exploitative practices, such as the creation of monopolies, the utilization of insider trading, and their not insignificant influence in politics.

- Spiritual leader Roger Williams originally settled in Massachusetts but was exiled for his views. Instead, he purchased land to found Providence and the new colony of Rhode Island in 1636.

- Metacom (also known as King Philip) was a leader of a confederation of Pauquunaukit, Wampanoag, and Narragansett peoples. Metacom advocated for Indigenous rights until 1675, when the execution of three Wampanoag men led him to organize an allied resistance. The war lasted for close to a year, ending in Metacom's death.

- Since the days of the Founding Fathers, johnnycakes have been a local staple. Made from finely ground white cornmeal and water, the cakes are fried and often eaten like pancakes.

- Founded in 1764, Brown University remains one of the country's preeminent research centers and is part of the Ivy League.

- Born in Warwick in 1742, Nathanael Greene was a member of the General Assembly who went on to become a Revolutionary War hero.

- One of the first renowned American artists, Rhode Island native Gilbert Stuart was famed for his portraiture, particularly that of President George Washington, which is on the $1 bill.

- By 1772, during heightening tensions between the colonists and British government, a Royal Navy vessel was dispatched. Hostilities between the ship's commander and the locals resulted in a group of colonists destroying the ship and her crew. The event is seen as a spark point for the American Revolution.

- The official state beverage is coffee milk: an aptly named drink made of milk and sweetened, coffee-flavored syrup.

RECORD ★ SETTERS

In 1776, Rhode Island became the first colony to officially declare independence from Great Britain with the Act of Renunciation.

STARS ★ OF ★ THE ★ STATE

ANNE HUTCHINSON

(c. 1591–c. 1643) Born sometime around 1591 in England, Anne Marbury Hutchinson went on to become one of Rhode Island's founders. Having arrived in the Massachusetts Bay Colony in 1634, Hutchinson soon began to question certain Puritan rules and beliefs, particularly those concerned with women's roles. Her active role as a spiritual leader directly opposed the conventional belief that men were the rightful spiritual authorities, and she was exiled from the colony in 1638. Moving to the newly formed colony of Rhode Island, which was known for its more liberal attitudes, Hutchinson and her family founded what is now Portsmouth. She remains known as an early feminist advocate.

- A Providence restaurant once served a salad made with sea snails.
- A food truck company from Providence has operated since 1893, when it started as a mobile food carriage pulled by horses.
- The state can be driven across in just one hour.
- The waters off Rhode Island hold more shipwrecks per square mile than any other state.

⯅ NIGHT LIGHT

A 23-foot-tall (7 m) sculpture on the campus of Brown University is part giant lamp and part blue teddy bear.

- One extermination company in Providence proudly displays a "Big Blue Bug" statue outside their office that is not only enormous—weighing 4,000 pounds (1,814 kg)—but decked out like Uncle Sam.
- The state never ratified Prohibition.
- Until 2020, the state's name was officially "State of Rhode Island and Providence Plantations."
- Rhode Island's first governor, Benedict Arnold, was the great grandfather of the famous Revolutionary War traitor of the same name.
- A Rhode Islander once did 302 successful skateboard ollies in a row.
- A cemetery in Exeter holds the grave of the country's last officially suspected vampire: a woman named Mercy Brown.

STORY OF THE SOUND Though he became known as the "Man Who Owned Broadway," George M. Cohan never seemed to forget his Rhode Island roots. Born in Providence in 1878 (likely on July 3, though his parents often claimed it was the 4th), Cohan grew up writing vaudeville tunes and original skits. He and his sister moved to New York in the early 1890s, where Cohan soon produced musicals—but rather than adapt to the current sounds of New York City, he infused Broadway with the historic patriotism of New England. With songs such as "You're A Grand Old Flag" to the iconic "I'm a Yankee Doodle Dandy," Cohan's music remains inseparable from the American identity. He was inducted into the Songwriters Hall of Fame in 1970.

- Locals are called **Rhode Islanders**.
- The state appetizer is **calamari**.
- The state name may come from its **red clay**, which explorers believed was similar to that found on the Greek island of Rhodes.
- **Striped bass** is Rhode Island's state fish.
- There is a state ship: the tall ship **U.S.S. Providence**.
- A rock known as **cumberlandite** is only found near Cumberland.

- **Quahog** is the state shell.
- In Newport, a 19th-century lighthouse keeper named **Ida Lewis** was said to have rescued at least 18 people from drowning.
- The state marine mammal is the **harbor seal**, known for its curiosity and playfulness.
- **Coffee cabinet** is a local dessert made by blending coffee milk with ice cream.
- The **American burying beetle** is the state insect.
- The state fruit is the **Rhode Island Greening apple**.

- A member of the Mustelidae family like its cousin the weasel, a local mammal called the **fisher** is common throughout parts of the state.
- The state mineral is **bowenite**.
- **Local-style clam chowder** features a light, clear broth without any cream.
- Rhode Island was the **last colony to ratify the U.S. Constitution**.
- The country's **first ferry service** was operated in Rhode Island.

⯅ RED MAPLE

Beloved for its fiery fall hue, the majestic red maple is the state tree.

BY THE NUMBERS

32% OF THE STATE IS COVERED BY WATER.

2013 the year same-sex marriage was legalized in the state

1876 the first game of polo is played in the U.S. near Newport

1904 THE YEAR OF THE FIRST JAIL SENTENCE GIVEN FOR AUTOMOBILE SPEEDING

500 the weight in pounds (226.8 kg) of the Independent Man, the statue atop the State House

3 the number of the most popular dishes in the state that include clams: clam cakes, clam chowder, clam stuffie

812 the elevation in feet (247 m) of Jerimoth Hill, the state's highest point

40,000 THE ROUGH NUMBER OF BOATS REGISTERED IN RHODE ISLAND

▼ WATER + FIRE

Part public art installation, part festival, Providence's WaterFire runs yearly during the fall. Featuring more than 80 bonfires, music, boats, and more, the event is a tribute to both Providence and public art.

- Since the Gilded Age, Newport has been a popular spot for vacationers. Visitors can still tour the enormous mansions such as the Vanderbilts' Breakers and Marble House, the Berwinds' Elms, the Astors' Beechwood, and more. Other popular attractions include the seaside Cliff Walk and the beaches themselves.

- Located on the Narragansett Bay since 1857, Point Judith Lighthouse has been privy to much of the state's history, including the WWII Battle of Point Judith.

- The site of Brown University and Rhode Island School of Design, Providence also offers the state capitol building, multiple museums, a largely cage-free zoo, a historic downtown, an arts district, and lovely urban parks.

- With 17 miles (27 km) of beaches, Block Island features everything from lighthouses to historic homes and farms, a maritime institute, boutiques, and restaurants.

- Narragansett is the state's preeminent destination for fans of the sea and seafood. The area attracts surfers, foodies, history buffs, fishers, and those looking to get away from it all.

- Outdoors and wildlife aficionados flock to Bristol for Colt State Park, the historic Blithewold estate gardens, and the world-class Audubon Society Environmental Education Center.

- The Touro Synagogue in Newport is America's oldest Jewish synagogue; construction was completed in 1763 to accommodate the local populations of Jewish settlers who had been arriving in the area since the 17th century.

- In Providence's Swan Point Cemetery is the grave of horror author Howard Phillips (H.P.) Lovecraft. Lovecraft created a universe of existential horror, which went on to inspire authors across the world including Stephen King, and more.

STARS ★ OF ★ THE ★ STATE

ELLISON BROWN

(c. 1914–1975) Known as Deerfoot to his Narragansett tribe, Ellison Myers "Tarzan" Brown was an Olympic-level runner famed for winning the Boston Marathon twice. Brown originally burst onto the national scene in 1936 when he overtook favored runner Johnny Kelley and became the first Indigenous person to win the Boston Marathon. He qualified for both the 1936 and 1940 Olympics, though he was unable compete in 1940 because of WWII. In 1939, Brown again won the Boston Marathon, this time setting a new world record. He was inducted into the American Indian Athletic Hall of Fame in 1973. ▪

THE PLACE OF EXCITING INNOVATION—WHERE THE ACTION IS—THAT'S RHODE ISLAND!

—Former governor Donald L. Carcieri

▶ MAKE WAVES

Newport is home to multiple regattas—races featuring yachts or boats—in addition to serving as the only North American stopover for a 38,000-nautical-mile (70,376 km) race around the world.

> **GROWING UP IN RHODE ISLAND, MY FRIENDS WOULD HAVE STRUNG ME UP IF I HAD BEEN A YANKEES FAN.**
>
> —Actor Charlie Day

SPORTING CHANCES

- Saunderstown resident Elizabeth Beisel is an Olympic swimmer who has won one silver and one bronze medal and who served as captain for the U.S. Olympic team.

- After he visited the Baseball Hall of Fame in the 1950s, Newport Casino owner Jimmy Van Alen decided to dedicate a similar hall of fame to tennis in Newport. Today, the hall represents 27 countries with some 262 inductees.

- The first U.S. Golf Open was played in Newport in 1895.

- Though the current iteration of the U.S. Open tennis tournament has been held in New York since 1968, it was born from an earlier version—the U.S. National Championship—first held in Newport in 1881.

- Brown University's mascot is Bruno the brown bear.

- The University of Rhode Island's ram mascot represents its history as a college of agriculture and mechanic arts.

- Meade Stadium—the state's largest stadium—only seats about 6,555.

- Providence College's mascot, Friar Dom, pays homage to the school's foundation by the Dominican Order in 1917. ▶

RECORD ★ SETTERS

Located in Newport since around 1673, the White Horse Tavern is the oldest continuously operating restaurant in the United States.

SOUTH CAROLINA

CAPITAL: Columbia **BIRD:** Carolina Wren **NICKNAME:** Palmetto State **ENTRY:** 1788

★ ★ ★ *"Prepared in Mind and Resources"* ★ ★ ★

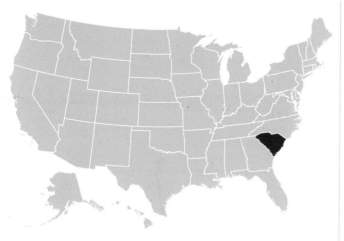

SC FACTS

- The easternmost state of the Deep South, South Carolina is the 23rd most populous and the 40th largest in area.

- Cherokee, Catawba, Creek, Yuchi, Cusabo, Edisto, Chicora, Pee Dee, Waccamaw, and Santee people have lived in the area for thousands of years.

- During the Revolutionary War, 137 battles were fought in South Carolina, more than in any other colony.

- On December 20, 1860, South Carolina became the first state to secede from the Union. The first shot of the Civil War was fired four months later on Fort Sumter. By the end of the war, some 12,922 South Carolina troops died in the war.

- Forests cover more than 67 percent of South Carolina; one of the state's biggest natural resources is the loblolly.

- South Carolina is usually divided into four geographic and cultural regions: the Lowcountry (the areas along the coast) and the Upcountry, as well as Pee Dee and the Midlands. ▼

▶ STATE FLOWER
Yellow Jessamine
Gelsemium sempervirens

This vine, which blooms with pops of bold yellow petals, climbs trees, fences, and latticework all over the state. It also appears on the South Carolina state quarter.

1732
The state was named after King Charles II of England. It was originally called Charles Town before adopting its present name in 1783.

COME QUICKLY, HAVE FOUND HEAVEN.

—Artist Alfred Hutty in a wire to his wife upon his first visit to Charleston

▶ **TREAD CAREFULLY**
Some 100,000 alligators as well as all four types of venomous snakes found in the U.S. live in South Carolina's Lowcountry.

- The state has more than 30 Sea Islands, the largest of which is 84-square-mile (218 sq km) Johns Island, the fourth largest barrier island in the U.S.

- The Sea Islands are home to a thriving Gullah Geechee community, many of whom are descendants of enslaved Africans with their own languages, dialects, and distinct cultures.

- The state is a top tire producer, and South Carolina–based companies manufacture approximately 110,000 tires daily.

- From 1851 to 2021, 44 tropical cyclones made landfall in the state.

- The most devastating hurricane to hit South Carolina was Hugo in 1989. It caused approximately $10 billion in damage, making it among the costliest hurricanes in U.S. history.

- In April 2022, eight tornadoes struck South Carolina in one day; the state has averaged 11 tornadoes each year since 1950.

- Wild pigs, bobcats, and river otters are among the mammals living in South Carolina.

- Every year in late summer about 800,000 purple martins roost on Bomb Island in Lake Murray, a bird sanctuary. ▪

▲ **STORY OF** THE TREE In South Carolina, pride for the palmetto tree runs deep. It's said that the trees—which in South Carolina average about 35 feet (11 m), unlike its much taller cousin, the palm tree—protected troops during the Revolutionary War (the British cannonballs bounced off the spongy logs surrounding Fort Moultrie near Charleston). So when it came time to adopt a state tree in 1939, the palmetto was a no-brainer—except another state supposedly wanted it, too. The story goes that State Senator Jeff Bates caught wind of this rumor and quickly drafted Senate Joint Resolution No. 63 to decree the tree South Carolina's own. The palmetto remains an icon of the state, adorning the state flag, license plates, T-shirts, key chains, and more. ▪

STARS ★ OF ★ THE ★ STATE

MARY McLEOD BETHUNE
(1875–1955) One of 17 children born to former enslaved people in Mayesville, Bethune rose from her impoverished beginnings to become a pioneer in education, women's rights, and civil rights. Her many roles include the founder of Bethune-Cookman College, the founding president of the National Council of Negro Women, and a consultant to the Secretary of War. Her legacy is honored with Dr. Mary McLeod Bethune Park and nature trail in Mayesville, and her portrait hangs in the South Carolina State House. ▪

Aiken-born Matilda Evans (1872–1935) was the first African American woman surgeon licensed to practice medicine in South Carolina. She also opened Columbia's first free clinic for Black children. In 2020, a street was named for her in the capital city.

▲ FROG ... LESS?

Frogmore stew, a local specialty, is not a stew—and does not contain frogs. Rather, it's a dish made with shrimp, corn on the cob, new potatoes, and smoked sausage.

WEIRD BUT TRUE

- In 2013, Saraswati, a white Bengal tiger at Myrtle Beach Safari Park, gave birth to the world's first confirmed white ligers—hybrids of a lion with a tigress.

- In 2019, Hurricane Dorian uncovered two Civil War–era cannonballs on Folly Beach.

- Due West, Ketchuptown, and Wide Awake are towns in South Carolina.

- Powdered coffee creamer once rained down on the town of Chester.

- Myrtle Beach is the "mini-golf capital of the world."

- Morgan Island, off the coast of Beaufort, is home to a population of some 4,000 rhesus monkeys.

- Lake Murray reportedly has its very own mysterious water monster known as "Messie."

- From 1964 to 2004, it was illegal to get a tattoo in South Carolina.

- In 2015, elementary students launched a toy boat equipped with a GPS tracker off the shores of South Carolina; months later it washed up in Wales.

MISCELLANY

- **The Shag**, which originated in the African American community and was popularized in the 1940s, is the official state dance.

- The state snack food is **boiled peanuts**.

- **Sumter** is home to the world's largest ginkgo farm.

- Writer Edgar Allan Poe's short story **"The Gold Bug"** was inspired by Charleston.

- Before it was the **"Palmetto State,"** South Carolina was known as the "Iodine State" because of the large percentages of the mineral found in the vegetation growing in the state.

- There are a series of **tiny mice sculptures** on Main Street in Greenville, inspired by the hidden mice in the children's book **Goodnight Moon**.

- On November 2, 1954, South Carolina's **Strom Thurmond** became the first U.S. senator elected by a write-in vote. He served in the Senate for 48 years.

- A nuclear bomb was accidentally dropped from a plane at **Mars Bluff** near Florence in 1958, leaving a 50-foot-wide (15 m) and 30-foot-deep (9 m) crater.

- Movies including **The Patriot, The Notebook, Deliverance**, and HBO's television show **Eastbound and Down** were all filmed in South Carolina.

- Blackville's **God's Acre Healing Spring** is said to have waters that can cure the sick and wounded; four British soldiers claimed they were healed of their wounds there during the Revolutionary War.

- In 1888, Dr. Charles Shepard founded the **Pinehurst Tea Plantation** in Summerville, the first commercial tea farm in the U.S.

- The **Isle of Palms**, first inhabited by the Sewee people, is estimated to be 25,000 years old.

▲ DRAYTON HALL

Built in 1738, Charleston's Drayton Hall is the oldest preserved plantation house open to the public.

BY THE NUMBERS

4,000 age in years of a mysterious circle of shells called the Sea Pines Shell Ring on Hilton Head Island. It's thought to have once been a ceremonial area for Native Americans.

13,200 the length in feet (4,023 m) of the Arthur Ravenel Jr. Bridge, North America's second-longest cable-stayed bridge, connecting historic Charleston and Mount Pleasant

297 the height in feet (91 m) of St. Matthew's Lutheran Church, the tallest structure in Charleston. At one point, it was also the tallest building in the state.

37 the population of Cope Town, South Carolina's smallest town

$25 cost of a plot of oceanfront land in Myrtle Beach in 1901. (You could get another plot of land for free if you built a house on the first plot.)

1,000+ number of graves at the cemetery of Charleston's Old St. Andrew's Parish Church, the oldest church in the state; one belongs to a man who died in 1733.

200 NUMBER OF KAZOOS ON DISPLAY AT THE KAZOOBIE KAZOOS FACTORY IN BEAUFORT, THE ONLY PLACE WHERE THE INSTRUMENTS ARE STILL MANUFACTURED IN THE U.S.

675,000 weight in pounds (306,175 kg) of the 40-foot-tall (12 m) "Busted Plug" sculpture in Downtown Columbia, built by a local artist to commemorate old-fashioned fire hydrants

One of the top destinations in the U.S., Charleston offers a bevy of beautiful buildings, antebellum architecture, and a buzzing nightlife to boot. Get your fill of history by taking a horse-drawn carriage ride through the city, and be sure to visit Rainbow Row, the pastel-colored historic homes located on East Bay Street, where you go to look for dolphins while strolling along the Battery, a seawall and promenade along Charleston Harbor.

DESTINATION: SOUTH CAROLINA

- Sail across Charleston Harbor to check out Fort Sumter, site of the 1861 attack by the Confederates that sparked the American Civil War. Fort Sumter and Fort Moultrie National Historic Park welcomed 385,472 visitors in 2022.

- Immerse yourself in the Congaree Wilderness in Hopkins by paddling down the 15-mile (24 km) Cedar Creek Canoe Trail. Look for local wildlife, including deer and river otters. Congaree has one of the largest concentrations of champion trees in the U.S.

- Scale to the top of the observation tower on Sassafras Mountain, the state's highest point at 3,553 feet (1,083 m) above sea level, which straddles the South Carolina/North Carolina line.

- Grab your clubs and take a swing on one of South Carolina's many golf courses. Harleston Green, the first golf club in the United States, was established in Charleston in 1786.

- Downtown Columbia hosts the South Carolina State Museum, a state-of-the-art venue featuring displays on everything from natural history to science to art. Housed in the Columbia Mills Building, the museum features a digital dome planetarium, and you can also see the world's first electric mill for textiles.

- The barrier island of Hilton Head stretches 12 miles (19 km) along the Atlantic coast, offering pristine beaches, stately homes, and luxurious resorts. It's also a sanctuary for sea turtles: In 2021, 283 nests were laid on Hilton Head beaches.

- Myrtle Beach is a magnet for sun lovers, with 60 miles (97 km) of coastline, plus a buzzing boardwalk and entertainment options galore. A veritable golfer's playground, Myrtle Beach boasts more than 90 courses.

STARS ★ OF ★ THE ★ STATE

JAMES BROWN

(1933–2006) Born in Barnwell, the "Godfather of Soul" began singing gospel music in church as a kid, teaching himself to play piano, guitar, and harmonica by ear. Brown's 1965 hit single, "Papa's Got a Brand New Bag," is one of the first funk songs ever written, and it popularized the genre. Throughout his four-decade career, Brown had 17 number one hits on the R&B charts, total sales of more than 50 million records, and was one of the first inductees of the Rock & Roll Hall of Fame. Later in life, Brown lived at his riverside estate in Beech Island until his death in 2006.

Tennis champion Althea Gibson, born in Silver in 1927, was the first Black tennis player to win the French Open (1956), Wimbledon (1957–58), and U.S. Open (1957–58) singles championships.

SPORTING CHANCES

- South Carolina has no major pro sports teams, but it is home to minor league baseball teams, including the Columbia Fireflies, Augusta GreenJackets, Charleston RiverDogs, Myrtle Beach Pelicans, and Greenville Drive.

- The first football matchup between rivals Clemson University and the University of South Carolina took place in 1896.

- In 2024, Clemson University ranked sixth among college football teams with the largest social media followings.

- The University of South Carolina has won eight national team championships. The wins came in women's basketball (2017, 2022), men's baseball (2010, 2021), equestrian (2005, 2007, 2011), and women's outdoor track and field (2002).

- Major league pitcher Bill Voiselle, who grew up in the town of Ninety Six and played for the Boston Braves in the 1940s, wore number 96.

- Built in 1926, Spartanville's Duncan Park is one of the oldest baseball stadiums in the country and is listed on the National Park Service's National Register of Historic Places.

- Home to more than 350 courses, South Carolina has more golf courses per square mile than anywhere in the U.S.

- In 1954, Henry Luce, publisher of *Time* and *Life* magazines, sent 67 writers and editors to Pine Lakes Country Club in Myrtle Beach to work on a new weekly sports magazine. The result? *Sports Illustrated* magazine, which is still published today.

- Joseph "Smokin' Joe" Frazier, one of the best heavyweight boxers in history, grew up in Laurel Bay, a rural Gullah community outside of Beaufort. Frazier was a 1964 Olympic gold medalist and was the undisputed world heavyweight champion from February 1970 to January 1973.

- Five South Carolina residents won gold at the Tokyo Olympics in 2021: Columbia's Wadeline Jonathas and North Charleston's Jasmine Camacho-Quinn (track and field); Charleston's Khris Middleton (men's basketball); Columbia's A'ja Wilson (women's basketball); and Greenwood's Allisha Gray (women's 3 × 3 basketball).

- Darlington Raceway was the first NASCAR superspeedway. The first race was held there in 1950.

- The Cooper River Bridge Run, a 10K race, has some 45,000 people participating each year.

- Each October, Winthrop University in Rock Hill hosts the U.S. Disc Golf Championships, considered one of the sport's most prestigious major events.

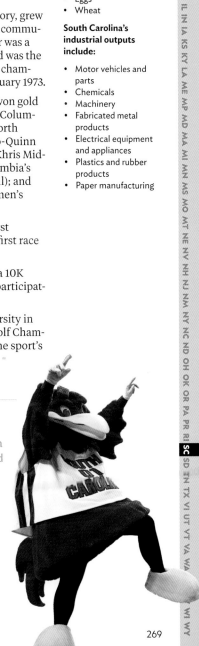

▶ GO! FIGHT!

The University of South Carolina mascot, the Gamecock, is named for Thomas Sumter, a famed guerrilla fighter of the Revolutionary War, who was known as "The Fighting Gamecock."

SOUTH DAKOTA

CAPITAL: Pierre **FLOWER:** American Pasque **NICKNAME:** Mount Rushmore State **ENTRY:** 1889

★ ★ ★ *"Under God the People Rule"* ★ ★ ★

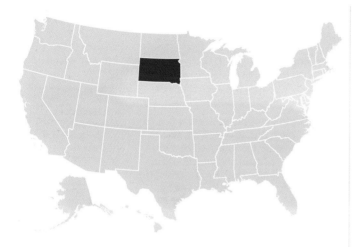

SD FACTS

- The population is 909,824.

- South Dakota joined the U.S. as the 40th state on the same day as North Dakota (the 39th).

- In addition to its rich Indigenous history, the state is known for its agricultural products, such as hay, honey, and rye.

- South Dakota has mining resources such as limestone, sand, granite, gravel, and—historically—gold.

- Today, federally recognized tribes include the Titunwan (Cheyenne River Sioux), Crow Creek Sioux, Dakota (Flandreau Santee Sioux), Kul Wicasa Oyate (Lower Brule Sioux), Oglala Lakota (Oglala Sioux), Sicangu Lakota Oyate (Rosebud Sioux), Sisseton Wahpeton Oyate (Sisseton-Wahpeton Sioux), and the Dakota and Lakota of Standing Rock (Standing Rock Sioux).

- The 1868 Treaty of Fort Laramie granted the area known as the Black Hills to what was then known as the Great Sioux Reservation.

- Thanks to the Black Hills Gold Rush of the 1870s, the region saw a major influx of German, Swedish, and Danish populations.

- Born Gertrude Simmons in Yankton, Zitkala-Ša was a Yankton Dakota Sioux writer, composer, and activist. He served as the Secretary for the Society of the American Indian.

- By the early 1900s, the state was home to large groups of Swiss and German Mennonites and Hutterites, who had arrived seeking religious freedom. Today, the groups are often referred to as the "South Dakota Amish."

▶ **STATE BIRD**
Ring-Necked
Pheasant
Phasianus colchicus

Originally found in central and eastern Asia, the ring-necked pheasant was introduced to the United States in the late 1800s, where it continues to thrive.

1876

Established in 1876 to serve the needs of the prospectors of the Black Hills Gold Rush, Deadwood was a boomtown famous for its outlaws and gunslingers. Such characters included Martha "Calamity Jane" Canary, a rugged frontierswoman equally known for her skill with a gun and humanitarian efforts for those afflicted with smallpox, and notorious gambler Wild Bill Hickok. ▼

WALKING IN A HARD DAKOTA WIND CAN BE LIKE STARING AT THE OCEAN: HUMBLED BEFORE ITS IMMENSITY, I ALSO HAVE A SENSE OF BEING AT HOME ON THIS PLANET.

—Author Kathleen Norris

- Mount Rushmore was designed by sculptor Gutzon Borglum, who remains infamous due to his ties with the hate group Ku Klux Klan. Construction of the four presidential heads began in 1927.

- At the time of Mount Rushmore's conception, ownership of the Black Hills remained contested. Lakota tribes were in the process of suing the U.S. government for the lands that had been taken from them in violation of the Treaty of Fort Laramie. It would not be until *United States v. Sioux Nation of Indians* in 1980 that the U.S. Supreme Court recognized the stolen lands and awarded the Lakota $17.1 million. The Sioux declined the compensation because they were advocating for the return of the Black Hills instead.

- Daughter of famed author Laura Ingalls Wilder, De Smet native Rose Wilder Lane focused her own writings on the political arena. She is considered one of the godmothers of libertarianism.

- In 1973, nearly 100 years after the U.S. government massacred some 150 Indigenous people—including Lakota leader Tatanka Iyotake (Sitting Bull)—at Wounded Knee, the American Indian Movement occupied the area for 71 days.

- Badlands—the dry, eroded areas that form gullies, buttes, and mesas—are found throughout much of the state.

- Fry bread, the official state bread, is made by deep-frying a dough made from wheat flour in hot oil or animal fat into a puffy disc. It is often topped with honey or powdered sugar.

STARS ★ OF ★ THE ★ STATE

BOB BARKER (1923–2023)

Born Robert William Barker in Washington, Bob Barker grew up with his mother on the Rosebud Indian Reservation in Mission as part of the Sicangu Lakota Oyate (also known as the Rosebud Sioux Tribe). After training as a Navy fighter pilot during WWII, Barker began a career in radio before being scouted to become a game show host. He became the host of *The Price Is Right* in 1972, which is the country's longest running television game show. In addition to winning 14 Emmy Awards, Barker was a dedicated activist and philanthropist for animal welfare.

271

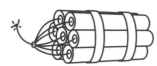

△ TNT
Almost all of Mount Rushmore was carved using dynamite.

WEIRD BUT TRUE

- An annual competition held in Clark involves wrestling in mashed potatoes.

- In South Dakota it is illegal to fall asleep in a cheese factory.

- Lutefisk, a dish brought over by Scandinavian immigrants and often eaten around Christmas, consists of whitefish soaked in lye.

- A South Dakotan Saint Bernard has the longest dog tongue in the world at more than seven inches (18 cm) long.

- Mount Rushmore contains a Hall of Records located behind Lincoln's head.

- One ranch store outside of Badlands National Park features a giant, six-ton (5.4 t) statue of a prairie dog.

- Located in Belle Fourche, a monument to the geographic center of the nation is actually ... off center.

- There is a 30-foot-tall (9 m) waterfall completely inside a Black Hills mountain.

- When North and South Dakota were admitted to the union, President Benjamin Harrison reportedly shuffled the papers and signed the documents without looking so that no one would know which was admitted first.

- If the Mount Rushmore presidents had bodies, they would be 46 stories tall.

RECORD ★ SETTERS
The first modern hot-air balloon—which relied on a propane gas burner—was flown in Sioux Falls in 1960.

△ STORY OF THE DANCE Wiwanyag Wacipi, also known as the Gazing-at-the-Sun Dance, is a traditional Lakota ceremony. Various forms of the Sun Dance have been (and continue to be) performed by multiple nations of the plains. Considered a time of renewal, ceremony participants traditionally include the entirety of the local community and involve the construction of a ritual circle or medicine lodge, where dancers practiced a ritual known as "sun gazing." The acts were often meant to symbolize the self-sacrifice and reciprocity of community. ▪

MISCELLANY

- Locals are called **South Dakotans**.

- The **coyote** is the state animal.

- **Milk** is the state drink.

- The **world's largest reptile zoo** is just outside Rapid City.

- The state fish is the **walleye**.

- The state jewelry is **Black Hills gold**.

- **Chislic**, a popular local dish, refers to salted and fried or grilled cubes of meat.

- In the **Dakota language**, Dakota can be translated as "friend" or "ally."

- The state fossil is the *Triceratops*.

- **Fairburn agate** is the state gemstone.

- The state's official dessert is **kuchen**, a traditional German treat that is a combination of cake and pie and often topped with custard.

- A former state governor, **Joseph Foss** was also a WWII marine fighter ace who was awarded the Medal of Honor.

- **Rose quartz** is the state mineral.

- Known as SUE, the world's **largest and most complete** *Tyrannosaurus rex* skeleton was found outside of Faith.

- The state tree is the **Black Hills spruce**.

BY THE NUMBERS

4,850
the weight in pounds (2,200 kg) of a sca turtle that swam 80 million years ago in the area that is now South Dakota

40
the top speed in miles an hour (64 kph) of a jackrabbit, an animal found across the state

2019
the year Kristi Noem became the state's first female governor

33,900
the number of acres (13,747 ha) that make up Wind Cave National Park

1,300
the approximate number of bison that live in South Dakota

2.5 million
the highest ever number of visitors to Mount Rushmore in one year

1965
the year South Dakota–born Hubert Humphrey became vice president of the United States

70+ years
THE LENGTH OF TIME CONSTRUCTION ON THE CRAZY HORSE MEMORIAL HAS BEEN ONGOING

Going from 54°F (12°C) to −4°F (−20°C) in just 27 minutes, Spearfish holds the world record for fastest known temperature drop.

DESTINATION: SOUTH DAKOTA

- Established in 1978, Badlands National Park features striking geological formations, ancient fossil beds, and wildlife such as bison, bighorn sheep, prairie dogs, and more.

- Falls Park features a series of impressive waterfalls in the Big Sioux River, which visitors can view from the observatory tower. Other local sites include the Arc of Dreams monument as well as the historic Cathedral of St. Joseph.

- Wall Drug in Wall has straddled the line between wacky tourist trap and historical cultural icon since 1931. Offering refreshments, a vintage apothecary, Black Hills gold, and jackalope-themed paraphernalia, what was once a stopover between state attractions has become one in its own right.

- Nature enthusiasts will delight in Custer State Park, which encompasses 71,000 acres (28,733 ha) of picturesque wilderness. Recreational activities include hiking, fishing, bird-watching, boating, and other water sports.

- Located in the Black Hills, Mount Rushmore features four 60-foot (18 m) busts of U.S. presidents carved into the mountainside. Also on hand are the Lincoln Borglum Visitor Center, the Avenue of Flags, and the Grand View Terrace. Nearby is the Crazy Horse Memorial, which is still under construction, as well as the Indian Museum of North America and the Native American Educational and Cultural Center.

- Wind Cave National Park features more than 150 miles (241 km) of charted passages some 500 feet (152 m) under the earth. Visitors can take tours of the complex underground system or enjoy camping aboveground, where they might spot coyotes, elk, bison, and more.

- Located in Vermillion, the National Music Museum features more than 15,000 instruments—including ones belonging to the likes of Elvis.

- Visiting Mitchell? Stop in at the World's Only Corn Palace, a mansion built of corn and featuring intricate murals.

- Located in Hot Springs, the Mammoth Site lets visitors tour an active archaeological dig site named for its excavation of a mammoth graveyard. The museum also offers junior paleontology programs for budding archaeologists.

- Standing 50 feet tall (15 m), the "Dignity of Earth & Sky" statue outside of Chamberlain is dedicated to women of the Lakota and Dakota nations.

- Though its original incarnation was as a hotbed of vice, the Deadwood of today caters to history buffs and family fun. Featuring historic reenactments, the area is also known for its live music, casinos, and breweries.

I AM BEGINNING TO LEARN THAT IT IS THE SWEET, SIMPLE THINGS OF LIFE WHICH ARE THE REAL ONES AFTER ALL.

—Author Laura Ingalls Wilder

SPORTING CHANCES

- Born in Bridgewater in 1934, George Lee "Sparky" Anderson was the first baseball manager to win the World Series in both the major and minor leagues.

- Located in Sioux Falls, the Denny Sanford Premier Center is an arena hosting events that range from Sioux Falls Stampede hockey games to indoor football matches to multiple monster truck shows.

- After more than a century without a moniker, South Dakota State University's jackrabbit mascot was given the name "Jack."

- The University of South Dakota's team colors are red and white.

- Known as the Queen of Spades, Sioux Falls native and WWE wrestler Shayna Baszler holds the record for the most days as the NXT Women's Champion.

- Born near Clarno Township in 1901, Cliff Lyons was a stuntman famous for his work in Western action movies.

- Huron native Billy Etbauer was a five-time World Champion Saddle Bronc Rider. He was inducted into the Pro Rodeo Hall of Fame in 2012.

- The University of South Dakota is home to the Coyotes—pronounced "KI-yotes."

- Located in Brookings, South Dakota State's Dana J. Dykhouse Stadium seats about 19,300.

MADE IN SD

South Dakota's agricultural outputs include:

- Soybeans
- Soy products
- Pork
- Cattle
- Grain
- Wheat
- Hay
- Sunflower seeds
- Corn
- Grain feed

South Dakota's industrial outputs include:

- Brewing waste
- Ethyl alcohol
- Farming equipment
- Bentonite
- Firefighting vehicles

I learned more about the economy from one South Dakota dust storm that I did in all my years of college.

—Vice President Hubert H. Humphrey

STARS ★ OF ★ THE ★ STATE

LAURA INGALLS WILDER

(1867–1957) Born in Wisconsin to a frontier family, Laura Ingalls moved through various territories as a child before her family finally settled in De Smet around 1879. There, Ingalls met her husband, Almanzo Wilder, and the two eked out a living as pioneers on the western frontier. In 1910, Ingalls Wilder's daughter began encouraging her to write down the stories of her youth. The first book of what would become Ingalls Wilder's smash hit *Little House* series, *Little House in the Big Woods*, was published in 1932. Ingalls Wilder continued to write well into her seventies, captivating young readers with her tales of pioneer living that remain iconic.

275

TENNESSEE

★ ★ ★
"Agriculture and Commerce"
★ ★ ★

CAPITAL: Nashville **FLOWER:** Iris **NICKNAME:** Volunteer State **ENTRY:** 1796

TN FACTS

- Tennessee is bordered by eight states—which ties it with Missouri for the most states on its borders.

- With a total area of 42,146 square miles (109,158 sq km), Tennessee is the 34th largest state.

- The state's population is 6.9 million.

- The capital, Nashville, has a population of 683,622. The state's other largest cities include Memphis (621,056) and Knoxville (195,889).

- Original inhabitants, dating back some 20,000 years ago, include the Creek, Choctaw, Chickasaw, Cherokee, Koasati, Shawnee, Yuchi, and Catawba.

- In 1567, the Spanish explorer Captain Juan Pardo was the first to use the word "Tennessee," which comes from the name "Tanasi," the one-time capital city of the Cherokee Nation.

- No presidents have been born in the state, but three grew up there: Andrew Jackson, James K. Polk, and Andrew Johnson.

- On average, 30 tornadoes touch down in Tennessee each year.

- There are about 6,000 black bears in East Tennessee.

▶ STATE GAME BIRD
Northern Bobwhite
Colinus virginianus

The state's official game bird, this small chicken-like bird has such a loud call, it can be heard for a quarter mile (400 m) in open country.

1819

Future president Andrew Jackson founded the city of Memphis on May 22, 1819, naming it after the ancient Egyptian city of Memphis—meaning "place of good abode"—which was located at the head of the Nile River Delta. ▼

WHEN YOU COME FROM MEMPHIS, MUSIC IS IN YOUR BLOOD.

—Singer Justin Timberlake

▶ **BONJOUR!**
There's a 60-foot (18 m) replica of the Eiffel Tower in Paris, Tennessee.

- Native Americans were forced to leave all lands east of the Mississippi River after the Indian Removal Act of 1830; today, there are no state-recognized tribes.

- Tennessee is known as the Volunteer State because of its high number of volunteers during the War of 1812.

- At 6,643 feet (2,025 km), Clingmans Dome in the Smokies is the highest point in Tennessee, and the third highest mountain east of the Mississippi.

- During the Civil War, Tennessee was the last state to secede from the Union—and the first to rejoin in 1866.

- Tennessee has more than 10,000 documented caves—the most in the U.S.

- Tennessee is one of the most religious states in the nation, with 73 percent of adult residents reporting to be "highly religious."

- Other animals found throughout the state include bats, red squirrels, foxes, bobcats, shrews, jumping mice, night herons, and frogs.

- The northern saw-whet owl, one of the smallest owls on the planet, lives in eastern Tennessee. ▪

▲ **MISTY MOUNTAINS**
Great Smoky Mountains National Park is America's most visited national park, attracting more than 14 million visitors in 2021.

STARS ★ OF ★ THE ★ STATE

DOLLY PARTON

(b. 1946) From a hardscrabble childhood deep in Appalachia to becoming a beloved cultural icon, Parton's career trajectory has been meteoric. The fourth of 12 children born to a poor family near Sevierville, Parton first showed off her musical prowess on a local radio station at six years old and performed at the Grand Ole Opry at the age of 13. A move to Nashville in 1964 led to her big break in the country music industry; she recorded her first number one hit six years later. She has since written more than 3,000 songs, had several major hits, and was inducted into the Country Music Hall of Fame in 1999. A generous philanthropist, Parton helped establish adequate health care facilities in her hometown, started a literacy initiative offering free books for children, and donated $1 million to fund research to develop a cure for COVID-19. ▪

- The Suck, the Skillet, and the Boiling Pot were all names of dangerous currents and whirlpools in the Tennessee River before dams made it safer for travelers to navigate.

- Tennesseans are sometimes referred to as "Butternuts," a reference to the tan uniforms of Civil War soldiers.

- Cotton candy was invented by a dentist from Nashville and was originally called "Fairy Floss."

- A pair of brothers from Knoxville created Mountain Dew soda, originally intended as a mixer for their bourbon.

- The AT&T Tower in downtown Nashville is nicknamed the Batman Building.

- A series of violent earthquakes in 1811 and 1812 created the state's only natural lake, the 15,000-acre (6,070 ha) Reelfoot in Tipton.

- Tennessee has 10 official state songs.

- The town of Columbia has been celebrating Mule Day for decades, featuring mule races and a parade.

- The RC Cola–MoonPie Festival in Bell Buckle honors the pairing of an ice-cold RC Cola and a fresh MoonPie, considered the South's "original fast food."

- Thousands of skeletons used to be housed under the University of Tennessee's Neyland Stadium in Knoxville as part of the anthropology department, which was commonly called the "Body Farm." (They have since moved to another location on campus.)

STORY OF THE MUSIC Country, bluegrass, blues, southern gospel, and rock 'n' roll all trace their roots directly to Tennessee. Specifically, to Nashville—known as Music City U.S.A. Country music really took off in the 1920s, when the Grand Ole Opry radio show was broadcast nationwide and Nashville soon became the epicenter for country music. Many artists have launched their careers from the Grand Ole Opry, including Loretta Lynn, Dolly Parton, and Garth Brooks.

MISCELLANY

- **President James K. Polk** and **First Lady Sarah Polk** are buried at the state capitol building.

- The capitol's architect, **William Strickland**, is also entombed inside the capitol's walls.

- Davy Crockett, the explorer known as the **"King of the Wild Frontier,"** went on to represent Tennessee in the U.S. House of Representatives.

- Nashville's **Centennial Park** is home to the only exact replica of the Greek Parthenon.

- Each April, Paris hosts the **World's Biggest Fish Fry**, where some 12,500 pounds (5,670 kg) of catfish are served.

- **Graceland**, in Memphis, is one of the most visited private residences in America, second only to the White House.

- The **Great Smoky Mountains** are known as the "Salamander Capital of the World."

- **FedEx** is based in Memphis, chosen because of its central location within the U.S. and because Memphis International Airport is rarely closed due to bad weather.

- In the 1940s, the U.S. government acquired 60,000 acres (24,281 ha) in East Tennessee to develop the **atomic bomb**.

- Camden is home to North America's only **freshwater pearl farm**.

- The University of Tennessee's mascot, **Smokey**, is a bluetick coonhound.

- **Copper Basin**—a stark landscape in the southeastern part of the state—was at one point so vast and barren that it could be seen from space.

- Dan Evins, a Smithville-born entrepreneur, opened the **first Cracker Barrel Old Country Store** and restaurant along Highway 109 in Lebanon.

- Foyil-born **Andy Payne** completed the 1928 Transcontinental Footrace in 573 hours.

- University of Tennessee's **Neyland Stadium** has a capacity of 102,455, making it the fifth largest in college football.

THIS LITTLE PIGGY WENT TO MARKET

Founded in Memphis in 1916, Piggly Wiggly was the first self-service grocery store in the U.S.

BY THE NUMBERS

500 the size in acres (202 ha) of farmland in Manchester designated for Bonnaroo, one of the largest music festivals in the world

2,238 the length in miles (3,602 km) of the entire Route 66, passing through eight states

11,000,000 the number of people who attended the 1982 World's Fair, also known as the Knoxville International Energy Exposition

16 the number of turtle species living in Tennessee. Reelfoot Lake, also known as the "Turtle Capital of the World," is home to several of those species, like sliders, stinkpots, mud turtles, and map turtles.

15,000 THE POPULATION OF THE LARGEST KURDISH COMMUNITY IN THE U.S., LOCATED IN NASHVILLE

5 the number of cities that have served as the state capital: Kingston, Knoxville, Memphis, Murfreesboro, and Nashville

7.5 the weight in pounds (3.4 kg) of the "Kookamonga" Burger, on the menu at the Kooky Canuck in Memphis

38 skiable acres (15.4 ha) at Ober Gatlinburg, a ski resort in the Great Smoky Mountains

400 the weight in tons (363 t) of the roof of the Millennium Manor Castle in Alcoa, a stone home built in 1945 meant to withstand an apocalypse. The exterior walls are more than two feet (0.6 m) thick.

DESTINATION: TENNESSEE

- Pay homage to Elvis Presley at Graceland, the estate where "the King" lived large (and is buried in the ground's meditation garden). Across the way, Elvis Presley's Memphis offers an impressive collection of artifacts from Presley's career, including his platinum records, his sparkly jumpsuits, and the various cars he owned.

- While in Memphis, check out any number of blues bars on the always-buzzing Beale Street, and make sure to sample the city's famous slow-cooked barbecue.

- The site where Martin Luther King, Jr., was assassinated in 1968 is now the National Civil Rights Museum, a comprehensive collection of interactive exhibits showcasing milestone events in civil rights history.

- Conquer the roller coasters at Dollywood in Pigeon Forge, Dolly Parton's joy-filled love letter to her hometown. After the thrills, visit Chasing Rainbows, a museum chock full of Parton's elaborate gowns and costumes, as well as many of her awards. ▼

▲ UP IN THE AIR

Tucked in the heart of the Great Smoky Mountains, Gatlinburg offers a series of adventures that are hard to, well, top. Several ways to soak up the impressive mountain views are available, from a ride to the peak of Anakeesta Mountain on the one-of-a-kind Chondola (a mash-up of a chairlift and a gondola) or on the Ober Gatlinburg Aerial Tram to a stroll along the SkyBridge, the longest pedestrian bridge in North America.

- The legendary Grand Ole Opry has been hosting live country music shows since 1925. But it's not the only place in Nashville to catch live music: From the honky tonks on Lower Broadway to larger performance halls like the Ryman Auditorium, there is something for everyone in Music City U.S.A. Can't get enough? Check out the Country Music Hall of Fame as well as the Johnny Cash Museum, both offering a journey into the genre's rich history.

- Every bottle of Jack Daniel's Old No. 7 Whiskey is made with water from a single spring in Lynchburg. Visit the site of the spring—which became the country's first registered distillery in 1866—to get your fill of whiskey tastings and local history.

STARS ★ OF ★ THE ★ STATE

ELVIS PRESLEY
(1935–1977) Influenced by the gospel music he heard in church and the rhythm & blues he absorbed on Beale Street in Memphis as a teenager, Elvis Presley helped introduce the world to rock and roll and changed the face of American music. In his two-decade career, Presley amassed a phenomenal array of accomplishments, from 14 Grammy nominations (he won three) to massive record sales, while developing a rabid fan base around the world. Despite his international fame, Presley never strayed too far from Memphis. He purchased his now famous home, Graceland, in 1957, and he lived there until his untimely death at the age of 42. Today, Graceland remains a tourist magnet welcoming over 500,000 visitors annually.

Tennessee's agricultural outputs include:

- Cattle and calves
- Soybean
- Broiler chickens
- Horticultural products
- Corn
- Cotton
- Dairy products
- Hay
- Tomatoes
- Eggs

Tennessee's industrial outputs include:

- Automotive and transportation products
- Processed foods and drinks
- Chemicals
- Electrical equipment and appliances
- Fabricated metals
- Machinery

SPORTING CHANCES

- In 2009, University of Tennessee's Pat Summitt became the first NCAA basketball coach to reach the 1,000-win mark, an NCAA record at the time. ▲

- Tennessee is home to four major professional sports franchises: the Tennessee Titans (NFL), the Nashville Predators (NHL), the Memphis Grizzlies (NBA), and the Nashville Soccer Club (Major League Soccer).

- There are four minor league baseball teams.

- Knoxville's Women's Basketball Hall of Fame is home to the world's largest basketball, measuring 30 feet (9 m) tall and weighing 10 tons (9 t).

- Bristol Motor Speedway is said to be the world's fastest half-mile (800 m) track, while Volunteer Speedway, in Bulls Gap, was touted as the world's fastest dirt track.

- Wilma Rudolph, who in 1960 became the first American woman to win three gold medals in track and field at a single Olympics, was born in St. Bethlehem.

- The University of Tennessee's varsity athletic teams have won 23 national team titles.

- Each April, some 20,000 walkers and runners hit the streets of the capital city for the Rock 'n' Roll Nashville Marathon.

- One hundred seventeen University of Tennessee athletes have competed in the Olympics, earning 39 gold medals in the process.

- The famous racehorse Iroquois, raised at Nashville's Belle Meade Plantation, was the first American winner of the English Derby in 1881. ▪

RECORD ★ SETTERS

Justice Martha Craig Daughtrey was the first woman to serve on the Tennessee State Supreme Court, and in 1993 was appointed to the U.S. Court of Appeals, where she became the first woman on the Sixth Circuit.

TEXAS

★ ★ ★
"Friendship"
★ ★ ★

CAPITAL: Austin **BIRD:** Mockingbird **NICKNAME:** Lone Star State **ENTRY:** 1845

TX FACTS

- With an area of 268,597 square miles (695,662 sq km) and with nearly 30 million residents, Texas is the second largest state in terms of both area and population.

- The state is home to three of the top 10 most populous cities in the United States: Houston (2,302,878), Dallas (1,299,544), and San Antonio (1,472,909).

- Austin, the capital, is the fourth largest city in Texas, with 974,447 residents.

- Texas has more species of birds than any other state.

- Today, the state is the leading producer of crude oil in the nation, accounting for 43 percent of crude oil production in the U.S.

- Several groups of Native Americans settled in Texas for thousands of years before the Europeans arrived, among the largest of which was the Caddo. Apache, Comanche, Wichita, and other tribes also lived there.

- Guadalupe Peak in the far west part of the state, also known as the "Top of Texas," is the highest point at 8,751 feet (2,667 m). ▼

▶ STATE FLOWER

Texas Bluebonnet
Lupinus texensis

This elegant blue-violet flower, often referred to as the "King of Spring," spreads over hills and valleys, and along roadsides throughout the state.

1845

In 1845, Texas became the 28th state to join the United States.

> ## THERE ARE NO SECRET HANDSHAKES BUT WHEN TEXANS MEET THERE'S A SPECIAL FRATERNITY.
>
> —Actor Matthew McConaughey

▶ TEXAS SIZED
If Texas was its own country, it would be the 40th largest in the world due to its land area.

- The name "Texas" comes from the Caddo Indian word *Tay-yas*, which is thought to mean friends. Spanish speakers referred to it as "Tejas," which later became "Texas."

- In 1519, Spanish explorer Alonso Álvarez de Piñeda and his crew were the first Europeans to view the entire Texas coast.

- After the Texas Revolution in 1836, Texas became its own country, known as the Republic of Texas, and remained an independent nation for nine years.

- The 1,900-mile-long (3,058 km) Rio Grande, which forms a border between Texas and Mexico, is the fifth longest river in North America.

- In 1900, Galveston was struck by a hurricane that's now considered the deadliest natural disaster in U.S. history.

- About 95 percent of land in Texas is privately owned.

- An average of 132 tornadoes touch down on Texas soil every year, usually occurring between the late spring and summer.

- An "oil boom" occurred in 1894 when the American Well and Prospecting Company accidentally came upon oil while looking for water.

- The state leads the country for installed wind power and is one of the largest wind energy producers in the world. ▼

▶ STORY OF THE MUSIC
While the actual origin of honky-tonks is up for debate, many a Texan will tell you that the boisterous cowboy bars—and the subgenre of music that emerged from them—began in the state. The term first appeared in the pages of Texas newspapers around the 1890s, and soon after boot-stomping dance halls like Sengelmann Hall and Coupland Hall opened for business. In the 1950s, honky-tonk began spreading across radio waves in the U.S., with tunes including a fiddle, a steel guitar, and a piano as well as honest (and often) heartbreaking lyrics. Texas-born singers like Waylon Jennings and Willie Nelson helped popularize honky-tonk, which remains as beloved today as it was decades ago. ▪

STARS ★ OF ★ THE ★ STATE

GEORGE W. BUSH
(b. 1946) When he was two years old, George W. Bush, the 43rd president of the U.S., moved to Midland from New Haven, Connecticut, after his father, President George H.W. Bush, got a job in the oil industry. He received a bachelor's degree in history from Yale University in 1968 before serving as an F-102 fighter pilot in the Texas Air National Guard, and eventually getting into politics, elected as the governor of Texas in 1994. The first governor in Texas history to be elected to consecutive four-year terms, Bush followed his father's footsteps into the White House in 2001, just the second time in American history that a president's son went on to fill the same role. Today, Bush and his wife, Laura, live in Dallas, but still own a home on a 1,600-acre (647 ha) ranch in Crawford, once known as the "Western White House." ▪

- There is a toilet-seat art museum in the city of The Colony.
- Bedford is home to the world's tallest living dog, a three-foot, 5-inch-tall (104 cm) Great Dane named Zeus.
- In 2022, it was reported that barnacle-covered dolls have been washing up along the beaches on Padre Island.
- A Texas woman spent $35 on a marble bust at a Houston thrift store that turned out to be a 2,000-year-old sculpture that once belonged to the king of Bavaria.
- In 1934, dust from Texas traveled so far that it coated ship decks in the Atlantic Ocean.
- There's a supposed alien gravesite from the 1800s in Aurora.
- It's illegal to shoot Bigfoot (also known as Woolly Booger) anywhere in the state.
- Silversmiths assembled the world's largest belt buckle in their Dallas showroom in 2021, measuring 10 feet 6 inches by 14 feet 6.4 inches (3.20 m by 4.43 m) and weighing more than 1,000 pounds (454 kg).
- During World War II, the British Broadcasting Corporation (BBC) banned Bing Crosby's "Deep in the Heart of Texas" from U.K. radio stations during work hours over concern that factory employees might neglect their machines to clap along with the catchy song.
- In 2005, the residents of Clark voted to change the town's name to Dish after the satellite TV company Dish Network offered them free service for 10 years.
- Earth, Texas, is perhaps the only town in the world to be named after the planet.

DON'T MESS WITH TEXAS.

—slogan developed by the Texas Department of Transportation for an anti-littering campaign

MISCELLANY

- One in every **12 Americans** lives in Texas.
- **Two U.S. presidents** were born in the state: Dwight Eisenhower (Denison) and Lyndon Baines Johnson (Stonewall).
- The **Tyler Rose Garden** features some 38,000 rose bushes of up to 500 species, making it one of the largest gardens of its kind in the country.
- Texas is the **battiest state** in the country, with 32 of the 47 species of the flying mammal calling the state home.
- The **George W. Bush Library** sits on 23 acres (9.3 ha) of the Southern Methodist University campus in Dallas.
- Students are required by state law to recite both the **U.S. Pledge of Allegiance and the Texas Pledge** each day.
- **Whole Foods** was founded in Austin in 1980.

- The **fastest speed limit** in the country, 85 miles an hour (137 kph), is on a stretch of Texas State Highway 130.
- Bonnie Parker and Clyde Barrow—the **infamous outlaws** who gained notoriety during the Great Depression for a series of bank robberies and the deaths of at least 13 people over the course of approximately two years—met in Dallas in 1930.
- Six Flags Amusement Park opened its gates in Arlington in 1961 and got its name from the number of flags that have **flown over Texas**: Spanish, French, Mexican, Texan, United States, and Confederate.
- *Paluxysaurus jonesi* is the **official state dinosaur**.

- The term **"maverick"** comes from Sam Maverick, an Alamo defender and Texas legend who left his unbranded cattle to roam freely. Originally used to describe unbranded cattle in general, the word is now likened to those who are independent-minded and have a "disposition to be different from the herd."
- Some residents of Fredericksburg and nearby areas speak **"Texas German,"** a dialect reflective of the German immigrants who settled in the area.
- There are **53 *Fortune* 500 Companies** based in the state, including AT&T, ExxonMobil, and Dell Technologies.

RECORD ★ SETTERS

In 2021, Lake Jackson–born Selena, the late Tejano icon, posthumously received the Grammy's Lifetime Achievement Award for her contributions to the music industry. She is the first Texan woman to receive the award.

BY THE NUMBERS

825,000 the size in acres (333,866 ha) of King Ranch in Kingsville. Covering more land than the state of Rhode Island, it is the largest ranch in the U.S.

30,000 the weight in pounds (13,607 kg) of wildflower seeds spread along Texas state highways each year

302 the height in feet (92 m) of the Texas State Capitol building in Austin, some 15 feet (4.5 m) higher than the U.S. Capitol Building in Washington, D.C.

24 the number of consecutive days the State Fair of Texas in Dallas runs each year, making it the longest-running state fair in the country

250 THE NUMBER OF LIVE MUSIC VENUES IN AUSTIN

627 the number of turbines at the Roscoe Wind Farm. They cover 100,000 acres (40,469 ha) of land, making it one of the largest onshore wind farms in the world.

320 the number of different species of birds living in the 44,413-acre (17,913 ha) Brazoria National Wildlife Refuge near Lake Jackson, including great blue herons, roseate spoonbills, and wood storks

23 THE NUMBER OF FLAVORS USED BY CHARLES ALDERTON, A PHARMACIST IN WACO, TO CONCOCT DR. PEPPER SODA, WHICH HE FIRST SERVED UP IN 1885. THERE'S A MUSEUM IN THE TOWN DEDICATED TO THE SODA'S JOURNEY.

◀ **SAN ANTONIO RIVER WALK**

There's a reason the San Antonio River Walk is considered a top attraction in the country: A stroll along the 15-mile (24 km) waterway offers riverfront dining, shopping, and a great place to relax and people watch. Want to see the city from the water? Hop on a river barge and get a guided tour.

DESTINATION: TEXAS

- From dive bars to high-end eateries and a little bit of everything in between, Austin is a party city through and through. In this "Live Music Capital of the World," there's a band to check out nearly anywhere you roam. The famed South by Southwest Conference and Music Festival takes place every March, attracting some 400,000 visitors from more than 100 countries.

- You can also go batty near Devil's Sinkhole in Rocksprings. The centerpiece of this state natural area is a 60-foot (18 m), 350-foot-deep (107 m) cavern, the largest single-chambered cavern in the state. From May to October, the cave is home to about three million Mexican free-tailed bats, who emerge like a tornado in the evenings. There are also guided nature hikes offered on the first and third Saturdays of every month.

- On November 22, 1963, John F. Kennedy was assassinated as he rode in a motorcade through Dallas's Dealey Plaza, becoming the youngest president to die in office. Today, the John F. Kennedy Memorial Plaza, located one block east of where he was shot, serves as a lasting homage. Nearby is the Sixth Floor Museum, located within the former Texas School Book Depository building, which showcases Kennedy's life, career, and assassination.

- A trip to Austin isn't complete without a sunset pit stop on Congress Bridge. Nearly each night at dusk from spring to fall, up to 1.5 million Mexican free-tailed bats swarm out from beneath the bridge in search of an evening snack; all told, the bats consume 10,000 to 30,000 pounds (4,536 to 13,608 kg) of insects every night.

- Everything's bigger in Texas—even its museums. Case in point? The Dallas Museum of Art is one of the largest art museums in America, situated in the nation's largest arts district. The museum occupies 515,520 square feet (47,893 sq m) and has more than 23,000 objects in its collection, dating from the third millennium B.C. to the present day.

> I HAVE SAID THAT TEXAS IS A STATE OF MIND, BUT I THINK IT IS MORE THAN THAT. IT IS A MYSTIQUE CLOSELY APPROXIMATING A RELIGION.
>
> —Author John Steinbeck

- The Alamo is another major draw in San Antonio. The centuries-old Spanish mission, the site of a drawn-out battle in the early 1800s, sits on 4.2 acres (1.7 ha). Tours, exhibits, demonstrations, and a Living History encampment featuring a glimpse of frontier life in early Texas make this a stop you'll always, well, remember.

- Sparkly blue water and wide sandy beaches line South Padre Island, located on the Gulf Shore on the southernmost tip of Texas. The longest barrier island in the world—and the largest stretch of undeveloped ocean beach in North America—"SPI" is flooded with spring breakers in February and March, but is a top family-friendly destination during the rest of the year.

Two years after the 19th Amendment granted women the right to vote, Edith Wilmans, a lawyer and mother of three, became the state's first woman legislator in 1922. A political pioneer, Wilmans also ran for governor.

MADE IN TX

Texas's agricultural outputs include:

- Cattle
- Milk
- Broiler chickens
- Cotton
- Corn
- Hay
- Sorghum
- Eggs
- Wheat
- Rice

Texas's industrial outputs include:

- Chemicals
- Petroleum and coal products
- Computer and electronic products
- Motor vehicles and parts
- Machinery

SPORTING CHANCES

- Texas is home to three different NBA teams (the San Antonio Spurs, the Dallas Mavericks, and the Houston Rockets); one WNBA team (the Dallas Wings); two NFL teams (the Houston Texans and the Dallas Cowboys); two MLB teams (the Houston Astros and the Texas Rangers); an NHL team (the Dallas Stars); and three professional soccer teams (FC Dallas, Austin FC, and the Houston Dynamos).

- The Cowboys have the second highest number of Super Bowl wins among all NFL teams, with five. It's also the only NFL team to have 20 consecutive winning seasons, from 1966 to 1985.

- AT&T Stadium is the largest enclosed stadium in the NFL.

- The Spurs, the Mavericks, and the Rockets have all won NBA championships.

- Some 108,713 fans packed into the 2010 NBA All-Star game at Cowboys Stadium in Arlington, setting a world record for attendance at a basketball game.

- A record 54,357 people attended the high school football game between Allen and Pearland High Schools in 2013.

- WNBA stars Ariel Atkins, of Duncanville, and Houston's Brittney Griner were both on the gold medal–winning women's basketball team at the 2020 Olympics.

- A total of 153 Olympic medals have been won by University of Texas Longhorns.

- The Circuit of the Americas in Austin, the first purpose-built Grand Prix facility in the U.S., hosts the Formula 1 U.S. Grand Prix.

- Babe Didrikson Zaharias, who grew up in Beaumont, is considered one of the greatest American athletes of all time. She excelled in basketball, won three Olympic medals in track and field at the 1932 games, and went on to help found the Ladies Professional Golf Association.

- Rodeo is the official state sport. The Houston Livestock Show and Rodeo is the largest rodeo in the state, with more than two million attendees annually.

- One of the world's first rodeos was held in Pecos, on July 4, 1883.

SIMONE BILES

(b. 1997) With a total of 34 Olympic and World Championship medals, Simone Biles is the most decorated gymnast of all time. Raised in the aptly named town of Spring, Biles began gymnastics early in her childhood and was a national champion at the age of 16. In addition to taking gold in the 2016 Rio Olympics, Biles is the first woman to have won six world all-around championships and introduced "The Biles," her signature move of a double layout with a half twist. While her accolades in gymnastics are extensive, Biles also received praise for speaking up about her mental health struggles during the 2020 Summer Olympics, when she withdrew from several events to focus on her emotional well-being. In 2022, Biles became the youngest person to receive the Presidential Medal of Freedom for her work advocating for athletes' mental health and safety, among other causes. Biles, whose family owns the World Champions Centre, a training facility in Spring, has a home in Houston.

U.S. VIRGIN ISLANDS

CAPITAL: Charlotte Amalie **FLOWER:** Yellow Trumpetbush **NICKNAME:** America's Paradise **ENTRY:** 1917

★ ★ ★ *"United in Pride and Hope"* ★ ★ ★

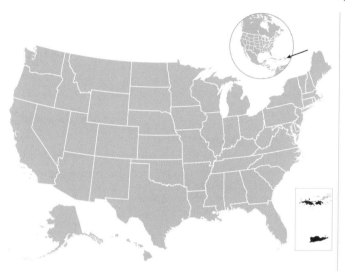

VI FACTS

- The territory is in the northeastern Caribbean Sea, some 40 miles (64 km) east of Puerto Rico.

- The population is 87,146.

- The U.S. Virgin Islands (USVI) is made up of three main islands—St. Croix, St. John, and St. Thomas—and approximately 50 smaller islets.

- Known for its relaxed island lifestyle and natural beauty, the territory's economy relies foremost on tourism. Other industries include government, manufacturing, finance, and real estate.

- Natural resources include fertile soil for growing sugarcane, tropical fruits (such as mango, passion fruit, coconut, and papaya), and plentiful seafood.

- The word "Caribbean" comes from Carib.

- English is the official language, but French and Spanish are widely spoken as well.

- As a territory, the islands are under the jurisdiction of

▶ **OFFICIAL BIRD**

Bananaquit
Coereba flaviola

Known for its yellow body and striped head, this small bird is nicknamed the "sugar bird" for its attraction to nectar.

1878

Black and Indigenous workers were kept in near-enslaved conditions as sharecroppers because of the Labor Law of 1849. In 1878, three women—Mary "Queen Mary" Thomas, Axeline "Agnes" Elizabeth Salomon, and Mathilda McBean—led an uprising that came to be known as the Fireburn Rebellion.

STARS ★ OF ★ THE ★ TERRITORY

AUDRE LORDE (1934–1992)

Renowned poet and author Audre Lorde was born in New York City in 1934 to Grenadan parents. An avid student of literature, Lorde published her first poetry volume in 1968. Over the next decade, her poetry explored social injustice, Lorde's identity as a Black lesbian woman, and the roles of women in society and politics. In the 1980s, Lorde made the USVI her chosen home, remaining in St. Croix for the rest of her life and changing her name to Gamba Adisa. In addition to her poetry, essays, and novels, Lorde is remembered as a pioneer of feminist theory and critical racial studies. ▪

> THE CARIBBEAN IS AN IMMENSE OCEAN
> THAT JUST HAPPENS TO HAVE A FEW
> ISLANDS IN IT. THE PEOPLE HAVE AN
> IMMENSE RESPECT FOR IT, AWE OF IT.

—Poet Derek Walcott

the United States. Residents are granted U.S. citizenship and passports but cannot vote in presidential elections.

- Camille Pissarro, one of the founders of the Impressionist artistic movement, was born in St. Thomas in 1830 to parents of Portuguese, Jewish, and Dominican heritage.

- The islands are thought to have been inhabited since around 1,000 B.C. by Arawak peoples who arrived from South America. Over time, this led to the development of the Taíno culture, an agriculture-based society that spread out over much of the Caribbean.

- Around the 15th century, the Carib people conquered the Taíno and came to dominate the islands.

- Among the first Europeans to the area were various pirates and privateers, who plundered and enslaved many Taíno and Carib people. Skirmishes between pirates of different nationalities lasted until Danish buccaneers took control of the islands in the 1600s, turning them into a pirate base.

- Over time, the presence of piracy gave way to the Danish West India Company, which cultivated the islands with cotton, tobacco, and sugarcane. For labor, the Danish forcibly enslaved and transported thousands of people captured in Africa. Today, the culture of the USVI reflects the varied origins of the islands' current inhabitants.

- In 1733, many of the enslaved people on St. John led a rebellion against the slavers, successfully taking control of a Danish fort and destroying some 50 plantations. However, with French aid, the Danish military retaliated and soon reconquered the island.

- During WWI, the U.S. government desired parts of the West Indies in order

▶ MOKO JUMBIES

Considered one of the preeminent cultural symbols of the USVI, Moko Jumbies are stilt walkers dressed in brightly colored clothes and cloth masks. Thought to originate in various parts of Africa, the performers are mainstays at celebrations such as Carnival.

to control certain water passage routes. Denmark, which remained neutral during the war, agreed to sell three of the islands for $25 million in 1917. Known as Transfer Day, this event is celebrated every year on March 31.

- Traditionally served on Transfer Day, red grout (also known as rødgrød) is a dessert of Danish origin made from a jelly of guavas and tapioca.

- In 1970, oceanographer and National Geographic Explorer Sylvia Earle led the first all-female team of divers as part of the Tektite II project off the coast of St. John. As part of the project, which aimed to examine the viability of underwater living and to study marine life in situ, the team lived for two weeks in an underwater laboratory.

- Myrah Keating Smith, born on St. Thomas in 1908, made revolutionary strides for health care in the USVI. After studying at the Tuskegee Institute, Smith returned to the territory in 1931 to work as a midwife. She was inducted into the Virgin Islands Women's Hall of Fame in 2005.

WEIRD BUT TRUE

- The local manchineel tree is so poisonous that even touching its sap can cause burns. ▶
- The USVI is the only location in the U.S. where people drive on the left side of the road.
- St. Croix was once willed to the Knights of Malta, an offshoot of the Knights Templar (but they sold it to the French West India Company).
- The sargassum frogfish, a fish which tends to live among the territory's mangroves, is known for its cannibalistic behavior.
- The capitol was once called "Taphus," the Danish word for tap house, because it had so many bars.

- St. John is famous for its wild donkeys. After being introduced to the island, they were left to roam free. ▲
- One island company offers customers the chance to dress up like a mermaid—complete with tail—and go for a swim.
- The Virgin Islands blind snake is not a snake—it is a form of legless lizard.
- One local pizza place operates on a boat and sells slices to snorkelers.
- Originally introduced to help curb the rat population in the 1800s, the mongoose now runs rampant on the islands. ▪

Located at the end of St. Croix, Point Udall in the U.S. Virgin Islands is the easternmost point in the United States.

MISCELLANY

- **Cocoa tea** is a chocolate drink made from roasted cocoa beans grated into a powder.
- A style of folk music known as *quelbe* is the official traditional music style.
- The USVI has coasts on **two geographic oceans**: the Atlantic and the Caribbean.
- **Two negotiation attempts** failed before the U.S. purchased the islands.
- **"Maroon"** was a 17th-century term for a formerly enslaved person who became a resistance fighter.
- **Pumpkin fritters** are made by frying bite-size pieces of pumpkin-based dough.
- Famed politician **Alexander Hamilton** was born in the West Indies and grew up on St. Croix.
- Made with spinach, okra, fish, and ham, the West African stew **callaloo** is often served on New Year's Eve.
- **Soursop**, a local knobby fruit, is often used to make ice cream.
- **Christopher Columbus** called the islands "Santa Úrsula y las Once Mil Vírgenes" after the Catholic legend of St. Ursula and the 11,000 virgins.
- Norman Island was the setting for **Robert Louis Stevenson's** *Treasure Island*.
- Called **banana figs**, one local fruit looks and tastes like a small, sweet banana.
- The remains of a **Taíno ball court**, the location for ceremonial games played with rubber balls, can be found in Salt River Bay.
- The **genip**, a small fruit with a rough, leafy exterior and a sweet, fleshy center, is similar to a lychee.
- St. Croix is home to a **baobab tree** planted more than 250 years ago.
- Named after a malevolent spirit of Caribbean folklore, **Jumbie Beach** is said to be haunted.
- One bat found in the USVI, the **greater bulldog bat**, is also known as the fisherman bat for its habit of snatching fish from rivers and coastlines.
- One local fish, the **flying gurnard**, has iridescent wings.
- 400 types of reef fish live around the islands.

STORY OF THE DRINK Invented sometime around 1650 in the West Indies, rum was an opportunistic side venture of the burgeoning sugar industry. The alcohol is made from distilling molasses, a byproduct of sugarcane, which allowed plantation owners to extend their profits. This beverage also extended the practice of slavery. Ships arriving in the West Indies with enslaved Africans were often given molasses. This was taken to New England, where it was turned into rum, transported back to the West Indies, and traded again for enslaved people. Despite its horrific origins, the drink itself remains a cultural icon of the USVI, which is home to several modern distilleries. ▪

BY THE NUMBERS

12,909
the size in acres (5,224 ha) of Virgin Islands National Park

2
the number of bioluminescent bays at St. Croix, one at Salt River Bay National Historical Park and the other at Altona Lagoon

1852
the year Judah P. Benjamin, born in St. Croix, became the first Jewish person elected to the U.S. Senate

1,556
THE HEIGHT IN FEET (474 M) OF CROWN MOUNTAIN, THE HIGHEST POINT IN THE ISLANDS

25,000,000
the number of dollars in gold used by the U.S. to purchase the islands in 1916

60
THE MAXIMUM HEIGHT IN FEET (18 M) OF A BREADFRUIT TREE

1760
the year the historic sugar mill at Estate Diamond was founded

1.6 inches
THE AVERAGE LENGTH (40 MM) OF A HAWKSBILL SEA TURTLE HATCHLING

- Bustling St. Thomas offers a wide array of entertainment and education, from the Pirates Treasure Museum to historic Main Street, from the Western Hemisphere's second oldest synagogue to various breweries, and from hiking up Mountain Top to taking the Skyride to Paradise Point.

- The Crucian Christmas Festival is a monthlong celebration in December on St. Croix that has taken place since the 1800s. Participants take part in pageants, musical competitions, parades (including one for children and one for adults), and plenty of eating.

- Covering nearly two-thirds of St. John, Virgin Islands National Park spans 7,259 acres (5,224 ha) of tropical forests and historic cultural sites. The park offers more than 20 hiking trails and near endless water activities.

- Though it is impossible to name any beach on the islands as the best, top contenders include St. John's Trunk Bay, which features striking white sands and turquoise waters; St. Thomas's Hull Bay, beloved for its surfing; and St. Thomas's Magens Bay, a top spot for families.

- Located off Trunk Bay, a 675-foot (206 m) underwater snorkel trail, part of Virgin Islands National Park, allows visitors to glimpse coral; myriad fish such as trumpetfish, tang, parrotfish, and more; as well as anemone, tube worms, and other marine animals.

- Each island celebrates Carnival—a Catholic festival that happens before Lent—in its own unique way. Each celebration includes parades, ornate costumes, public music and dancing, and plenty of food.

RECORD ★ SETTERS

In 1917, USVI native Alton A. Adams became the first Black bandmaster to serve in the U.S. Navy.

- A popular stopover for cruise ships, Charlotte Amalie is known for its shopping and high-end dining. Historic sites also abound, such as Market Square, Fort Christian (not to be confused with Fort Christiansvaern), and the Government House.

- The largest island, St. Croix is a favorite destination of foodies and history buffs alike. Popular sights include the Danish Fort Christiansvaern, historic plantation ruins, rum distilleries, and tide pools.

- Located some two miles (3.2 km) south of St. Thomas, the Buck Island National Wildlife Refuge was designated in 1969. The island and local waters serve as nesting and feeding grounds for green sea turtles.

▼ ST. JOHN

Likely the least crowded of the main islands, St. John is only accessible by ferry. It offers unparalleled access to nature, plenty of hiking trails, and easy access to Virgin Islands National Park.

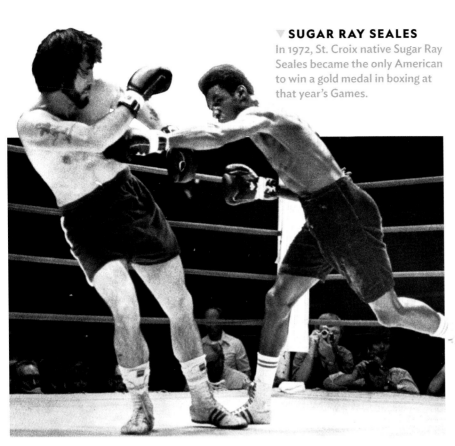

▼ SUGAR RAY SEALES

In 1972, St. Croix native Sugar Ray Seales became the only American to win a gold medal in boxing at that year's Games.

MADE IN VI

USVI's agricultural outputs include:

- Peanuts
- Fish
- Previously exported sugar and molasses (but no longer)

USVI's industrial outputs include:

- Rum
- Petroleum
- Light oils
- Motorboats
- Jewelry
- Gold items
- Platinum items
- Electronic parts
- Gravel products

SPORTING CHANCES

- The St. Thomas International Regatta is a premier yacht-racing event for boaters around the world.

- Set in St. Croix, the Coral Reef Swim is an annual open water racing event with matches catering to everyone from children to world-class open water swimmers.

- With drops of more than 13,000 feet (3,962 m), the USVI is known for hosting some of the best wall scuba diving in the world.

- Born in St. Thomas, Peter Holmberg is an Olympic sailor who earned top ranking in match racing.

- The University of the Virgin Islands (UVI) mascot is the Buccaneer.

STARS ★ OF ★ THE ★ TERRITORY

DAVID HAMILTON JACKSON

(1884–1946) Born in St. Croix, David Hamilton Jackson was an activist and labor union revolutionary who fought for better working conditions in what were then the Danish West Indies. Jackson received his legal training at the University of Chicago in Illinois before returning home to St. Croix, where he founded a newspaper criticizing Danish colonial rule and led a successful strike for increased wages on sugar plantations and reduced working hours. Jackson also strongly advocated for the sale of the colonies to the U.S., as he believed this would offer higher protections for workers. To this day, the USVI celebrates November 1 as David Hamilton Jackson Day. ▪

▼ PIRATE BOOTY

According to legend, 17th-century St. Thomas governor Adolph Esmit was famous for helping pirates avoid capture—in return for loot.

UTAH

★ ★ ★

"Industry"

★ ★ ★

CAPITAL: Salt Lake City **BIRD:** California Gull **NICKNAME:** Beehive State **ENTRY:** 1896

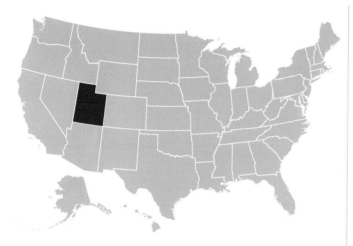

UT FACTS

- The population is 3,380,800.

- The 45th state, it is the 12th largest in area.

- Utah has been inhabited for at least 10,000 years. The original inhabitants of the area included the Nimi' (Bannock), Diné (Navajo), Newe (Goshute), Nuwuvi (Paiute), Shoshone, and Nuciu (Ute). Today, federally recognized tribes are the Confederated Tribes of the Goshute Reservation, Uintah and Ouray (Ute), Navajo Nation, Paiute Indian Tribe of Utah, Skull Valley Band of Goshute, and Northwestern Band of the Shoshone Nation.

- The earliest European expedition into the area may have been in 1541 under Captain García López de Cárdenas. The lands became part of Mexico after the country declared independence in 1810.

- In 1832, two years after self-proclaimed prophet Joseph Smith published his *Book of Mormon*, a 31-year-old Brigham Young decided to join the Church of Jesus Christ of Latter-day Saints (LDS). Young went on to lead his congregation west, establishing Salt Lake City as the Mormon base.

- In 1850, the region became an American territory. Mormon settlers wished to join the Union as the state of Deseret, but the territory was admitted as the state of Utah.

- Utah scones are puffy, fried rounds of bread topped with powdered sugar and honey. Historians think these local treats may have been adapted by Mormon pioneers from recipes for Indigenous fry bread.

- Born in 1926 in Salt Lake City, Neal Cassady became a renowned writer and formative figure of the 1950s Beat Generation. In addition to creating works notable for their stream-of-consciousness style writing, Cassady served as muse to iconic American writers Jack Kerouac and Allen Ginsberg. ◄

▶ STATE FLOWER

Sego Lily
Calochortus nuttallii

Designated in 1911, this summertime bloom was chosen to represent both the natural beauty of Utah's rangelands and the state's reliance on it as a source of sustenance during hard times.

1847

First founded in 1847, the Tabernacle Choir consists of 360 Church of Jesus Christ of Latter-day Saints members. Often accompanied by an enormous pipe organ and a 110-person orchestra, the choir has performed choral music at world's fairs, presidential inaugurations, and around the world.

MOTHER NATURE IS A MASTER SCULPTOR AND IN NO PLACE IS THAT MORE EVIDENT THAN AT ARCHES NATIONAL PARK.

—Stefanie Payne, *A Year in the National Parks*

▼ **LOOK UP**
The state draws countless stargazers each year thanks to its reputation as the place with the highest concentration of Dark Sky Parks on the planet.

- After President Lincoln signed the Pacific Railway Act in 1862, the Union Pacific Railroad and Central Pacific Railroad companies began work on the tracks from opposite directions, starting in Nebraska and California. In 1869, the railroad united at Promontory Point.

- Known for desert and natural beauty, the state sees much tourism. Its economy also relies on aerospace companies, data centers, and digital media.

- With the arrival of the railroad came copper prospectors who poured into the state in the 1870s and '80s. In 1903, the Utah Copper Company formed and began mining at Bingham Canyon. Mining expanded rapidly, and the company soon merged with two others. The Kennecott copper mine, as it became known, remains one of the world's largest human-made, open-pit copper mines.

- Natural resources in Utah include potassium chloride, uintaite, copper, and stones such as red beryl, bertrandite, and topaz.

- Not only does Utah consume the most Jell-O per capita, it has also declared the wiggly dessert an official state snack. ▲

STARS ★ OF ★ THE ★ STATE

EARL BASCOM

(1906–1995) Born near Vernal in 1906, Earl Bascom is known to many as the "father of modern rodeo." Bascom began riding at a young age and started his competitive career at the age of 10, becoming well-known for his saddle bronc riding, bareback riding, bull riding, and steer wrestling. He is credited with inventing multiple game-changing pieces of rodeo equipment, including the side-delivery rodeo chute, the first hornless bronc saddle, and the first one-handed bareback rigging. Over the course of his career, Bascom was inducted into four separate halls of fame.

PICKLES AND BEANS

A diner in Bicknell serves pies made with pickles and pinto beans.

WEIRD BUT TRUE

- The Mormon cricket, so named for the group of Mormons who discovered it, is often cannibalistic.

- One roadside stop in Moab features a modern home carved directly into the side of a mountain.

- The Cosmic Navel, a rock formation in Grand Staircase-Escalante National Monument, has a belly-button-like appearance.

- There is a micronation known as the Republic of Zaqistan located in Box Elder County.

- The Bonneville Salt Flats are home to a 90-foot-tall (27 m) statue, known as the Tree of Life, that locals refer to as "Momen's Meatballs."

- One museum in Hurricane has a piece of wedding cake more than 100 years old.

- A tunnel winding through a mountain in Zion National Park includes windows built into the tunnel wall.

- A work of art in Great Salt Lake only appears during droughts.

- Located in the Logan City cemetery, one tombstone features a fudge recipe.

- Officials constructed an animals-only overpass over a highway near Parley's Summit.

▶ **STORY OF** THE SOUND: Born and raised in Ogden to a Mormon family, the Osmonds were a vocal group that shot to stardom in the 1970s. The band that started singing together, and eventually included five of their nine siblings, was known for their catchy, wholesome tunes such as "One Bad Apple." Thanks to their family-friendly image and bubblegum meets country stylings, the Osmonds soon topped the charts in both the U.S. and the U.K. The group has sold more than 100 million albums around the globe.

MISCELLANY

- Locals are called **Utahans**.

- The state animal is the **elk**.

- A **Dutch oven**, a covered iron pot once used by pioneers to prepare meals over campfires, is the state cooking pot.

- Though the origins of **funeral potatoes** are somewhat uncertain, historians think they got their start when the Church of Jesus Christ of Latter-day Saints' Relief Society brought the casserole to grieving families. The dish consists of creamy, cheesy potatoes topped with potato chips or corn flakes.

- The state emblem is the **beehive**.

- **Bonneville cutthroat trout** is the state fish.

- A popular local condiment is **fry sauce**: a mix of mayo and ketchup often served over fries.

- The state fossil is the **Allosaurus**.

- **Cherry** is the state fruit.

- Utah's name comes from the **Apache word for "people of the mountains."**

- Often colorless, gleaming **topaz** is the state gem.

- **Coal** is the state rock.

- Utah is part of the **Four Corners**: the boundary where Utah, New Mexico, Arizona, and Colorado meet.

MARS DESERT RESEARCH STATION

Located near Hanksville, the Mars Desert Research Station runs simulations for the study of life on Mars.

BY THE NUMBERS

290
THE LENGTH IN FEET (88 M) OF LANDSCAPE ARCH IN ARCHES NATIONAL PARK

1879
the year Utah's oldest continually operating bar opened

46
the length in miles (74 km) of Nine Mile Canyon which features pictographs, some of which are 1,000 years old.

12,215
THE NUMBER OF PEOPLE WHO ONCE PARTICIPATED IN A GAME OF SIMON SAYS IN CEDAR CITY

1927
the year Utahan Philo Farnsworth invented the all-electronic television system

13,528
the elevation in feet (4,123 m) of King's Peak, the highest point

5
the highest number on the Salt Lake City–based Utah Avalanche Center's danger scale

- Utah is famous for its 14 skiing and snowboarding areas, including Park City, the country's largest ski resort. Other top destinations include Alta, an advanced skier's paradise; Deer Valley, a resort known for its high-end ski lodging; and Brian Head, a family-friendly resort.

- Located outside Salt Lake City, Alta resort allows only skiers during the winter.

- Held in Park City each January, the Sundance Film Festival celebrates independent filmmaking and is regarded as one of the most esteemed film festivals.

- The largest saltwater lake in the Western Hemisphere, Great Salt Lake was once part of the massive, prehistoric Lake Bonneville. The lake is salty because while the lake is fed by mineral-bearing rivers and streams, it has no outlet. Visitors go for the bird-watching, and to visit Antelope Island, which is home to bison, antelope, and bighorn sheep.

- The state's first national park, Zion National Park is perhaps the best known. It is famous for its dramatic, wind-carved geological formations such as hoodoos and rock bridges. The park, which was founded in 1909, caters to campers, rock climbers, horseback riders, photographers, and more. ▽

RECORD ★ SETTERS | Salt Lake City native Florence Ellinwood Allen became the country's first woman to serve on a state supreme court in 1922.

- The perfect jumping-off point to visit Great Salt Lake or Bonneville Flats, Salt Lake City also boasts access to other outdoor activities such as paragliding, hiking, white-water rafting, and skydiving.

- Located within Salt Lake City, Temple Square is a 35-acre (14 ha) compound that serves as the Church of Jesus Christ of Latter-day Saints headquarters.

- Visitors to Anasazi State Park can explore a 1,000-year-old ancestral Puebloan village and visit the museum to learn about ancient artifacts.

- The country's largest Holi festival, also known as the Festival of Colors, is celebrated at the Sri Sri Radha Krishna Temple in Spanish Fork. A Hindu festival that originated in India, Holi is a celebration of the triumph of good over evil most commonly associated with the practice of throwing colorful powder among participants.

- Visitors to the state would be remiss to skip its myriad national parks. The most popular among them include Arches, so named for its wind-carved stone formations; Bryce Canyon, which boasts pink and red cliffs; and Canyonlands, a testament to the power of rivers.

- In 1863, a group of pioneers traveling through Panguitch to Parowan encountered a seemingly impassable snowstorm. However, by laying their quilts over the snow, the travelers were able to cross the drifts without sinking. Today, Panguitch's Quilt Walk Festival celebrates this historic event.

THIS WILL BECOME THE GREAT HIGHWAY OF NATIONS.

—Brigham Young, second president of the Church of Jesus Christ of Latter-day Saints

MADE IN UT

Utah's agricultural outputs include:

- Cattle
- Dairy
- Hay
- Hogs
- Turkeys
- Mink pelts
- Greenhouse plants and equipment
- Wheat

Utah's industrial outputs include:

- Gold
- Circuitry
- Civilian aircraft parts
- Safety airbags
- Medical instruments
- Metal scraps
- Gas
- Coal

SPORTING CHANCES

- The Bonneville Salt Flats are a popular destination for speed racing. ▲
- The Utah Jazz have won two NBA conference championships: in 1997 and 1998.
- Established in 2005, the Real Salt Lake soccer team won the MLS championship in 2009.
- In 2002, Salt Lake City hosted the Winter Olympic Games.
- In 2019, the city also hosted the ISU World Cup Speed Skating Final.
- In 2022, Utah became the first state outside of Hawaii to host the Iron Man World Championship.
- The University of Utah offers a total of 19 varsity sports.
- Cosmo the Cougar has been the mascot of Brigham Young University for more than 60 years.
- The Aggie, the mascot of Utah State, is a reference to the school's origin as an agricultural university.
- Jeff Griffin of the Utah Wheelin' Jazz has tied for the record for the most wheelchair basketball free throws in one minute, with 25.
- In 2007, former Utah Jazz player John Amaechi became the first retired NBA player to publicly come out as gay.
- The University of Utah's Rice-Eccles Stadium can seat more than 51,000.
- In 1912, Alma Richards became the first Utahan to win a gold medal at the Olympics.

STARS ★ OF ★ THE ★ STATE

JUANITA BROOKS

(1898–1989) An author, historian, and researcher, Juanita Brooks was born in Nevada and settled in Utah as an adult. She is most famous for her exposé of the Mountain Meadows Massacre, an event in 1857 in which around 120 pioneers were slaughtered during the Utah War. Her research brought to light that the tragedy, which had previously been asserted as perpetrated solely by local Indigenous peoples, had actually been carried out by some 50 to 60 Mormon militiamen alongside Indigenous allies. Though concerned with discipline from the Mormon Church, Brooks successfully pushed for a correction of the record both publicly and within the church. ▪

VERMONT

★ ★ ★

"Freedom and Unity"

★ ★ ★

CAPITAL: Montpelier **FLOWER:** Red Clover **NICKNAME:** Green Mountain State **ENTRY:** 1791

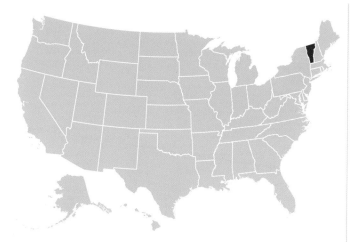

VT FACTS

- Bordered by Canada to the north, New York to the west, Massachusetts to the south, and New Hampshire to the east, Vermont is one of the six states to make up New England.

- With a recorded population of some 647,064, it's the state with the second smallest population (after Wyoming) and is eighth smallest in area.

- With a population of about 8,000, Montpelier is the smallest state capital. Vermont's largest city, Burlington, has a population of around 45,000.

- Before being settled by Europeans, the land was occupied by the Abenaki, the Mohican, the Pennacook, the Pocomtuc, and other tribes for nearly 13,000 years.

- Some 4.5 million acres (1.8 million ha) of Vermont—or 74 percent of the state—is covered in forests. Top trees include sugar maple, red maple, eastern hemlock, and American beech.

- The state's highest point is Mount Mansfield, with a summit that peaks at 4,393 feet (1,338 m) above sea level. ▼

▶ STATE BIRD

Hermit Thrush
Catharus guttatus

This small brown bird is nicknamed the "American nightingale" for its pleasant song. Its habitat of choice? Forest interiors with ponds or meadows close by.

1777

Once part of New York, Vermonters declared their own independence in 1777, and they remained separate from the U.S. for 14 years. Operating as its own country, Vermont had a distinct currency, a constitution, and a president, Thomas Chittenden.

VERMONT IS A JEWEL STATE, SMALL BUT PRECIOUS.

—Author Pearl S. Buck

▶ THE CHECK IS IN THE MAIL

On January 31, 1940, Brattleboro's Ida May Fuller received a check for $22.54, becoming the first beneficiary of recurring monthly Social Security payments.

- The 1777 constitution made slavery illegal—ahead of the other colonies—but only liberated enslaved people of a specific age range, so the practice continued until the early 1800s.

- Today, there are four state-recognized Abenaki tribes, or bands, that still live in Vermont.

- In 1791, Vermont joined the U.S. as the 14th state and the first addition to the original 13 colonies.

- Known as the Green Mountain State, Vermont's name derives from the French *montagne verte*.

- It's the largest producer of maple syrup in the country, generating between 1.5 and two million gallons (5.7 to 7.6 million L) each year, enough to fill about 40,000 bathtubs.

- Vermont has one of the largest number of ski resorts and ski areas in the U.S., including Killington, the biggest ski resort in the eastern U.S. Killington also has New England's largest vertical drop, at 3,050 feet (930 m).

- Vermont is the only New England state with no ocean coastline, but it does have 800 lakes and ponds, 23,000 miles (37,014 km) of rivers and streams, and 300,000 acres (121,406 ha) of wetlands.

- Fifty-six percent of Lake Champlain—out of its total 435 square miles (1,127 sq km)—is in Vermont. The rest is in New York and Quebec. ▲

- Some 260 species of birds such as barred owls, ospreys, peregrine falcons, ruffed grouse, and American robins live here.

- Moose, white-tailed deer, gray and red foxes, and American martens are found throughout the state.

- There are 40 reptile and amphibian species in the state. ▪

STORY OF THE SONG "These Green Mountains" may be the official song, but the most recognized tune about the state is undoubtedly "Moonlight in Vermont," a jazz standard written by Karl Suessdorf and John Blackburn in 1944. The song draws on Blackburn's impressions of the state while attending Bennington College, with lyrics like "People who meet in this romantic setting/are so hypnotized by the lovely/evening summer breeze." The song has since been recorded by artists such as Ella Fitzgerald, Louis Armstrong, Billie Holiday, Frank Sinatra, and Willie Nelson, helping to popularize it as a timeless jazz classic. ▪

STARS ★ OF ★ THE ★ STATE

BERNIE SANDERS

(b. 1941) Although he didn't move to Vermont until 1968, Sanders, a self-proclaimed democratic socialist, has made a lasting impact on the state as a politician known for focusing on working families and narrowing the growing gap between the rich and everyone else. After his tenure as mayor of Burlington from 1981 to 1989, Sanders went on to serve in the U.S. House of Representatives and has run for U.S. president twice. Sanders, a father of four and grandfather of seven, remains the longest serving independent member of Congress in American history. He lives in Burlington and has a vacation home in North Hero, an island community in Lake Champlain. ▪

WEIRD BUT TRUE

- Chittenden used to be known as the "spirit capital of the universe," after two brothers who lived there in the 1870s claimed to have psychic powers.

- Native Vermonters refer to non-locals as "flatlanders."

- Montpelier is the only state capital that doesn't have a McDonald's.

- There are no billboards in Vermont, by law.

- In 2000, Vermont-based Cabot Creamery made the world's largest grilled cheese sandwich, weighing 320 pounds (145 kg).

- Vermont is the only state that does not have any buildings taller than 124 feet (38 m).

- There's a "Flavor Graveyard" at the Ben & Jerry's headquarters in Waterbury, where the company has headstones honoring discontinued flavors, like Vermonty Python.

- Some old farmhouses in the state feature "witch windows," which are windows set on a diagonal that are said to prevent a witch on a broomstick from flying through.

- Devils Gap, Terrible Mountain, and Vulture Mountain are all Vermont landforms.

- "Queen Connie," a two-story concrete gorilla holding a full-size Volkswagen Beetle, can be found near Salisbury.

- There are tales of UFO abductions, cross-dimensional wormholes, and strange beasts in the woods in Bennington Triangle.

- In the late 1700s, Matthew "Mad Matt" Lyon, one of the state's founding fathers, was re-elected for the U.S. House of Representatives while in prison.

- Each July, Bristol residents race in homemade outhouses down West Street for the town's Great Outhouse Race.

▶ WHAT A CHAMP

"Champ," Lake Champlain's mysterious sea monster, is said to be a giant serpent with silver scales and razor-sharp teeth.

▲ TWICE AS NICE

Two U.S. presidents were born in the state: Chester A. Arthur (born in North Fairfield in 1829), at left, and Calvin Coolidge (born in Plymouth in 1872).

MISCELLANY

- On **Town Meeting Day**—the first Tuesday in March—state offices and schools close so residents can gather, debate, and vote on local issues.

- **Danby Quarry**, in Dorset Mountain, is the world's largest underground marble quarry.

- **Cougars**—locally referred to as catamounts—once prowled the Green Mountains before being declared extinct in 2018.

- Vermont is considered **one of the least devout states** in the country, with only 34 percent of adults reporting to be "highly religious."

- There is a **thriving community of Somalis** in Chittenden County who arrived after escaping conflict in the African country. The state has also become home for refugees from Afghanistan, Bosnia, Kosovo, Sudan, Syria, Vietnam, and other countries.

- Vermont is **among the "greenest" states** based on factors of air quality, water quality, soil quality, motor gasoline consumption in barrels, and renewable energy consumption.

- Woodstock's **Billings Farm**, established in 1871, is one of the oldest registered Jersey dairy farms in the United States.

- Almost **90 percent of Vermont residents report their race as white**, but the state's minority population is increasing: From 2010 to 2020, the Hispanic population grew by 68.4 percent, the third largest percentage increase in the country, and a 44 percent increase of Black residents was the seventh largest jump among all states.

- A serving of soft-serve ice cream is called a **"creemee"** in Vermont. Hot tip: Order a maple and black raspberry twist.

BY THE NUMBERS

85 length in miles (135 km) of the Lamoille, the longest river entirely within the state

1762 the year Bennington's Old First Church was established as the first Protestant church in Vermont, making it the oldest church in the state

35,000+ number of Vermonters who fought in the American Civil War, some 10 percent of the state's population at the time

1 NUMBER OF NATIONAL PARKS IN VERMONT: MARSH-BILLINGS-ROCKEFELLER NATIONAL HISTORIC PARK, IN WOODSTOCK

3,000 estimated number of moose that roam around Vermont, along with 5,700 black bears and some 50,000 turkeys

600 depth in feet (183 m) of Graniteville's Rock of Ages Granite Quarry, the world's largest "deep hole" granite quarry

100+ the number of covered bridges, some of which were first constructed as early as 1820, found throughout the state

3 NUMBER OF FREE PINTS OF ICE CREAM BEN & JERRY'S EMPLOYEES GET TO BRING HOME EACH DAY THEY WORK

802 Vermont's one and only area code

AL AK AS AZ AR CA CO CT DE FL GA GU HI ID IL IN IA KS KY LA ME MP MD MA MI MN MS MO MT NE NV NH NJ NM NY NC ND OH OK OR PA PR RI SC SD TN TX VI UT VT VA WA DC WV WI WY

On April 26, 2000, Vermont became the first state to adopt a same-sex civil-union law. Nine years later, it was the fourth state to legalize same-sex marriage.

▲ SUNDAE FUNDAY

A trip to Vermont isn't complete without a stop at Ben & Jerry's Ice Cream Factory in Waterbury. Built in 1985, the factory manufactures some 350,000 pints per day. See how the ice cream magic happens, then grab a free sample (or some cones) in the Flavor Room.

DESTINATION: VERMONT

- Some seven decades ago, Georg and Maria von Trapp built their family lodge in the hills of Stowe. Today, *Sound of Music* fans flock to the Austrian-style hotel to drink in the history of the real-life version of the singing von Trapps, plus gain access to the 2,500 acres (1,012 ha) of pristine landscape and mountain views.

- Red Rocks Park, in South Burlington, features awesome views (think: soaring cliffs jutting out over Lake Champlain) as well as hiking and mountain biking trails looping through some 100 acres (40 ha) of hemlock and pine forests.

- Manchester's Hildene was once the summer home of Abraham Lincoln's son, Robert. Today, the 8,000-square-foot (743 sq m) mansion is open to the public, as well as historic buildings including a schoolhouse (there's also a goat farm and cheese-making facility on-site). Visit in the winter and snowshoe or cross-country ski along the property's trails, while thousands of peonies bloom in the estate's garden each spring and summer.

- Focused on preserving the history and culture of the region, the Bennington Museum boasts the world's largest public collection of paintings by Grandma Moses, the American folk artist who lived in nearby Eagle Bridge, New York, during the early to mid 1900s.

- Ride a bike on the Colchester Causeway, a rail-to-trail path in Chittenden County. The four-mile (6.4 km) causeway, made from white marble from quarries in nearby Rutland, extends across Lake Champlain, offering spectacular views.

▼ FARM-TASTIC

Get an up-close-and-personal look into a real working dairy farm at Shelburne Farms. Once the country estate of railroad mogul Dr. William Seward Webb and Eliza "Lila" Vanderbilt, the 1,400-acre (567 ha) farm was designated a national historic landmark in 2001. Visitors can tour the facility, sample award-winning cheese and maple syrup, admire the formal gardens, and grab a meal at the farm-to-table Inn at Shelburne Farms.

▲ PHAT AIR
Londonderry's Ross Powers won gold at the 2002 Olympic Games in Salt Lake City in the snowboarding half-pipe event.

SPORTING CHANCES

- There are no major professional sports teams in the state.

- Some 38 Vermonters have made it to baseball's major leagues, including Hall-of-Famer Carlton "Pudge" Fisk.

- Rudyard Kipling, who lived in Vermont in the 1890s, is said to have invented snow golf—he painted his golf balls red so he could find them in the snow.

- In 1977, Jake Burton Carpenter founded Burton Snowboards. Today, the company, based in Burlington, is the largest snowboard brand in the world.

- John LeClair, the first Vermont-born NHL player, has a foundation that awards grants to nonprofit Vermont organizations focusing on programs for children.

- Woodstock is home to the nation's first ski tow, built in 1934 on Gilbert's farm in Woodstock—and powered by a Ford Model T.

- Vermont is one of the top producers of U.S. Olympic skiers and snowboarders in the nation, including snowboarder Lindsey Jacobellis, who trains at Stratton Mountain and won gold at the 2022 Winter Olympics.

- Skiing pioneer Suzy Chaffee, a Rutland native, was the first woman to serve on the U.S. Olympic Committee Board.

- In 2022, Starksboro's Ryan Cochran-Siegle won the silver medal in the men's super-G at the Beijing Winter Games, 50 years after his mom won gold in the women's slalom at the 1972 Games.

- Olympian (2020 Olympic Games) and highly decorated runner Elle Purrier St. Pierre grew up on a dairy farm in Montgomery.

- The state's largest sporting event, the Vermont City Marathon draws some 7,500 runners to the streets of Burlington. ▪

STARS ★ OF ★ THE ★ STATE

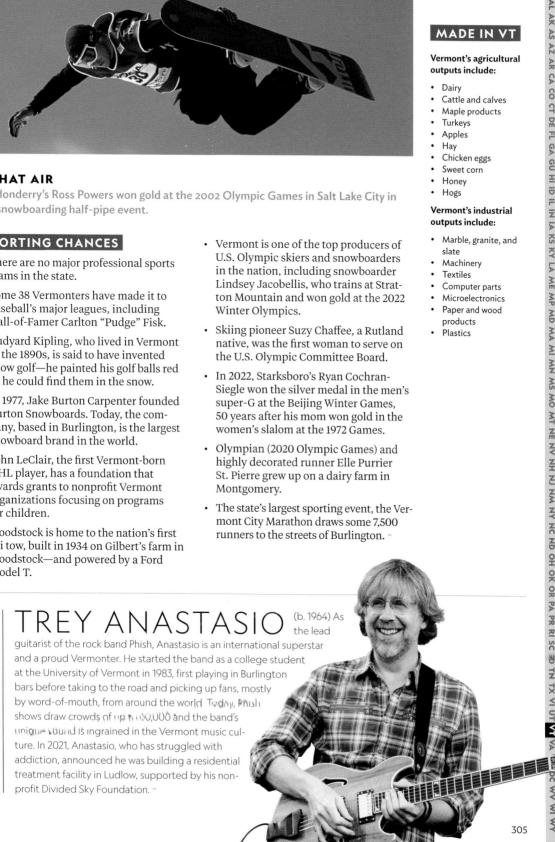

TREY ANASTASIO (b. 1964)
As the lead guitarist of the rock band Phish, Anastasio is an international superstar and a proud Vermonter. He started the band as a college student at the University of Vermont in 1983, first playing in Burlington bars before taking to the road and picking up fans, mostly by word-of-mouth, from around the world. Today, Phish shows draw crowds of up to 80,000 and the band's unique sound is ingrained in the Vermont music culture. In 2021, Anastasio, who has struggled with addiction, announced he was building a residential treatment facility in Ludlow, supported by his nonprofit Divided Sky Foundation. ▪

VIRGINIA

★ ★ ★

"Thus Always to Tyrants"

★ ★ ★

CAPITAL: Richmond **FLOWER:** American Dogwood **NICKNAME:** Old Dominion **ENTRY:** 1788

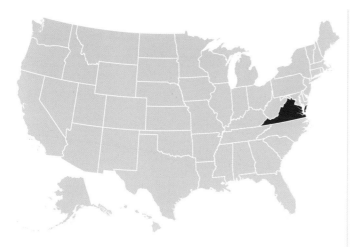

- Original inhabitants of the area included the Catawba, Ani-Yun-Wiya (Cherokee), Croatoan, Powhatan Confederacy, Tuscarora, Yesan (Tutelo) and Saponi, and Tsoyaha (Yuchi). Today, tribes include the Chickahominy, Eastern Chickahominy, Mattaponi, Monacan, Nansemond, Pamunkey, Cheroenhaka Nottoway, Nottoway, Patawomeck, Rappahannock, and Upper Mattaponi.

- In 1606, King James I granted a charter to a local joint-stock venture known as the Virginia Company to establish a settlement in North America. One year later, three ships bearing settlers arrived on what would become Jamestown Island. However, the settlement struggled greatly. By 1624, King James I had revoked the charter, converting the area into a colony instead.

- One of the first colonial rebellions took place some 100 years before the Revolutionary War—though Bacon's Rebellion, as it was called, likely reflected a power struggle among colonial leaders rather than a growing desire for colonial independence. In 1676, tensions grew between local governor William Berkeley and militia leader Nathan Bacon—and the resulting battle saw Jamestown burned to the ground.

- Born at a Virginia plantation in 1743, Thomas Jefferson is considered one of the nation's Founding Fathers. In addition to helping draft the Declaration of Independence in 1776, Jefferson became the country's third president in 1801 and founded and designed the University of Virginia in 1819.

- Some of the oldest mountains on Earth, the Appalachians have been inhabited for at least 14,000 years. Beginning in the 1600s, the Appalachian region became home to European settlers from Ireland, Scotland, and Germany, as well as enslaved people forcibly transported

▶ STATE BIRD

Northern Cardinal
Cardinalis cardinalis

How can you tell a male northern cardinal from a female? Males boast bright red plumage, while females are light brown with red accents.

1781

In 1781, with the Revolutionary War well under way, British general Lord Cornwallis made a hasty retreat before arriving at a coastal peninsula in Virginia's Yorktown. There, he was flanked by General George Washington and French allies such as the Marquis de Lafayette. On October 19, Cornwallis surrendered, ending the war.

VA FACTS

- The population is 8,683,619.

- The 10th state admitted to the union, Virginia is the 37th in area.

- Known for its history, beautiful rolling lands, and beaches, the state relies on its corporate services, food and beverage processing, IT, manufacturing, aerospace, mining, military, and agricultural industries.

- Virginia's natural resources include forests, fertile land, coal, sand, rocks, and watersheds.

> **VIRGINIA IS FOR LOVERS.**
>
> —Virginia tourism slogan

to the colonies. Over time, various aspects of music, language, cooking, dancing, and more from these distinct cultures intermingled, along with those of local Indigenous populations. The resulting Appalachian culture became known for its self-reliance, tight-knit community, and deeply creative traditions in music and art.

- By the 1800s, Virginia relied economically on its plantations for cotton, peanuts, and—most importantly—tobacco. Plantation owners exploited the forced labor of the enslaved (largely comprised of Black people stolen from Africa, their descendants, and Indigenous people). Refusing to give up its reliance on enslaved labor during the Civil War, Virginia seceded from the Union in 1861 and relocated the capital of the Confederacy from Montgomery, Alabama, to Richmond until its surrender in 1865.

- Likely native to South America, peanuts arrived in Virginia in the first half of the 19th century. Today, the crop remains a staple—as does peanut pie. Similar to pecan pie, the treat is a sticky-sweet combination of sugary syrup and peanuts baked into a pie crust.

- In 1917, the Commandant of the Marine Corps established a Marine Barracks in Quantico, and the Marine Corps School

▲ **THE PENTAGON**

Completed in 1943, the Pentagon—so named for its five-sided shape—in Arlington serves as the headquarters of the U.S. Department of Defense. On September 11, 2001, the Pentagon was struck by a hijacked plane as part of a terrorist attack, which resulted in the deaths of 184 innocent people. Today, the Pentagon remains one of the world's largest office buildings.

in 1920. The school and complex have been used to train Marines and to develop amphibious warfare technology. In 1935, the FBI also established its Training Academy at the Marine base.

- Square dancing is the state's official dance. The dance's unique structure may have originated in the formal dances of 1600s Europe, while traditional square dance music—as well as the called-out dance formation changes—likely developed in the area among enslaved Africans.

STARS ★ OF ★ THE ★ STATE

BOOKER T. WASHINGTON

(1856–1915) Born to an enslaved mother in Franklin County, Booker Taliaferro Washington was an educator and activist. Following emancipation, Washington spent his youth studying at various schools and then college, often paying his way by working as a janitor. In 1881, he was selected to help establish a school for Black students in Tuskegee, Alabama. Though the school opened in a one-shack shanty, the Tuskegee Normal and Industrial Institute soon grew to span more than 540 acres (218 ha) and host more than 400 students, with Washington as its first president. Washington went on to publish 40 books and founded the National Negro Business League in 1901.

WEIRD BUT TRUE

- One farm in Centreville has a full-size replica of Stonehenge made of foam and dubbed Foamhenge.

- Located at Kiptopeke State Park, there is a decaying fleet of concrete ships that were commissioned during WWII.

- In a grave near Chancellorsville lies Confederate leader Stonewall Jackson's arm, which was amputated in 1863.

- A museum in Williamsburg is devoted entirely to former and current presidents' pets.

- One house in Richmond was built using repurposed tombstones.

- Virginia House, located on Richmond's Agecroft Hall estate, was transported piece by piece from England.

- Cementiscope is a giant, 3,000-pound (1,361 kg) kaleidoscope housed in a cement mixer located in Norfolk.

- The city of Bristol is located in two states, directly on top of the Virginia-Tennessee border.

- Virginia Beach's Mount Trashmore is a park built on a landfill.

- One museum in Waverly is entirely peanut-themed.

▼ PLANESPOTTERS

Located near Ronald Reagan National Airport, Arlington's Gravelly Point is situated right beneath a highly used flight landing path. The spot draws visitors who want to picnic under the low-flying planes.

▷ STORY OF THE "COMPUTERS"

In the 1930s, NASA's predecessor—the National Advisory Committee for Aeronautics (NACA)—relied not on automated computers, but on women mathematicians dubbed the "computers." Beginning in the 1940s, NACA began hiring Black women as well as white, though these Black women faced the double hurdles of sexism and racism and were subject to ongoing segregation. Despite the bigoted working conditions, the Black women of the West Area Computing Unit in Langley made enormous strides in engineering during WWII.

GIVE ME LIBERTY, OR GIVE ME DEATH!

—Statesman Patrick Henry

MISCELLANY

- Virginia was the **first colony** in North America.

- The state bat is the **Virginia big-eared bat**.

- Thought to have originated in Brunswick County, **Brunswick stew** is traditionally made with squirrel.

- Virginia's state seal features an **Amazonian woman defeating tyranny**.

- The state dog is the **American foxhound**.

- Virginia's state beverage is **milk**.

- Virginia boasts more than **300 wineries**.

▷ ROAR!

Striped like its namesake, the tiger swallowtail butterfly is the state insect.

- The **striped bass** and the **brook trout** are the state fish.

- The state fossil is the **Chesapecten jeffersonius**, an extinct type of scallop.

- Some of the Thanksgiving turkeys pardoned by the president live out the rest of their lives at **Kidwell Farm** in Herndon.

- **George Washington's Rye Whiskey** is the state spirit.

- The state rock is **nelsonite**.

- Virginia was named after Britain's Queen Elizabeth I, who was often called the **"Virgin Queen."**

- Found in **Luray Caverns**, the Great Stalacpipe Organ is the largest musical instrument in the world.

- The **first known recipe for sweet tea** appeared in an 1879 Virginia cookbook called *Housekeeping in Old Virginia*.

RECORD ★ SETTERS

Born in Richmond in 1922, Samuel Lee Gravely, Jr., became the U.S. Navy's first Black commander, captain, rear admiral, and vice admiral.

BY THE NUMBERS

18,000 the number of enlisted Confederate men buried in the Hollywood Cemetery in Richmond

1693 THE YEAR THE COLLEGE OF WILLIAM & MARY WAS CHARTERED

20 the upper number of joeys in a Virginia opossum litter

300,000 the approximate number of American veterans at rest in Arlington National Cemetery

2 the number of extinct volcanoes located in the state

5,729 THE ELEVATION IN FEET (1,746 M) OF MOUNT ROGERS, THE STATE'S HIGHEST POINT

- Richmond is at once historic and cutting-edge. Fans of the outdoors can go tubing down the James River; history buffs can visit Civil War–era ruins; fans of art might spend hours at the Institute for Contemporary Art; and foodies won't want to miss the city's beer trail.

- With more than 200,000 acres (80,937 ha), Shenandoah National Park is beloved for its rolling hills, abundant wildlife, and, in the fall, fiery coloring. Running through the park is Skyline Drive, some 105 miles (169 km) of winding scenic road.

- At the Chincoteague National Wildlife Refuge, visitors can spot wild Chincoteague ponies. Visitors can also attend the yearly Chincoteague Pony Swim or the Chincoteague Fireman's Carnival.

- Virginia Beach offers boardwalk activities, sand dunes, and water activities. There is also a vibrant arts scene, family-friendly museums and aquariums, and a bustling nightlife.

- Arlington National Cemetery is home to the Tomb of the Unknown Soldier, the John F. Kennedy Eternal Flame, the memorial to the space shuttle *Challenger*, the former home of Confederate general Robert E. Lee, and more.

- At George Washington's Mount Vernon estate, visitors can learn about the country's first president and his family as well as the lives of the people he enslaved at Mount Vernon. Tours cover

A hiker's delight: There are more miles of the Appalachian Trail in Virginia than in any other state.

the home, slave quarters, farms, and family tombs, and reenactors offer visitors the chance to ask questions.

- Set in the more than three-centuries-old city of Williamsburg, Colonial Williamsburg is the country's largest outdoor educational living museum.

- Owned by third U.S. president Thomas Jefferson, Monticello was a working plantation. Visitors today can tour the grounds and learn about the lives of the more than 400 enslaved people forced to live and work there. The grounds also include exhibits on Jefferson's role as a slave owner, his role in drafting the Constitution, and his time as president.

- Known as the nation's horse and hunt capital, Middleburg is famous for its equestrian activities.

- Home to the University of Virginia (UVA), Charlottesville is a charming college town steeped in history.

- A primary player in the Civil War, the state is home to numerous battlegrounds and Civil War sites. Those interested in history can tour the Virginia Civil War Trails.

STARS ★ OF ★ THE ★ STATE

POCAHONTAS

(c. 1596–1617) Born Amonute around the area that would be settled as Jamestown, Pocahontas, as she came to be known, was a Powhatan ambassador and translator. Daughter of the Powhatan chief Wahunsenaca (known to the English as Powhatan), Pocahontas was around 11 years old when British captain John Smith was captured and brought before Chief Wahunsenaca. As told by Smith, Pocahontas rescued him from being killed; according to historians, Smith either grossly misunderstood a welcome ritual or simply fabricated the tale. Over the years, Pocahontas became something of a folk legend to the colonists and later Americans as a symbol of peace between Indigenous nations and settlers. However, according to Mattaponi oral history, the truth was much grimmer: Pocahontas was a skilled translator and ambassador who was eventually kidnapped by the English and likely murdered. Today, she is remembered for her intelligence and bravery and her work as an emissary.

SPORTING CHANCES

- Born in Newport News, Gabby Douglas is an Olympic gymnast who has won three gold medals and one silver. She was the first woman of color of any nationality and first Black American woman to become the Individual All-Around Champion, and the first American gymnast to win gold in the individual all-around and the team competitions within the same games. ▶

- Located in Chantilly, the Smithsonian's Steven F. Udvar-Hazy Center hosts thousands of aviation and space artifacts, including the space shuttle *Discovery*, space suits, WWII airplanes, and more.

- Founded in 1950 by Stuart native Glen Wood, Wood Brothers Racing is the oldest continuously operating NASCAR Cup Team.

- Rodney the Ram is the mascot of Virginia Commonwealth University.

- Founded in 1947, Martinsville Speedway is the shortest track on the NASCAR Cup Series circuit.

- Since the 19th century, fans of UVA have chanted "Wahoowa" during matches, potentially in reference to the university's reputation as a party school.

- Also known as "The Mayor," South Boston native Jeff Burton has 21 NASCAR Cup Series career victories.

- Virginia Tech's mascot is a turkey, known as the HokieBird.

- Renowned tennis coach Dr. Robert Walter "Whirlwind" Johnson helped change the history of the sport by using his influence in the tennis world to secure the inclusion of Black athletes.

- Born in Richmond, Arthur Ashe was a world-class tennis player who trained under Dr. Johnson. He was inducted into the International Tennis Hall of Fame in 1985, and was awarded the Presidential Medal of Freedom in 1993. ▪

MADE IN VA

Virginia's agricultural outputs include:

- Chickens
- Cattle
- Milk
- Turkey
- Soybeans
- Corn
- Hay
- Tobacco

Virginia's industrial outputs include:

- Industrial machinery
- Electrical machinery
- Cars and auto parts
- Plastics
- Oil
- Aircrafts
- Paper
- Coal

RECORD ★ SETTERS

More presidents were born in Virginia than any other state: George Washington, Thomas Jefferson, James Madison, James Monroe, William Henry Harrison, John Tyler, Zachary Taylor, and Woodrow Wilson.

STARS ★ OF ★ THE ★ STATE

GEORGE WASHINGTON

(1732–1799) A native of the colony of Virginia, George Washington is considered by many to be the Father of the United States. Growing up, Washington's primary focuses were his work as a surveyor and overseeing his family estate, Mount Vernon. In 1774, Washington was elected one of the Virginia delegates to both Continental Congresses, and—as hostilities turned to war—appointed commander in chief of the Continental Army in 1775. At the war's end, he helped lead the Constitutional Convention, and he was unanimously elected the nation's first president by 1789. ▪

WASHINGTON

★ ★ ★

"Alki"
(Native American word
meaning "Bye and Bye")

★ ★ ★

CAPITAL: Olympia **FLOWER:** Coast Rhododendron **NICKNAME:** Evergreen State **ENTRY:** 1889

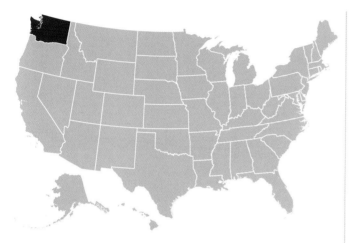

▶ STATE BIRD
American Goldfinch
Spinus tristis

You can spot flocks of this golden bird among the trees, bushes, and fields across the state nearly all year long.

1980

The eruption of Mount St. Helens in 1980 was the deadliest and most economically destructive volcanic event in recent U.S. history, with 57 deaths and some $860 million in damage.

WA FACTS

- Sitting in the northwestern corner of the 48 conterminous states, Washington borders British Columbia to the north, Idaho to the east, Oregon to the south, and the Pacific Ocean to the west.

- Covering some 71,000 square miles (184,666 sq km) of land, it is the 20th largest state by size and ranks 13th in population, with 7,785,786 residents.

- The capital of Olympia is the 22nd largest city in the state and has a population of some 55,669.

- Some 51 percent of Washington's total land area is covered in forest.

- Seattle is the most populated city in Washington with a population of 749,256; close to 52 percent of Washington residents live in the Seattle metropolitan area.

- Washington is home to Native American tribes including the Chinook, tribes from Coast Salish, and the Yakama, whose ancestors have been living on the land for 10,000 years. Today, there are 29 federally recognized tribes with reservations across the state.

- Through the Oregon Treaty of 1846, the U.S. gained control of the region from the British and took over land that included Washington, Oregon, Idaho, and parts of Wyoming and Montana. In 1853, Congress created Washington Territory, which was admitted into the Union as the 42nd state in 1889.

- Named in honor of George Washington, it is the only U.S. state named after a president.

- Mount Rainier National Park's Grove of the Patriarchs is home to some of the country's oldest trees, with some dating back 1,000 years.

- Olympic National Park near Port Angeles is the site of the Hoh Rain Forest, one of the largest temperate rainforests in the country.

- Mount Rainier, along with Mount St. Helens, Mount Baker, Glacier Peak, and Mount Adams, are all active volcanoes that are part of the Cascade Range, which extends from British Columbia to northern California.

- More than 1,000 earthquakes occur in the state each year, mostly in the western part of the state.

- The San Juan Islands are known for having the largest concentration of bald eagles in the continental U.S., with some 150 pairs of breeding birds found there.

IF THAT BE NOT THE HOME WHERE DWELL THE GODS, IT IS BEAUTIFUL ENOUGH TO BE, AND I THEREFORE CALL IT MOUNT OLYMPUS.

—Explorer John Meares

▼ OLYMPIC MOUNTAINS

Washington's capital, Olympia, was named for the Olympic Mountains, which were named after Mount Olympus of Greek legend.

- The state of Washington is the second largest wine-producing region in the country, with more than 1,000 wineries and more than 60,000 acres (24,281 ha) of wine grapes.

- Not to be outdone by wine, more than 75 percent of the country's hops are grown in the Yakima Valley, helping to make it a hot spot for craft breweries.

- With a record annual rainfall of 184 inches (467 cm) in one spot, Washington is home to several of the rainiest spots in the U.S. The wettest town on average is Forks at 119.7 inches (304 cm).

- Grand Coulee Dam, on the Columbia River west of Spokane, is the largest hydropower producer in the U.S. It creates enough power to supply some two million households with electricity for one year.

- Washington produces more apples than any other state in the country.

- At 14,410 feet (4,392 m) tall, Mount Rainier is the highest point in the state. The area surrounding the mountain became a national park in 1899, one of three national parks in Washington.

- Standing 550 feet (168 m) high and stretching 5,223 feet (1,592 m), Grand Coulee is also one of the largest structures ever built by humans.

- The waters of the Salish Sea, including Puget Sound, are home to pods of southern resident orca whales. ▪

STARS ★ OF ★ THE ★ STATE

WILLIAM "BILL" GATES

(b. 1955) Born in Seattle, Gates created Microsoft in 1975 with business partner Paul Allen. The company ultimately gained massive success—and made 31-year-old Gates the youngest billionaire at the time. As Microsoft grew, so did Gates's fortune, and he spent 13 years as the world's richest man. His home, a lakefront estate in the Seattle suburbs, is valued at some $131 million and includes a 60-foot (18 m) pool, a trampoline room, and a salmon- and trout-stocked stream. Gates has also used his fortune to create a nonprofit foundation to fund such causes as vaccines for children in the world's poorest countries. ▪

WEIRD BUT TRUE

- Seattle is believed to be the first city in the U.S. to play a Beatles song on the radio.

- Seattle's Magnuson Park was the site of one of the world's longest line of rubber ducks, with some 17,782 of the squeaky bath toys assembled.

- A man dressed like Elvis Presley once finished the Seattle Marathon in 2 hours, 42 minutes, and 52 seconds.

- The Fremont Troll, an 18-foot-tall (5.5 m) concrete sculpture, greets visitors under the Aurora Bridge in Seattle. ▼

- Since the early 1990s, hundreds of thousands of pieces of chewing gum have been placed on the side of a Seattle theater, affectionately known as the "gum wall."

- There's a museum dedicated to giant shoes in Seattle's Pike Place Market, including a size 37 wingtip once owned by Robert Wadlow, the world's tallest man.

- No one has actually died at the Wall of Death, a public art installation made of 10 metal spires and a giant orange ring.

- Created for a 1950s cowboy-themed gas station, "Hat 'N' Boots," said to be the largest pair of boots and accompanying cowboy hat in the country, are on display in Oxbow Park.

▶ **"KENNEWICK MAN"**
8,400 years is the age of the "Kennewick Man," one of the most complete ancient human skeletons ever discovered.

MISCELLANY

- On January 19, 2020, Washington reported the **first confirmed case of COVID-19 in the U.S.** from a 35-year-old man from Snohomish County who had recently traveled from Wuhan, China. In the following months, the Seattle area became the epicenter of an early U.S. outbreak.

- The **Dungeness crab** is named after the Dungeness Spit on the Olympic Peninsula; at 5.5 miles (8.9 km) long, it's the longest natural sand spit in the country.

- Washington State is home to more reported **Bigfoot (aka Sasquatch)** sightings than any other state in the nation.

- The **Evergreen Point Floating Bridge** connecting Seattle to Bellevue is the longest floating bridge in the world.

- The **first Starbucks coffee shop** opened in 1971 at Seattle's Pike Place Market.

- Spokane is the **smallest city to ever host a world's fair**, which it did in 1974 with more than 5.2 million people in attendance. (Seattle also hosted a world's fair in 1962.)

- In 1994, Jeff Bezos started **Amazon** out of a garage in Bellevue as an online marketplace for books. When he stepped down as CEO 27 years later as the world's richest person, the company was worth $1.6 trillion.

- With a depth of 7,900 feet (2,400 m), **Hells Canyon**, a small section of which is in Washington, is the deepest gorge in North America.

- Seattle is home to the **first Costco warehouse store**, which opened its doors in 1983. The company remains headquartered in Washington.

- Spokane resident Sonora Smart Dodd is credited with creating **Father's Day** in 1910 as a way to honor her own dad—although it did not become a federal holiday until 1972.

- At 350 acres (142 ha), **Harbor Island**, located in the mouth of Seattle's Duwamish Waterway, is one of the largest artificial islands in the world.

- Washington was the first state to pass a **texting ban** for drivers in 2007.

- **Cape Alava** in Olympic National Park is the westernmost point in the continental U.S.

▼ **HERE, KITTY KITTY**
The Olympic marmot, a house-cat-size rodent found in the Olympic Peninsula, is the official state endemic mammal.

BY THE NUMBERS

33 the height in feet (10 m) of a tsunami that engulfed the Washington coastline in 1700, triggered by a large earthquake in the Pacific Ocean

50 THE NUMBER OF DIFFERENT KINDS OF PETRIFIED TREES RESIDING IN GINKGO PETRIFIED FOREST STATE PARK IN KITTITAS

28 the length in miles (45 km) of Long Beach Peninsula, the longest contiguous beach in the U.S.

24 the number of lightning rods on the roof of the Seattle Space Needle, which help it withstand lightning strikes

1,100 the number of dams found throughout the state

3,026 the number of miles (4,870 km) of coastline in Washington

3,000 the number of glaciers in Washington, including more than two dozen on Mount Rainier alone, making it the most glaciated of the 48 contiguous states

268 the height in feet (82 m) of Snoqualmie Falls— about 100 feet (30 m) higher than New York's Niagara Falls

59% of people in Seattle have a college degree, making it the country's most educated city.

47% OF MENUS IN WASHINGTON RESTAURANTS FEATURE PRAWNS, ACCORDING TO ONE SURVEY.

315

DESTINATION: WASHINGTON

- You can't miss the Seattle Space Needle, the 605-foot (184 m) landmark built for the 1962 World's Fair. Take an elevator ride some 520 feet (158 m) up to the top for sweeping views—and grab a drink at the Loupe Lounge, featuring the world's first revolving glass floor. ▲

- Want to see a fish fly? Head to Pike Place Market in downtown Seattle, where mongers are known to toss fresh-caught fish before they wrap them up for customers. The vibrant market also features restaurants and shops all showcasing local fare and flair.

- Washington State operates the largest ferry system in the U.S., and a ride on one of the boats that crosses Puget Sound and the Greater Salish Sea each day offers unrivaled views of the sound, the Cascade and Olympic mountain ranges, and the Seattle skyline. Keep your eyes peeled for orca whales.

STORY OF THE REBUILD On June 6, 1889, the entire central business district of Seattle quite literally went up in smoke after a raging fire sparked by an overheated pot of glue in a cabinet shop ravaged some 25 blocks of the city's downtown. And instead of rebuilding as it was before, local leaders decided to place the city at a higher level, grading the streets using dirt from the surrounding hills, and elevating the neighborhood. The new buildings, made with stone and iron, were constructed on top of the former street level, leaving a ghost town below. Today, visitors can tour what remains beneath the streets, offering a glimpse of life in the city late in the 19th century. ▪

- Seattle's Museum of Pop Culture showcases iconic artifacts from TV, rock 'n' roll music, and exhibits on musicians that got their start in the Pacific Northwest, including Nirvana, Pearl Jam, and Jimi Hendrix.

- Olympia may be one of the state's smaller cities, but its capitol campus stands out with the tallest masonry dome in North America. Take a complimentary guided tour of the Legislative Building, constructed in 1928, which also features decorative marble and a five-ton (4.5 t) Tiffany chandelier.

- The Boeing Future of Flight Aviation Center in Mukilteo allows visitors to learn about the assembly of 747, 777, and 787 Dreamliner airplanes. ▪

- In 2013, the crowd at a Seahawks game hit 136.6 decibels to produce the "largest crowd roar at a sports stadium" record. (The mark has since been beaten by Kansas City Chiefs fans.)

- The faces of the football players who participated in a legendary 1938 touch football game are carved into a six-story cedar tower known as the Codger Pole in Colfax.

- The Seattle Dojo, founded around 1907, is the oldest judo academy in North America.

- Washington State is home to seven professional sports teams, including the Seattle Seahawks (NFL), the Seattle Mariners (NFL), the Seattle Kraken (NHL), the Seattle Sounders FC (MLS), OL Reign (National Women's Soccer League), the Seattle Seawolves (Major League Rugby), and the Seattle Storm (WNBA).

- Debbie Armstrong, who won a gold medal in alpine skiing at the 1984 Olympic Games, grew up in Seattle and learned to ski at Alpental on the Snoqualmie Pass.

- Swimmer Nathan Adrian, an eight-time Olympic medalist (with five golds), was born and raised in Bremerton.

- When he retired from his helm at Washington State University in 1994, Chuck "Bobo" Brayton was the fourth winningest NCAA Division I baseball coach, with a 68.9 percent winning average in a nearly three-decade long career. The Pullman school's baseball field is now named after him.

MADE IN WA

Washington's agricultural outputs include:

- Apples
- Sweet cherries
- Red raspberries
- Spearmint oil
- Cattle
- Hops
- Grapes
- Onions

Washington's industrial outputs include:

- Lumber
- Hydroelectric power
- Computer software
- Aircraft
- Aluminum refining

SPORTING CHANCES

- In 2021, Phil Shinnick of Spokane was recognized for setting a world record in the long jump—58 years after the fact. The University of Washington alum was initially denied the record due to an official's procedural error, but campaigned for decades to get it back.

- Each year, Spokane hosts Hoopfest, the world's largest three-on-three outdoor basketball tournament, featuring more than 6,000 teams and 425 courts spanning 45 city blocks.

- In 2014, the Seattle Seahawks won Super Bowl XLVIII, and the Seattle Storm has brought back WNBA titles in 2004, 2010, 2018, and 2020.

STARS ★ OF ★ THE ★ STATE

MEGAN RAPINOE (b. 1985)

A forward for Seattle's OL Reign, the Washington State transplant made a name for herself as one of the city's—and the country's—most dynamic athletes. As captain of the U.S. team in the 2019 Women's World Cup, Rapinoe was the first woman to start in three consecutive World Cup finals, and she won the Golden Ball for the tournament's best player and the Golden Boot for its top scorer. She was also a member of the U.S. Olympic squad that won a bronze medal in Tokyo in 2021. A player on the Reign from 2013 to 2023, Rapinoe lives in Seattle with her partner, Sue Bird, star of the WNBA's Seattle Storm.

WASHINGTON DISTRICT OF COLUMBIA

BIRD: Wood Thrush **NICKNAME:** "D.C.," "The District," and "Chocolate City" **ENTRY:** 1790

★ ★ ★ *"Justice for All"* ★ ★ ★

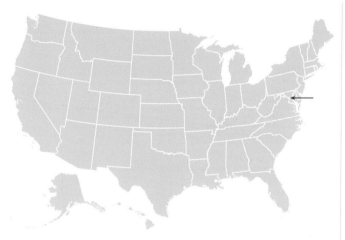

DC FACTS

- The population is 671,803.

- Located on the borders of Virginia and Maryland, D.C. is just 68 square miles (176 sq km).

- The seat of the country's government, the District is also highly involved in tourism, hospitality, and security IT.

- D.C. sits in an area originally occupied by the Nacotchtank (also known as the Anacostans).

- Begun in 1969, D.C.'s mostly underground train transport system, known as the Metro, features more than 117 miles (188 km) of track and 91 stations.

- During the War of 1812 British soldiers burned down much of D.C.—including the White House and the Capitol Building.

- Dedicated before some 50,000 people in 1922, the Lincoln Memorial is a monument to President Abraham Lincoln.

- Designed by Robert Mills, the Washington Monument was erected in honor of the nation's first president. ▼

▶ OFFICIAL FLOWER

American Beauty Rose
Rosa 'American Beauty'

The district's unofficial flower, the American beauty variety of rose is known for its lovely fragrance, cupped petals, and vivid fuchsia shade.

1790

Washington, D.C., was established as the nation's capital in 1790. The exact location was intended as a compromise to various states and political parties, each of which desired the capital to be in their jurisdiction.

THE 51ST STATE

Though the concept of statehood for D.C. has been voiced since the 1880s, the 1980s saw the rise of formal suggested legislation. In 2020 and in 2021, the House passed the Washington, D.C., Admission Act, bringing national attention to the issue.

END TAXATION WITHOUT REPRESENTATION

—D.C. license plate slogan

- The White House was built by enslaved laborers over the course of eight years.

- The Capitol Building is where Congress meets. Designed by Dr. William Thornton, it was begun in 1793 but not completed until 1829.

- Following the assassination of Martin Luther King, Jr., on April 4, 1968, chaos erupted across the District. Riots lasted for four days, ending with 13 deaths and the deployment of some 13,000 National Guard troops.

- During the Civil War, Clarissa "Clara" Harlowe Barton was famous for her tireless work as a battlefield nurse. In 1881, she founded the American Red Cross, whose headquarters remain in D.C.

- As a district, D.C. is not considered a state. Its residents are U.S. citizens who pay taxes, but do not have voting representation in Congress.

- Born in 1939, D.C. native Marvin Gaye was a soul singer and songwriter. Among his most iconic tunes are "What's Going On" and "Sexual Healing."

- To design the city, President George Washington appointed French architect Pierre Charles L'Enfant, whose designs drew on surveys by Benjamin Banneker, a free Black mathematician.

FREE AT LAST

In 1963, legendary Civil Rights leader and activist Martin Luther King, Jr., led the March on Washington where he delivered his iconic "I Have a Dream" speech.

- D.C. has served as a destination for protests and marches—from the 1913 Woman Suffrage Procession to the 1963 March on Washington for Jobs and Freedom to the annual March for Life—for more than a century.

- Designed in 1981 by then 21-year-old artist and architect Maya Lin, the Vietnam Veteran's Memorial is made up of 70 granite panels inscribed with more than 58,000 names of those killed during the war.

STARS ★ OF ★ THE ★ STATE

DUKE ELLINGTON

(1899–1974) Considered one of the greatest jazz musicians of all time, Duke Ellington was born Edward Kennedy Ellington in Washington, D.C. Ellington began studying as a pianist at the age of seven, performing professionally by the time he was 17. Ellington moved to New York's Harlem, where he helped develop big-band jazz during his time at the Cotton Club. In addition to his skill at the piano, Ellington became known for his unparalleled abilities as a band leader, songwriting and composing, and performances with fellow musicians Ella Fitzgerald, Louis Armstrong, and others.

◀ (UN)LUCKY DIAMOND

One of the most famous (or infamous) items in the Smithsonian's collections is the supposedly cursed Hope Diamond.

WEIRD BUT TRUE

- Dancing was once banned at the White House.

- President Arthur once auctioned off a pair of Abraham Lincoln's pants to help finance renovations at the White House.

- During his time at the White House, President John Adams had a pet dog named Satan.

- During the DC Half and Half Marathon, contestants run a half marathon, pausing halfway through to eat a half smoke—a local, hot dog–like sausage sandwich often packed with chili and onions

- During the blooming season of the U.S. Botanic Garden's corpse flowers, which smell similar to rotting flesh, visitors stand in line for up to an hour to get a whiff.

- Washington National Cathedral has Darth Vader as one of its gargoyles. ▼

- A local restaurant serves fried sugar toads, an invasive type of puffer fish.

- The collection of Smithsonian's National Air and Space Museum includes a studio model of popular television show *Star Trek*'s starship *Enterprise*.

- The ghost of former first lady Dolley Madison reportedly haunts her old home, located on Lafayette Square.

- D.C. residents were not allowed to vote for the president and vice president until 1961. ▪

▶ STORY OF THE SOUND

From jazz to soul music, D.C. has long had a rich musical history. But perhaps no genre best encapsulates the sound of the city as well as go-go. An upbeat mix of funk and Latin American percussion, go-go was developed in the 1970s by musical pioneers such as Chuck Brown, Rare Essence, Experience Unlimited, and Trouble Funk. For decades, the danceable, homegrown music reflected the District's status as a hub of Black culture. Today, it also reflects the challenges and marginalization faced by the District's Black residents. Go-go has become the sound of much of the city's activism and protests, such as the Black Lives Matter movement to end political violence against people of color, as well as the Don't Mute D.C. movement against gentrification and the displacement of marginalized people. ▪

▲ OFF THE HOOK

The local wharf has the oldest continually operating open-air fish market in the U.S.

MISCELLANY

- People from D.C. are called **Washingtonians**.

- The official dinosaur is *Capitalsaurus*.

- The District is named after both **George Washington** and **Christopher Columbus**.

- Each year in June, D.C. hosts a month-long LGBTQ+ celebration known as **Capital Pride**.

- The official tree is the **scarlet oak**.

- Born in D.C., former vice president **Al Gore** won the Nobel Peace Prize in 2007 for his work to fight climate change.

- D.C. is home to the largest concentration of **Ethiopians** outside of Africa.

- The official rock is **Potomac bluestone**.

- D.C. has a **larger population** than either Wyoming or Vermont.

- D.C. streets are **organized alphabetically**.

- **DMV** stands for D.C., Maryland, and Virginia, and it refers to D.C. and its immediate suburbs.

- There is a **labyrinth of underground tunnels** below the Capitol Building.

- **American University** became the first U.S. university to achieve carbon neutrality.

- **Cherry** is the official fruit.

The Smithsonian Museum of Natural History houses the world's largest cut aquamarine, a 10,000-carat obelisk known as the Dom Pedro.

BY THE NUMBERS

570 GALLONS (2,158 L) OF PAINT IS REQUIRED TO COVER THE OUTSIDE OF THE WHITE HOUSE

200+ the number of historic sites on the African American Heritage Trail

3 THE NUMBER OF PRESIDENTS—JAMES K. POLK, ANDREW JOHNSON, AND DONALD TRUMP—WHO DIDN'T HAVE A PET WHILE SERVING IN OFFICE

24,000,0000 the approximate number of visitors to the National Mall each year

1800 the year Congress moved from Pennsylvania to D.C.

100,904 number of letters to military members once collected in one month by the Daughters of the American Revolution

383 THE LENGTH IN MILES (616 KM) OF THE POTOMAC RIVER

500,000+ the number of people who attended the 2017 Women's March for women's rights in D.C.

1,754 the size in acres (710 ha) of Rock Creek Park

21 STORIES: THE DEPTH OF ONE OF D.C.'S METRO STOPS

DESTINATION: WASHINGTON, D.C.

- Located at 1600 Pennsylvania Avenue, the White House and its surrounding grounds offer an up-close view of the nation's history.

- Monuments dotting the National Mall include the Washington Monument, an Egyptian-style obelisk that is the tallest building in D.C.; the Lincoln Memorial, a monument to equality and unity; the Martin Luther King, Jr. Memorial; the Vietnam Veterans Memorial; and many more.

- D.C. is famous for its myriad museums, many of which offer free admission. Top destinations include numerous Smithsonian Institution museums—such as the National Museum of African American History and Culture, the National Museum of the American Indian, the National Museum of Natural History, the National Portrait Gallery, and more.

- Capitol Hill is home to the U.S. Capitol, the Supreme Court, the Library of Congress, the U.S. Botanic Garden, and more.

- In 1864, Gallaudet University became the first school for the advanced education for deaf and hard of hearing people.

- Founded in 1888, the National Geographic Society is an organization dedicated to geographic knowledge and conservation. Visitors to its headquarters in D.C. can explore changing exhibits at the museum.

With more than 164 million items in nearly all formats and languages, the federal Library of Congress is the largest library in the world.

- Founded in 1867, Howard University is a historically Black university established to support advanced studies for Black students. Its famous former students include U.S. Supreme Court Justice Thurgood Marshall, Vice President Kamala Harris, author Toni Morrison, actor Chadwick Boseman, and others.

- Ford's Theater and Museum was the site of President Abraham Lincoln's assassination.

- Originally a separate settlement, Georgetown was established as a tobacco port town. Today, it is a historic neighborhood home to some of D.C.'s oldest houses, Georgetown University, landmarks, fine dining, and plenty of shops.

- When it opened in 1910, the Howard Theatre was the "largest colored theatre in the world." With performers such as Duke Ellington, Ella Fitzgerald, and Chuck Brown and the Soul Searchers, the venue became a place that shaped the sounds of jazz and go-go.

▼ THINK PINK

Held each spring, the National Cherry Blossom Festival celebrates the blooming cherry blossom trees originally given to the District by the mayor of Tokyo in 1912. Events include a kite festival, opening ceremony, parade, and more.

▲ PRESIDENTIAL RACE

The Presidents' Race is a mascot-only race at baseball's Nationals Park where contestants must dash to the finish line while wearing enormous presidential mascot costumes.

SPORTING CHANCES

- It wasn't until 1998 that the NHL Washington Capitals, which had been founded in 1974, secured a major win with the Eastern Conference Championship. In 2018, they won another—and the Stanley Cup.

- Originally based in Montreal and called the Expos, the Washington Nationals (MLB) won the World Series in 2019.

- Professional men's soccer team D.C. United has won four MLS Cups.

- In 2020, after years of protests from activists championing Indigenous representation, the Washington NFL team changed its name to the Commanders.

- Located in Penn Quarter, Capital One Arena is home to the NBA Wizards, the WNBA Mystics, and the NHL Capitals.

- D.C.'s professional women's soccer team, the Washington Spirit, won the NWSL Championship in 2021.

- Known as "The Great Eight" in reference to his jersey number, NHL player Alex Ovechkin leads the Capitals in career goals scored with more than 800. Ovechkin is also the oldest NHL player in history to score 50 goals in one season.

- Known as the D.C. Divas, the D.C. female football team plays in the Women's Football Alliance.

- Georgetown athletic teams are known as the Hoyas, which may have originated from an early cheer, "Hoya saxa!" The cry, which comes from ancient Greek and Latin, translates to "What rocks!"

MADE IN D.C.

Washington, DC's industrial outputs include:

- Parts of airplanes and helicopters
- Electrical parts
- Ships and boats
- Military weapons
- Works of art
- Vehicles
- Antiques
- Medical equipment

WASHINGTON ISN'T A CITY, IT'S AN ABSTRACTION.

—Poet Dylan Thomas

HELEN HAYES

(1900–1993) Born Helen Hayes Brown in Washington, D.C., in 1900, Hayes is often considered the "First Lady of American Theater." She first appeared on Broadway at the young age of nine, gaining notoriety some eight years later in the touring titular role of Pollyanna. Hayes later transitioned into film, winning an Academy Award in 1931 for *The Sin of Madelon Claudet*. In 1946, she earned her first Tony with a return to Broadway, continuing to balance her career between the stage and the screen for the rest of her life. In 1986, Hayes was awarded the Presidential Medal of Freedom.

STARS ★ OF ★ THE ★ STATE

WEST VIRGINIA

CAPITAL: Charleston **BIRD:** Northern Cardinal **NICKNAME:** Mountain State **ENTRY:** 1863

★ ★ ★ *"Mountaineers Are Always Free"* ★ ★ ★

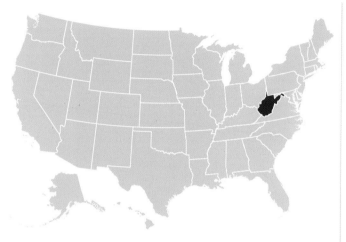

WV FACTS

- The population is 1,775,156.

- The 35th state, West Virginia is the 10th smallest in area.

- Inhabited for at least 14,000 years, the area's original peoples included the Shawano (Shawnee), Ani-Yun-Wiya (Cherokee), Yesan (Tutelo), and Saponi. Today, there are no federally recognized tribes.

- West Virginia natural resources include timber, salt, coal, gas, and, historically, iron ore.

- The most famous beverage of the state is likely moonshine: a whiskey originally made by 18th-century immigrants from the U.K. who adapted their home recipes to use the region's abundant corn.

- Coal mining became the area's major industry by the mid 1800s thanks to the rise of steamboats and coal furnaces. With the rise of industrialization, coal mining grew exponentially. Many miners suffered unsafe working conditions and health issues. By the 1960s, the industry was in steep decline due to foreign competition, mechanization, and a dwindling reliance on coal. ▼

▶ STATE FLOWER
Rhododendron
Rhododendron maximum

In 1903, public school children across the state selected the rhododendron over honeysuckle and the wild rose as the official state bloom.

1861

After Virginia seceded from the Union in 1861, Union and Confederate armies immediately began vying for control of the western portion of the state. In one of the first land battles of the Civil War, Union Colonel Benjamin Franklin Kelley was deployed to seize Philippi.

GRAN ALWAYS SAID OUR WEST VIRGINIA MOUNTAINS IS LIKE THE BOSOM OF THE ALMIGHTY, KEEPING US PROTECTED AND STILL IN HIM.

—Marilyn Sue Shank, *Child of the Mountains*

- In 1774, the colonial governor, Lord Dunmore, led two armies to attack local Shawano tribes in order to cripple Indigenous resistance efforts and expand areas of settlement. Known as the Battle of Point Pleasant, the end result was Shawano defeat and further colonization of the region.

- Born in Yawkey in 1921, Virginia Ruth Egnor—known to the world as Dagmar—went on to become one of the best-known television celebrities of the 1950s.

- In the 1880s, an infamous feud between two Appalachian families, the Hatfields and the McCoys, drew national attention and even the involvement of the U.S. Supreme Court.

- In response to the dangerous working conditions facing coal miners, advocacy groups such as the Knights of Labor began to spring up in the 1860s. The early 1900s saw violent clashes between labor leaders and local officials known as the Mine Wars.

- Gatherings known as mountain dances, with bluegrass or old-time music, are a product of the intermingling of Irish, Scottish, English, British, German, Indigenous, and African cultures.

- Though the state has historically been known for its coal mining, a rising interest in the outdoors has contributed to a large ecotourism industry. ▲

- Music often includes the fiddling of various Indigenous nations, ballad singing of Scotch-Irish origin, African instruments and traditions such as the banjo and call-and-response stylings, and more.

- Other industries include chemicals, metals, lumber, glass, and biotech.

- The state has strong ties to Appalachian culture, known for its self-reliance, tight-knit community, and deeply creative traditions in music and art. ▪

STARS ★ OF ★ THE ★ STATE

BILL WITHERS

(1938–2020) A soul musician, singer, and songwriter, Bill Withers was born in Slab Fork in 1938. While serving in the U.S. Navy, he became interested in music, and he moved to Los Angeles to pursue a career in the 1960s. Withers burst onto the scene with his 1971 song "Ain't No Sunshine," which won a Grammy Award and climbed to the number three spot in the radio charts. The following year, "Lean on Me" reached number one on the Billboard charts. Withers won his second Grammy in 1981 and received the ASCAP Rhythm & Soul Heritage Award in 2006. He was inducted into the Songwriters Hall of Fame in 2005 as well as the West Virginia Music Hall of Fame in 2007. ▪

A member of the U.S. Senate for 51 years and 177 days, Robert Byrd of WV was the longest-serving U.S. Senator.

WEIRD BUT TRUE

- A store in Harpers Ferry sells authentic re-creations of candy from past centuries, such as candied rose petals and stained-glass sugar. ▲

- Colonists in the area originally wanted to create a 14th colony called Vandalia, or a separate state called Westsylvania.

- A slice of corn bread served in a glass of milk is a popular local treat.

- In Berkeley Springs State Park, there is an annual event celebrating the ruins of a bathtub used by George Washington.

- In 1888, one Philippi man patented a method for preserving human mummies—two of which are still on display today.

- Cell phones, microwaves, and televisions are not allowed in the town of Green Bank (because of the risk of interference with a nearby radio telescope).

- Holding some 760 pounds (335 kg) of birdseed, the world's largest bird feeder is located in Keister.

- There is an annual Roadkill Cook-Off in Pocahontas County.

- Visitors to Seneca State Forest in Dunmore can spend the night in a real historic fire tower. ▪

STORY OF THE NAME Originally part of the colony of Virginia, the region was named in honor of England's Queen Elizabeth I, known as the Virgin Queen. However, as more German and Scotch-Irish frontier settlers colonized the western region of the state, an independent culture began to emerge. Although many settlers wished to separate themselves from the majority British citizens of eastern Virginia by the early 1800s, it wasn't until the Civil War that the process was set in motion. Many Virginian westerners, who did not rely on the forced labor of enslaved people, wished to remain with the Union, and split from Virginia upon the state's secession. ▪

MISCELLANY

- The state amphibian is the northern **red salamander**.

- The **black bear** is the state animal.

- The **golden delicious apple** is the state fruit.

- In 1882, journalist J.R. Clifford founded the **Pioneer Press**, the state's first Black newspaper.

- The state butterfly is the **monarch**.

- West Virginia colors are **old gold and blue**.

- There is a secret, never-used congressional bunker located beneath **Greenbrier Resort**.

- **Brook trout** is the state fish.

- **Megalonyx jeffersonii**, a type of giant prehistoric ground sloth named in honor of President Jefferson, is the state fossil.

- During the 1700s, the state was the nation's major **supplier of iron**.

- Not technically a gemstone but instead mineralized remains of coral some 325 million years old, **fossil coral** is the state gem.

- **Sugar maple**, a tree used for tapping maple syrup, is the state tree.

- The state reptile is the **timber rattlesnake**.

- Said to haunt the skies of Point Pleasant, the **Mothman** is a cryptid that is supposedly part man, part moth.

- The state rock is **bituminous coal**.

- An official state intertribal tribe is the **Appalachian American Indians of West Virginia**.

- During the 1800s, **the steamboat** was among the state's primary modes of transportation.

PEARL S. BUCK

(1892–1973) Born Pearl Comfort Sydenstricker in Hillsboro, Pearl S. Buck was an award-winning author and humanitarian. Thanks to her Presbyterian missionary parents, Buck spent the first 18 years of her life in China. She published her first novel, *East Wind, West Wind*, in 1930, and in 1932 was awarded a Pulitzer Prize for her second, *The Good Earth*. Six years later, she became the first American woman to win both a Pulitzer Prize and the Nobel Prize in Literature. In addition to her work as an author, Buck was a passionate activist for adoption and child sponsorship. In 1949, she founded the Welcome Home adoption program and in 1964 established the Pearl S. Buck Foundation, a child sponsorship organization. ▪

THE SUN DOESN'T ALWAYS SHINE IN WEST VIRGINIA, BUT THE PEOPLE DO.

—Former senator Richard Ojeda

BY THE NUMBERS

1866
THE YEAR THAT LOCAL DOCTOR MAHLON LOOMIS CONDUCTED THE FIRST KNOWN RADIO COMMUNICATION

1778
the year Greenbrier Resort opened

60 TO 80%
estimated percentage of local soldiers who fought for the Union during the Civil War

4,863
ELEVATION IN FEET (1,482 M) OF SPRUCE KNOB, THE HIGHEST POINT

84
the age of the oldest BASE jumper to parachute off the New River Gorge Bridge, which sits 876 feet (267 m) above the river. It is the highest bridge east of the Mississippi.

12,884
the size in acres (5,214 ha) of Seneca State Forest

1914
the year President Woodrow Wilson officially made Mother's Day a national holiday after West Virginian Anna Jarvis organized celebrations

The Green Bank Observatory houses the world's largest radio telescope, which weighs more than a whopping 17 million pounds (7.7 million kg).

STORY OF THE FOLK HERO In the 1870s, many recently emancipated Black Americans migrated to the state in search of paying jobs in the booming railroad construction industry. It was around this time that the ballad of John Henry first appeared. In the legend, John Henry is a free Black railroad worker who defeats a steam drill in a race to drill a tunnel but dooms himself to death by overexertion in the process. While the origins are unclear, some historians believe they may have been inspired by a real man. Regardless, the legend remains as an ode to defiance and resilience, as well as a warning against entrapment by labor. ▪

DESTINATION: WEST VIRGINIA

- In the winter, visitors to Snowshoe Mountain spend their time skiing the 60 trails or relaxing at the lodge. In the warmer months they can enjoy hiking and lake activities.

- During Bridge Day at New River Gorge, daredevils from around the country BASE jump off New River Gorge Bridge.

- Located in Riverton, the 460-million-year-old cave system known as Seneca Caverns hosts cave tours and gem mining for family-friendly fun.

- Built in 1866, the West Virginia Penitentiary in Moundsville functioned as a prison for more than a century. Today it conducts ghost tours.

- Charleston offers multiple museums, a historic center, and the nearby Kanawha State Forest.

- For more than 80 years, Richwood has held the annual Feast of the Ramson Festival—a celebration of wild ramps, a local leek-like vegetable that can only be obtained by foraging.

- The site of abolitionist John Brown's raid, Harpers Ferry is part living history museum, part nature escape. Visitors can tour the spots where Brown and his supporters seized the federal armory and made their stand, watch Civil War reenactments, and visit historic shops.

- Known as the Little Bahamas of the East, Summersville Lake has the depth, warm water, and visibility to make for top-notch scuba diving.

- Blackwater Falls State Park is named for its 57-foot (17 m) waterfall. The park is a popular destination for viewing changing fall leaves.

- Established in 1920, Monongahela National Forest is a top destination for camping, fishing, hiking, and bird-watching. ▼

COUNTRY ROADS, TAKE ME HOME TO THE PLACE I BELONG/ WEST VIRGINIA, MOUNTAIN MOMMA/ TAKE ME HOME, COUNTRY ROADS

—John Denver, "Take Me Home, Country Roads"

▲ CHUCK YEAGER

In 1947, U.S. Air Force officer and Myra native Chuck Yeager became the first person to break the sound barrier in flight.

SPORTING CHANCES

- Thanks to its multitude of rapids, the state is considered one of the world's best spots for white-water rafting.

- First proposed in 1921 and completed in 1937, the Appalachian Trail's 2,190-mile-long (3,525 km) hiking route spans 14 states and takes some five to seven months to complete when done as a thru-hike. Two sections of the Appalachian Trail run through the state.

- One local company offers flights in WWII-era planes.

- Born in Fairmont, Mary Lou Retton is an Olympic gymnast with one gold medal, two silver, and three bronze.

- Following his exceptional career in the NBA, Charleston-born Rodney Clark "Hot Rod" Hundley went on to become a beloved basketball broadcaster.

- Each West Virginia University (WVU) victory is celebrated at the Milan Puskar Stadium with the John Denver song "Take Me Home, Country Roads."

- Huntington native Hal Greer was named an NBA All-Star 10 times.

- In 1971, Ona Speedway hosted the West Virginia 500, a NASCAR Winston Cup Series event.

- Since 1934, the WVU mascot has been the Mountaineer.

- Raised in Coalwood, Homer Hickam, Jr., went on to specialize in training astronauts at NASA.

▶ ALEXIS HORNBUCKLE

In 2008, Charleston native Alexis Hornbuckle became the only basketball player to win WNBA and NCAA titles in the same year.

WISCONSIN

★ ★ ★
"Forward"
★ ★ ★

CAPITAL: Madison **BIRD:** Robin **NICKNAME:** Badger State **ENTRY:** 1848

WI FACTS

- Situated in the central northern area of the U.S., Wisconsin is within the Midwest and Great Lakes regions.

- The area was part of the Wisconsin Territory from July 3, 1836, until May 29, 1848, when an eastern portion of the territory was admitted to the Union as the state of Wisconsin.

- The discovery of ancient mammoth bones with human-made tool marks near Kenosha County suggests that people have lived in this region for more than 14,500 years.

- The name is believed to stem from the Algonquin word *Meskonsing*, meaning "this stream meanders through something red," referring to the Wisconsin River.

- Native American tribes such as the Dakota Sioux, Winnebago, Menominee, Ojibwe, Potawatomi, Fox, and Sauk have all lived in the region for thousands of years.

- Green Bay is the oldest city in the state. Jean Nicolet started a small trading post there in 1634. ▼

▶ STATE FLOWER

Wood Violet
Viola papilionacea

This small flower blooms in wet woodland and meadow areas, and along roadsides between March and June.

1763

The area came under British rule at the end of the French and Indian War in 1763 and remained that way until the War of 1812.

GOT MILK?
14% of U.S. milk production comes from Wisconsin.

ON, WISCONSIN! ON, WISCONSIN! PLUNGE RIGHT THROUGH THAT LINE!

—from the official state song, "On Wisconsin"

- With a population of some 5,892,539, it is the 20th most populous state in the U.S. Its total area of 65,496 square miles (169,635 sq km) makes it the 25th largest state.

- Eleven federally recognized American Indian tribes still live in Wisconsin today.

- Madison was incorporated in 1856. It is the second largest city in the state with a population of 272,903.

- The state's largest city, Milwaukee, has a population of some 563,305.

- The highest point in the state is Timms Hill, at 1,952 feet (595 m). The lowest? Lake Michigan, at 581 feet (177 m).

- Home to 15,074 lakes, water covers almost 3 percent of the state's area at nearly one million acres (405,000 ha).

- The state's Great Lakes coastline stretches for more than 800 miles (1,300 km), and there is nearly 200 miles (325 km) of Mississippi River shoreline.

- The highest temperature ever recorded in Wisconsin was 114°F (45°C). The lowest was −55°F (−48°C).

- There are some 64,400 farms in the state, covering a total of 14.3 million acres (5.8 million ha).

▲ **GREAT LAKE**
At 30 miles (48 km) long and 10 miles (16 m) wide, Lake Winnebago is the state's largest inland lake.

STORY OF THE NICKNAME Wisconsin's nickname, "the Badger State," has less to do with the short-legged omnivores and more to do with the state's history. The story goes that miners who flocked to the state seeking lead in the 1820s often dug tunnels in the hillside as a cozy spot to rest. This habit was similar to that of badgers, and the miners soon picked up the animal's moniker. It stuck, and eventually the University of Wisconsin ran with it, choosing the badger as its mascot. As for the actual animal? While there are some in the state, they are rather evasive and rarely seen.

STARS ★ OF ★ THE ★ STATE

ORSON WELLES

(1915–1985) Born in Kenosha, Welles went on to become a prolific writer, producer, actor, and one of the greatest and most influential filmmakers of all time. Welles, who attended school as a boy in Madison, made his first major impression in the entertainment industry with an adaptation of the H.G. Wells novel *The War of the Worlds*, which aired on the radio in 1938. Welles's major moment came in 1941, when his film *Citizen Kane* debuted, earning nine Academy Award nominations, including a win for best screenplay—and a reputation as the greatest movie ever made. Welles's childhood home is now a Kenosha landmark.

WEIRD BUT TRUE

- Green Bay, where the first splinter-free toilet paper was invented in the 1930s, is known as the "Toilet Paper Capital of the World."

- The Fox River is one of the few rivers in the nation that flows north.

- Cheese brine—the salt-saturated liquid left over from the cheesemaking process—is used to treat icy roads in Polk County.

- Mount Horeb is called the "Troll Capital of the World" and features hand-carved trolls lining its streets.

- In 2010, a group from the University of Wisconsin campaigned to make *Lactococcus lactis*, the bacterium used to make Colby, Cheddar, and Monterey Jack cheeses, the first official state microbe in the U.S.

- A 20-pound (9 kg) piece of the Soviet satellite Sputnik IV fell out of orbit and landed in Manitowoc in 1962.

- In 2021, a watermelon-size chunk of ice crashed through the roof of a home in Elk Mound, narrowly missing the person who lived inside.

- A scientifically accurate re-creation of Samson—a silverback gorilla who once lived in the Milwaukee Zoo—won "best in show" and "best in world" at the World Taxidermy Championships.

- Cows and other livestock get the right of way on Wisconsin roads.

- "Claire d' Loon," a 16-foot (5 m), 2,000-pound (907 kg) fiberglass bird greets visitors with its amplified loon sounds at the Mercer Chamber of Commerce.

- Some scientists believe Wisconsin once had a tropical climate and was home to some of the world's first coral reefs.

The first kindergarten classes in the U.S. were held in 1856 at the home of Margarethe Meyer Schurz in Watertown.

▶ BOGGED-DOWN

Each September, the town of Warren (population: 400) draws some 100,000 visitors for the world's largest cranberry festival.

▶ HOT DIGGITY

A sheriff in Waukesha County once pulled over the Oscar Mayer Wienermobile for a moving violation.

MISCELLANY

- During the Civil War, the state became an important part of the **Underground Railroad**.

- The **Republican party** was established in Ripon on March 20, 1854, as a faction that would defend against the expansion of slavery.

- Wisconsin's motto, "Forward," adopted in 1851, speaks to the **socially progressive** nature of its residents.

- The **first dairy school** in the U.S. was established at the University of Wisconsin-Madison in 1890.

- There are some **752 shipwrecks** lurking on the bottom of Wisconsin's waterways.

- Wisconsin stores about **1.2 quadrillion gallons (4.5 quadrillion L) of water underground**. If it was all aboveground, it would submerge the state in 100 feet (30.5 m) of water.

- **25 percent of the nation's cheese** is made in Wisconsin.

- The **first sundae**—a dish of ice cream with chocolate sauce on top—was served in Two Rivers in 1881.

- Wisconsin has the **third largest Hmong population** in the U.S., with more than 58,000 people.

- It's said that the Virgin Mary appeared in October 1859 on the grounds of **New Franken's Our Lady of Good Help**, making it the site of the first and only Catholic Church–confirmed apparition of the saint.

- The **methunky**, a cracker made from flour, salt, cracklings, and sauerkraut, is a popular snack.

- Wisconsin is home to an **estimated 24,000 black bears**.

- Wisconsin's state fish, the **muskellunge**, can grow to be six feet (1.8 m) long and weigh almost 70 pounds (32 kg).

- The **average snowfall** is about 46 inches (117 cm) annually.

BY THE NUMBERS

Wisconsin Dairy

3,470,000,000 pounds (1.57 billion kg) of cheese is made in the state each year.

1895 the year Wisconsin established a law prohibiting the sale of yellow margarine in order to support the dairy industry. (It was repealed in 1967.)

$45.6 billion the amount of money the dairy industry contributes to Wisconsin's economy each year

21% OF THE TOTAL NUMBER OF U.S. DAIRY FARMS ARE LOCATED IN WISCONSIN.

55,000 the number in pounds (24,948 kg) of cheese that spilled onto a Wisconsin highway in March 2020

95% OF WISCONSIN DAIRY FARMS ARE FAMILY OWNED.

8 the number of gallons (3.8 L) of milk produced by each Wisconsin dairy cow each day

1,280,000 the number of dairy cows in the state, which produce 2.44 billion pounds (1 billion kg) of milk per month.

90% of Wisconsin milk is made into cheese.

600 the number of varieties of cheese produced in Wisconsin—more than double that of any other state

▲ FRANK LLOYD WRIGHT

Born in Richland Center in 1867, American architect Frank Lloyd Wright left a legacy that can be traced across the state. The self-guided Frank Lloyd Wright Trail through southern Wisconsin has nine stops stretching from Kenosha County to Richland County, all homes that Wright designed, including Wingspread, the largest of his Prairie-style houses, in Wind Point.

- The Great Wisconsin Cheese Festival in Little Chute celebrates all things cheesy: There's a parade, music, cheese tastings, a cheese carving demo, a cheese curd eating contest, and more.

- Known as the "Waterpark Capital of the World," the Wisconsin Dells has plenty of places to splash around, including Noah's Ark Waterpark, the largest in the country, featuring 51 slides and two wave pools.

- Sea caves, dramatic cliffs, sparkling water, charming lighthouses, and more than 800 species of plants are just a few of the standout features of Apostle Islands National Lakeshore, a group of 22 islands in Lake Superior. The largest, Madeline Island, is 15 miles (24 km) long and three miles (3.8 km) wide.

- A tour of the Wisconsin State Capitol in Madison offers an insider glimpse of the stunning architecture for the building, which was completed in 1917 with 43 types of stone from six countries and eight states. The dome is the largest by volume in the nation.

- Each summer, the population of Door County swells from 27,000 to 250,000, and for good reason: Perched on the banks of Lake Michigan, it offers more than 50 beaches and outdoor activities galore, from stand-up paddleboarding to hiking.

700

feet (213 m) of Rib Mountain bedrock stands near Wausau, the highest mound in the state.

STARS ★ OF ★ THE ★ STATE

MARISSA MAYER

(b. 1975) Google's first female engineer and the former CEO of Yahoo, Mayer hails from Wausau, where she was one of two children born to an engineer and an art teacher. Calling her childhood in Wisconsin "wonderful," Mayer participated in ice skating, ballet, piano, and worked as a cashier at a local supermarket. Always maintaining a strong interest in computer programming, Mayer migrated toward the field while at Stanford University, where she earned degrees in computer science and symbolic systems specializing in artificial intelligence that led her to land a role at Google. While at Yahoo, Mayer became the first CEO of a *Fortune* 500 Tech company to give birth, sparking change in family leave at the company. Mayer left Yahoo in 2017, after which she launched her own company.

RECORD ★ SETTERS

Tammy Baldwin became the first woman elected to represent Wisconsin in Congress in 1998. She was also the first openly gay senator in U.S. history.

SPORTING CHANCES

- Wisconsin has four major professional sports teams: the Milwaukee Brewers (MLB), the Milwaukee Bucks (NBA), Forward Madison FC (MLS), and the Green Bay Packers (NFL).

- The Green Bay Packers have won 13 league championships, the most in NFL history, and four Super Bowl victories.

- The Wisconsin Glo, a women's professional basketball team, is based in Oshkosh and plays in the Global Women's Basketball Association.

- The Pettit National Ice Center in Milwaukee has served as a training center for many current and former elite speed skaters, including Olympic gold medalists Eric Heiden, Bonnie Blair Cruikshank, and Dan Jansen.

- The World Championship Snowmobile Derby—the largest and most prestigious snowmobile competition in the sport—is held each January in Eagle River.

- The American Birkebeiner, the largest cross-country ski marathon in the U.S., brings upward of 5,000 competitors to Cable each February.

- The Milwaukee Mile, an oval track opened in 1903, is the oldest operating motorsports venue in the world.

- In July 2021, the Milwaukee Bucks won their first NBA title in 50 years.

- At the 1980 Lake Placid Winter Games, Eric Heiden won all five speed skating events. Born in Madison, he was the first person in history to win five gold medals in the same Olympics.

MADE IN WI

Wisconsin's agricultural outputs include:

- Dairy
- Soybeans
- Feed and feed grains
- Cranberries
- Whey
- Ginseng root
- Sweet corn

Wisconsin's industrial outputs include:

- Industrial machinery
- Medical and scientific instruments
- Electrical machinery
- Pharmaceutical products
- Vehicles and parts
- Plastic parts
- Paper products

SAY CHEESE

◀ Packers fans are known as "cheeseheads" and wear bright yellow, triangular foam hats that look like chunks of cheese.

WYOMING

★ ★ ★

"Equal Rights"

★ ★ ★

CAPITAL: Cheyenne **BIRD:** Meadowlark **NICKNAME:** Equality State **ENTRY:** 1890

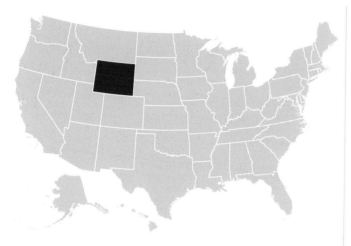

WY FACTS

- The population is 581,381.

- The 44th state to join the nation, it is the ninth largest in area.

- Perhaps best known as the home of Yellowstone National Park, the state is famous as a tourist destination for its outdoors, cowboy lifestyle, and ranches.

- As the ranching and cowboy lifestyle spread across the state, so did chuck wagons: wagons carrying food supplies used to feed cattle drivers while on the range.

- Some 2.1 million years ago, a hot spot under what is now Yellowstone created one of the largest volcanic eruptions known to history. The supervolcano exploded several times more, forming the Yellowstone caldera.

- The state's wide-open plains and tall grasses tended to attract cattle drivers and ranchers. Soon, this ranching lifestyle was romanticized and vacationers headed to the region. In the 1880s, some of the first guesthouses specially targeted at these vacationers—known as dude ranches—began to spring up.

- The first Americans to explore the region were trappers, traders, and mountain men such as John Colter, Jim Bridger, and Jedidiah Smith.

- One of the earliest establishments was Fort Laramie, which was built as a fur trading post in 1834 and later evolved into a military post.

- Residents of the state follow a "Code of the West," which was signed into law in 2010. The code encourages integrity and hard work.

- One of the most iconic attractions of the state, Yellowstone's Old Faithful can be credited as the inspiration for Yellowstone National Park. The geyser "faithfully" erupts every 60 to 75 minutes. ◀

▶ STATE FLOWER

Indian Paintbrush
Castilleja linariifolia

Famed for their vivid color, the prairie fire's "blooms" are actually leaves—the real flowers are hiding within.

1869

In 1869, Wyoming became the first state to grant women the right to vote.

> THERE CAN BE NOTHING IN THE WORLD MORE BEAUTIFUL THAN ... THE CANYON OF THE YELLOWSTONE, THE THREE TETONS; AND OUR PEOPLE SHOULD SEE TO IT THAT THEY ARE PRESERVED FOR THEIR CHILDREN AND THEIR CHILDREN'S CHILDREN FOREVER, WITH THEIR MAJESTIC BEAUTY ALL UNMARRED.
>
> —President Theodore Roosevelt

- Wyoming's natural resources include coal, petroleum, uranium, and bentonite.

- Beginning largely in the 1860s, the U.S. government began entering into treaties with varying Indigenous nations—such as the 1863 Fort Bridger Treaty—which set aside "reservations" of land the government promised not to encroach upon. However, the government subsequently either broke these treaties or forced further reductions upon the reservations.

- Living in the region for some 12,000 years, the area's original inhabitants included the Inuna-Ina (Arapaho), Tsis tsis'tas (Cheyenne), Apsáalooke (Crow), Newe (Shoshone), and Nuciu (Ute). Federally recognized tribes today include the Inuna-Ina and Newe.

- Said to have been first spotted in Douglas, the jackalope is a cryptid that resembles a jackrabbit with the horns of an antelope.

- Born in 1860 in Philadelphia, author Owen Wister was an East Coaster who spent time in Wyoming. His turn-of-the-20th-century novels often centered on cowboy folk, and he is considered the "father of Western fiction."

- After explorers in the 1840s discovered a pass through the Rocky Mountains known as the South Pass, pioneers heading west flooded into the area. ▲

- After oil was discovered in the state, President Warren G. Harding appointed Albert Fall, secretary of the interior, to oversee the resource. In what became known as the Teapot Dome scandal, Fall was convicted of taking bribes from private oil companies wishing to secure access to the oil reserves.

- Though Yellowstone National Park has long been home to abundant wildlife, many of these animals were targeted by hunters or ranchers seeking to protect their livestock. Thanks to ongoing conservation efforts, populations have somewhat rebounded.

- The image of a bucking horse and rider is the official trademark of the state. ▪

CHIEF WASHAKIE

(c. 1804–1900) Born in the early 1800s to a Shoshone mother and a father who may have been Umatilla or Séliš, Chief Washakie was a renowned warrior and Shoshone leader who attempted to preserve his people's way of life through diplomacy. With the relentless encroachment and invasion of American settlers into Native territory, Indigenous nations often had to decide whether to fight for their rights or secure them through negotiation. According to Chief Washakie, a vision instructed him that the only way forward would be through political discussions. Chief Washakie led many Shoshone into negotiations and occasional alliances with the U.S. government, even aiding soldiers in certain battles. Critics of this method argue that Washakie's actions helped destroy the Shoshone way of life, while proponents claim that diplomacy preserved the Shoshone nation against American slaughter. ▪

- A local drive-in chain serves cheese wheels: deep-fried cheeseburgers.

- Served across the state, Rocky Mountain oysters are deep-fried bull testicles.

- Located near Afton, the Periodic Spring (or Intermittent Spring) is said to constantly flow for 18 minutes, stop for 18 minutes, and flow again.

- Some brewers use microorganisms found in Yellowstone to test their beer quality.

- Outside of Medicine Bow is a cabin built out of nearly 6,000 fossils.

- Register Cliff is home to some historic graffiti: Oregon Trail travelers carved their names into the bluffs for decades.

- There are only two escalators in the state.

- The sand dunes at Killpecker "sing."

- Taxidermied from various animals, there is a giant, ride-able "jackalope" statue in Dubois. ▼

RECORD ★ SETTERS

In 1906, a volcanic formation known as Grizzly Bear Lodge (also called Devils Tower) became the country's first national monument.

MISCELLANY

- Locals are called **Wyomingites**.

- The state amphibian is the **blotched tiger salamander**.

- According to one Apsáalooke legend, Bighorn Canyon was once home to an **enormous Bighorn Sheep named Big Metal**, so called for its metal horns.

- **Sheridan's green hairstreak butterfly** is the state butterfly.

- Located in Jackson Hole, the **T.A. Moulton Barn** may be one of the most photographed barns in the world.

- Wyoming's state dinosaur is the **Triceratops**.

- The state fossil is **Knightia**, a type of fish.

- Now reminiscent of a ghost town, **Jeffrey City** was once a uranium mining site.

- Discovered in the region in 1937 (which led to a mining rush), **jade** is the state gemstone.

- Once roaming the area by the tens of millions and nearly hunted to extinction, the **bison** is the state mammal.

- The state reptile is the **horned toad**.

- Perhaps around 1,000 years old, the **Bighorn Medicine Wheel** was likely used for Indigenous astronomical purposes.

- Known as the **chokecherry**, a local shrub produces fruit often used to make jelly and wine.

- **Elk and bison** are popular local meats.

- The name "Wyoming" comes from a contraction of the word **mecheweamiing**, given to the area by the Lenape (Delaware) and meaning "at the big plains."

- The state coin is the **Sacagawea golden dollar**.

- There are two state holidays: **Native American Day** and **Wyoming Day**.

STARS ★ OF ★ THE ★ STATE

NELLIE TAYLOE ROSS

(1876–1977) Born in Missouri in 1876, Nellie Tayloe Ross (née Wynns) became the country's first female state governor. After meeting and marrying William B. Ross in the 1890s, she moved with her husband to Cheyenne, where the pair settled. A Democrat interested in the newly forming concepts of progressivism, William Ross entered into politics, becoming the state's governor in 1922. When he died unexpectedly in 1924, a devastated Nellie Ross expressed an interest in running, much to the dismay of friends and family. Acting against their warnings that politics was a man's realm, she accepted the Democratic nomination. Upon winning and being inaugurated in 1925, Ross advocated for laws protecting laborers and women. ■

BY THE NUMBERS

Natural Treasures

13,804 the elevation in feet (4,207 m) of Gannett Peak, the state's highest point

1995
THE YEAR WOLVES WERE REINTRODUCED TO YELLOWSTONE NATIONAL PARK

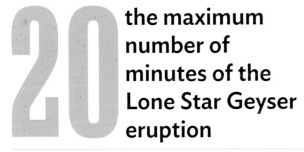

20 the maximum number of minutes of the Lone Star Geyser eruption

100,000+
THE NUMBER OF ACRES (40,469 HA) COVERED BY STATE PARKS

2 THE NUMBER OF OCEANS INTO WHICH ISA LAKE DRAINS. IT'S THE ONLY NATURAL LAKE TO DRAIN INTO TWO OCEANS.

91 the length in miles (146 km) of the Flaming Gorge Reservoir

550 the number of miles (885 km) of the Continental Divide Trail in Wyoming

Home to the largest bison herd in North America, Yellowstone National Park contains some 5,500 roaming American bison.

DESTINATION: WYOMING

- With 4,860,537 visitors in 2021, the highest visitation on record, Yellowstone National Park is one of the nation's most popular destinations. Top attractions include the multicolored Grand Prismatic Spring, Mammoth Hot Springs, more than 500 geysers, and 5,000-plus bison scattered throughout the park.

- Thermopolis also offers plenty of family fun. Visitors seek out the Wyoming Dinosaur Center, Hot Springs State Park, Legend Rock Petroglyph Site, and Wind River Canyon.

"IN WYOMING, THE BEAUTY OF OUR MOUNTAINS IS MATCHED ONLY BY THE GRIT OF OUR PEOPLE."

—Politician Liz Cheney

- Dubois is a delight with its National Bighorn Sheep Center, full of stunning badlands, ranches, lakes, and parks.

- The primary sight at Grand Teton National Park is the Grand Teton Mountain Range. People also come for the scenic drives and hikes, river and lake activities, and spectacular camping. ▼

- According to Inuna-Ina (Arapaho), Tsis tsis'tas (Cheyenne), and Apsáalooke (Crow) legends, Devil's Tower Monument (also called Bear's Tipi, Bear Lodge, or Bear's Home) got its unique formation when it was scratched by a giant bear (though the reason for the scratching varies from legend to legend).

- Cody was founded in 1896 by Wild West showman William "Buffalo Bill" Cody. Today, the town features multiple museums about the Old West and precolonial Indigenous life, as well as chuck wagon dinners, music shows, and day ranches.

- Cheyenne has plenty to offer those interested in the Old West, from its history as America's "railroad capital" to its lawmen-and-outlaws reenactments to its rodeos and ranches.

- In addition to top-tier skiing, Jackson Hole's winter activities include snowmobiling, ice skating, sleigh rides, cross-country skiing, and more. In summer, visitors come to mountain bike, fish, golf, and kayak.

- Fossil Butte National Monument contains one of the largest deposits of fossilized freshwater fish in the world.

- Hole in the Wall is a natural pass in the red sandstone Big Horn Mountains that functioned as an outlaw hideout for the likes of Butch Cassidy, Black Jack Ketchum, Jesse James, and others. ▪

MADE IN WY

Wyoming's agricultural outputs include:

- Cattle
- Pigs
- Sheep
- Hay
- Sugar beets
- Dry beans
- Barley
- Grain feed

Wyoming's agricultural outputs include:

- Petroleum
- Bentonite
- Propane
- Transportation equipment
- Machinery parts
- Disodium carbonate

SPORTING CHANCES

- The annual Cody Ice Climbing Festival draws ice climbers from near and far to partake in ice climbs—the act of using gear to climb up vertical ice faces.

- The University of Wyoming's (UW) athletic teams are the Cowboys and Cowgirls.

- War Memorial Stadium at UW can seat nearly 30,000.

- Rodeo is the state sport. For more than 125 years, Cheyenne Frontier Days has featured rodeos, Wild West shows—including those of Buffalo Bill—and aerial acrobatics.

- Born in Green River, Curt Gowdy was a sportscaster who broadcast 13 World Series and 16 MLB All-Star games.

- In the early 1900s, Steamboat was a 1,100-pound (499 kg) horse legendary for throwing his riders.

- World champion professional bareback rider Chris LeDoux was also a singer known for pioneering "rodeo rock 'n' roll."

- Known as the "father of extreme skiing," Bill Briggs is famous for his daredevil descents of the Grand Tetons.

STORY OF THE PARK

Though humans have lived in the Yellowstone area for some 11,000 years, its history as a national park is much more recent. Around the year 1807, explorer John Colter split off from the Lewis and Clark expedition and headed south, becoming the first American citizen to record the area that is now Yellowstone National Park. Over the next 70 years, three more expeditions followed. Thanks to the photographs, paintings, and sketches of these expeditions, which captured the region's stunning beauty and diverse wildlife, President Ulysses S. Grant established Yellowstone as the nation's first national park in 1872. However, the park soon came under threat of poachers and woodcutters to the point that the U.S. Army was deployed. The army remained in place until 1916, when President Woodrow Wilson approved the National Park Service Organic Act and care of the park was entrusted to newly appointed park rangers.

CREDITS

COVER

Front cover: Dan Thornberg/Shutterstock (baseball); lexaarts/Shutterstock (flag); dibrova/Shutterstock (Statue of Liberty); FloridaStock/Shutterstock (eagle); back flap: Alina Zamogilnykh/Shutterstock

FRONT MATTER

p2, lexaarts/Shutterstock; p4, Romiana Lee/Shutterstock

ALABAMA

p6 (le), Paul Nicklen/NGIC; p6 (rt), Nicholas Courtney/Shutterstock; p7 (up), Daniel Paul; p7 (ctr), Doug Benc/Staff/Getty Images; p7 (lo), Bettman/Getty Images; p8, Buyenlarge/Getty Images; p9, Chase D'Animulls/Shutterstock; p10 (up), Bastiaan Slabbers/iStock/Getty Images; p10 (lo), Bettman/Getty Images; p11, Derek Hudson/Getty Images

ALASKA

p12 (le), Vilor/Shutterstock; p12 (rt), Michael Roeder/Shutterstock; p13 (up), Daniel Paul; p13 (lo), Duane Prokop/Stringer/Getty Images; p14 (up), Andrea Izzotti/Shutterstock; p14 (lo), Loren Holmes/Alamy; p15 (up), Drakuliren/Shutterstock; p15 (lo), Museum of London/Heritage Images/Getty Images; p16 (up), Incredible Arctic/Shutterstock; p16 (lo), Daniel Paul; p17 (up), doleesi/Shutterstock; p17 (lo), Angela Weiss/Getty Images

AMERICAN SAMOA

p18 (le), Tarn Pisessith/Shutterstock; p18 (rt), SCStock/Shutterstock; p19 (up), Aaron/Adobe Stock; p19 (lo), Anna Moneymaker/Staff/Getty Images; p20, Jumus Davis Photography/Alamy; p21, Hadi Zaher/Getty Images; p22 (up), Daniel Paul; p22 (ctr), Danita Delimont/Shutterstock; p22 (lo), Daniel Paul; p23, Gregory Shamus/Getty Images

ARIZONA

p24 (le), Mary E. Eaton/NGIC; p24 (rt), Katrina Brown/Adobe Stock; p25 (up), Reid Dalland/

Shutterstock; p25 (lo), Charles Ommanney/Getty Images; p26, Jon Chica/Shutterstock; p27 (up), Evelyn/Adobe Stock; p27 (lo), Nate Hovee/Shutterstock; p28 (up), Pamela Au/Adobe Stock; p28 (lo), Daniel Paul; p29 (up), Daniel/Adobe Stock; p29 (lo), Library of Congress Prints & Photographs Division, #3a21666

ARKANSAS

p30 (le), FotoRequest/Shutterstock; p30 (rt), Jeremy Janus/Shutterstock; p31 (up), Marti Bug Catcher/Shutterstock; p31 (lo), Joseph Sohm/Shutterstock; p32, Paul/Adobe Stock; p33 (up), OGphoto/iStock/Getty Images; p33 (lo), mwessellsphotography/Shutterstock; p34 (up), Don Smetzer/Alamy; p34 (lo), ABC Television/Getty Images; p35, Science History Images/Alamy

CALIFORNIA

P36 (le), Mary E. Eaton; p36 (rt), Bettman/Getty Images; p37 (up), Daniel Paul; p37 (lo), EpicStockMedia/Adobe Stock; p38 (up), BlueBarronPhoto/Shutterstock; p38 (lo), Bettman/Getty Images; p39, Bannosuke/Shutterstock; p40, Paul-Ibc/Shutterstock; p41, Sunset Boulevard/Contributor/Getty Images

COLORADO

p42 (le), Mary E. Eaton/NGIC; p42 (rt), Gary/Adobe Stock; p43 (up), Brian/Adobe Stock; p43 (lo), Hulton Deutsch/Contributor/Getty Images; p44 (le), Legacy Images/Shutterstock; p44 (rt), Niko Bono/Shutterstock; p45, Mark C Stevens/Getty Images; p46, Stan Hill/Shutterstock; p47 (up), Daniel Petty/Contributor/Getty Images; p47 (lo), Nik Wheeler/Contributor/Getty Images

CONNECTICUT

p48 (le), Mr.Coffee/Shutterstock; p48 (rt), Winston Tan/Shutterstock; p49 (up), Daniel Paul; p49 (lo), Ernest Bachrach/John Kobal Foundation/Getty Images; p50 (up), Universal History Archive/Getty Images; p50 (lo), Daniel Paul; p51, S. Vidal/Shutterstock; p52 (up), Bettman/Getty Images; p52 (lo), Romiana Lee/Shutterstock; p53 (up), David Hahn/Icon Sportswire/Getty Images; p53 (lo), Reuters/Almay

DELAWARE

p54 (le), Mary E. Eaton/NGIC; p54 (rt), Chicago History Museum/Getty Images; p55 (up), Heritage Images/Getty Images; p55 (lo), Lev Raden/Shutterstock; p55 (rt), Daniel Paul; p56 (up), Visual Intermezzo/Adobe Stock; p56 (lo), lunamarina/Adobe Stock; p57 (le), JayPierstorff/Shutterstock; p57 (rt), Ethan Quin/Shutterstock; p58, Walter Bibikow/Getty Images; p59 (up), casa.da.photo/Shutterstock; p59 (lo), National Baseball Hall of Fame Library/Getty Images

FLORIDA

p60 (le), Mary E. Eaton/NGIC; p60 (rt), Global_Pics/Getty Images; p61 (up), Felix Mizioznikov/Shutterstock; p61 (lo), Corbis Historical/Getty Images; p62, Blackdiamond67/Adobe Stock; p63 (up), Lux Blue/Shutterstock; p63 (lo), Image Source Trading Limited; p64, ampueroleonardo; p65 (up), Lynn Pelham/Contributor/Getty Images; p65 (lo), S_Buckley/Shutterstock

GEORGIA

p66 (le), John L. Absher/Shutterstock; p66 (rt), MCT/Contributor/Getty Images; p67 (up), Bob Krist/Getty Images; p67 (lo), MM Photos/Shutterstock; P68 (up), Daniel Paul; p68 (lo), banglds/Adobe Stock; p69, kurdistan/Shutterstock; p70, Andru Goldman/Shutterstock; p71 (up), Bettman/Getty Images; p71 (lo), Donaldson Collection/Getty Images

GUAM

p72 (le), langg Stock Photo/Shutterstock; p72 (rt), Denis Moskvinov/Shutterstock; p73 (up), abimages/Shutterstock; p73 (lo), Saul Loeb/Staff/Getty Images; p74 (le), Daniel Paul; p74 (rt), Matt Roberts/Stringer/Getty Images; p75, Byungsuk Ko/Shutterstock; p76 (up), Danita Delimont/Shutterstock; p76 (lo), Reuters/Alamy Stock; p77, Bennie Lynn/Getty Images

HAWAII

p78 (le), Matt Jordan/Shutterstock; p78 (rt), Yvonne Baur/Shutterstock; p79 (up), Daniel Paul; p79 (center), Lotuscolor/Shutterstock; p79 (lo), Mark Reinstein/Shutterstock; p80 (up), Lorraine

Logan/Shutterstock; p80 (lo), liquid studios/Shutterstock; p81, Paula Cobleigh/Shutterstock; p82, Damien Verrier/Shutterstock; p83 (up), Theodore Trimmer/Shutterstock; p83 (lo), Streeter Lecka/Getty Images

IDAHO

p84 (le), Double Brow Imagery/Shutterstock; p84 (rt), CSNafzger/Shutterstock; p85 (up), Daniel Paul; p85 (center), Wirestock Creators; p85 (lo), Idaho State Historical Society; p86 (up), Alena Demidyuk/Shutterstock; p86 (lo), M L Pearson/Alamy Stock; p87 (ctr le), Diamon Jewelry/Adobe Stock; p87 (lo rt), Mehmet Gokhan Bayhan/Adobe Stock; p87 (up le), Andreas Foll/Shutterstock; p87 (up rt and lo), ijp2726/Adobe Stock; p88, PNG Studio Photography; p89 (up), Daniel Paul; p89 (lo), Jeff Haynes/Getty Images

ILLINOIS

p90 (le), Volosina/Shutterstock; p90 (rt), Chicago History Museum/Getty Images; p91 (up), Michael Ochs Archives/Getty Images; p91 (lo), Library of Congress; p91 (rt), Daniel Paul; p92, AGF srl/Alamy Stock; p93, Felix Lipov/Shutterstock; p94 (up), Kent Raney/Shuttstock; p94 (lo), Luis Boucault/Shutterstock; p95 (up), Rich Kane Photography/Alamy Stock; p95 (lo), Everett Collection Historical/Alamy Stock Photo

INDIANA

p96 (le), Louis Agassiz Fuertes/NGIC; p96 (rt), Grindstone Media Group/Shutterstock; p97 (up), Daniel Paul; p97 (lo), Michael Ochs Archives/Stringer/Getty Images; p98 (up), Richard/Adobe Stock; p98 (lo), Bettmann/Getty Images; p99, HodagMedia/Shutterstock; p100 (up), drewthehobbit/Shutterstock; p100 (lo), Michael Ochs Archives/Getty Images; p101, Chicago History Museum/Getty Images

IOWA

p102 (le), Pavaphon Supanantananont/Shutterstock; p102 (rt), Lena Platonova/Shutterstock; p103 (up), Jim Cork/Shutterstock; p103 (lo), Stock Montage/Getty Images; p103 (up), Daniel Paul; p104, Northallertonman/Shutterstock; p105, Barnorth/Shutterstock; p106, Graphica-Artis/Getty Images; p107 (up), David Madison/Getty Images; p107 (lo), Silver Screen Collection/Getty Images

KANSAS

p108 (le), Lidia Fotografie/Shutterstock; p108 (rt), RaksyBH/Shutterstock; p109 (up), Daniel Paul; p109 (lo), *The Washington Post*/Getty Images; p110 (up), Emory Kristof/NGIC; p110

(lo), Silver Screen Collection/Getty Images; p111, Danita Delimont/Alamy; p112 (up), Ricardo Reitmeyer/Shutterstock; p112 (lo), Bettmann/Getty Images; p113, Jamie Squire/Getty Images

KENTUCKY

p114 (le), Mary E. Eaton/NGIC; p114 (rt), Alexey Stiop/Shutterstock; p115 (up), Daniel Paul; p115 (ctr), Getty Images; p115 (lo), The Stanley West Archive/Getty Images; p116 (up), Alan Powdrill/Getty Images; p117 (up), WNstock/Shutterstock; p117 (lo), Thomas Kelley/Shutterstock; p118 (up), Ko Zatu/Shutterstock; p118 (lo), Alberto E. Rodriguez/Getty Images; p119, Thomas Kelley/Shutterstock

LOUISIANA

p120 (le), Robin Mackenzie/Shutterstock; p120 (rt), Erika Goldring/Getty Images; p121 (up), Daniel Paul; p121 (ctr), RJPhotography/Adobe Stock; p121 (lo), Bettmann/Getty Images; p122, Natalia Lisovskaya/Shutterstock; p123, LeonardoVillasis/Adobe Stock; p124, Nathan Steele/EyeEm/Getty Images; p125 (up), David Madison/Getty Images; p125 (lo), Randy Holmes/Getty Images

MAINE

p126 (le), Mary E. Eaton/NGIC; p126 (rt), Sean Pavone/Shutterstock; p127 (up), *Portland Press Herald*/Getty Images; p127 (lo), Silver Screen Collection/Getty Images; 128 (up), Daniel Paul; p128 (lo), Seregraff/Shutterstock; p129, Romiana Lee/Shutterstock; p130, Pernelle Voyage/Shutterstock; p131 (up), Bettmann/Getty Images; p131 (lo), Everett Collection/Shutterstock

N. MARIANA ISLANDS

p132 (le), Mark J Meyers/Shutterstock; p132 (rt), Everett Collection/Shutterstock; p133 (up), Daniel Paul; p133 (lo), AFP/Getty Images; p134, Ivan Jiang/500px/Getty Images; p135, RaklsyBH/Shutterstock; p136, Alex Ship/Shutterstock; p137 (up), *South China Morning Post*/Getty Images; p137 (lo), U. S. District Court for the Northern Mariana Islands

MARYLAND

p138 (le), Quang Ho/Shutterstock; p138 (rt), Yvonne Navalaney/Shutterstock; p139 (up), MPI/Stringer/Getty Images; p139 (lo), Everett Collection/Shutterstock; p140, *The Washington Post*/Getty Images; p141, WilliamSherman/Getty Images; p142 (up), The Old Major/Shutterstock; p142 (lo), Bettman/Getty Images; p143, Salty View/Shutterstock

MASSACHUSETTS

p144 (le), chas53/Getty Images; p144 (rt), jejim/Shutterstock; p145, Library of Congress; p146 (up), Dora Zett/Shutterstock; p146 (lo), John Bryson/Getty Images; p147 (up), Katkami/Shutterstock; p147 (lo), Vladimir Dimchenko/Shutterstock; p148, nevada.claire/Shutterstock; p149 (le), Marcio Jose Bastos Silva/Shutterstock; p149 (rt), Daniel Paul; p149 (lo), PhotoVrStudio/Shutterstock

MICHIGAN

p150 (le), Phant/Shutterstock; p150 (rt), Susan/Adobe Stock; p151 (up), EQRoy/Shutterstock; p151 (lo), Ron Howard/Popperfoto/Getty Images; p152 (up), Doug Lemke/Shutterstock; p152 (lo), Judy Tomlinson/500px/Getty Images; p153, ehrlif/Shutterstock; p154 (up), Benjamin/Simeneta/Shutterstock; p154 (lo), Library of Congress; p155, Christian Petersen/Staff/Getty Images

MINNESOTA

p156 (le), Edgar E Espe/Shutterstock; p156 (rt), Paul Brady Photography/Shutterstock; p157 (up), Edgar E Espe/Shutterstock; p157 (lo), Bettmann/Getty Images; p158, Edgar E Espe/Shutterstock; p159, Frank Kennedy MN/Shutterstock; p160 (up), BlueBarronPhoto/Shutterstock; p160 (ctr), Daniel Paul; p160 (lo), Michael Ochs Archives/Getty Images; p161, Star Tribune/Getty Images

MISSISSIPPI

p162 (le), Paul Winterman/Shutterstock; p162 (rt), F11photo/Shutterstock; p163 (up), Daniel Paul; P163 (lo), Everett Collection/Shutterstock; p164 (up), Bettmann/Getty Images; p164 (lo), TDC Photography; p165, Melinda Fawver/Shutterstock; p166 (up), Sewan Pavone/Shutterstock; p166 (lo), Michael Levin/Getty Images; p167, Scott Cunningham/Getty Images

MISSOURI

p168 (le), Arthur A. Allen/NGIC; p168 (rt), Everett Collection/Shutterstock; p169 (up), Sean Pavone/Shutterstock; p169 (lo), Hulton Archive/Getty Images; p170, jmanaugh3/Shutterstock; p171 (le), RozenskiP/Shutterstock; p171 (rt), Keystone-France/Getty Images; p172 (up), M.Curtis/Shutterstock; p172 (lo), Michael Ochs Archives/Getty Images; p173, Harry Engels/Getty Images

MONTANA

p174 (le), Mary E. Eaton/NGIC; p174 (rt), wanderluster/Getty Images; p175 (up), Historical/Getty Images; p175 (lo), Hulton Archive/Getty

Images; p176 (up), Daniel Paul; p176 (ctr), Eric Isselle/Shutterstock; p176 (lo), Scott E Read/Shutterstock; p177, Tory Kallman/Shutterstock; p178, Vaclav Sebek/Shutterstock; p179 (up), Sergei Bachlakov/Shutterstock; p179 (lo), Michael Ochs Archives/Getty Images

NEBRASKA

p180 (le), Mary E. Eaton/NGIC; p180 (rt), soupstock/Adobe Stock; p181 (up), MPI/Stringer/Getty Images; p181 (lo), NBC/Getty Images; p182 (up), marekuliaSZ/Shutterstock; p182 (lo), Steve Russell/Getty Images; p183, Treveller70/Shutterstock; p184, Bettmann/Getty Images; p185, Joe Raedle/Getty Images

NEVADA

p186 (le), Mary E. Eaton/NGIC; p186 (rt), Galyna Andrushko/Shutterstock; p187 (up), Millenius/Shutterstock; p187 (lo), Bob Martin/Getty Images; p188 (up), Daniel Paul; p188 (ctr), Que Images/Shutterstock; p188 (lo), DiegoMarriottini/Shutterstock; p189, Sean Pavone/Shutterstock; p190 (up), Lukas Bischoff Photography/Shutterstock; p190 (lo), AP Photo/Laura Rauch, file; p191, Brian Steffy/Getty Images

NEW HAMPSHIRE

p192 (le), Louis Agassiz Fuertes/NGIC; p192 (rt), David Boutin/Shutterstock; p193 (up), spatuletail/Shutterstock; p193 (lo), Ray Fisher/Getty Images; p194, Everett Collection/Shutterstock; p195, critterbiz/Shutterstock; p196 (up), yuziS/Shutterstock; p196 (lo), Ed Vebell/Getty Images; p197 (up), *Star Tribune*/Getty Images; p197 (lo), Kean Collection/Getty Images

NEW JERSEY

p198 (le), Rabbitti/Shutterstock; p198 (rt), Bettmann/Getty Images; p199 (up), Daniel Paul; p199 (ctr), Sean Pavone/Shutterstock; p199 (lo), Ilya S. Savenok/Getty Images p200 (up), Bettmann/Getty Images; p200 (lo), Kevin Winter/Getty Images; p201, Olesya/Adobe Stock; p202, EQroy/Shutterstock; p203, Sasha/Getty Images

NEW MEXICO

p204 (le), Olga Mazo; p204 (rt), Bettmann/Getty Images; p205 (up), Reid Dalland/Shutterstock; p205 (lo), Fred Stein Archive/Getty Images; p206 (le), Maria Dryfhour/Shutterstock; p206 (rt), Nick Fox/Shutterstock; p207, Doug Meek/Shutterstock; p208, Historical/Getty Images; p209 (up), Transcendental Graphics/Getty Images; p209 (lo), Tony Roberts/Getty Images

NEW YORK

p210 (le), Quang Ho/Shutterstock; p210 (rt), anek.soowannaphoom/Shutterstock; p211 (rt), Andrei Mayatnik/Shutterstock; p211 (lo), Bill Spilka/Getty Images; p212 (up), Barry Winiker/Getty Images; p212 (lo), Foodio/Shutterstock; p213, Mirco Chianucci/Shutterstock; p214 (up), Daniel Paul; p214 (lo), haveseen/Shutterstock; p215 (up), David Madison/Getty Images; p215 (lo), Ovidiu Hrubaru/Shutterstock

NORTH CAROLINA

p216 (le), Le Do/Shutterstock; p216 (rt), NBC/Getty Images; p217 (up), Vereshchagin Dmitry/Shutterstock; p217 (lo), Jack Robinson/Getty Images; p218 (up), Skipper Pappy D/Shutterstock; p218 (low), HQ3DMOD; p219, Rivers Setliff/Shutterstock; p220, Margaret.Wiktor/Shutterstock; p221 (up), Onelinestock/Shutterstock; p221 (lo), RacingOne/Getty Images; p221 (ctr), Daniel Paul

NORTH DAKOTA

p222 (le), Jack Bell Photography/Shutterstock; p222 (rt), Zak Zeinert/Shutterstock; p223, Stock Montage/Getty Images; p224, northlight/Shutterstock; p225, Joseph Sohm/Shutterstock; p226 (up), Jacob Boomsma/Shutterstock; p226 (lo), Patrick Faricy/National Geographic Partners; p227 (up), GR Photo/Shutterstock; p227 (lo), Universal Images Group/Getty Images

OHIO

p228 (le), Mary E. Eaton/NGIC; p228 (rt), MPI/Getty Images; p229 (up), Kathy Burns/Adobe Stock; p229 (lo), Daniel Boczarski/Getty Images; p230 (le), Kenneth Sponsler/Shutterstock; p230 (rt), *Denver Post*/Getty Images; p231, Richard345/Shutterstock; p232 (up), Hendrickson Photography/Shutterstock; p232 (lo), Bettmann/Getty Images; p233, Bettmann/Getty Images

OKLAHOMA

p234 (le), Brett Lawson/Shutterstock; p234 (rt), Andreas Stroh/Shutterstock; p235 (up), Keith Ladzinski/NGIC; p235 (lo), J. Kempin/Getty Images; p236, DFree/Shutterstock; p237, Andrey Bayda/Shutterstock; p238 (up), Hum Images/Getty Images; p238 (low), Kit Leong/Shutterstock; p239 (lo), David Madison/Getty Images; p239 (rt), Werner Forman/Getty Images

OREGON

p240 (le), Le Do/Shutterstock; p240 (rt), Rigucci/Shutterstock; p241 (up), Nadia Yong/Shutterstock; p241 (lo), Tara Ziemba/Getty Images; p242 (up), chanakon/Adobe Stock; p242 (lo), WoodsyPhotos/Shutterstock; p243, Lazyllama/Shutterstock; p244, Wollertz/Shutterstock; p245 (up), Leo Mason/Popperfoto/Getty Images; p245 (lo), Volgi Archive/Alamy

PENNSYLVANIA

p246 (le), Louis Agassiz Fuertes/NGIC; p246 (rt), GraphicaArtis/Getty Images; p247 (up), Daniel Paul; p247 (lo), Bettman/Getty Images; p248 (up), Lee Snider Photo Images/Shutterstock; p248 (lo), Vivienstock/Shutterstock; p249, Opis Zagreb/Shutterstock; p250 (up), Derek Hudson/Getty Images; p250 (lo), Bettmann/Getty Images; p251, Moviestore Collection Ltd./Alamy Stock

PUERTO RICO

p252 (le), Julio Salgado; p252 (rt), Mariette Pathy Allen/Getty Images; p253 (up), Joseph/Shutterstock; p253 (lo), Silver Screen Collection/Getty Images; p254 (up), Marvin del Sid/Getty Images; p254 (lo), Film Favorites/Getty Images; p255, Felix Lipov/Shutterstock; p256 (up), Aneta Waberska/Shutterstock; p256 (lo), Rich Polk/Getty Images; p257, Bettman/Getty Images

RHODE ISLAND

p258 (le), Louis Agassiz Fuertes/NGIC; p258 (rt), Jose L Vilchez/Shutterstock; p259, Bettman/Getty Images; p260 (up), Pernelle Voyage/Shutterstock; p260 (rt), David TB/Shutterstock; p261, Felix Lipov/Shutterstock; p262, James Kirkikis/Shutterstock; p263 (up), Leightonoc/Shutterstock; p263 (lo), Icon Sportswire/Getty Images

SOUTH CAROLINA

p264 (le), Mary E. Eaton/NGIC; p264 (rt), Nate Rosso/Shutterstock; p265 (up), James M. Davidson/Shutterstock; p265 (lo), Chicago History Museum/Getty Images; p266 (up), p kyriakos/Shutterstock; p266 (rt), cer1126/Shutterstock; p267, Susanne Pommer/Shutterstock; p268 (up), f11photo/Shutterstock; p268 (lo), Lawrence Lucier/Getty Images; p269, Icon Sports Wire/Getty Images

SOUTH DAKOTA

p270 (le), Louis Agassiz Fuertes/NGIC; p270 (rt), fotoroarch/Getty Images; p271 (up), Traveller70/Shutterstock; p271 (lo), Mark Davis/Getty Images; p272 (le), Daniel Paul; p272 (rt), *Fort Worth Star-Telegram*/Getty Images; p273, Volodymy Burdiak/Shutterstock; p274, critterbiz/Shutterstock; p275 (up), Getty Images; p275 (lo), Album/Alamy Stock

TENNESSEE

p276 (le), Bonnie Taylor Barrie/Shutterstock; p276 (rt), Kevin Ruck/Shutterstock; p277 (up), Lamar Sellers/Shutterstock; p277 (lo), Ian Gavan/Getty Images; p278, *Denver Post*/Getty Images; p279, Brian Lasenby/Shutterstock; p280 (up), Miro Vrlik Photography/Shutterstock; p280 (ctr), Michael Gordon/Shutterstock; p280 (lo), Michael Ochs Archives/Getty Images; p281, Jim McIsaac/Getty Images

TEXAS

p282 (le), Mary E. Eaton/NGIC; p282 (rt), Victoria 'Tori' Meyer/Shutterstock; p283 (up), Gregory Smith/Getty Images; p283 (lo), Joseph August/Getty Images; p284, Barbara Laing; p285 (up), jdross75/Shutterstock; p285 (lo), Anton Starikov/Shutterstock; p286, Sean Pavone; p287, Tom Pennington/Getty Images

U.S. VIRGIN ISLANDS

p288 (le), guentermanaus/Shutterstock; p288 (rt), Jack Mitchell/Getty Images; p289, EA Given/Shutterstock; p290 (up), Darryl Brooks/Shutterstock; p290 (lo), EQroy/Shutterstock; p291, Wangkun Jia/Shutterstock; p292, SCStock/Shutterstock; p293 (up), Ernie Leyba/Getty Images; p293 (lo), Kevin McFadin

UTAH

p294 (le), Salil/Adobe Stock; p294 (rt), Allen Ginsberg LLC/Getty Images; p295 (up), jonbilous/Adobe Stock; p295 (lo), HandmadePictures/Shutterstock; p296 (up rt), domnitsky/Shutterstock; p296 (up le), EM Arts/Shutterstock; p296 (lo), IrinaK/Shutterstock; p297 (up), Darren J. Bradley; p297 (lo), Bettman/Getty Images; p298, SWMC/Shutterstock; p299 (up), Adam Duckworth/Alamy Stock; p299 (lo), Utah State Historical Society

VERMONT

p300 (le), Photo Spirit/Shutterstock; p300 (rt), mdfahey/Shutterstock; p301 (up), Alexander Ryan Thompson/Shutterstock; p301 (lo), Joseph Sohm/Shutterstock; p302 (le), Library of Congress; p302 (rt), Library of Congress; p303, Bob Pool/Shutterstock; p304 (up), enchanted_fairy/Shutterstock; p304 (lo), vermontal/Shutterstock; p305 (up), Al Bello/Getty Images; p305 (lo), Paul R. Giunta/Getty Images; p306, Rob Palmer Photography/Shutterstock

VIRGINIA

p306, Louis Agassiz Fuertes/NGIC; p307 (up), Everett Collection/Shutterstock; p307 (lo), Library of Congress; p308 (lo), Bill Chizek/Shutterstock; p308 (up) Mircea Costina/Shutterstock; p309 (le), Rachel Fischer/Shutterstock; p309 (rt), aceshot1/Shutterstock; p310 (up), Frank Staub/Getty Images; p310 (lo), Library of Congress; p311 (up), Dilip Vishwanat/Getty Images; p311 (lo), Everett Collection/Shutterstock

WASHINGTON

p312, FotoRequest/Shutterstock; p313 (up), Merrill Images/Getty Images; p313 (lo), Jamie McCarthy/Getty Images; p314 (up le), Checubus/Shutterstock; p314 (up rt), Brittney Tatchell, Smithsonian Institute; p314 (lo), Virginie Merckaert/Shutterstock; p315, Mariusz S. Jurgielewicz/Shutterstock; p316, Xuanlu Wang/Shutterstock; p317 (up), Keystone/Getty Images; p317 (lo), Elsa/Getty Images

WASHINGTON, D.C.

p318 (le), Anakumka/Shutterstock; p318 (rt), Sean Pavone/Shutterstock; p319 (up), CNP/Getty Images; p319 (lo), Bettman/Getty Images; p320 (up), Daniel Paul; p320 (ctr), eurobanks/Shutterstock; p320 (lo), Eva Hambach/Getty Images; p321, Albert Pego/Shutterstock; p322, f11photo/Shutterstock; p323 (up), Diamond Images/Getty Images; p323 (lo), Bettmann/Getty Images

WEST VIRGINIA

p324 (le), Al Petteway and Amy White/NGIC; p324 (rt), Bettman/Getty Images; p325 (up), Harrison Shull/Getty Images; p325 (lo), Gilles Petard/Getty Images; p326, Jon Bilous/Shutterstock; p327, Dynamic Photography/Shutterstock; p328, Jon Bilous/Shutterstock; p329 (up), Bettman/Getty Images; p329 (lo), Barry Gossage/Getty Images

WISCONSIN

p330 (rt), Jacob Boomsma/Shutterstock; p330 (le), margo555/Adobe Stock; p331 (up), Aaron of L.A. Photography/Shutterstock; p331 (lo), John Springer Collection/Getty Images; p332 (up), Aaron of L.A. Photography/Shutterstock; p332 (lo), Joshua Rainey Photography/Shutterstock; p333, dcwcreations/Shutterstock; p334 (up), Photo 12/Alamy Stock; p334 (lo), ZUMA Press Inc./Alamy Stock; p335, Jonathan Daniel/Getty Images

WYOMING

p336 (le), Mary E. Eaton/NGIC; p336 (rt), Susanne Pommer/Shutterstock; p337 (up), Archive Photos/Getty Images; p337 (lo), Peter Ptschelinzew/Alamy; p338 (le), melissamn/Shutterstock; p338 (rt), Bettman/Getty Images; p339, Agnieszka Bacal/Shutterstock; p340, Matt Anderson Photography/Getty Images; p341 (up), Kerem Yucel/Getty Images; p341 (lo), Naughtynut/Shutterstock

All state flags from National Geographic Society

INDEX

Since 1888, the National Geographic Society has funded more than 14,000 research, conservation, education, and storytelling projects around the world. National Geographic Partners distributes a portion of the funds it receives from your purchase to National Geographic Society to support programs including the conservation of animals and their habitats.

National Geographic Partners, LLC
1145 17th Street NW
Washington, DC 20036-4688 USA

Get closer to National Geographic Explorers and photographers, and connect with our global community. Join us today at nationalgeographic.org/joinus

For rights or permissions inquiries, please contact National Geographic Books Subsidiary Rights: bookrights@natgeo.com

Produced for National Geographic Books by WonderLab Group, LLC

Design by Fan Works Design, LLC

The information in this book has been carefully checked and to the best of our knowledge is accurate. However, details are subject to change, and the publisher cannot be responsible for such changes, or for errors or omissions.

ISBN: 978-1-4262-2257-3

Printed in China

24/PPS/1